Awqaf-led Islamic Social Finance

This book provides an authoritative and comprehensive overview of Waqf (endowment), addressing specific issues, models, solutions, structures and practices. As Islamic finance has gained in significance, so too has the institution of Waqf, working towards creating an enterprising and an entrepreneurial community across the globe, in order to meet the underlying objectives of the sustainable development goals (SDGs) by targeting the low-income group in particular.

The book analyses the historical context of Waqf as well as its revival in the digital era. It addresses the laws and policies affecting the management of Waqf, such as Maqasid al-Shari'ah, law and policies, law and fiscal reform, regulations applied within Muslim countries, judicial procedures and dispute resolutions and covers the core issues concerning the formalities of Waqf, its management and corporate governance questions. The book includes a series of specialized chapters focusing on the products and services of Waqf, covering product innovation, product development, and then assesses the risk factors in Waqf and Waqf Takaful. Finally, it focuses on the challenges of Waqf and offers recommendations for the way forward.

A timely and practical guide, comprising a literature review and future research directions, as well as a number of international case studies, this book will be a key reference for academics, students, researchers, practitioners and policy makers.

Mohd Ma'Sum Billah is Professor of Finance and Insurance at the Islamic Economics Institute, King Abdulaziz University, Jeddah, Kingdom of Saudi Arabia.

Islamic Business and Finance Series

Series Editor: Ishaq Bhatti

There is an increasing need for western politicians, financiers, bankers, and indeed the western business community in general to have access to high quality and authoritative texts on Islamic financial and business practices. Drawing on expertise from across the Islamic world, this new series will provide carefully chosen and focused monographs and collections, each authored/edited by an expert in their respective field all over the world.

The series will be pitched at a level to appeal to middle and senior management in both the western and the Islamic business communities. For the manager with a western background the series will provide detailed and up-to-date briefings on important topics; for the academics, postgraduates, business communities, manager with western and an Islamic background the series will provide a guide to best practice in business in Islamic communities around the world, including Muslim minorities in the west and majorities in the rest of the world.

Halal Logistics and Supply Chain Management in Southeast Asia
Edited by Nor Aida Abdul Rahman, Azizul Hassan and Mohammad Fakhrulnizam Mohammad

A History of Interest and Debt
Ancient Civilizations
Edited by Murat Ustaoğlu and Ahmet İncekara

Awqaf-led Islamic Social Finance
Innovative Solutions to Modern Applications
Edited by Mohd Ma'Sum Billah

For more information about this series, please visit: www.routledge.com/Islamic-Business-and-Finance-Series/book-series/ISLAMICFINANCE

Awqaf-led Islamic Social Finance

Innovative Solutions to Modern Applications

Edited by
Mohd Ma'Sum Billah

Professor of Finance and Insurance
Islamic Economics Institute
King Abdulaziz University
Kingdom of Saudi Arabia.

Routledge
Taylor & Francis Group
LONDON AND NEW YORK

First published 2021
by Routledge
2 Park Square, Milton Park, Abingdon, Oxon OX14 4RN

and by Routledge
52 Vanderbilt Avenue, New York, NY 10017

Routledge is an imprint of the Taylor & Francis Group, an informa business

British Library Cataloguing-in-Publication Data
A catalogue record for this book is available from the British Library

Library of Congress Cataloging-in-Publication Data
Names: Mohd. Ma'sum Billah, 1968– editor.
Title: WAQF-led Islamic social finance : innovative solutions to modern applications / edited by Mohd Ma'Sum Billah.
Description: Milton Park, Abingdon, Oxon ; New York, NY : Routledge, 2021. | Includes bibliographical references and index.
Identifiers: LCCN 2020015250 (print) | LCCN 2020015251 (ebook)
Subjects: LCSH: Waqf. | Finance—Islamic countries. | Finance (Islamic law)
Classification: LCC BP170.25 .W375 2021 (print) | LCC BP170.25 (ebook) | DDC 361.7/632091767—dc23
LC record available at https://lccn.loc.gov/2020015250
LC ebook record available at https://lccn.loc.gov/202001525

ISBN: 978-0-367-40537-3 (hbk)
ISBN: 978-0-429-35657-5 (ebk)

Typeset in Bembo
by codeMantra

This book is, dedicated to the remembrance of my most beloved parents *Allamah Mufti Nur Mohammad (r)* and *Ustazah Akhtarun Nisa' (r)* who have nourished me with their love and wisdom. May *Allah (swt)* shower them with His Love and Mercy and grant them *Jannat al-Ferdaus Nuzulah.* I would also like to dedicate this book to my lovely wife Dr Khamsiah Binti Nawawi and our heart-touching children Dr Ahmad Mu'izz Billah, Ahmad Mu'azz Billah (OP-Cadet), Ahmad Muniff Billah (OP-Cadet) and Akhtarun Naba' Billah for their continuous support and sacrifices. Also, heartiest appreciation to Mrs Eman Bawazir, Abdullah M Alabdulraheem and Noor M AlAbdurraheem.

May all be blessed with *Muwaddau Wa Rahmah, Qurratu A'yun* and *Mardhaati Allah (swt)* in their life and the next.

This book is also dedicated to the *Ummah* and the whole of humanity.

Mohd Ma'Sum Billah, PhD
Islamic Economics Institute
King Abdulaziz University
Saudi Arabia

Contents

List of figures xi
List of tables xiii
Acknowledgement xv
Foreword xvii
Preface xxi
About the author xxiii
List of contributors xxv

Introduction 1

PART I
Awqaf: its world view 3

1 **Emergence of *Awqaf* development centre: a mind-mapping idea** 5
MOHD MA'SUM BILLAH

2 **Awqaf-led neo-endowment in supporting socio-economic development** 11
MOHAMMED FAWZI AMINU AMADU AND MOHD MA'SUM BILLAH

3 **Objectives of awqaf within the classical discourse and their modern implications** 23
MOHAMMAD ABDULLAH

4 **Role of awqaf as an economic driver** 39
HISHAM DAFTERDAR

5 **The perception of waqf as a financial institution – a lesson from the French literature on Ottoman Empire** 52
ABDERRAZAK BELABES

6 **Contemporary approach in productive awqaf development** 71
HENDRI TANJUNG, IMAM TEGUH SAPTONO AND IMAM NUR AZIZ

7 **Utilizing awqaf in modern Muslim minority societies** 83
SHEIKH HAITHAM AL-HADDAD AND UMER SULEMAN

PART II
Awqaf: its law and policies 101

8 **Gender justice in the law of awqaf** 103
SYED KHALID RASHID

9 **Developing a waqf market and reconceptualising awqaf governance via regtech** 116
ZAKARIYA MUSTAPHA AND AISHATH MUNEEZA

PART III
Awqaf: its applications and experiences 135

10 **Poverty alleviation through Islamic social finance in agro-sectors – an experience of northern Ghana** 137
ABDUL-JALIL IBRAHIM AND MOHD MA'SUM BILLAH

11 **Developing awqaf through cash waqf** 155
HICHEM HAMZA

12 **Islamic social finance reform – Hibah a catalyst for Awqaf advancement** 166
NOOR SHAHALINA BINTI JAMALUDIN AND SHAIKH HAMZAH ABDUL RAZAK

13 **Edu-Waqf model – an analysis of selected OIC member countries** 191
MUSTAFA OMAR MOHAMMED, MOHAMED CHERIF EL AMRI AND SOUHAILA GUEDIRA

14 **Smart *Waqf* City for Education – an experience in Darussalam Gontor, Indonesia** 207
MAGDA ISMAIL ABDEL MOHSIN AND AMINUDDIN MARUF

15 **Empirical investigation on *awqaf* and its socio-economic impact in Malaysia** 218
MUHAMMAD IQMAL HISHAM KAMARUDDIN, MUSTAFA MOHD HANEFAH AND ROSNIA MASRUKI

16 **Awqaf – its ASEAN experiences and a lesson to learn** 234
LISA LISTIANA AND DIAN MASYITA

17 **Integrated social and productive awqaf in Indonesia** 245
ASCARYA, RADITYA SUKMANA AND MUHAMAD NADRATUZZAMAN HOSEN

18 **Waqf-led social finance in poverty alleviation – an experience in Khyber Pakhtunkhwa, Pakistan** 260
S. GHISAUL HAQ AND SUHAIL AHMAD

19 **Youth empowerment and the application of cash waqf – an experience in Kano State, Nigeria** 270
NURA ABUBAKAR GWADABE AND ASMAK BINTI AB RAHMAN

Index 281

Figures

1.1	Flagship: research and publication	7
1.2	Flagship: academic development	8
1.3	Flagship: professional development	8
1.4	Flagship: industrial solutions	8
1.5	Flagship: industrial models/products	8
1.6	Strategic plan: short term	9
1.7	Strategic plan: long term	9
2.1	WAQF model 1	14
2.2	WAQF model 2	14
2.3	WAQF model 3	14
2.4	WAQF model 4	14
2.5	Benefits of WAQF to partners	19
3.1	Conceptual origin of *waqf*	27
3.2	*Waqf*: the representative terms	28
3.3	The shariah basis of *waqf*	29
3.4	Role of *waqf* in refugee crisis management	33
3.5	Parallel *waqf*: a proposed model	34
5.1	Variety of financing methods in Bosnia-Herzegovina before the idea of the awqāf bank emerged	57
5.2	Waqf as a power issue between diverse forces	61
5.3	Spread dynamics of the idea of bank of awqāf between Bosnia-Herzegovina and Turkey (1900–1992)	63
5.4	Modelization of the spread of the idea of awqāf bank between Bosnia-Herzegovina and Turkey	63
6.1	Cash Waqf -linked Sukuk (CWLS) scheme	75
10.1	Ghana economic structure	139
10.2	Agriculture waqf fund structure and stakeholders	146
12.1	Wealth distribution channel	180
12.2	Proposed framework: Waqf Investment Corporation	183
13.1	Cash Waqf model for educational institutions	195
16.1	Structure of Cash Waqf Linked Sukuk	236
16.2	Structure of waqf shop	237
17.1	General scheme of social waqf	247

17.2 General scheme of productive waqf 248
17.3 General scheme of integrated social and productive waqf model-1 249
17.4 General scheme of integrated social and productive waqf model-2 250
17.5 The scheme of Firdaus Memorial Park 251
17.6 Current development of Firdaus Memorial Park 251
17.7 The scheme of Rumah Sehat Terpadu – Dompet Dhuafa (RST-DD) Hospital 252
17.8 The scheme of Jogokariyan Islamic Center 254
17.9 The scheme of Kuttab Al-Fatih – Sinergi Foundation 256
18.1 Management and distribution of awqaf and zakat in the province of Khyber Pakhtunkhwa (KP) of Pakistan 264
19.1 Prototypical application of cash waqf for youth empowerment in Kano State 275

Tables

3.1	Different classifications of the earliest *waqf*	26
5.1	Methodology of the historical approach to the project of a bank of awqāf which appeared in Bosnia–Herzegovina in 1900	53
5.2	Number of Muslims in Bosnia-Herzegovina in the years 1878–1918 (census of 1879, 1885 and 1910)	56
8.1	Women awqaf in Kuwait	108
12.1	Total number of depositors of TH	171
12.2	Population by ethnic group, Selangor (2018)	177
12.3	Respondents' marital status	181
12.4	ASNB depositors	183
14.1	Boarding schools and the number of students and teachers in 2018	210
14.2	Number of students based on the faculties in 2018	212
14.3	Number of foreign students based on their origin countries	213
14.4	Gontor's business units as per 1970–2007	214
14.5	Land owned by Gontor	215
14.6	Expansion of *Waqf* assets (2017–2018)	216
15.1	*Waqf* projects under the Ninth Malaysia Plan (2006–2010)	222
15.2	Socio-economic impact indicators for the best *waqf* reporting practices	224
15.3	*Waqf* socio-economic impact disclosure on cash *waqf* scheme	228
15.4	*Waqf* socio-economic impact disclosure on share *waqf* scheme	229
15.5	*Waqf* socio-economic impact disclosure on *waqfkhas* project	230

Acknowledgement

There is no strength and power except in *Allah (swt)*, To Him comes the praise, the Savant, the Wise, the Omniscient, the most beautiful names belong to Him. May the blessing of Allah (swt) and peace be upon *Muhammad (saw)* and all the Prophets (*aws*) from the first to the last.

First of all, I would humbly like to acknowledge King Abdulaziz University, Kingdom of Saudi Arabia and its prestigious wing Islamic Economics Institute for supporting us with every facility in research, academic, human capital and professional development activities outreaching the global *Ummah*. It is also a great honor for me to humbly acknowledge His Excellency Professor Dr Abdulrahman Obaid AI-Youbi, the President of King Abdulaziz University, Professor Dr Yousef Abdul Aziz Al Turki, the Vice President of King Abdulaziz University and Dr Abdullah Qurban Turkistani, the Dean of the Islamic Economics Institute (IEI), King Abdulaziz University (KAU), Dr Mohammad A. Naseef (Vice Dean, IEI-KAU), Dr Faisal Mahmoud Atbani (Head, Department of Insurance, IEI-KAU), Prof Dr Abdulrahim Al-Saati, Dr Omar Hafiz, Mr Mohammed Alabdulraheem and respected fellow-colleagues from the IEI, King Abdulaziz University for their continuous supports and encouragements towards dynamic professional development, excellent academic contributions and specialized advance scientific research activities. I would like to express my heartiest thanks with appreciation to H.E. Ms Nathalie Fustier, UN Resident Coordinator, Riyadh, Saudi Arabia and some other dignitaries of the UN and UNDP for supporting this research with applied ideas particularly with SDGs. Further acknowledgement is extended to public & private sectors, universities, industries and professional firms whose direct and indirect supports with knowledge, experiences and resources are full-heartedly recorded.

Mohd Ma'Sum Billah, PhD
Islamic Economics Institute
King Abdulaziz University
Saudi Arabia

Foreword

In the inception of 2020, the entire globe witnesses numerous catastrophes, namely the global attack by the novel Coronavirus outbreak (COVID-19), negative hit on the global oil price, political turmoil in several parts of the world, racial and ethnic war in many parts of the world, which destabilize in the world eco-peace and smooth forward of the socio- economic and financial movement. It has recently been predicted that the social finance may play a significant role in rescuing the global economic future from the existing catastrophic *status quo*. In the contemporary century, the world has been enjoying with advancement of science and technology in the cyberspace in almost every sectors of day to day life and culture, be one personal, private, domestic, social, political, economic, global or cyber. The economic, corporate, financial or trade sectors have still been dominated by traditional culture in coping up with gradual science and technological way uphill. It has been observed that, in the recent phenomena, the economic, financial and non-financial corporate sectors appreciate social financing with multiple smart mechanisms and structures in facilitating the contemporary socio-economic solutions. Despite such phenomena optimized by the eco-financial industries, there are obstacles and challenges in social financial movement, which slows the smooth way forward in true achievement. It may be recorded that, among those obstacles are lack of regulatory standard, less political support, poor understanding the impact, misuse and fraud cultures, poor system, inefficient professionalism and skills, unskilled corporate governance, lack of confidence, non-etiquette and insufficient support and cooperation from decision makers and policy controllers. However, most of these challenges might be due to invention with new dimension, but with temporary effect, perhaps. Such challenges may not last long in the promising journey or the emerging era of the social finance with its skilled dynamism and friendly offerings. Shari'ah compliance eco-financial industries are not exception in coping up with the global emergence of social finance through the noble application of *Awqaf* in their products and quality services, but within the rules of *Maqasid al-Shari'ah* (Divine objectives)in no parallel, but dichotomizing with the culture adapted in the conventional financial industries. The *Awqaf* led Social finance with divine ethical compliance may be an added value to the existing solutions particularly in this socio-economic catastrophic era in the 1st quarter of the 21st century.

Appreciating an *Awqaf* led social financial mechanisms in corporate or financial industries may be among the sustainable solutions to the contemporary eco-turmoil of the globe. Economic and financial authorities, regulators, decision makers, operators and customers are moving with greater prospects towards appreciating the socio-impact and or value-based financial system with promising benefits and better services with rational returns and sharing. Such achievement phenomenon is not realized only among the socio-economically developing states, but a rising global dimension. The contemporary Islamic financial market is growing faster than conventional counterpart, with an annual growth rate ranging from 13% to 23% with sustainability appreciated by all irrespective of religion, nationality, color, gender, status and or age across the today's world of economy. It is observed that, Islamic corporate and financial industries optimize *Awqaf* and *Zakat* led social financing opportunity in their master plan, policies, system, products, services and marketing within the rules of *Maqasid al-Shari'ah* aiming at serving the society with satisfaction and comfortness compatible with possible best offerings of the global practices of socio-eco-culture. Hence, *Halal* corporate and financial industries today foresee the emerging social financing led by *Awqaf* is the pushing factor of the impact investment or CSR with innovation to global platform with a furtherance legacy to position itself as an able alternative to the conventional counterpart with significant results and added benefits for all with universal value within the holistic spirit of *Maqasid al-Shari'ah*. To record that, among the OIC and non-OIC other states leading the advancement of social finance led by *Zakat* and *Awqaf* are Kingdom of Saudi Arabia, Malaysia, United Arab Emirates, Indonesia, Pakistan, Bahrain, Kuwait, Qatar, Turkey, Bangladesh, Oman, Brunei, Maldives, Sri Lanka, India, Iran, Sudan, Egypt, Gambia, Jordan, Uganda, Kenya, Afghanistan, Syria, Iraq, Hong Kong, Thailand, New Zealand, Ghana, Nigeria, South Africa, Bosnia, UK, Philippine, Singapore, USA, Australia, Germany, Russia, Canada are notable. The socio-political and financial authorities, corporate and professional entities, researchers and decision makers are among those who earnestly pushing, supporting and innovating the legal framework, technical know-how, operational mechanisms of *Awqaf* led social finance in their innovative system, products, services and marketing. *Awqaf* led social finance crowdfunding, SCR, SRI *sukuk*, VBI, Impact investment, *Waqf* cooperation, *Zakat* management, online social financial services, and social financial services through mobile banking are among those opportunities that are already in action through the *Shari'ah* compliance social financing within the spirit of *Maqasid al- Shari'ah*.

Undoubtedly, **Prof Dr Mohd Ma'Sum Billah** is a world-renowned Islamic finance scholar who has initiated in producing this unique book *Awqaf-Led Islamic Social Finance: Innovative Solutions to Modern Applications* as timely to meet the emerging demand of the global socio-economic environment with numerous solutions to *Awqaf* for socio-humanitarian causes within the holistic *Shari'ah* ethical frameworks. The book is thus a value-added empirical solution to Islamic socio-economic environment by contributing several notable chapters on specialized issues of *Awqaf* led social finance. It is thus an honor for me to appreciate and acknowledge that, this unique book is a solution to core issues of *Awqaf* led social finance, which is rightfully produced by Prof Billah of **Islamic Economics Institute, King Abdulaziz University, Saudi Arabia,** along with the cooperation and intellectual contributions of reputable researchers from different parts of the world as contributors, which is timely to meet the global demand of researchers, academia, professionals, industrialists, financial authorities, decision makers, technical experts, students, NGOs and other humanitarian organizations. The book therefore may be a useful reference in understanding and technical know-how of *Awqaf* led social finance and mechanisms within the principles of *Shari'ah* and may significantly contribute to socio-humanitarian needs and applications of *Awqaf* in the post-COVID-19 era in particular, *enSha Allah (swt).*

Sheikh Fawaz Mohammed Bashraheel
Chairman
Pharan Holding
Kingdom of Saudi Arabia (KSA)

Preface

The institution of *Awqaf* is a divine paradigm to care about all creatures as to one's well-being by cooperative helping hands. *Awqaf* is not a mere charitable component in satisfying the needy in their day to day life, but it is a holistic medium of contributing towards a sustainable balanced economy and development for the benefit of individual, family, society, nation as well as globe as to one's basic needs with food, clothing, healthcare, education, shelter, environment, spiritual enrichment, personality development and other needs and comforts, which are with much wider scope than the coverage of the SDGs. There are huge *Awqaf* defined wealth (realized or unrealized) available across the world, which may reach to trillions. They can be in the form of property, asset, wealth, currency, reserves, mining and so on with value impact. Such *Awqaf* wealth may significantly contribute to the rise of the global economy should they be carefully identified by professional research organizations, structured and managed with socio-economic impact within the *Maqasid al-Shari'ah*. However, due to poor constructive and effective research, ineffective structuring and unskilled management, the *Awqaf* wealth has failed to contribute with a socio-economic impact as ought to be. Thus, an attempt is made in this book to share different impact-oriented solutions to *Awqaf* in its holistic sustainable capacity as a socio-economic vehicle with impact in today's reality. The book however contributes with **innovative solutions to modern applications of *Awqaf*-led social finance** by addressing some core and specialized issues, which are divided into four parts with 21 different chapters besides an introduction, a bibliography and an index.

Part I provides a worldview of *Awqaf*, which consists of eight chapters addressing different core issues of *Awqaf*. Chapter 1 contributes to Emergence of *Awqaf* Development Centre: A Mind-Mapping Idea. Chapter 2 provides a paradigm of *Awqaf*-Led Neo Endowment in Supporting Socio-Economic Development. Chapter 3 analyzes the Objectives of *Awqaf* within the Classical Discourse and their Modern Implications. Chapter 4 analyzes the Role of *Awqaf* as an Economic Driver. Chapter 5 presents a paradigm of Genesis of *Awqaf* – A Lesson to Learn from the French Literature on Ottoman Empire. Chapter 6 goes on analyzing the Contemporary Approach in Productive

Awqaf Development. Chapter 7 analyzes the Utilizing *Awqaf* in Modern Muslim Minority Societies.

Part II focuses on Law and Policies governing *Awqaf,* which consists of two chapters. Chapter 8 provides Gender Justice in the Law of *Awqaf.* Chapter 9 discovers Developing a *Waqf* Market and Reconceptualizing *Awqaf* Governance via Regtech.

Part III focuses on the Application and Experiences of *Awqaf* in today's reality. This part deals with different applied issues and experiences of *Awqaf* in relevant chapters. Chapter 10 discusses the Poverty Alleviation through Islamic Social Finance in Agro-sectors – An Experience of Northern Ghana. Chapter 11 analyzes the Developing Awqaf through Cash *Waqf.* Chapter 12 contributes to an Islamic Social Finance Reform – *Hibah* a Catalyst for *Awqaf* Advancement. Chapter 13 analyzes Edu-*Waqf* Model – An Analysis of Selected OIC Member Countries. Chapter 14 provides a comprehensive analysis of Smart *Waqf* City for Education – An Experience in Darussalam Gontor, Indonesia. Chapter 15 discusses the Empirical Investigation of *Awqaf* and Its Socio-Economic Impact in Malaysia. Chapter 16 analyzes the *Awqaf* – Its ASEAN Experiences and a Lesson to Learn. Chapter 19 contributes to Integrated Social and Productive *Awqaf* in Indonesia. Chapter 18 analyzes *Waqf*-Led Social Finance in Poverty Alleviation – An Experience in Khyber Pakhtunkhwa, Pakistan. Chapter 19 provides an analysis on the Youth Empowerment and the Application of Cash *Waqf* – An Experience in Kano State, Nigeria.

It is needless to submit that the idea of *Awqaf* and its emergence are capturing the attention and appreciation of all levels of mankind across the contemporary world; yet no significant or comprehensive research with applied solution on *Awqaf* is to be used as a reliable reference for continuing academic or industrial research in meeting the demand of practical market niche and develop further with technical know-how, except mostly with jurisprudential thoughts available in the library or as occasional research or in the social media. Thus, ***Awqaf-Led Islamic Social Finance:* Innovative Solutions to Modern Applications** is expected to be among the pioneers with organized and comprehensive applied solutions to social finance led by a holistic approach of *Awqaf,* which may be a guide to academia, researchers, practitioners, decision makers, programmers, professionals, promoters and students for their technical know-how, future research and development of furtherance niche products. It is not impossible for this book to have any shortcomings. We would be thus grateful to all readers should any shortcomings be notified to us for further improvement.

Mohd Ma'Sum Billah, PhD
Islamic Economics Institute, King Abdulaziz University, Saudi Arabia

About the author

Mohd Ma'Sum Billah, PhD, is a Professor of Finance, Insurance, Fintech and Investment at the Islamic Economics Institute, King Abdulaziz University, Kingdom of Saudi Arabia. Billah has been serving and contributing both academic and corporate industries for more than 20 years in management, teaching, research, solution proving and sharing of strategic and technical thoughts towards the advancement of Islamic finance and insurance *(Takaful)* besides *Halal* standard. Billah has published 33 books and chapters in books besides more than 200 articles in journals and social media. He has presented more than 300 conferences, seminars, executive workshops and industrial trainings in different parts of the world. In addition, he was also affiliated with corporate, academic and financial industries including central banks, international corporate organizations, governments and NGOs in his capacity as a member in boards, advisor, strategic decision maker, transformer and reformer with strategic solution provider. Among the areas of his interest and contributions are Islamic finance, insurance (*Takaful*), crowd-funding, investment, Waqf, capital market (*Sukuk*), social finance, SDGs, petroleum finance, trade, fintech and cryptocurrency models and standards.

Contributors

Asmak Binti Ab Rahman, PhD, is currently an Associate Professor and Head of the Department of Syariah and Economics, Academy of Islamic Studies, University of Malaya. She obtained her PhD in Islamic Economics, Masters in Syariah and Bachelors of Syariah from the University of Malaya. She is an expert in the areas of Takaful, Islamic Banking, Economics of Waqf, Peace Economy, among other Islamic Finances. She has published many articles in peer-reviewed journals, books and chapters.

Suhail Ahmad, MBA, is currently a PhD Research Scholar in the Department of Business Administration in the Sarhad University of Science and Information Technology, Peshawar, Pakistan. After graduating with a BBA HONS in Finance with ***Distinction*** and awarded ***Certificate of Merit*** from the Govt. Post Graduate College of Management Sciences Thana, Malakand, University of Malakand, Chakdara, Pakistan, I obtained my MBA/MS in Finance with a research thesis on *Issues & Problems of Islamic Banking in Pakistan with special reference to poverty alleviation* from the University of Malakand, Chakdara, Pakistan. Suhail Ahmad's area of interest is Islamic Finance, Poverty Alleviation through Islamic Finance and Microfinance and desires to alleviate poverty in the economy, not only in Pakistan but also across the globe. Suhail Ahmad has published research papers in the field of finance, Islamic finance, microfinance, poverty alleviation, etc. and has recently published a paper titled "Developing and Proposing a Model for Zakat Management System: A Case of the Malakand District of KP, Pakistan, with Special Reference to Poverty Alleviation in the District" in the *International Journal of Zakat* (Volume 04 No. 01, 2019), an Indonesian-based journal, which won the **Best Paper Award** with a cash prize.

Mohammed Fawzi Aminu Amadu, MBA, is a Management Consultant and Social Commentator with 18 years of experience. His consultancy covers work with Government of Ghana, Private Corporations – both local and international – as well as local NGOs. Currently, he is the Director of Business Development for GM Ambassadors – a management consulting firm. Amadu is also a Director with Africa Islamic Economic Foundation, an international NGO. Through his office at the Africa Islamic

Economic Foundation, he is currently working with the Government of Ghana (through the Ministry of Foreign Affairs and the Bank of Ghana) to develop an enabling environment for the adoption of Islamic Finance. His consultancy has covered a wide range of fields including Information Technology issues, Education, Commodity Trading, Real Estate Development, Finance – especially with regard to Islamic Finance, Agriculture, as well as transport and logistics.

Ascarya, PhD, is a Magister of Economics and Waqf at the University of Darussalam Gontor, Indonesia. He serves as the editorial team member of several international scientific journals (SCOPUS indexed) and an Editorial Board Member of other international scientific journals. He is also a reviewer for several international (SCOPUS Indexed) and national scientific journals. He is an expert in the field of Islamic Economics, Monetary, Banking, Islamic Microfinance and Islamic Social Finance (especially Zakat and Waqf), as well as a lecturer in several universities. In addition, he is a trainer in the Analytic Network Process (ANP) and Data Envelopment Analysis (DEA) research methods. He holds a PhD in Islamic Economics and Finance from IEF-Trisakti University, Jakarta, Indonesia. He has also received PhD in International Development, MBA in Finance and MSc in Management Information System from the University of Pittsburgh, PA, USA. He has produced 26 international journals and books, 70 international papers, 22 national journals, 23 national papers, 41 working papers, 3 occasional papers, 22 books, 4 proceedings, 12 periodical publications, and 6 research notes. He has presented in 70 international conferences and 90 national conferences. He has received four International Best Paper Awards in 2013, 2014, 2015 and 2016.He has also received BAZNAS Award 2018 as "Tokoh Pendukung Kebangkitan Zakat".

Imam Nur Aziz, PhD, is a member of the Indonesian Waqf Board and co-founder of Alwyni International Capital. He obtained his bachelor's degree from Diponegoro University and did his postgraduate studies in International Political Economy from Leeds University in 2001 and in development economics and international development from Fushinkang College in 2012.

Abderrazak Belabes, PhD, currently serves as a Professor of Economics at the Islamic Economics Institute, King Abdulaziz University, Saudi Arabia. He holds an engineering degree in electronics, a Masters in Science in econometrics and PhD in economic analysis and policy from the School of High Studies in Social Sciences (EHESS, Paris). His main research interests – beyond the subject matter – focus on the economic methodology, in the broadest sense of the term, which includes the distinction between the existence of the object (ontology), its representation (imago) and the way to know it (epistemology). This led him gradually to the deconstruction of the discourse on Islamic economics, finance and banking to better understand the complex interactions between religion and economics, and the inconsistencies between intention and action, theory and facts, beyond the conceptual smokescreen. This approach is a continuation of his PhD thesis, which investigated the complex interaction between ideology and economics beyond the Schumpeterian dichotomy 'science/ideology'. It aims to identify the conditions for the emergence of a discourse, its limitations and inconsistencies in the light of research works on comparative literature, archeology of knowledge, history and philosophy of science, sociology of knowledge, history of economic life and institutions, and ethics of science and technology.

Hisham Dafterdar, PhD, is an Advisor at the International Islamic Institute of Waqf, Malaysia, a consultant of International Islamic Rating Agency, Bahrain and a partner of Jeyad Advisory Services, Bahrain. He is the Founder and Chairman of Awkaf Australia Ltd, a founding member of the National Awqaf Foundation of Canada (Awqaf Canada), Director of Awqaf New Zealand and Deputy President of World Awqaf Forum, Switzerland. He is also a Lecturer at the Bahrain Institute for Banking and Finance. Dafterdar is an experienced Islamic banker with more than 30 years of practice. Previously, he was a Business Development Manager at the Islamic Development Bank, where his responsibility included Awqaf fund management and development of Awqaf projects and investments. He represented IDB on the board of banks and investment companies, and served as a member of the Product Development Committee of the International Islamic Financial Market in Bahrain. He was also a Senior Advisor at Bank Al-Khair, Bahrain, leading a team on the development of Awqaf properties and advising on all matters relating to mergers and acquisitions, product development and endowment funds. Dafterdar co-authored books on Awqaf and delivered a number of research papers and speeches at conferences and served as a panelist and discussant at international seminars and roundtables on Awqaf and Islamic banking.

Mohamed Cherif El Amri, PhD, is working as an Assistant Professor at the Faculty of Business and Management Sciences Specialized Islamic Economics and Finance, at Sabahattin Zaim University. He completed his Bachelor's degree in Islamic Studies from Ibn Tofail University in Morocco. He had his Masters in Islamic Jurisprudence and its principles and his PhD in Islamic banking and finance from International Islamic University Malaysia. He worked as an intern at several Islamic Financial Institutions, such as the Islamic Capital Market Business Group, Securities Commission, Kuala Lumpur Malaysia, and Maybank Islamic. He worked as a researcher at the Institute of Islamic Banking and Finance, Malaysia. He was an Associated Consultant at Amanie Advisors, Kuala Lumpur, Malaysia. He is a member of the Scientific Committee of the *International Review of Entrepreneurial Finance Journal* and *International Journal of Islamic*

Economics and Finance. He has multiple research publications and presentations in the field of Islamic Finance and Economics.

Nura Abubakar Gwadabe, MA, is from Kano State of Nigeria. She obtained a bachelor's degree in Islamic Studies from the University of Maiduguri, 2007, Master in Fiqh from Al-Madinah International University, Malaysia, 2014 and is currently a PhD candidate at the Department of Syariah and Economics, University of Malaya, Malaysia, since 2018. She is a lecturer in the Department of Islamic Studies, Faculty of Humanities, Yusuf Maitama Sule University, Kano State Nigeria. Nura has published a quite number of articles related to Islamic Economics and Finance in many peer-reviewed journals.

Shaykh Haitham al-Haddad, PhD, was born in Saudi Arabia and studied Islamic jurisprudence, Hadith, Arabic and other sciences for many years with various scholars from different countries. Shaykh Haitham holds a BSc Honours in Law and Shari'ah from Sudan. He also holds a BSc in Computer Science from Saudi Arabia and has obtained his PhD in Islamic Law at SOAS in London. Shaykh Haitham sits on the board of advisors of a number of key Islamic organizations in the United Kingdom and other European countries. Shaykh Haitham al-Haddad's specialty is in principles of Islamic jurisprudence, Islamic law and Islamic finance. He wrote a number of books in Arabic and English. He also authored many articles in Arabic and English. He is an international speaker and academic who participated in many academic conferences around the world. He also appears regularly in many Islamic channels. He delivered hundreds of lectures and courses in many Muslim and European countries. He serves as a Muslim judge for British and European Muslims and also runs an open fatwa line.

Hichem Hamza, PhD, holds a doctoral degree in Economics from the University of Economics and Management in Clermont-Ferrand, France. He started his career at Tunis Higher School of Business in 2003. Since 2016, he is an Associate Professor and Researcher at the Islamic Economics Institute, King Abdulaziz University. His research interests include Islamic finance and banking, monetary and financial economics, Awqaf (Endowments) and non-profit organizations. Dr. Hamza published, among others, his studies in *Research in International Business and Finance*, *Studies in Economics and Finance*, *International Journal of Islamic and Middle Eastern Finance and Management*, *Journal of Islamic Accounting and Business Research* and *Borsa Istanbul Review*.

Mustafa Mohd Hanefah, PhD, is a Professor of Accounting, shariah auditing and zakat at the Faculty of Economics and Muamalat, Universiti Sains Islam Malaysia (USIM). He was a former Deputy Vice-Chancellor (Research and Innovation) at the USIM and the Dean of Research and Innovation at the Faculty of Economics and Muamalat. He also was a Visiting Professor at the Economic Research Centre, Nagoya University (2011) and Aoyama Business School, Aoyama Gakuin University (2016), Japan. Dato' Dr Mustafa obtained his Bachelor Degree in Accounting (Hons) from Universiti Kebangsaan Malaysia (UKM). Later, he obtained his Master Degree in Accountancy from the University of Wollongong, Australia, and his PhD in Islamic Accounting from Memphis University, USA. He has published many papers in international journals and books in the areas of Islamic financial reporting and accounting, shariah auditing, taxation, zakat and waqf. He also serves as a member of the editorial boards in a number of international journals.

Sahibzada Ghiasul Haq, PhD, is currently a Professor and the Dean of Faculty of Management Sciences at the Sarhad University of Science and Information Technology, Peshawar, Khyber Pakhtunkhwa, Pakistan. He holds PhD in economics from Glasgow University, UK. He is one of the top supervisors and supervised many doctorate scholars in the university in the field of economics and management sciences. He has vast experience in the field of economics and management sciences. He published different research papers in the field of economics, and Islamic economy and Islamic finance. He also worked on SMEs financing in Khyber Pakhtunkhwa, Pakistan.

Souhaila Guedira, M.Sc, is currently, a PhD candidate in the field of Islamic Economics and Finance in Istanbul Sabahattin Zaim University (IZU) in Turkey. Born in Morocco, she pursued her Bachelor studies in France and completed her Master in Management majoring in Audit and Finance in KEDGE Business School in Marseille, France (2017). She holds a Master of Science (MSc) in Islamic Finance from INCEIF, The Global University of Islamic Finance, Malaysia (2019). Her research interests include education, empirical studies and research in Islamic finance, social finance, data analysis and Econometrics. She speaks Arabic (native), French (bilingual), English (advanced), and Turkish (elementary) languages.

Muhamad Nadratuzzaman Hosen, PhD, is currently a Senior Lecturer at State Islamic University Syarif Hidayatullah, Jakarta, since 2003. He holds PhD in economics from University of England, Armidale, Australia. He is a Treasurer at the Indonesian Council of Ulama as well as at the National Shariah Board. He published several books and articles in international journals. He was the Vice Chairman for National Waqf Board from 2005 to 2008.

Abdul-Jalil Ibrahim, MSc, is a PhD student in Islamic Finance and Economy at Hamad Bin Khalifa University in Doha, Qatar, where he previously pursued his second Master's degree in Islamic Finance. He earlier received an MSc in Energy Studies from the University of Dundee, UK, where he graduated with a distinction in 2012. He also graduated with a first-class degree from the Kwame Nkrumah University of Science and Technology, where he pursued a BSc in Business Administration (Accounting).

His research interests include sustainability and Islamic finance, climate risks and financial stability, Islamic venture capital and entrepreneurship and application of fintech in Islamic finance. He was the lead consultant for a project on a study of the viability of improved cookstove producers in Ghana commissioned by the SNV Netherlands Development Organisation in 2018. Abdul-Jalil has over seven years of varied experience in financial services sectors and SMEs advisory. He is co-founder of Data Partners and Dar Al Istithmar (Islamic fund management and investment advisory company based in Accra). He has also worked with Standard Chartered Bank Ghana and Coface Ghana as Operations Assistant and Sales Representative, respectively. Abdul-Jalil has written and presented research papers, including a paper on energy-water-environment nexus and the transition towards a circular economy in Qatar at the University of Cambridge in 2019. He also co-authored a book on energy sector development in Ghana. His recent co-authored paper on "Digital era and Islamic monetary policy with special reference to systemic liquidity" received the best paper award at INCEIF-ISRA Inaugural Conference on Islamic Economics and Finance in the Digital Era in November 2019 at Kuala Lumpur, Malaysia.

Noor Shahalina BINTI Jamaludin, MSc, is a Professional Mawarith Consultant who helps Malaysian Muslims and finance professionals plan their wealth management for Islamic Inheritance to ease the beneficiaries' claim in future. She is also a Remisier (a registered Dealer's Representative with Securities Commission) with a stock broking firm since 1996. With a successful career helping investing clients, Noor Shahalina now helps them with more extensive Islamic Inheritance awareness and services. Noor Shahalina graduated from INCEIF with a Master in Islamic Finance Practice. Noor Shahalina is available for marketing and writing projects, as well as private consultations.

Muhammad Iqmal Hisham Kamaruddin, MA, is a USIM Graduate Fellow and a PhD student at the Faculty of Economics and Management, Universiti Kebangsaan Malaysia (UKM). He received his Bachelor Degree in Accounting with Honours (2014) and Master Degree in Economics and Muamalat Administration (2016) from Universiti Sains Islam Malaysia (USIM). He was a recipient of the Royal Education Award for his bachelor degree and the Accounting Best Student Award 2014 from the Malaysian Institute of Accountants (MIA). He also received the Faculty Book Award (Master by Research) for his Master Degree. Currently, he is writing a thesis on Financial Management, Financial Governance and Accountability in Islamic Social Enterprise (ISE) in Malaysia. His area of expertise is Islamic accounting, Shariah audit and governance and Islamic social finance. He has also presented and published a number of articles and chapter in books in various national and international conferences, journals and book publications. He has also published two books entitled *Shariah Audit and Assurance: Process and Programme* and *Shariah Governance and Assurance in Islamic Financial Sectors.*

Lisa Listiana, MSc, is founder of Waqf Center for Indonesian Development and Studies (WaCIDS). Currently she is pursuing PhD program at Institute of Islamic Banking and Finance (IIiBF), International Islamic University Malaysia (IIUM) with full scholarship from Indonesia Endowment Fund for Education (LPDP). She has strong passion and research interest on waqf, undertakes PhD research related to waqf, and established WaCIDS as a think tank and independent research institution. WaCIDS provides a forum for researchers and practitioners to collaborate in developing waqf in Indonesia and hosts various programs to promote awareness on waqf, especially among millennials (Instagram address: @wacids.official). She was the Best Talent of LPDP 2017. Some of her papers related to waqf were awarded as best papers in 4th Annual Islamic Finance Conference (AIFC) Call for Paper 2019, Hajj Financial Management Agency (BPKH) Call for Paper 2018, Shariah Economic and Finance Forum (FREKS) Call for Paper 2018. She has presented papers related to waqf in the 5th international Ibn Khaldun Symposium, Turkey (2019); 6th Global Waqf Conference, Thailand (2018); International Conference on Religion, Culture, and Governance, Malaysia (2018); International Postgraduate Colloquium on Waqf Research, Malaysia (2018); 5th Global Waqf Conference, Indonesia (2017); and Muktamar Waqf Iqlimi IV, Malaysia (2017). She holds master's degree in accounting from University of Indonesia with full scholarship from the same sponsor. Previously, she worked as an accountant for four years in ExxonMobil, auditor in Ernst and Young, also a part-time lecturer and research fellow in Indonesian universities.

Aminudin Ma'ruf, MSc, holds a Master's Degree in Islamic Finance from INCEIF, Malaysia. Prior to that, he graduated in Shari'ah and Islamic Jurisprudence from IIUM. His interest is on the topic of Shari'ah, Ethical Finance and Islamic Social Finance.

Rosnia Masruki, PhD, is a Senior Lecturer at the Faculty of Economics and Muamalat, Universiti Sains Islam Malaysia (USIM). She holds a PhD in Accounting, specialising in reporting and disclosure for Islamic Financial Institutions (IFIs) and non-profit organisations (NPOs) such as government agencies, charities, cooperatives, faith-based organisations and waqf (endowment) institutions. In fact, her PhD thesis is about Majlis Agama Islam in Malaysia, which triggers the interest to enhance this area of research further. At present, she teaches financial accounting, management accounting and public-sector accounting at the bachelor and master degree programs. She was the Head of the Accounting program at her previous university in Malaysia. She has also served as an adviser in the field of education. She has been a trainer and invited speaker in business accounting and finance for corporations and universities. Currently, she is the Head of Accounting Programme in the Faculty of Economics and Muamalat, USIM. She is actively researching the best practices of reporting, performance measurement and socio-economic impact for NPOs and corporate governance. Dr Rosnia found that waqf is an area that needs further attention on the accounting and reporting aspects, particularly waqf's impact for the benefit of Muslims and society. She can be reached at rosnia@usim.edu.my.

Dian Masyita, PhD, is an Associate Professor at the Faculty of Economics & Business, Universitas Padjadjaran. She completed her PhD in Islamic Finance from Durham University, UK, in 2012. She was the first member of the R&D division in Badan Wakaf Indonesia (BWI) in 2007. She was awarded "The TOP 10 Most Influential Women in Islamic Business and Finance 2019" by Cambridge IFA, UK, "The Best Syariah" from Investor Magazine in 2019 and "The Top 8 Outstanding Lecturers in Indonesia in 2018" by Kemenristekdikti. Since 2015, she has been appointed as a Project Manager of Waqf Core Principles by Bank Indonesia and a Senior Specialist in Islamic Finance at Lab Innovative Financing – UNDP. The World Resources Institutes, USA, invited her to participate in focus group discussions with MIT's System Dynamics Group at MIT, USA, 2018. She is one of the authors of the book titled *Islamic Microenterprises* published by Bank Indonesia in 2016. She had presented papers in many conferences i.e., the System Dynamics Conference, MIT-USA (2005), IRTI-IDB's Islamic Financial conference (2007) in Brunei Darussalam, Moral Value in Milan Italy (2009), DFIP-Kyoto University Workshop in Durham (2010 & 2012), Ethics in Financial in Melbourne (2011); two IRTI IDB Conferences in Sudan and Doha-Qatar (2011), Durham-Monash Conference (2014), ISRA-IRTI-Durham Roundtable (2014), UC Berkeley USA (2016), Umm Al Qura, Makkah (2016), ARI-NUS Singapore (2017), Ankara, Turkey (2018). She has published her papers in more than 10 Scopus indexed journals until 2019.

Mustafa Omar Mohammed, PhD, is presently the Head and an Associate Professor at the Department of Economics, International Islamic University Malaysia (IIUM), where he has been teaching for more than 15 years now. He has published more than 50 refereed journal articles and presented more than 70 papers, mostly at international conferences. He is actively involved in funding and commissioning research projects. His present research areas of interest are in *Waqf*, *Zakat*, Islamic Microfinance and *Maqasid al-Shari'ah*. He has supervised more than 45 dissertations at PhD and Master Levels. He is also a journal editorial member and reviewer panel to 11 academic entities. He has received several quality awards for teaching and research. He was part of a committee responsible for setting up the Institute of Islamic Banking and Finance and recently, the Department of Islamic Finance at IIUM. He also has long experience in translations, Arabic and English. He undertook projects for several organizations, including MIFC, IBFIM, AIBIM, IFSB – affiliates of the Central Bank of Malaysia. He offers consultancy and has conducted several training on Islamic economics, banking and finance in several countries including Kazakhstan, Singapore, Sri Lanka, Bangladesh, Philippines, Indonesia, South Africa and Uganda. Dr Mustafa holds Bachelor and Master degrees in Economics from IIUM and PhD in Finance from Universiti Sains Malaysia.

Magda Ismail Abdel Mohsin, PhD, is currently an Associate Professor at the International Centre for Education in Islamic Finance (INCEIF). She obtained her doctorate in Islamic Civilization/Islamic Economy from the International Institute of Islamic Thought and Civilization (ISTAC), the International Islamic University Malaysia (IIUM) in 2003. Prior to joining INCEIF in 2007 she taught many subjects in Islamic economics and Islamic finance at the International Islamic College (IIC) and was appointed as the Head of Economic Department for two years and as Deputy Chief Executive Academic for two years in the same college. She presented many papers at national and international levels held in different countries such as Washington DC, UK, Singapore, Maldives, India, Indonesia, Turkey, UAE, Kuwait, Qatar, Algeria, Tunisia and Sudan besides local conferences in Malaysia. Moreover, she conducted many trainings on waqf and zakah locally and internationally: locally with Redmoney, the International Centre for Waqf Research (ICWR) and the International Federation of Red Cross and Red Crescent IFRC; and internationally by IRTI & the National Awqaf Foundation of South Africa in South Africa, the Singapore Institute of Management (SIM) in Singapore, Le Centre Nationale de la Recherche Scientifique in Algeria, BAZNAS in Indonesia and Bilim Ve Sanat Vakfi in Turkey. With reference to the research, she is the author of two books on waqf entitled *Cash Waqf: A New Financial Product* and *Corporate Waqf: From Principle to Practice*, both published by Pearson Malaysia Sdn. Bhd. In 2009 and 2014, respectively. She is also the editor of her latest book on waqf entitled *Financing the Development of Old Waqf Properties: Classical Principles and Innovative Practices around the World*, published by Palgrave Macmillan, 2016. Moreover, she published many articles on waqf, zakah, Islamic microfinance, Islamic economics and more recently on fintech and blockchain. Furthermore. She is the recipient of two awards on waqf publications: best/outstanding paper award for the paper "Financing through cash-waqf: A new innovation for the 21st Century" by Emerald Group in 2013 and best book on *Corporate Waqf; from Principle to Practice*, which had been translated into Arabic by Imam Muhammad ibn Saud Islamic University Riyadh, Saudi Arabia, in collaboration with Sheikh Rashid bin Dail Research Chair for Endowments Studies 2015. In 2016 she also received the Outstanding Women Achiever for the contribution and achievement in the field of Islamic Economics and Finance, given under the seal of Venus International Foundation, India. In 2018 she was recognised by Cambridge Analytica IF as one of the top 30 most influential women in Islamic finance.

Aishath Muneeza, PhD, is an Associate Professor at INCEIF. She is the first female Deputy Minister of Ministry of Islamic Affairs and is the Deputy Minister of Ministry of Finance & Treasury of Republic of Maldives. She is also the Chairwoman of Maldives Center for Islamic Finance. She is considered as the founder of Islamic finance in Maldives. Her contribution to Islamic finance includes structuring of the corporate sukuks and sovereign private sukuk of the country, including the Islamic treasury instruments. She also drafted the Islamic Capital Market framework of the country and is the only registered Shari'ah adviser for Islamic capital market in the country since 2013. She played a key role in setting up of the Tabung Haji of Maldives, Maldives Hajj Corporation and was the first chairperson of it. She sits in various *Shari'ah* advisory bodies nationally and internationally and is chairman for many of these *Shari'ah* advisory bodies including the apex Shari'ah Advisory Council for capital market in Maldives. She has assisted more than eleven institutions to offer Islamic financial products/services. She won various national and international awards for her contribution made towards the development of Islamic finance industry. She is also a role model and a mentor for females who aspire to build their careers in Islamic finance industry and is the Vice President of Women on Boards, an NGO advocating women representation on boards of companies. She is an invited speaker in Islamic finance conferences and events held in different parts of the world. She was listed in 2017 as number seven among the 50 Influential Women in Business and Finance by ISFIRE, which is an official publication of Islamic Bankers Association based in London and she is among the most influential 500 in Islamic Economy. She is a member of the Association of Shari'ah Advisors in Islamic Finance Malaysia (ASAS), Malaysia. She holds a doctorate in law from International Islamic University of Malaysia.

Zakariya Mustapha, LLM, practices law in Nigeria where he is an advocate and solicitor of Nigeria's Supreme Court since 2008. In 2010, he joined Faculty of Law, Bayero University Kano, Nigeria, as a lecturer where he taught conventional and Islamic banking and finance law, alongside other Islamic law courses until 2017. He specializes on legal and *Shari'ah* issues in Islamic banking and finance and offers legal and Islamic financial advisory services about legal framework, dispute resolution and Shari'ah-compliant product development in Islamic banking and finance. He has published numerous articles and he has presented research papers in national and international conferences. He holds a LLB, LL.M, BL with membership of Nigerian Bar Association and Nigerian Institute of Management (Chartered). He is currently pursuing his PhD in Islamic finance law at Faculty of Law, University of Malaya, Kuala Lumpur.

Mohammad Abdullah Nadwi, PhD, is an expert in the theory and practices of Islamic Sciences, Islamic Jurisprudence and Islamic finance. Abdullah is a well-trained and highly experienced Shariah Scholar, providing Shariah consultancy and advisory services to various Islamic financial institutions in Europe, South America and the UAE. He is a reputed researcher and has produced a number of research papers and book chapters on the comparative study of *Waqf* and English trust, *Shariah* governance, Islamic finance and development studies. Dr Abdullah holds a Bachelor degree in Shariah Sciences from Darul Uloom Nadwatul Ulama, Lucknow, India, and Masters in Islamic Banking, Finance and Management from the Markfield Institute of Higher Education, UK. Abdullah received his PhD at the University of Gloucestershire (UK) and he is a Certified Shariah Advisor and Auditor (CSAA) by the AAOIFI. Abdullah frequently presents research papers and he has presented a number of research papers on different aspects of Islamic banking and finance in different American, European and Asian countries including Germany, Norway, Italy, Ireland, Scotland, UK, Trinidad & Tobago, Indonesia, Malaysia, India and Dubai. He is currently based in UAE.

Syed Khalid Rashid, PhD, served as a Professor of Law at the Ahmad Ibrahim Kulliyyah of Laws, International Islamic University, Malaysia, for 25 years (1990–2015). He has 50 years of research and teaching experience, mainly in Waqf laws and management in four different universities in Malaysia, India and Nigeria. In 1971, his PhD thesis on "Waqf laws and administration in India" was awarded the first doctorate in Islamic Laws by Aligarh Muslim University in India in its century long history. For 10 years, he served as a Professor of Law and Dean at Usmanu Danfodiyo University, Sokoto, Nigeria (1980–90). For a total of 12 years, he was Associate Professor of Law at Aligarh Muslim University and Kurukshetra University, India. His publication includes 13 books and 88 papers, of which 8 books and 27 papers are on Waqf laws and management. He won the best Researcher Award in Law at IIUM during 2004. Islamic Development Bank, Jeddah, Saudi Arabia, invited him as a Visiting Scholar (Waqf) in 2011 and JAWHAR (Prime Minister's Department, Federal Government of Malaysia) appointed him as the chief consultant (Waqf) during 2010–11. He was the founding director, International Centre for Waqf Research, IIUM during 2014–15. In 2019, he was awarded the "Lifetime Achievement Award" by the Deputy Prime Minister of Malaysia, conferred by the Global Waqf Conference 2019 held in Kuala Lumpur, organized by the Al-Madinah International University, for excellence in Waqf research.

Shaikh Hamzah Abdul Razak, DBA, is an Associate Professor at INCEIF, teaching Wealth Management as well as Takaful. His areas of research include Islamic social finance, waqf, inheritance, etc. He joined INCEIF in November 2006 upon graduating from USM after INCEIF's inception as a private university. He is also involved with consultancy work. Prior to joining, Shaikh Hamzah was with Malayan Banking Berhad (Maybank), a local bank since 1974 as a clerical staff until 2001 as a Manager of Komtar Branch, Penang. He left the bank under voluntary separation scheme (vss) to pursue his DBA at Sains University of Malaysia (USM) in Penang, which he graduated in 2006. At USM, he was a part-time lecturer of corporate finance with the School of Continuing Education Distance Learning as well as a tutor for Investment Portfolio under Professor Ruhani. While pursuing his DBA he acted as insurance unit manager from 2002 to 2004.

Imam Teguh Saptono, PhD, is a member of the Indonesian Waqf Board. Prior to this, he was the president director of Global Waqf Corporation and president director of BNI Syariah. He obtained his Ph.D. in Business Management from IPB University and his master's in Agribusiness Management from the same university in 1994.

Raditya Sukmana, PhD, is currently a Professor in Islamic Economics in Department of Islamic Economics, Faculty of Economics and Business, Universitas Airlangga. Besides being a lecturer, he is also a member of East Java National Waqf Board, provincial waqf regulator. He got his Bachelor Degree from Universitas Airlangga, Master of Arts in Economics from Georgia State University, USA. He holds PhD from International Islamic University Malaysia. His area of specialization is Waqf, Islamic Bank, and Capital Market. He has published in several reputable journals such as *Economic Modelling, Economic Notes, International Journal of Islamic & Middle Eastern Finance and Management.* He has presented papers on Islamic Economics and Finance in several prestigious universities such as Harvard University (USA) in 2014, Cambridge University (UK) in 2012 and Oxford University (UK) in 2005. Furthermore, he has written books on Islamic Capital Market and Waqf, and worked as an external examiner at INCEIF Malaysia. He shares opinions on waqf and Islamic Economics in national newspapers.

Umer Suleman, PG Dip GRC, has over 15 years of experience within the assurance and risk management arena, advising across a variety of businesses and sectors. He is known for establishing fit-for-purpose risk frameworks that enable businesses to manage their key risks in line with their strategic objectives. During his 7 years at HSBC, Umer was Head of KYC Risk globally within their Global Banking & Markets business, Head of Business & Conduct Risk for MENA within Retail Banking and headed up the CCO function for Digital (GLCM) within the UK with a global remit. Umer has regularly managed high performance teams and runs C-suite Risk & Performance forums. Umer is also an SME in the Shariah Governance space and successfully managed the Shari'ah certification of Yielders, the UK's first FCA approved fintech. He has also advised the UK government on alternative finance schemes and is currently serving as a non-executive advisor to a number of tech start-ups and NGOs. Umer holds a PG Diploma in Governance Risk & Compliance from Manchester Business School and started his career in Ernst & Young as part of the specialist PFI group.

Hendri Tanjung, PhD in economics from the International Institute of Islamic Economics, International Islamic University Islamabad, Pakistan in 2012. Author of 33 books; reviewer and editor of 14 journals; 66 publications in newspaper and magazines; 40 publications of research papers; 1958 citations, h-index 11, google scholar version. Vice-director of the Post Graduate School, University of Ibn Khaldun, Bogor, Indonesia; Chairman of International Council of Islamic Finance Educators (ICIFE) Indonesia Chapter; Commissioner of Waqf Board Indonesia.

Introduction

The institution of *Awqaf* (endowment) is a holistic wealth bank contributed by individual, family, group, organization or state on account of concern and due care for others. The application of *Waqf* was originated from the ancient era and has been flourishing since the golden time of Islam through the divine spirit of the Holy Prophet Mohammad (*saw*) followed by *Khulafay-e-al-Rashedun* and a non-stop chain to date within the holistic principles of *Maqasid al-Shari'ah*. The institution of *Waqf* contributes unlimitedly for the individual, family, society and public benefits in general. The contribution of *Waqf* extends its care through knowledge and professional development, creating community with skills and professionalism, helping hand towards healthcare, religious activities, shelter, food, clothing, cultural cohesion, caring for the economic well-being of needy, poor and helpless ones, public utilities, nature and environmental well-being, caring for creatures, humanitarian care and concern, and universal peace and progress.

The conventional alternative of endowment, on the other hand, has been indeed observed and experienced with sustainable existence in humanitarian causes like education, healthcare, shelter, food, clothing, public utilities, religious activities and other charitable actions. Despite both institutions generally aim at humanitarian care and concern, the fundamental difference between them is one (*Waqf*) is regulated and operated strictly within the principles of *Maqasid al-Shari'ah* for the humanitarian causes and caring for creatures within the universal value while the conventional alternative like endowment, trust, half-secret trust, social foundation, humanitarian action and so on are regulated and managed based on laws and policies of concerned country. In the smart economic chapter of the contemporary reality the emergence of *Waqf* is significantly realized with utmost appreciation both in Muslim and non-Muslim environment with significant impact.

No doubt that the growth of Islamic finance today is significantly realized and in no exception of the institution of *Waqf* and its emergence towards creating an enterprising and an entrepreneurship-based community across the world, so to meet the underlying objectives of the sustainable development goals (SDGs) by targeting the low-income group in particular by designing an Awqaf-led entrepreneurship model with a cooperative culture for the needy, poor, helpless and destitute ones in the society.

It is submitted that if the different classes of Awqaf are discovered by effective research and are designed with appropriate structures, may create a size of USD 5–7 trillion, which may be three times of what the SDGs annually require. Such effective research, discovery, structures, models and strategic action plan may not confine with the property waqf, but in cash, gold, other precious metals, mining, business entities, reserved wealth, sanctioned wealth, doubtful wealth and wealth of uncertain ownership. The strategic structure may be extended to individual waqf, family waqf, social waqf, public waqf, temporary waqf, sukuk al-waqf, sukuk al-Intifa' led by waqf, SRI sukuk led by waqf, green sukuk led by waqf, edu-waqf, healthcare-waqf, shelter-waqf, humanitarian care waqf, climate change-waqf, impact investment led by waqf, crowdfunding led by waqf and other causes of helping hands led by waqf.

There are numerous research works on *Waqf* available in the market, which are mainly on conceptual and jurisprudential with *Fiqhi* treatment and regulatory frameworks, but a very little focus on the practical models, products, industrial solutions, experiences and digital mechanisms of *Waqf*. Thus, such phenomena may fail to meet the demand of the *Waqf* solutions in the wake of globalization.

The prime objective of this book is to contribute with an innovative and practical solution to *Awqaf* in the socio-economic reality. It may be a unique reference and a guide to academia, researchers, industrialists, decision makers and students in the field of *Awqaf* with applied solutions. Moreover, the project aims at focusing more on a practical model structure than on conceptual analysis. An attempt is however made in this research to produce a practical solution to *Awqaf* in the contemporary socio-economic environment through SWOT analysis, different categories of *Awqaf* products, models, industrial experiences, smart operations and further solutions to reality.

Part I

Awqaf

Its world view

1 Emergence of *Awqaf* development centre

A mind-mapping idea[1]

Mohd Ma'Sum Billah

Central idea

While the contemporary world is dominated by debt-based economy along with selfishness of the habitual capitalist culture in ignoring the basic eco-social rights of those destitute, poor and helpless ones, the Islamic economic renaissance tries to create some possible ways to care about those underprivileged ones based on the holistic principles of "just distribution" through the institutions of *Zakat*, *Waqf*, *Hibah* and others. Despite the earlier fact, the divine institutions of *Zakat* and *Waqf* are growing more under the umbrella of conceptual solutions far from the desired practical solutions in the socio-economic reality of today. It is undeniably understood that if the institutions of *Zakat* and *Waqf* are effectively organized, the socio-economic distress in the Third World particularly among those underprivileged ones may diminish for a better lives.

It is thus timely to initiate an effective strategic action plan to design the institution of Waqf with result-oriented products and services in order to create an enterprising and an entrepreneurship-based community across the world aimed at rescuing those underprivileged ones from socio-economic curse and sufferings.

Considering the global track-record of the rapid growth of Islamic financial or professional activities in developing and promoting the contemporary Islamic economics and finance with no exception of *Awqaf* thoughts and with utmost appreciation through research, teaching and sharing, it is thus the right time to establish "Waqf Development Centre", also named as "**International Awqaf Development Center (IADC)**", to develop the comprehensive research, solutions and practical models for global players, operators, policymakers, students and future researchers in order to make the Waqf institution as an effective vehicle to help those underprivileged ones to enjoy their basic socio-economic rights.

Rational outlook

Followings are the underlying objectives:

1. To develop the institution of Waqf through professional research, teaching and sharing by considering the socio-economic demands today.
2. To standardize the Waqf Model for the benefit of all.
3. To create the institution of *Waqf* as a practical model to upgrade the socio-economic status of the underprivileged ones in particular.

Concerned issues and problems

The institution of *Waqf* (endowment) is not merely a religious entity, but is an important socio-economic chapter, which has influence on the individual, domestic, spiritual, economic, community, political, social and educational concern. *Waqf* covers a wide range of issues from socio-economic to the human capital; it can be attributed as one of the instrumental platforms to uplift one's pride and dignity within the Divine supremacy. Hence, the issue of *Waqf* cannot be free to run itself on the whims without adhering to the standard policies (*Shari'ah*), rules and acceptable management systems within *Maqasid al-Shari'ah* (*Shari'ah* objectives). Application of the standard management systems and principles along with modern practical mechanisms and the institution of *Waqf* may provide the basis for excellence of operations to achieve the overall efficiency and result-oriented outcome.[2]

The appropriateness in the management of *Waqf* with its true Islamic spirit was hindered due to some historical reasons, which were mainly attributed to the Western influence on Muslim countries. Thus, it is timely to address the effectiveness of *Waqf* management systems in OIC including the factors influencing proposals for further improvement of the overall performance. Referring to the experience of practitioners and researchers in the field of *Waqf* in OIC nations, the management of the institution of *Waqf* in OIC nations faces numerous challenges. The main problem starts with the *State Islamic Religious Council* of OIC nations, which is the sole trustee of all *Waqf* in OIC countries.[3] Once the Religious council is entrusted with *Waqf* property, it should be managed by qualified, knowledgeable and professional managers who are well acquainted with Islamic as well as country laws to manage the institution rightfully.

People involved in managing the *Waqf* properties are *Mutawalli* (*waqf* manager) who are in some situation found not to be qualified with required skills and professionalism. Even in some cases the *Waqf* lands are managed by non-Muslims who are not really competent to run the venture. It is curious on how an authority can trust one who does not have faith in Islam. Hence, *Waqf* property should be granted to the right *Mutawalli* by considering their sound footings in ability, willingness and beliefs to utilize the asset with trust and confident. Furthermore, in the management of *Waqf* asset the properties in issue are left idle due to some complexity in the management process.

The notable factors that lead to the complexity consist of properties given out orally without any registration and documentation, and thus, one's accounting practices are not in compliance with the *Shari'ah* standard. Moreover, the problem in the possession of *Waqf* properties puts restrictions on their sale and purchase, while in leasing and renting these properties are often devalued. There is instance where the land is leased to a man for $250 who afterwards rented it to another person for over $2,500.[4] Such a difference between the leased value and the market value of the properties may open the door for the opportunists.

There is also complication faced in the spontaneous development process of the *Waqf* properties. For example, the *Waqf* properties are beyond the control of MAIN that gives rise to subsequent problems such as defaulting land tax and other kinds of tax related to charges against the *Waqf* properties. As a result, the *Waqf* land is seized by land office and duly sealed by local authorities like a caveat. Among other problems in the *Waqf* management are revenues generated in the *Waqf* management are insufficient to suffice the operational cost, *Waqf* properties have no self-generating income and are unproductive, delay in the earning of the compensation in the acquisition of *Waqf* properties and irregularity in receiving the benefit of the *Waqf* properties by the *mauquf alaih* (beneficiaries).[5]

There is inconsistency between the expectation and the existence of presence of all factors that make the *Waqf* systems ineffective. It is thus understood that due to the earlier mentioned diverse problems *Waqf* management systems are facing various challenges to make it dynamic, transparent, productive and innovative in the utilization of the *Waqf* properties that deserve attention to reorient the total systems.[6] Thus, the following sections provide possible recommendations in improving the management and administrative systems of *Waqf* properties in OIC nations.

Flagships

There are five flagships that the total master plans to the establishment of an "Awqaf Development Center" may be achieved (Figures 1.1–1.5):

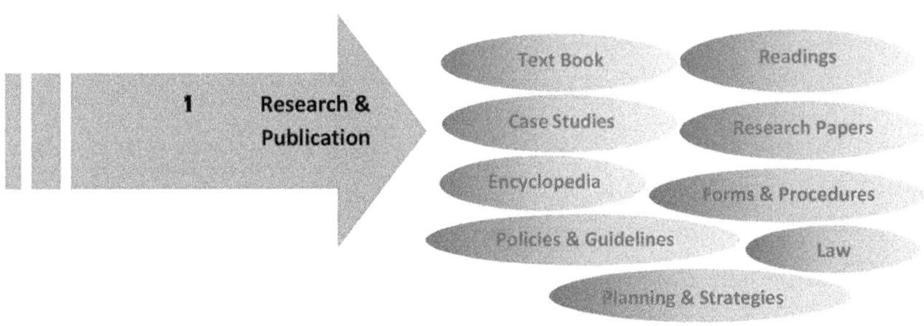

Figure 1.1 Flagship: research and publication.

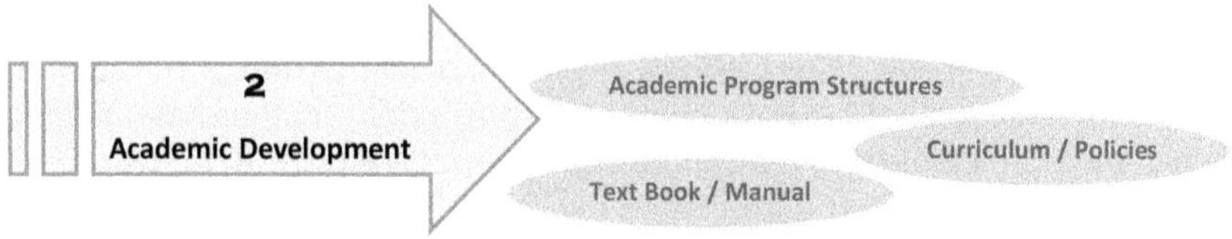

Figure 1.2 Flagship: academic development.

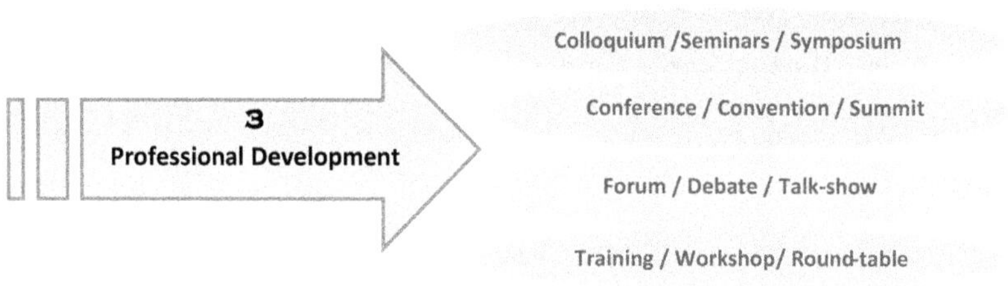

Figure 1.3 Flagship: professional development.

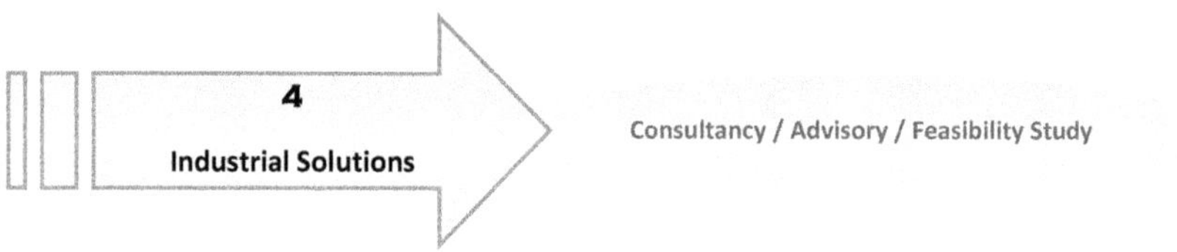

Figure 1.4 Flagship: industrial solutions.

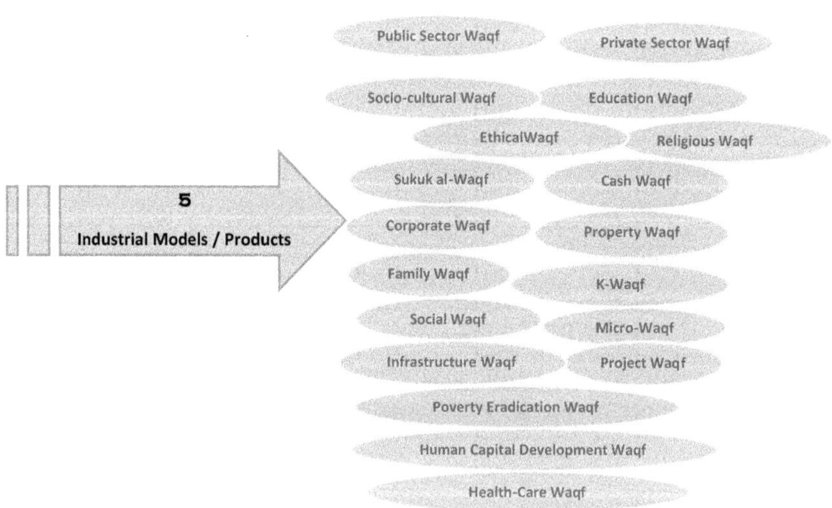

Figure 1.5 Flagship: industrial models/products.

Strategic plan

Two (02) strategic plans are suggested, namely, short-term plan, which can be treated as a pilot scheme for the academic year of 1438H, and long-term plan, which can be launched and duly achieved during 1439–1441H. Activities of both plans are outlined as follows (Figures 1.6 and 1.7).

Conclusion

It is thus understood that the institution of *Waqf* is undoubtedly a holistic vehicle in caring about the socio-economic well-being of the underprivileged society through a cooperative care and concern. Among the OIC countries, the government, corporate and the people generally are seriously concerned with the development, management and achievement of the true goal of *Waqf* through verities of its products, activities and services today, namely, land, properties and assets, cash *Waqf*, *Sukuk Al-Waqf* and corporate *Waqf*. Yet, there are some shortcomings encountered in the dynamic management of *Waqf* in *Waqf* property due to the influence of traditional mechanisms that are adapted particularly in the management of *Waqf* land besides being hampered by insufficient skills and professionalism within the management itself. Hence, it is timely for the authorities, operators and experts to work hand in hand towards reforming the *Waqf* management standard particularly on the *Waqf* properties so as to ensure the right benefits bestowed for the beneficiaries within the *Maqasid al-Shari'ah*.

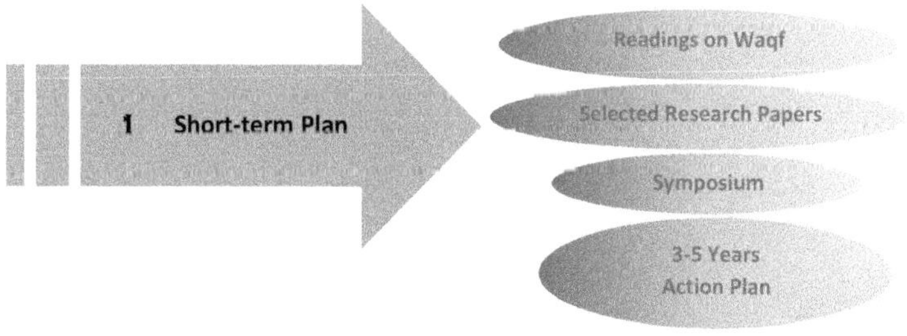

Figure 1.6 Strategic plan: short term.

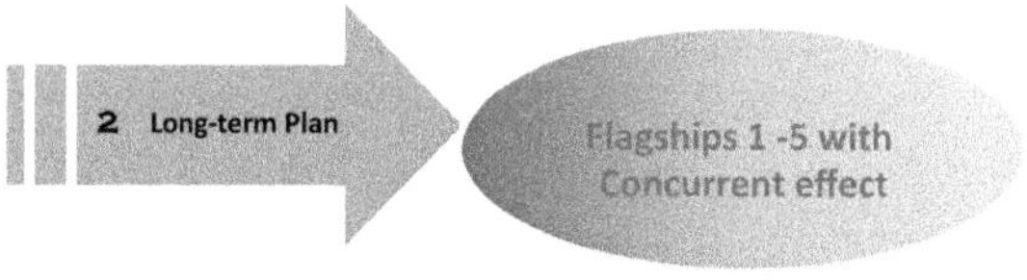

Figure 1.7 Strategic plan: long term.

Notes

1 This chapter shall not be treated as a research paper, because it is a mere mind-mapping idea on the emergence of an International Awqaf Development Center in view of promoting the idea of Awqaf with a socio-economic impact, which may open up the door for future research. The original idea was shared by the author a couple of years ago during an academic meeting held at the Islamic Economics Institute, King Abdulaziz University, Saudi Arabia.
2 Chowdhury, M.S.R. et al. (n.d.). "Problems of Waqf administration and proposals for improvement: a study in Malaysia" *Journal of Internet Banking and Commerce* (ISSN: 1204-5357), at p. 2.
3 Ibid.
4 Ibid.
5 Abdullah, M.S. (2010). Malaysia needs transformation of Waqf management, Travelodge PhD Wakaf @ MohamadSallehAbdullah, blog entry, Malaysia needs transformation of Waqf management. Retrieved from: http://sallehabdullah.blogspot.com/2010/01/artikalmalaysia-perlukantransformasi.html (accessed 27 February 2011).
6 Chowdhury, ibid.

References

Abdullah, M.S. (2010). Malaysia needs transformation of Waqf management, Travelodge PhD Wakaf @ Mohamad Salleh Abdullah, blog entry, Malaysia needs transformation of Waqf management. Retrieved from: http://sallehabdullah.blogspot.com/2010/01/artikalmalaysia-perlukantransformasi.html (accessed 27 February 2011).

Chowdhury, M.S.R. et al. (n.d.). "Problems of Waqf administration and proposals for improvement: A study in Malaysia" *Journal of Internet Banking and Commerce* (ISSN: 1204-5357), at p. 2.

2 Awqaf-led neo-endowment in supporting socio-economic development

Mohammed Fawzi Aminu Amadu and Mohd Ma'Sum Billah

Introduction

Islamic endowments (Awqaf) have played as a force for socio-economic developments for many centuries[1] and can still be made relevant in light of existing socio-economic challenges that governments and their economies face around the world. Given that there is vast information on Awqaf (plural for Waqf) and how they have been used for socio-economic intervention, it would be a wise decision that the concept of Waqf be revisited to understand how it was used and how it can be used given today's dynamics. The recent publication of The New Waqf Law[2] goes to emphasize that there is belief that Waqf is relevant to solving challenges that exist in the world's economies and it would be unfortunate if such a powerful tool is not leveraged to help overcome the existing challenges.

Waqf is a powerful tool because none other than Allah is the one who calls on the believers to give Him a goodly loan,[3] and this is what a Waqf is an example of. Because of this there is a high chance of getting believers to support in the creation of Awqaf. It is in light of this continuous relevance and the high probability to get support to create Awqaf that the concept of Waqf needs to be studied with an aim on leveraging its benefits as a catalyst for socio-economic development.

Literature review

Waqf has continued to be relevant as a tool for social intervention. There are research papers, magazine and religious edicts that are continually being produced on this concept. Given the Allah's call to believers to promote all that is good and forbid all that is otherwise, it is incumbent on Muslims to help the world leverage the concept of Waqf for economic good. Existing literature demonstrates how Awqaf has been successfully used in the past (Cizakca 1997) and there is literature on new efforts at revitalizing Waqf (Elasrag 2017). Together this information on what Waqf has done and can do is the reason why efforts to develop solutions for using Waqf in newer ways to solve new challenges are necessary. This work is an effort in that direction.

What is Waqf

A Waqf is an Arabic or more appropriately an Islamic concept which means a charitable endowment of value given as a gift in the name of Allah for use in support of good courses acceptable in light of the Shari'ah. Hussein states

> ...Waqf refers to religious endowment i.e. voluntary and irrevocable dedication of one's wealth or portion of it - in cash or in kind (such as a house or a garden) and its disbursement for Shari'ah compliant projects (such as Mosques or religious schools...).[4]

Simply put, a Waqf is a private initiative to help in socio-economic development and we may add religious development by donating a thing of economic value to be held in the name of Allah and to be managed in an agreed manner and the proceeds from such management used for agreed socio-economic intervention(s).The important thing about Waqf therefore is that, in it, there is a mechanism that is available for use in socio-economic intervention. And so in every time and place, in line with the concept of Adalah[5] (equity and justice) and Ihsan[6] (doing things in the best way), Muslims should look at ways to leverage Waqf in support of social needs in their respective communities.

How Waqf was used

Waqf can be directly said to be related to answering Allah's call to give Him a goodly loan (Qard Hassan) (Qur'an 2:245)[7] as well as to Prophet Muhammad's saying that "the best Muslim is he who is most useful to the people".[8] In this regard, Waqf was and is still a means by which a Muslim, a servant of Allah, seeks to gain the pleasure of Allah by investing in a good – through giving a thing of socio-economic value to the people, so that by serving them through it, they may gain divine favour.

A great example of a Waqf that still produces benefit to this day is the endowment left by the third Khalifa of Islam, Uthman ibn Affan. He bought and endowed a well for the Muslim community in Medina[9]; the well was then used to develop a date farm as dates had begun to grow around it. The government through the Ministry of Agriculture oversees the farms and sells the dates; then its proceeds are split into two – half of it is used to support orphans and the poor whilst the other half is put in an account in the name of Sayyidinaa Uthman and managed by the Ministry of Endowment. Proceeds from the endowment have recently been applied to build accommodation (a Hotel) for pilgrims.

A cursory look at Awqaf (plural of Waqf) around the world will show that various Waqf have been used for many varying projects that fall under socio-economic development as long as the project is Shari'ah compliant. And it is in this light that this study proposes to look at innovative ways to help the people and government of Ghana to use Waqf to augment existing means of supporting socio-economic development.

Tapping into the potential of Waqf

It is due to the exhibited potential of Awqaf around the world juxtaposed with the lack of any well structured Waqf in Ghana as well as the increasing burden on government for socio-economic intervention that we are working on a case to engage the system of Waqf in Ghana in order to help lessen the burden of socio-economic pressure on government and other entities that want to offer support.

The model

The model of Waqf being promoted will engage various socio-economic entities (referred to as Facilitating Partner in Figure 2.1) with the need for capacity to support their social and economic work to reach out to landowners (primarily Chiefs, referred to as Partner 2 in Figure 2.1) to allocate land to be dedicated as Waqf. Once a Chief allocates land and it is dedicated as a Waqf, the Waqf Manager (referred to as partner 4 in Figure 2.1) will agree with the Facilitating Partner and the landowner on the agreed use of the land – as per the case presented for the creation of the Waqf (the first phase of the scheme will concentrate on agricultural projects).

Once the project that the dedicated Waqf land will be used for is agreed upon, the partners in the project, i.e. the Facilitating Partner, the landowner (usually they would be a silent partner) and the Waqf Manager (the Waqf Manager may not always be a partner but will simply manage for a fee [indicated in Figures 2.2 and 2.4 with a clear cell and without the term partner by the name], the dynamics of each project will determine whether the Waqf Manager is a partner or just a Manager for a fee), will work on the project feasibility and business plan. The Waqf Manager is then tasked with the responsibility of finding an investor (Partner: 3 in Figures 2.1 and 2.2) with whom to undertake the project. The investor may be a businessman in which case they enter into an equity partnership or they may be a philanthropist in which case they will simply support the project without needing to be a partner (an investor that invests as a philanthropic gesture will have no interest in sharing the returns generated by managing the waqf) and this scenario is shown in Figures 2.3 and 2.4.

In one of the possible structures as mentioned earlier, the partners agree that the Waqf Manager is a full partner (Figures 2.1 and 2.3). This is the case when the manager participates in the process of land acquisition, project identification and project design, that is the manager is instrumental in acquiring the land, determining which project is to be undertaken on the land,

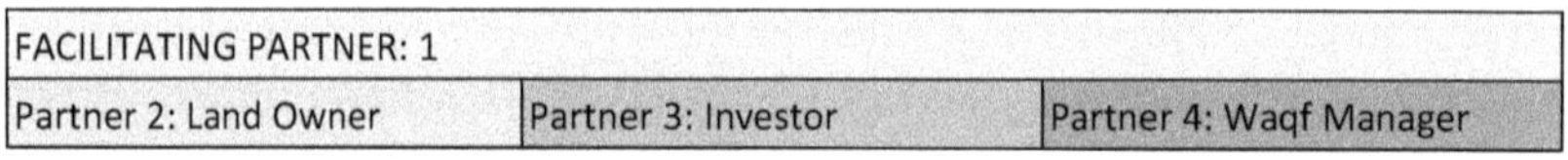

Figure 2.1 WAQF model 1.

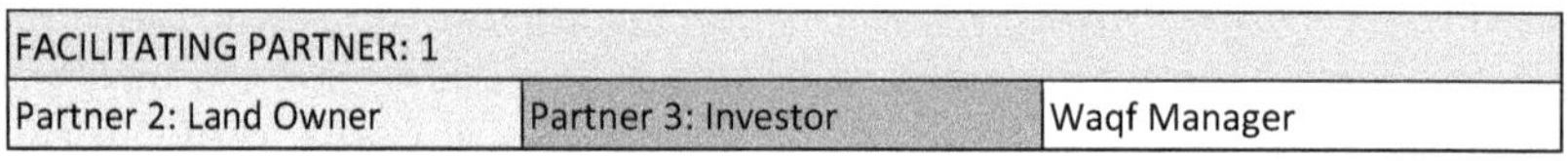

Figure 2.2 WAQF model 2.

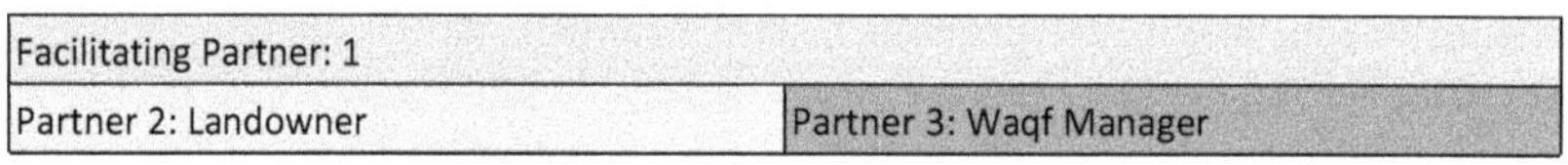

Figure 2.3 WAQF model 3.

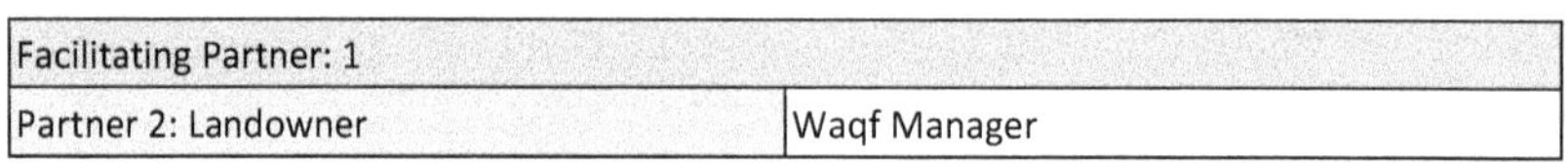

Figure 2.4 WAQF model 4.

as well as finding an investor for the project. It is envisaged that the early stages of such types of Waqf projects will be modelled in this way as the project model is a new innovation that is being promoted by the Waqf Manager.

However, going forward it is envisaged that various entities, learning from the early stage examples, will find their own land, design their own projects and identify their own investor(s) but then they would want to leverage the expertise of a Waqf Manager; in this case the manager will not be a full partner and thus will be paid a management fee only (indicated in Figures 2.2 and 2.4). The management fee can be a predetermined fee or one that is wholly or partially based on generated revenues.

From the foregoing the Shari'ah compliant business model of the Waqf would be structured on either a Mudaraba[10] or a Musharaka[11]; this will depend on whether the Waqf Manager will be a partner or just a manager. Where the Waqf Manager only manages, the model will be a Mudaraba (Figures 2.2 and 2.4); where the Waqf Manager invests into the project along with the investor, the model will be a Musharaka (Figures 2.1 and 2.3).

The idea or concept of a Facilitating Partner is a very critical and novel one that is specially created to cater to the needs of government entities. Otherwise the term will simply be a Partner. As a Facilitating Partner, their remuneration will be in the form of commission, for it is critical that they should have no management responsibility in line with the best practices provided in the International Waqf Management Standards.[12]

Aside from leaving government out of the direct management of the Waqf, local considerations also advise this position to leave government out of Waqf management. Government involvement would usually come along with bureaucratic inefficiencies, politicization of the project and potential interference in the management process. Considering these factors, allowing the government to have oversight in the form of a guarantor of sorts is the best means of having them participate.

Critical success factors

No state interference

Given that the Waqf is proposed in collaboration with government entities, it is important that as a Waqf, the government does not interfere in its operations; the government is offered a part of the profits from the Waqf as a perpetual voluntary (charitable) donation and not based on them having a share in the ownership of the Waqf. The Waqf once created is a gift to Allah and this must be the understanding of both the landowner and the government, indeed all parties involved with the Waqf.

The critical need to keep the state from interfering in the Waqf as well as to fend off government bureaucracy by way of legal regulations or political interest is the reason why the government entity in the partnership is positioned as a facilitator with oversight responsibility. This (the oversight and decision on the use of the land) will form the basis of the commission the government entity will be entitled to from the proceeds (profits to be exact) of the project.

The oversight by the government will give comfort to both the landowner and the investor, while being the final approver of the land will justify the landowners release of the land knowing that the social responsibility of the government entity is the basis for the use of the land. (In essence the landowner is saying, "I will use the land to support government's course by working with a selected partner to deliver the objective).

The contract will stipulate that the landowner shall not take back the land as long as it is used for the stated purpose as well as state that the Waqf Manager shall at no time have rights to the land except where it is being used for the agreed objective and that if for any unforeseen reason the land cannot be used for the stated purpose, the Waqf agreement be terminated. Hussien Elasrag (2017) points out that the Maliki Madhhab does recognize temporary Waqf, though the other ones do not. West Africa though is dominated by the Maliki Madhhab[13] and the land be returned to the owner or whoever the owner stipulates in the agreement or in a will or otherwise as per traditional dictates.

As a facilitator with oversight responsibility, the program remains a tripartite program but one that relieves the government entity from any obligations which would otherwise transfer the encumbrances of government onto the project.

Despite this, the government entity will have oversight through its presence on the board (but never as Chairman as this will defeat the idea of government not having management control) as well as participate by being a mandatory party to the final decision to approve the project to be implemented.

Transparency

From the very outset, all parties to the Waqf must understand that the land given cannot be taken back and that the partners are free to use the land for its agreed purpose at the time of acquisition (land laws need to be catered for – renewal and rezoning). Information on how the land is used and how that is in accordance with the agreed reason for creating the Waqf must always be made public and periodic reports on how the land is being used to achieve its goal must be made available.

The disbursement of funds from the Waqf management must be transparent for all qualified beneficiaries to be able to access support under the laid down agreement.

Accountability

Every aspect of the program must be managed in an accountable manner so that all parties to the project and even third parties to the deal will be able to understand how the system is being run. Proper record keeping and reporting will be invaluable to the continuous and smooth running of the Waqf.

Important considerations

The land actually never changes ownership in reality though it becomes endowed to God; ownership still rests with the landowner, and so there is no cumbersome process of land acquisition. Rather a partnership is created for the use of the land and a Waqf Manager was appointed as an agent to manage the land.

Since Ghana does not currently have an endowment law and as Ghana's law cannot in its current form recognize Waqf, the clause that stipulates that the landowner cannot take back the land from the project has the same effect as God becoming the owner of the land.

Abuse of land use by the Waqf Manager is curbed by the oversight of the related government entity given its duty as the decision maker on the use of the land – this ensures that the Waqf Manager cannot arbitrarily at any time change the purpose for which the land is to be used.

The dissociation of the project from the effective control of government also supports the Waqf requirement that the Waqf Manager be a Muslim, a necessary condition for a Waqf as per Islam. This is because with government not having a say in choosing the Waqf Manager, there is little possibility that they would interfere with the team that initiated the project in the first place.

The case

The specific case that this chapter is looking at implementing the Waqf with is that of The Tamale Teaching Hospital (TTH),[14] the only teaching hospital located in the Northern Region and the northern part of Ghana – thus serving as a referral hospital for the three (now five Northern Regions since the creation of two new regions after partitioning the Northern Region) Northern Regions,[15] a region that has the third highest poverty headcount in Ghana.[16]

The management of the TTH has constantly complained about the difficulty of running the hospital as most of the patients are very poor to pay for the services offered by the hospital as well as lacking capacity to afford some of the necessary equipment and infrastructure required to help the hospital deliver on its mandate.

Though the Northern Region is currently poor, it is blessed with vast amounts of arable land which is very rich for use for commercial agriculture and these lands are vested in the hands of traditional Chiefs of the regions.

Lack of funding though means that these rich arable agricultural lands are currently not being used for commercial agriculture. It is this lack of funding, coupled with the availability of vast lands that are in the hands of the traditional Chiefs whose subjects are mostly poor to afford the health services at the TTH, that affords a case for the creation of a Waqf based on the earlier suggested model in order to generate funds to subsidize health support to the subjects of the traditional Chiefs.

In line with the earlier suggested Waqf Model, the TTH, whose mandate is set by Act 525 of the Ghana Health Service and Teaching Hospitals Act of 1996[17]and thus making the hospital a government institution, will be the Facilitating Partner (Partner 1) to the Waqf project. The traditional Chiefs (Partner 2) will be the ones to donate the land (about 100,000 acres) to be made into a Waqf. Dar Al Istithmar – a company duly registered with the Registrar General of Ghana and a company specializing in Waqf Management among others services, will be the Waqf Manager (Partner 4). Finally, it is the responsibility of Dar Al Istithmar to identify a suitable investor (Partner 3) with whom to enter into a partnership to use the 100,000 acres of land for an agreeable commercial agricultural project.

The Waqf proposal

Dar Al Istithmar has proposed the TTH that together they must approach the overlord of the three major tribal groupings who own millions of acres of land between them to dedicate 10,000 acres of land as Waqf towards the support of the health services of the Hospital and for the general health of the poor subjects of the overlord.

The lands will be used for a commercial agricultural project through support of, in this case, other Awqaf from the Gulf or Turkey (there have been some agreement in principle). The investors will invest money and technology into the partnership to undertake commercial farming of Soybean and Sorghum, both highly desired agricultural products that are widely used, especially in the Gulf.

The partners to the project will share in the revenue generated from management of the land for agricultural projects. The landowner would be given 10% of the proceeds from the profits of the project, the manager would get an estimated 10% (the actual amount will be determined by results from actual execution), the investor is expected to get between 20% and 30% of the profits leaving TTH with between 50% and 60% of the revenues. Should the investor decide to not demand a share or decide to give an interest free loan (Qard al-Hasan),[18] TTH would be entitled to 70%–80% of the revenues.

Interventions to be made with funds from management of Waqf

The TTH has many needs for which they need additional funding and thus for which the Waqf would be a helpful source of financing akin to an Internally Generated Fund. Of these needs, subsidizing the cost of services and medicine and developing accommodation for staff of the hospital, especially medical doctors, are some of the priority areas where the revenue generated from the Waqf would be used. The management of the hospital will make their case for interventions that they need and then in consultation with the Waqf Manager, available funds allocated for the hospital from returns accrued from management of the Waqf would be applied towards the identified priority areas insofar as these areas are in accordance with the agreement that formed the basis of the Waqf.

Benefits of the Waqf project – direct and indirect

This innovative use of Waqf would bring enormous benefit to the economy and participants; this shows how invaluable the concept of Waqf is. With regard to the TTH project specifically there are benefits to government (i.e. TTH), landowners, the subjects of the landowners and for investors. These are illustrated in Figure 2.5.

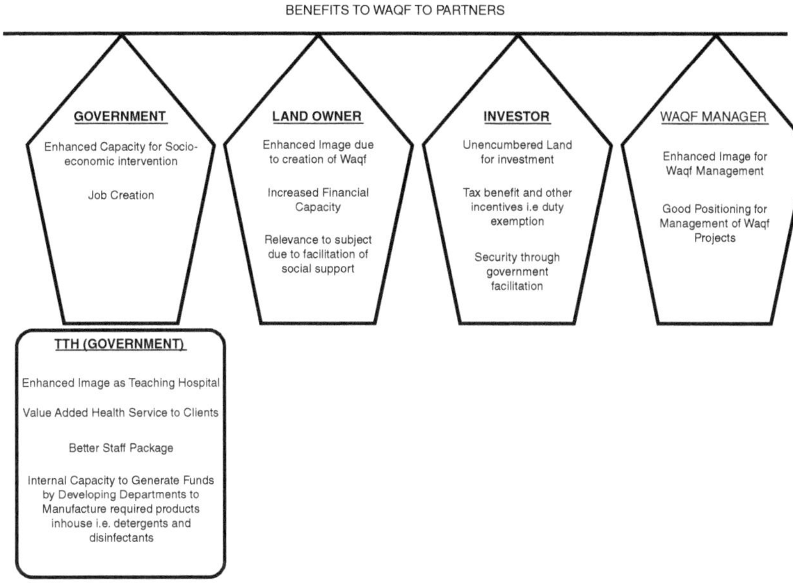

Figure 2.5 Benefits of WAQF to partners.

For the government and the TTH, which is the entity directly involved as a stakeholder, the use of Waqf reduces the burden on government for providing social services. Government through the augmentation of social services by Waqf-based projects is strengthened financially as it is able to deliver critically needed services without having to find the funding themselves. Further government is able to create jobs for the people and this is both good for the government and for the economy of the country.

In the case of the TTH, service delivery to customers will be enhanced because they can be capacitated by the Waqf to build a healthy financial position that will allow them to better support their clients in ways that are a burden for them currently. The image of the TTH as a teaching hospital is suffering at the moment because medical doctors refuse to work for them due to lack of housing and equipment needed for them to do their work; however, through the intervention of Waqf it is expected that these challenges would be significantly alleviated. The TTH internally needs funds to undertake activities like building a soap manufacturing plant within the hospital to support the very critical issue of keeping the hospital disinfected and clean; it is expected that this too would be catered for by revenues generated by the Waqf.

Kings who are the traditional owners of land and a stakeholder in the Waqf have the responsibility to support their subjects who are not capable on their own. The Waqf project will provide the Kings an opportunity to be seen to be more concerned about their people due to the fact that they have set up the Waqf to support the subjects under them. There is also the matter of the Kings getting a portion of the revenue generated by the Waqf; this revenue will be used to properly manage the Royal Affairs at the court; some of this will be used to directly support some of the subjects of the Kings directly and thus enhance the reputation of the Kings even further.

The dependants of the King (patients of the hospital) will enjoy subsidized medical services as well as an overall enhanced service from the hospital with an expected quality of services in terms of availability of doctors and their commitments because, the Waqf is generating funds to support the hospital accordingly. This key factor of providing better healthcare services to the subjects is the underlying reason for the creation of the Waqf.

Another aspect of the benefit of having a Waqf is the creation of jobs – directly and indirectly. Directly, the Waqf land is used for commercial agriculture which will create a significant number of direct jobs (both full-time and part-time); many indirect jobs will also result from such a commercial venture. This will have a multiplier effect to the economy and that alone is a significant boost for the image of Waqf as a socio-economic institution.

Investors as partners to a Waqf will get secure land that is free of encumbrances from landowners who is one of the partners in the project and thus the investor can fully concentrate on the project. Furthermore, because the land is facilitated by government, the investor has an added layer of security and can avail government incentives such as free duty on imported equipment that will be brought in for the commercial venture coupled with other incentives that the investor or other stakeholders can apply to government for on behalf of the Waqf.

Finally, there is the Waqf Manager who will benefit from the opportunity to manage such a huge commercial project as it will further enhance his chance of being offered similar opportunities in other jurisdictions or under other entities who want to create similar endowments.

Recommendation

The attempt to use Waqf to solve contemporary challenges will be a welcome and well advised effort, as Islam would always want to drive activities to be in line with peaceful existence ultimately. However it is important that the process of implementing the new Waqf projects is constantly monitored and assessed to ensure that the implementation is in line with the objectives of Shari'ah. Any potential misstep must be quickly corrected for; the credibility of the process is the most important critical success factor. Should the public have a sense that the Waqf is being abused, support for such projects would suffer.

Conclusion

There should be no doubt about the potential of Waqf for socio-economic intervention. Properly designed and managed the Waqf can become a leading and very useful source of funding for various communities in education, health, and many other social support areas. Understanding the local dynamics and localizing the structure of the Waqf accordingly are very important. In Ghana where politicization of programs are a usual thing, the Waqf programs to be developed must do well to ring fence the Waqf from government involvement that can lead to politicians manipulating the management of the Waqf. Changes in government should have no effect on the management of the Waqf as we see in other areas of Muslim affairs – this is critical to ensure that the value proposition of these Waqf programs endures.

Notes

1 Elasrag, H (2017), *Towards a new role of the institution of Waqf*, CreateSpace Independent Publishing Platform.
2 Cizakca, M (2013), The New Waqf Law prepared by IDB/IRTI and The Kuwait Public Foundation, INCEIF.
3 Qur'an 2:245 "Who is he that will lend to Allah a goodly loan so that He may multiply it to him many times?..." – Waqf is an example of this goodly loan.
4 Elasrag, ibid.
5 Arbounia, H & Sexton, M, (2006), *Islam and sustainable development, in house publishing*, Rotterdam, Netherlands.
6 Ibid.
7 Qur'an 2:245 "Who is he that will lend to Allah a goodly loan so that He may multiply it to him many times?..." – Waqf as an example of this goodly loan.
8 Al-Mu'Jam Al-Awsaṭ 6192, Ibn Umar reported: The messenger of Allah, peace and blessings be upon Him, said: The most beloved people to Allah are those who are most beneficial to the people.
9 AWQAF SA, Waqf hotel "Uthman ibn 'Affan" (RA), viewed 10/31/2019, https://Awqafsa.Org.Za/Waqf-Hotel-Uthman-Ibn-Affanra/
10 "Mudarabah" is a special kind of partnership where one partner gives money to another for investing it in a commercial enterprise. The investment comes from the first partner who is called "Rabb-Ul-Mal", while the management and work is an exclusive responsibility of the other, who is called "Mudarib". Usmani, M T (1998), *An introduction to Islamic finance*. https://www.amazon.com/introduction-Islamic-finance-Muh%CC%A3ammad-%CA%BBUs%CC%B2ma%CC%84ni%CC%84/dp/B0006FD3H6
11 "Musharakah" is a word of Arabic origin which literally means sharing. In the context of business and trade it means a joint enterprise in which all the partners share the profit or loss of the joint venture. Usmani, ibid.
12 Cizakca, ibid.
13 Elasrag, ibid.
14 http://Www.Tth.Gov.Gh/
15 http://Www.Moh.Gov.Gh/Tamale-Teaching-Hospital/
16 Ghana Statistical Service Report, Ghana Poverty Mapping Report, 2015.
17 http://Www.Moh.Gov.Gh/Tamale-Teaching-Hospital/
18 This is a type of loan that is interest free.

References

Arbounia, H & Sexton, M, (2006), *Islam and sustainable development, in house publishing*, Rotterdam, Netherlands.

Çizakça, M. (1997), 'Towards a Comparative History of the Waqf System', Al-Shajara (ISTAC, Kuala Lumpur), 2 (1): 18–32.

Elasrag, H (2017), *Towards a new role of the institution of Waqf*, Create Space Independent Publishing Platform, Munich Personal RePEc, MPRA.

3 Objectives of awqaf within the classical discourse and their modern implications

Mohammad Abdullah

Introduction

> Anyone who has spent time studying the history of Islamdom has formed some idea of the institution of the Islamic endowment, or *waqf*... No one would question its central importance in the social and economic history of the Islamicate regions, particularly in the twelfth to nineteenth centuries, and most scholars consider it the single most important institution for the provision of community social services in Islamdom.
>
> (McChesney, 1991: 3)

The concept of *waqf* originated in an early Islamic environment which was overwhelmingly charged with the spirit of voluntary spending (Singer, 2008). *Waqf* not only served to insulate the primitive Islamic community from socio-economic financial contingencies but also contributed to institutionalise charity forever (Lev, 2005; al-Sibai, 1985; Abu Zuhra, 1972). Technically, the mechanism of *waqf* meticulously responded to the need of a versatile property-conveyance tool. *Waqf* entailed both: the essentials of a private wealth redistributive mechanism, and the attributes of a perpetual charitable institution (Abdullah, 2019).

In juristic terms, *waqf* refers to an Islamic charity that can be exercised by alienating the ownership of a tangible or intangible property or valuable for the benefit of specific persons/s or purposes (Zaid, 1996). A *waqf* is created as a token of voluntary charitable disposition for the purpose of securing an on-going spiritual reward by the *waqif* (endower). According to the Accounting and Auditing Organisation for Islamic Financial Institutions (AAOIFI), *waqf* is defined as "...making a property invulnerable to any disposition that leads to transfer of ownership, and donating the usufruct of that property to beneficiaries" (AAOIFI, *Shariah* Standard 2/1, 2015).

The institution of *waqf* has its own objectives which could be identified and located by referring to the original sources of *shariah* as well as the classical jurisprudential discourse of *waqf* (Abdullah, 2018a). This study attempts to analyse the origin, significance, jurisprudential framework and objectives of *awqaf*. It examines the objectives of *waqf* as enshrined in the classical *waqf* literature followed by exploring the framework of *waqf* application in line with the objectives of the institution. The aim of examining the objectives of *waqf* is to contextualise the modern application of *waqf* in a dynamic manner. By examining the mechanism, *shariah* premises and socio-economic objectives of *waqf*, this study analyses the impacts and implications of *waqf* objectives on the socio-economic effectiveness of the institution. The purpose of this study is to identify the key policy implications that can be drawn for enhancing the modern *waqf*.

By determining the common theme of *waqf* objectives, this study provides a *maqasid*-oriented comprehensive pitch for the application of *waqf* with a contextualised approach. The study is based on qualitative research paradigm, and it utilises the available literature to conduct a desk-based analysis by employing the socio-legal research methodology.

The chapter is divided into four main sections other than the introduction and conclusion sections of the study. The second section of the study endeavours to explore the *shariah* origin and conceptual mechanism of *waqf*. The objectives of *waqf* are analysed in the third section. The fourth section deliberates and discusses contextualisation of *waqf* objectives in the current scenario and provides some policy recommendations for enhancing the role of *waqf* in the modern world.

The origin and conceptual mechanism of *waqf*

In the context of *waqf*, many Islamic jurisprudential books begin by relating the story of Omar (R.A), who had acquired a piece of land in Khayber and sought the consultation of the Prophet (pbuh) on how to treat that land in the best *shariah* recommended manner (al-Jazayri, 2000; Ibn al-Qudamah, 1997). According to the most jurists, the endowment of that land by Omar (R.A) was the first example of *waqf* in the Islamic history (al-Shawkani, 2008; Othman, 1983). In contrast, some scholars believe that the first act of *waqf* was exercised by Othman (R.A) in the form of a famous well of Medina – known as *Byr al-Rumah* (Kahf, 2003). The background of this narration is referred to be a situation where the Prophet (pbuh) had asked his companions to buy the well and endow it for free public utility (Kahf, 2003). Othman (R.A) is reported to have responded to this call and was known as the first *waqif* (Kahf, 1999).

In addition, one may rightly assume that since Abu Talha (R.A), the companion of the Prophet (pbuh), was the first to act on the prescription of the *Quranic* verse which exhorts to dispense the most beloved property or wealth in charitable causes to (Chapter, 3 verses: 92), he was the first *waqif* of Islamic history. It is reported that in the wake of revelation of this verse, Abu Talha approached the Prophet (pbuh) and expressed his will to endow his famous orchard called '*Bairuha*' for the sake of Allah (Qurtubi, 2003). This donation of Abu Talha could be the first instance of *waqf* (Othman, 1983).

In comparison, there are some narrations that assert a very different account of the history of *waqf*. According to one narration, it was the Prophet himself who founded the very first *waqf* by endowing the orchard of Mukhairiq

(Gil, 1998). Compared to this, there are also opinions that the land of *Ka'bah* in Mecca and *Bait al-Muqaddas* in Palestine should be considered as the first instances of *waqf* (al-Zarqa, 1947).

Based on the available *waqf* literature, there seem to be two ways to decide the earliest example of *waqf*. First, the existing forms of all *waqf* can be categorised into two kinds – i.e. *waqf* made by human action, and *waqf* created by Divine assertion. In the light of this division, if all of these mutually contradicting claims are put in order, the task of determining the first *waqf* is accomplished without any further hazard. It is asserted in the *Quran* that the first house of worship built for humans is the one that is in Mecca (Chapter, 3 Verse: 96). Thus, there remains no scope for doubt that the *Ka'bah* constitutes the first example of *waqf*, which arose by Divine assertion. As far as the first *waqf* by human action is concerned, there should not be any objection in referring the Mosque of Quba as the first *waqf*. The Mosque of Quba came into existence while the Prophet (pbuh) was still on his way to Medina from Mecca (al-Zarqa, 1947). Having identified the first two examples of *waqf*, it is worth noting that by its given purpose, a *waqf* can be divided into three categories, namely *waqfkhayri* (philanthropic), *waqfahli* (for posterity) and religious *waqf* (al-Amin, 1994: 113). Thus, the scholars who are of the view that the first *waqf* in the Islamic history is the Mosque of Quba might have meant the religious one, while those who view the *waqf* of the Prophet or Othman (R.A) as first might have taken into account the philanthropic one. The *waqf* of Abu Talha (R.A) can be considered as earliest in terms of being first *waqfahli* (family *waqf*), while the *waqf* of Omar (R.A) can be deemed first for being established with the explicit recommendation of the Prophet (pbuh).

In one of the earliest and most detailed books on *waqf* doctrines by *imam* al-Khassaf (d. 261 *hijri*), it has been reported that among the companions of the Prophet (pbuh), generally, there were two diverging opinions in relation to the earliest *waqf*. Al-Khassaf (1904) narrates that Miswar bin Rifa'ah reported, "The endowment of the Prophet (pbuh) was the first *sadaqah* (*waqf*) in the history of Islam". Rifa'ah says: I pleaded to Ibn-e-Ka'ab that people say the endowment of Omar (R.A) was the first. On this, Ibn-e-Ka'ab replied: Mukhairiq was killed after 32 months of *hijrah* in the battle of *Uhad*, and he had already expressed his will that if he would have died, his property should go to the Prophet (pbuh), and upon his death the Prophet (PBUH) made immediately endowed his orchards as *waqf*. Ibn-e-Ka'ab continued to elaborate that this endowment of the Prophet (pbuh) came in the third year of *hijrah*, whereas the *waqf* of Omar (R.A) was not made until the Prophet (pbuh) returned from the battle of Khayber in the seventh year of *hijrah* (al-Khassaf, 1904: 4–5). In view of this story, seemingly there remains little scope for any speculation on the first deed of philanthropic *waqf* in Islam. However, contrary to this report, Ibn-e-Omar was of the opinion that *waqf* of *thamag* by Omar (R.A) in Khayber was the first reported *sadaqah* in Islam (al-Khassaf, 1904: 5). Table 3.1 summarises the list of *waqf* deeds each of which could be possibly classified as the earliest *waqf* based on different criteria and perspectives.

Table 3.1 Different classifications of the earliest *waqf*

Earliest waqf	*Status*
• The land of Ka'ba	• Earliest *waqf* (by Divine assertion)
• Mosque of Quba	• Earliest religious *waqf* (by human action)
• *Byr al-Rumah*	• Earliest philanthropic *waqf*
• *Byruha*	• Earliest family *waqf*
• Khayber Orchard	• Earliest *waqf* with jurisprudential characteristics
• Orchard of Mukhairiq	• Earliest *waqf* by a non-Muslim companion of the Prophet

To capture a holistic picture of *waqf* and its objectives, understanding the Islamic approach towards voluntary spending is vital. The Islamic vision of charity, charitable spending and voluntary dispensation of wealth is broadly covered under the umbrella term '*infaq*' (literally, spending). By dissecting the term *infaq* and its different branches, the epistemology of *waqf* can be grasped. The term *infaq* constitutes one of the most comprehensive terms which finds frequent usage in the Quran. The term '*infaq*' is more comprehensive than the term '*sadaqah*' in one sense, and narrower than that in another. *Infaq*, in its broader sense, encompasses *sadaqah* into its fold. However, compared to *infaq*, the term '*sadaqah*' assumes broader scope in implying the benevolent expressions, gracious gestures and good physical actions along with covering the pecuniary spending. Though, at occasions, in *Quranic* usage both the terms have been employed interchangeably, they differ in their terminological underpinnings and implications. According to Zaman (1991: 57), "the concept of *sadaqah* in spite of its narrowness has a moral superiority over *infaq* as far as it involves ethics and courtesies in addition to material giving".

Sadaqah is further sub-divided into obligatory and non-obligatory. In its technical construct, the non-obligatory *sadaqah* can be classified into absolute and non-absolute. The non-absolute version of *sadaqah* constitutes three possibilities: (a) it entitles the beneficiaries to benefit from the usufruct only, e.g. *maniha* (gift of usufruct); (b) it entails the transfer of ownership to the beneficiary, albeit with the provision of its equivalent repayment, e.g. (*qard-hasan*); or (c) it entails the suspension of the ownership with the allocation of the recurring benefits to the assigned beneficiaries (Nomani, 1904). This, the last form of non-absolute *sadaqah*, is, in fact, defined as *waqf* (Abdullah, 2018a). Figure 3.1 explains the relationship of the organic term '*infaq*' with its specific branch, i.e. *waqf*.

In the classical *fiqh* literature, *waqf*, in general, has been referred as *habs*, albeit, in specific contexts; the term *sadaqah* too has been employed to imply *waqf* (al-Khassaf, 1904). However, to highlight the underlying distinction between a *waqf* and an absolute *sadaqah*, jurists have suffixed with it some other qualifications. Figure 3.2 contains the main terminologies which have been employed by the classical jurists to imply *waqf*.

The difference of *waqf* over other forms of Islamic charities is discernible from the above-mentioned terminological distinction of the same. The

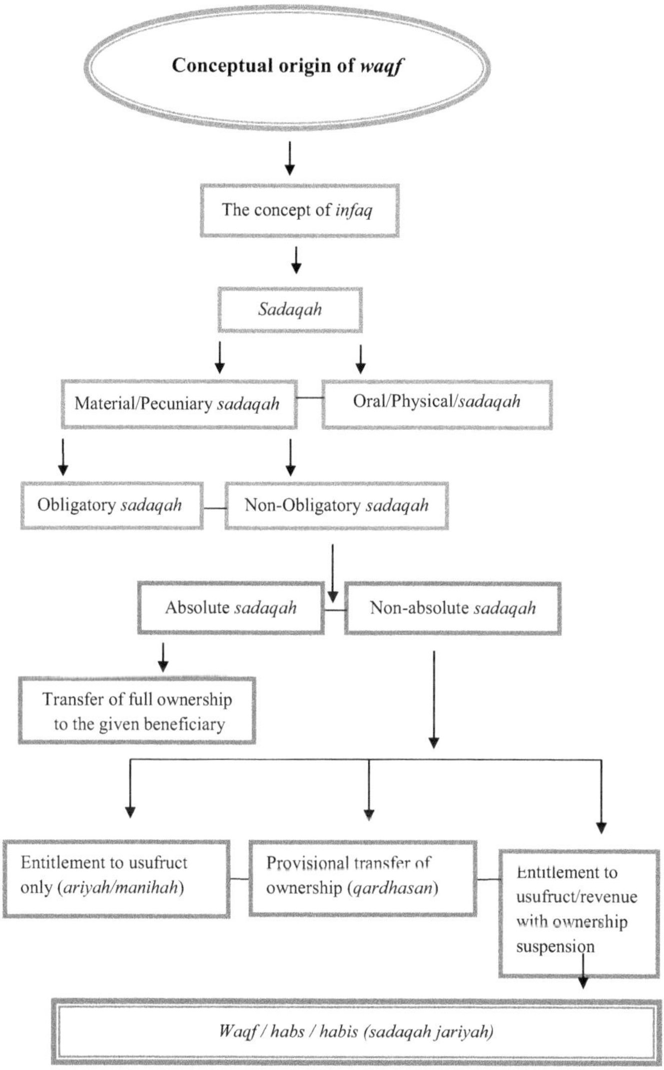

Figure 3.1 Conceptual origin of *waqf*.

conceptual origin of *waqf* is deduced in the light of the *hadith* describing the concept of *sadaqahjariyah* (Çizakça, 2000). The Prophet (pbuh) said:

> when a child of Adam dies, the scope his good deeds is closed except in three cases; (1) one who established a perpetual charity, (2) a scholar who left behind him a legacy of knowledge that benefits people, and (3) a pious child of the deceased who constantly seeks Allah's mercy for him.
>
> (Muslim, 1999)

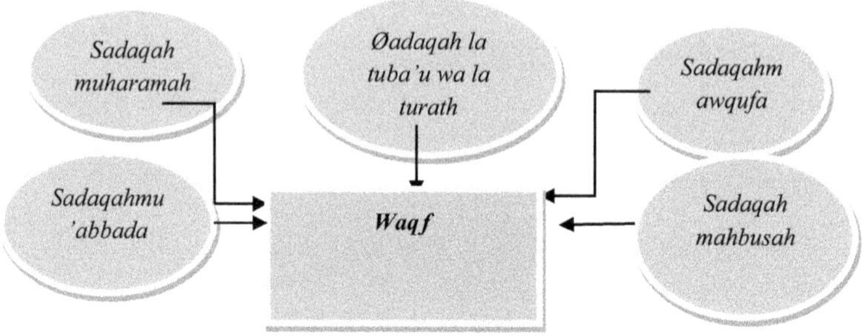

Figure 3.2 Waqf: the representative terms.

Figure 3.3 attempts to present a consolidated synthesis of the sources which provided evidence for the *shariah*-permissibility of *waqf*.

The objectives of *waqf* in *shariah*

The underlying technical difference between a *waqf* and an absolute *sadaqah* can be located by delving into the legal status of their corpuses in *shariah*. Whereas an absolute *sadaqah* entails transfer of complete ownership, *waqf* provides permissibility (*al-ibahah*) of enjoying its benefits (*ghallah*) to the beneficiary (al-Shaybani, 1997; al-Shafi'i, 1990). It is due to this distinction of *waqf* over an absolute *sadaqah* that the scope of a *waqf* is wider which encompasses both the rich and poor in terms of bestowal of its benefits. In comparison, an absolute *sadaqah* is confined to benefitting either poor people or pious purposes only (al-Shaybani, 1997: 263). In other words, while the benefits of a *sadaqah* can be offered only to poor, pauper or other needy people; the revenue, usufruct and utility of a *waqf* is potentially open for all, irrespective of an underlying beneficiary's financial background.

Waqf arose in the early Islamic period in its own context. The true objectives of *waqf* can be properly grasped by putting the mechanism of the institution in perspective. A critical review of the structural setting of *waqf* and its functional mechanism reveal that *waqf* has been envisaged to be a multi-functional institution, filling the existing gaps of resources between the public needs and supply (Shatzmiller, 2001). The institution of *waqf* is distinguished for its need-oriented approach and objective-based application. Thus, the objective of the institution can be materialised only by maintaining the need-orientation as well as its effective application. The backgrounds of the first few *awqaf* of the Islamic history provide evidence and support to this theory. For example, the Mosque of Quba,[1] which can be considered as the first instance of *waqf*, came into existence to provide for the immediate need of the Muslim community for a Masjid. Similarly, the *waqf* of *Byr al*-Rumah[2] (the well) was declared by the companion

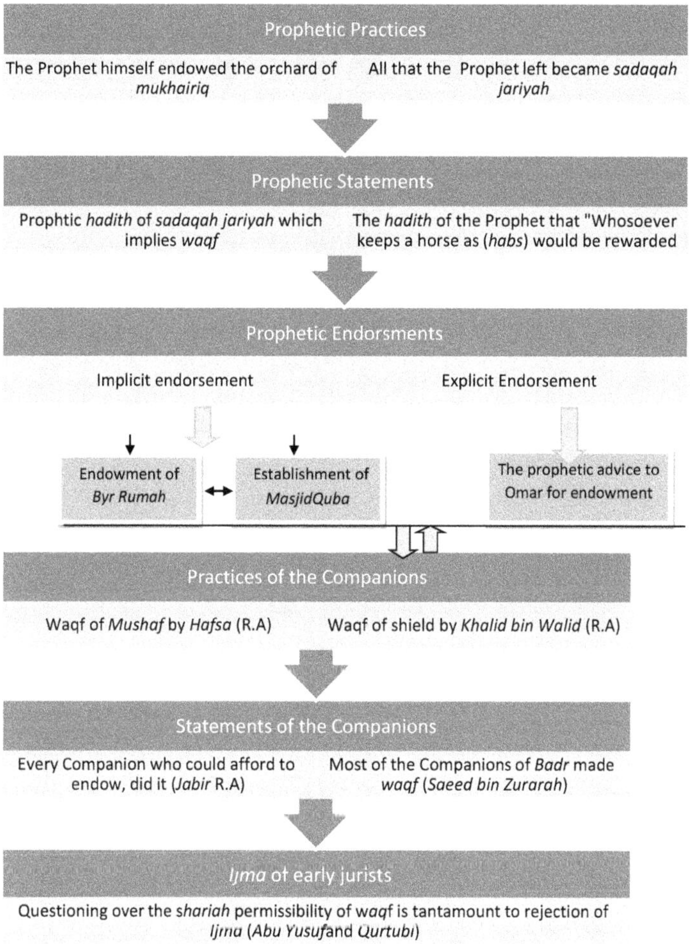

Figure 3.3 The shariah basis of *waqf*.

Othman (R.A) to fill a gap in the supply of free drinking water for the general public in Medina. The endowment of Bayruha (the orchard) by Abu Talha (R.A) was to provide for the basic necessities of his poor relatives. In addition, the objectives of the *waqf* by Omar (R.A) of a land in Khayber reflect the embodiment of the true spirit of the institution to fill any existing gap between the demand and supply of the basic necessities (Samhudi, 2001; Saleh, 2000; Badr, 1993). Reflecting on the objectives of early *awqaf* made by the companions of the Prophet (pbuh) can help to understand the nature and spirit of the *waqf* institution. Since all the above-mentioned *awqaf* were made with the consultation of the Prophet (pbuh), assessing the objectives of these *awqaf* would provide the guidance on how the Prophet (pbuh) envisaged a *waqf* to be made and used in a need-oriented manner. In the context of *waqf* beneficiaries, the Prophet (pbuh) directed the companions as per the need of the time and circumstances. Thus, the companions endowed for different objectives which fulfilled the need-orientation criteria of the time and circumstances which included endowment of land for a mosque, *waqf* of horse *jihad*, *waqf* for the benefits of poor, pauper, wayfarer, as well as for the family members of the endower (Abdullah, 2018b).

Some of the distinctive features of a *waqf* are a combination of voluntarism, charity, spirituality along with the flexibility of control and authority of the *waqif* over an endowed property (Layish, 1997). Hence, the objectives which can be fulfilled by a *waqf* can rarely be accomplished through other modes of charity (Khaleel and Abdullah, 2016). The device of *waqf* effectively fulfils the spiritual, financial, charitable, commercial, private and other forms socio-economic needs and objectives (Anderson, 1951). Also, a *waqf* can be resorted to achieve a wide array of shariah-permissible objectives in a self-defined manner of *waqif*. With the evolution of *waqf* as an institution, its role has been central in establishment of mosque, madarsa (Islamic educational institutions), hospitals and other institutions of public utility (Abdullah, 2015).

In historical terms, *waqf* fulfilled diverse socio-economic needs of the community (Kahf, 2003). The scope of *awqaf* extended as wide as to encompass the welfare of birds, animals and environment within its range. Similarly, the classical *awqaf* participated in deploying funds for the purposes, which may easily qualify for the modern concept of social finance (Abdullah, 2019). In the contemporary scenario, by virtue of its underlying massive potentials, the institution of *waqf* can prove a catalyst towards the sustainable development communities (Abdullah, 2018a). To this end, it is pertinent to underline that the model of *waqf* suitably matches the sketch of contemporary social enterprise, and there is huge scope for transforming many existing and potential *awqaf* into the proper mould of modern social enterprises.

The need-oriented approach of *waqf* makes it relevant in restrictive as well as flexible contexts. Keeping the spiritual merit of *waqf* aside, the institution caters to the existing socio-economic needs of individuals, families as well as the society as a whole. Historically, the social norms of Islamic societies have been vital in upholding the need-oriented application of *waqf* in different situations (Kuran, 2001). There are numerous examples where the endowers have explicitly favoured their disadvantaged or economically weak offspring through family *waqf*. As per Layish (1983: 20), "many persons prefer to make dedication in favour of their wives and of poor people of both sexes (other than relatives) rather than of wealthy siblings". There are also cases in which the founders of *waqf* favoured their orphaned grandchildren in equal terms (Layish, 1983). The usage of *waqf* in its historical context reflects the pragmatic pattern and normative behaviour of Islamic societies which enabled the endowers to withhold the philosophical underpinnings of *waqf* which is to bridge the existing gap in the supply of public good or to support the disadvantaged members of family through voluntary but perpetual charity (Lev, 2005; Shatzmiller, 2001).

Contextualising the *waqf* and policy recommendations

Waqf as a philanthropic institution and as an innovative socio-legal device facilitates accomplishing the spiritual and socio-economic objectives of *shariah* (Layish, 1997). Even though the model and mechanism of *waqf* was suggested by the Prophet (pbuh) himself, the detailed jurisprudential rulings and operational framework of the institution were developed by the classical jurists in subsequent centuries (Abdullah, 2018b). Later on, the socio-economic dynamics demanded that the domain of *waqf*-doctrines is augmented through the application of analogical reasoning (Kahf, 1999). Over the last few centuries, *awqaf* stagnated and mired in the precipitous decline. In this process, the institution received criticism for its inability to remain viable and sustainable. Interestingly, the criticism directed to the institution's inability in remaining viable is sourced both from within the Muslim community itself and from the outsiders (Kuran, 2001; Schoenblum, 1999).

In order to restore its previous glory, several aspects of *waqf* need to be tweaked in alignment to the objective of the institution. For this, some dynamic and innovative practices need to be introduced for the revival as well as a rejuvenated role of the institution in the current scenario.

In the modern context, the institution of *waqf* can possibly play a critical role towards achievement of Sustainable Development Goals (SDGs), in particular, among the Muslim-majority countries. In targeting the SDGs which aim to achieve 17 social, economic and environmental goals by 2030 (Sachs, 2012), global *awqaf* can emerge as a crucial contributor (Securities Commission Malaysia, 2015). It is estimated that globally there are *awqaf* of more than $1 trillion worth, which, if utilised diligently, may add great value in the context of SDGs (Abdullah, 2018a).

Other than this, the institution of *awqaf* can potentially make huge difference in accommodating and supporting refugees particularly across the Muslim nations. Based on different research reports, a vast number of total refugees across the world are either Muslim or the citizens of the Muslim-majority countries. From the perspective of *maqasid al-shariah* (higher objectives of *shariah*), provision of accommodation, protection and means of sustenance to these war-driven or internally displaced people is above all other developmental priorities (Abdullah, 2018a). Effective and strategic utilisation of awqaf in this respect can be critical to the relief and rehabilitative efforts. In this regard, a collaboration of both national and international *awqaf* institutions with the refugee-host countries is imperative to fulfil the maqasid-based vision of the institution.

From the prism of the *maqasid al-shariah* approach, the refugees as well as other war-affected people who lack basic necessities must be protected and provided for (Siddiqui, 1988). For this, the responsibilities should be shared by the international community in general and by Muslims in particular. In fact, due to the phenomenon of globalisation the onus to respond and redress the mass-human suffering in any region of the world transcends the national boundaries. In this, international *awqaf* can take a lead to provide critical resources. According to UNHCR (2015), statistically there are more than 59 million people who have been displaced for fleeing from their homes due to either civil war or internal conflicts. Effectively, these refugees are the most vulnerable people in the world. The application of *maqasid* approach would necessitate rehabilitation of and provision for these refugees on priority.

Remarkably, more than 50% of all the refugees across the world are children. In terms of geographical locations, over 85% of the cumulative world's refugees and forcibly displaced are scattered around the developing countries (Amnesty International, 2015). Out of this, a huge proportion of these refugees is concentrated in Muslim countries (Amnesty International, 2015). The world data on refugees reveal that more than three million refugees from Syria are being hosted by Turkey and Lebanon alone. Other than these, there are a huge number of refugees and internally displaced who have taken refuge in and around Jordan, Iraq, Egypt, Pakistan and other African countries (Amnesty International, 2015). By all means, these people fall within the necessities zone of *maqasid*-based priorities, and thus invariably qualify for the immediate relief and developmental resources.

The focus of the global *waqf* and its development policies need to be shifted so that it can accommodate the requirements of emergency relief as well as long-term settlement of these marginalised people. *Waqf* is of special importance to this discussion, as its involvement is central for the very existence of Muslim population in any society. In regions where these refugees are concentrated for many years, the material, non-material and religious needs of these people can best be provided by *awqaf*. In a nutshell, excluding the emergency relief requirements, the basic necessities of Muslim refugees include Mosques, graveyards, Madarsa, schools, vocational training centres and other financial and non-financial services. In this, the role of global *awqaf* can be pivotal. *Awqaf* proceeds from different regions can be utilised to accommodate these needs with the agreement of refugee-hosting regions. Additionally, the existing *awqaf* properties within the host regions can be employed for this purpose. For instance, there is scope for the host regions to swap the *waqf* lands which are dispersed across the different regions with the ones where refugees need shelters, mosques, graveyards, schools, etc. Also, there is scope for the international *awqaf* institutions to enter into negotiations with these host regions to establish new *awqaf* for the refugees. For these new Awqaf, the governmental bodies in the host regions can play the role of *mutawalli* (trustee) for the agreed amount of monetary contributions to be paid by the international *awqaf* institutions. Figure 3.4 further elucidates how this mechanism may work.

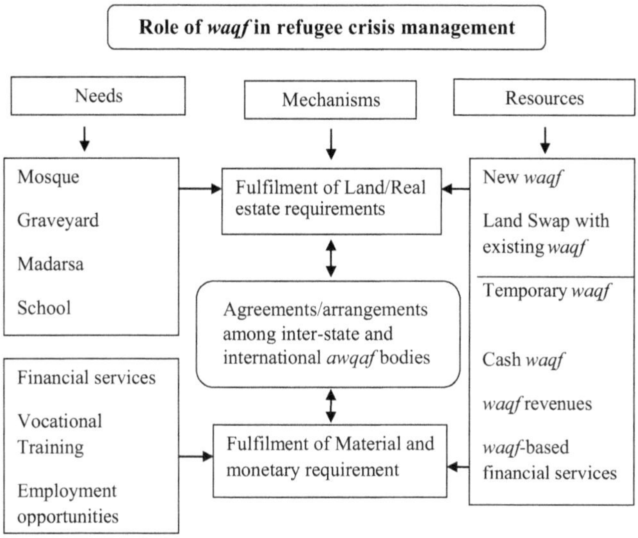

Figure 3.4 Role of *waqf* in refugee crisis management.
Source: Authors.

To sum it up, as an institution, the involvement of *waqf* is critical in providing for the necessary resources to the community. It is envisaged that *awqaf* should spearhead the philanthropic sector in providing both emergency relief and rehabilitative support to the refugees, facilitating the fulfilment of other basic necessities of the community at large.

To this end, while setting up new *awqaf* is profoundly appreciated, the practice of adding up over the existing *awqaf* should also be promoted and encouraged. This, as a result, can entail the benefits of economies of scale on the one hand, and on the other hand, this practice could ensure longer existence of the older *awqaf* as well. To this effect, in the classical discourse there are clear indications that the early generations of Muslims have practically appreciated this point. For example, there are reports that not only Hafsa (R.A), daughter of Omar, added in the existing *waqf* of Omar (R.A), but so did Ibn Omar (R.A) and Othman (R.A) (al-Khassaf, 1904: 9–11).

In addition, towards the enhancement of *waqf*'s effectiveness and efficiency, this chapter proposes that the concept and mechanism of parallel *waqf* can play a crucial role, particularly, in the context of existing large size family *waqf*. However, for this, the concept of parallel *waqf* needs to be recognised in *shariah* and promoted. Precisely, a parallel can be defined as allocation of a beneficial right by an affluent family-*waqf* beneficiary in favour of a more deserving third-party beneficiary. Thus, a nominated beneficiary may as well participate in the spiritual benefits of *waqf* (Abdullah, 2018a). Although the concept and mechanism of parallel *waqf* have scarcely been discussed in the available *waqf* literature, this study postulates its definition. Figure 3.5 explains the model of parallel *waqf*.

The scope of parallel *waqf* concept is possible as per those scholars who permit the *waqf* of usufruct (*manfa'ah*) (Abdullah 2018b; Kahf, 1999). In this way, while the beneficiary-cum-*waqif* may enjoy the merit and reward of an original *waqif* on the one hand, an optimal usage of *waqf* resources can be accomplished on the other. Similarly, in scenarios of family *waqf* where, with the passage of time, the number of beneficiaries of a *waqf* has increased manifold with the continuous expansion in the progeny of the original *waqif*, the wealthy ones may decide to forgo their entitlements for the benefit of the underprivileged ones through parallel *waqf*.

Perhaps, implementing the concept of adding up new *awqaf* in the existing ones wherever needed, as well as recognising the mechanism of parallel *waqf* may help enhance the effectiveness of the institution. In addition, this will sharpen the confidence of the community in the institution, for these practical measures may significantly augment the width and breadth of the potential benefits from the existing *awqaf*.

Finally, learning from the past experience of *waqf*'s decay and the alleged reasons of this fall, the planning for the development and administration of

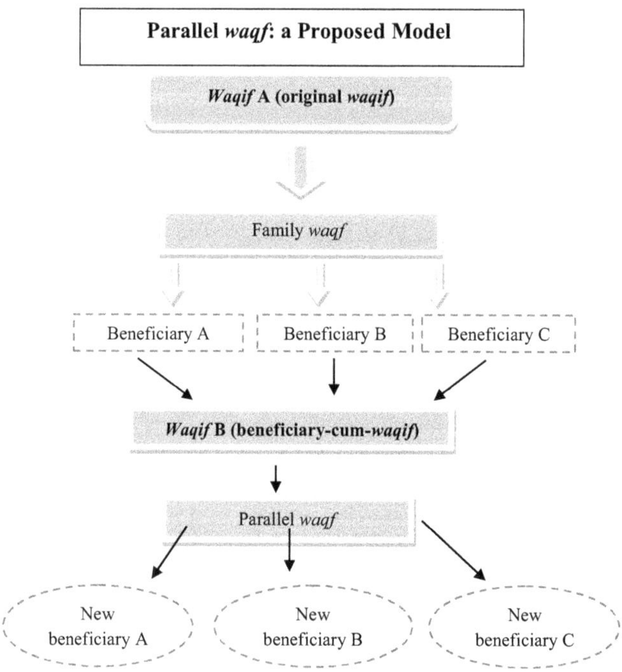

Figure 3.5 Parallel *waqf*: a proposed model.
Source: Author.

modern *awqaf* needs to drawn so that the past shortcomings of the institution can be effectively remedied. Based on the available literature on the factors of *waqf*'s downfall, it may be argued that the role of *waqf* started stagnating in Islamic society due to apparently two prominent factors. First, since most of the endowers began to create *waqf* in a random manner "without any reference to the needs and priorities of the society, depending on the intentions and visions of the contributors" (Sadeq, 2002: 271), it diluted the special character of the institution, which was to bridge the existing gap between the immediate needs of the society and the scarcity of public resources. Second, *awqaf* fell underprivileged on management frontier, due to the incompetency coupled with alleged insincerity of many *mutawallis* (Boudjellal, 2005). Thus, these two loopholes must be addressed by emphasising on the need-oriented and objective-based application of the awqaf in the current scenario.

Conclusion

Over the last few decades, the institution of *waqf* has attracted a great deal of interest from researchers of various academic backgrounds and disciplines. That *waqf* has successfully fascinated the scholars from various backgrounds is well evidenced by the enormous amount of academic literature that has been produced by them while analysing the role of the institution from the angle of their own academic fields and disciplines. Two aspects of the institution – namely the jurisprudence of *waqf* and its role in the Islamic history – have received detailed treatment in the extant literature and scholarly discourse; however, little has been written on the true objectives and priorities of *awqaf*. Keeping in view the dearth of scholarly research on the objectives of *waqf* within the classical jurisprudential discourse, this study attempted to fill this gap in the literature. The study endeavoured to analyse the jurisprudential premises of *waqf* in shariah, followed by deliberating the spiritual, financial as well as socio-economic objectives of the institution in its early Islamic period.

Among the key findings of this chapter includes the argument that the early *awqaf* of Islamic history were founded with the consultation of the Prophet (pbuh), and were directed to fill the immediate needs of the society. Be it the *waqf* of land for the Masjid Quba, Masjid Nabawi, *waqf* by Abu Talha (R.A) of his orchard or *waqf* by Othman (R.A) of Byr al-Rumah (the Well) in Medina, all of these *awqaf* were directed to meet the needs of the time and circumstances. Similarly, the *waqf* by Omar (R.A) in Khayber showcased the broad objectives of *waqf* which included supporting the family, relatives, poor, widow as well as other pious purposes in line with the need-oriented spirit of the institution. In a nutshell, there is rarely any instance of *waqf* in the early Islamic history which may had been created randomly without a firm objective.

However, in later centuries, being plagued by some unceremonious characteristics, Muslim societies began conditioning the institution of *awqaf* in a random as well as reactive manner instead of maintaining its proactive and need-oriented approach. In this reactionary process, many endowers failed to uphold the axioms of Islamic charitable paradigm, which seeks to focus on filling the gaps existing between the immediate needs of the society and scarcity of allocated resources for it.

This chapter argued that in order to contextualise the functions and role of *waqf* institution in the modern context, the true objectives of the institution need to be diligently explored and duly applied. The recognition and promotion of the *waqf*'s objectives are critical towards enhancing the modern relevance of the institution. For this, the chapter contended for the promotion of need-oriented approach and context-specific application of *waqf*. Thus, the priorities of the *waqf* institution cannot be of a static nature or standard across the different regions and jurisdictions; rather the essence of *waqf* lies in its dynamic setting, which needs materialisation.

The chapter provided some key policy recommendations for improving the effectiveness of the *waqf* institution, which included recognition of the parallel *waqf* concept along with implementation of adding up new *awqaf* in the existing ones as and wherever needed. In addition, this chapter recommended to contextualise the relevance of global *awqaf* with reference to the United Nations-promoted programme of SDGs in particular among the Muslim-majority nations. Finally, the chapter deliberated and discussed how the objectives of *waqf* are a natural fit to address the refugee crisis, particularly, across the Muslim countries and regions.

Notes

1 Quba is located in the outskirts of Medina. On the eve of his emigration to Medina, the prophet (Pbuh) stayed there for few days and built there the very first mosque of Islamic history.

2 Rumah was a famous well owned by a Jew in Medina. He used to charge individuals for supplying water from the well. The prophet (Pbuh) asked his companions to buy and donate the well for the sake of Allah. Othman, the third Caliph of Islam, responded to the call and, after paying the price of well, endowed it for free public utility.

References

AAOIFI (Accounting and Auditing Organisation for Islamic Financial Institutions) (2015) *Shariah Standards*. Manama, Bahrain.

Abdullah, M. (2019) Waqf and trust: the nature, structures and socio-economic impacts, *Journal of Islamic Accounting and Business Research*, Vol. 10, No. 4, pp. 512–527.

Abdullah, M. (2018a) Waqf, sustainable development goals (SDGs) and maqasid al-shariah, *International Journal of Social Economics*, Vol. 45, No. 1, pp. 158–172.

Abdullah, M. (2018b) Evolution in *Waqf* Jurisprudence and Islamic financial innovation, *Journal of Islamic Monetary Economics and Finance*, Vol. 4, No. 1, pp. 161–182.

Abdullah, M. (2015) A new framework of corporate governance of Waqf: a preliminary proposal, *Islam and Civilisational Renewal*, Vol. 6, No. 3, pp. 353–370.

Abu Zuhrah, M. (1972) *Muhadarat fil waqf*. Cairo: Darul Fikr al-Arabi.

Al-Amin Hasan, A. (1994) *Idaratu wa Tathmiru Mutamallakatul Awqaf.* Jeddah: IRTI, p. 107.

Amnesty International (2015) Global refugee crisis in numbers. Available at: https://www.amnesty.org/latest/news/2015/06/global-refugee-crisis-in-numbers/ (Accessed on 13th March, 2018).

Anderson, J.N. (1951) 'The religious element in *Waqf* endowment, *Journal of the Royal Central Asian Society*, Vol. 38, pp. 292–299.

Badr, A. B. (1993) *al-Tarikh al-Shamil lil-Madinah*.al-Medina al-Munawarah, Publisher not given.

Boudjellal, M. (2005) The Need for a new approach of the socio-economic developing role in Waqf in the 21st Century, in Haneef, M. A. & Anwar, M. (eds.) *Studies in Islamic Economics in the 21st Century, Shariah Foundations, Theory and Institutions.* Malaysia: IIUM.

Çizakça, M. (2000) *A History of Philanthropic Foundations: The Islamic World from the Seventh Century to the Present.* Istanbul: Bogazici University Press.

Gil Moshe, (1998) The earliest Waqf foundations, *Journal of Near Eastern Studies*, Vol. 57, No. 2, pp. 125–140.

Ibn al-Qudamah, M. A. (1997) *al-Mughni.* Riyadh: Dar Qalam al-Kutub (Vol. 8, pp. 231–32).

Al-Jazayri, A. (2000) *Al-Fiqh Ala Madhahib al-Arba'a.* Istanbul: Hakikat Kitabvi (Vol. 3rd).

Kahf, M. (2003) *The Role of Waqf in Improving the Ummah Welfare.* Available at: http://monzer.kahf.com/ (Accessed on 12th April, 2015).

Kahf, M. (1999) *Towards the Revival of Awqaf: A Few Fiqhi Issues to Reconsider.* Available at: http://monzer.kahf.com/ (Accessed on 12th April, 2015).

Khaleel, F. and Abdullah, M. (2016) Waqf (Islamic endowment), human capital and humanitarian aid, *Interdisciplinary Journal of Economics and Business Law*, Vol. 5, No. 2, pp. 36–52.

al-Khassaf, A. B. (1904) *Ahkam al-Awqaf.* Egypt: Dewan Umum *al-Awqaf* al-Misriyah.

Kuran, T. (2001) The provision of public goods under Islamic law: origins, impacts and limitation of the *Waqf* system, *Law and Society Review*, Vol. 35, pp. 841–898.

Layish, A. (1997) The family Waqf and the Shariah law of succession in modern times, *Islamic Law and Society*, Vol. 4, No. 3, pp. 352–388.

Layish, A. (1983) The Maliki Family Waqf according to Wills and Waqfiyyat, *Bulletin of the School of Oriental and African Studies*, Vol. 46, pp. 1–32.

Lev, Y. (2005) *Charity, Endowments and Charitable Institutions in Medieval Islam.* Gainesville, FL: University Press of Florida.

McChesney, R. D. (1991) *Waqf in Central Asia: Four Hundred Years in the History of a Muslim Shrine, 1480–1889.* Princeton, NJ: Princeton University Press.

Muslim, al- Sahih (1999) Kitab al-wasiyah, in Salih, A. (ed.), *Mawsuah al-Hadith al-Sharif.* Riyadh: Darussalam, (Hadith No. 1017).

Nomani, S. (1951) *Waqf Awlad: Maqalat-i-Shibli.* Azamgarh, India: Dar al-Musannifin.

Othman, M. Z. (1983) Origin of the Institution of Waqf, *Hamdard Islamicus*, Vol. 6, No. 2, pp. 3–23.

Qurtubi, A. (2003) *al-Jame' li Ahkam al-Quran*, (Verse 92: chapter 3). KSA: Dar Alam al-Kutub.

Sachs, J. D. (2012) *From Millennium Development Goals to Sustainable Development Goals.* Available at: http://www.thelancet.com/journals/a/article/PIIS0140-6736%2812%2960685-0/fulltext (Accessed on 20th September, 2015).

Sadeq, A. (2002) *Waqf*, perpetual charity and poverty alleviation, *International Journal of Social Economics,* Vol. 29, No. 1, pp. 135–151.
Saleh, A. M. (2000) *al-Masjid Jami wa Jamiah.* Riyadh: Maktaba Malik Fahad.
Samhudi, N.A. (2001) *Wafa al-Wafa fi Akhbar Dar al-Mustafa.* Medina: Muassasah al-Furqan lil-Turas.
Schoenblum, J. A. (1999) The role of legal doctrine in the decline of the Islamic *Waqf*: a comparison with the trust, *Vanderbilt Journal of the Transnational Law,* Vol. 32, pp. 1191–1203.
Securities Commission Malaysia (SCM) (2015) *'Harnessing Waqf into a Bankable Social Financing and Investment Asset Class*, Proceedings of the SC-OCIS Roundtable 2014, Kuala Lumpur: SC.
Al-Shafi'i, M. (1990) *Al Umm.* Beirut: Darul Ma'rafah, (Vol. 4).
Shatzmiller, M. (2001) 'Islamic institutions and property rights: the case of the 'public good' Waqf, *Journal of the Economic and Social History of the Orient*, Vol. 44, No. 1, pp. 44–74.
Al-Shawkani, M. (2008) *Nailul Awtar: Sharhu Muntaqa al-Alkhbar.* Available at: http://www.islamhouse.com/p/140690 (Accessed on 23rd January, 2012).
Al-Shaybani, M. (1997) *Sharah Kitab al-Siyar al-Kabir.* Beirut: Darul Kutub al-Ilmiyah, (Vol. 5, pp. 249–283).
Al-Sibai, M. (1985) *Min Rawai'i Hadaratina.* Beirut: al-Maktaba al-Islami, pp. 121–161.
Siddiqui, M. N. (1988) The guarantee of a minimum level of living in an Islamic state, in Iqbal, M. (ed.) *Distributive Justice and Need Fulfilment in an Islamic Economy.* Leicester: The Islamic Foundation, pp. 251–281.
UNHCR (2015) Families forced to flee their homes. Available at: http://donate.unhcr.org/gbr/general?gclid=CjwKEAjwq-OsBRDd95aryprR9wQSJACQnU3GTV1aNAMkvuaQ23EpAnTwvBPn_NK5rR8zh4QqWwcvgBoCT_Hw_wcB&gclsrc=aw.ds (Accessed on 23rd March, 2018).
Zaid, A. (1996) *Ahammiyatul Waqf wa Ahdafuhu.* Riyadh: Dar al-Taibah.
Zaman, S. M. (1991) *Economic Functions of an Islamic State: the Early Experience.* Leicestershire: The Islamic Foundation.
Al-Zarqa, M. (1947) *Ahkam al-Awqaf.* Damascus: Syria University Press.

4 Role of awqaf as an economic driver

Hisham Dafterdar

Introduction

The institution of waqf is a *sunna* – sayings and practices – established by the Prophet (pbuh) that became the base upon which the Islamic socio-economic development model is built. As a feature of the Islamic civilisation, the history of awqaf is rich with impressive achievements in the field of social work and human development. Awqaf served the poor in particular and society in general. Awqaf services ranged from education and healthcare to economic development and social welfare. Awqaf also contributed to the protection of the environment and the preservation of religious and cultural heritage. Grand mosques and impressive shrines, major hospitals and universities, libraries and museums, orphanages and homes for the elderly, animal shelters and sanctuaries are few examples of awqaf-worthy beneficiaries.

Despite these achievements, the history of awqaf is dotted with turbulent events. Over the years, due to a variety of reasons including the legacy of the colonisation of Muslim countries, the role of the waqf as an effective tool for socio-economic development has become neglected and somewhat forgotten. After independence, many governments considered awqaf as public property and part of the national wealth. They exercised disproportionate control over awqaf affairs and interfered in operational matters. They established ministries and directorates as government agencies to manage awqaf and tweaked rules and regulations to realise economic outcomes. These policies led awqaf to fall into the hands of the state which took over the assets and revenues and covered the administrative expenses from the national budget.

The control of awqaf by governments did more to stifle the sector than to vitalise it. To date in many Muslim countries, awqaf has not been able to fulfil its purpose as a vehicle of social welfare and stimulus for economic growth. One of the major impediments to awqaf is the lack of the enabling legal environment. Legislative reforms and the implementation of effective corporate governance framework are needed to enable the development of awqaf as a driver of social welfare and economic development in the country.

While awqaf have generally been overlooked, a few countries did embark on developing this sector and built substantial portfolios of awqaf properties and investments. They recognised the potential of awqaf as an effective economic institution with a social role to combat poverty and enhance welfare. Saudi Arabia, Kuwait, Qatar, the UAE, Turkey, Malaysia and Indonesia are some of the countries that took effective measures to harness the potential that awqaf present in enhancing social welfare and economic development. However, despite these efforts, the sector remains lacklustre and fundamentally constrained. The need is dire for and more devoted work in order to realise its tangible effects on social and economic welfare.

Historical overview

The institution of waqf has played a major developmental role throughout Islamic history. The concept of endowing property by Muslims as an ongoing charity (*sadaqajariya*) was established by the Noble Prophet (PBUH). The practice of waqf was known before the advent of Islam, although with different names, where people donated assets for the benefit of priests and temples. However, Islam expanded the circle of beneficiaries and included human and non-human life, public utilities and the environment. According to Sheikh Mustafa Zarqa, "everything in waqf is subject to *ijtihad* and there is no single ruling in it that gained unanimity except that the waqf purpose must be benevolent (*birr*)".[2] Islam was the first religion to develop a comprehensive regulatory framework that promotes, guides, protects and fosters the development of the institution of waqf. Everything that the West developed later on in this field is derived from the waqf system.

Since the earliest days of Islam, awqaf has featured prominently in the social and economic development of Muslim societies. It has long been the lifeboat of the economy. Awqaf was the main provider of many of the social services that today are financed by the state such as education, healthcare, infrastructure and national security. Awqaf was also the means of achieving equitable distribution of income and wealth and introducing inter-generational social investments in society.

The foundation of waqf reached its zenith during the 16th and 17th centuries at the height of the Ottoman Empire, as many sultans and other public figures and prominent people created numerous waqfs in the form of mosques, schools, hospitals, shelters and agricultural land. It was reported that more than one third of the agricultural land of the Ottoman Empire was waqf, providing food and creating employment.

By the turn of the 20th century, many Muslim governments had established ministries and directorates that placed awqaf firmly under government control. The government's firm grip on awqaf had several negative impacts that led not only to much less new awqaf being established, but also to the expropriation of large areas of awqaf land.[3] Many awqaf properties were left undeveloped or fell into disrepair and much of the latent wealth of awqaf remains to date largely untapped and underutilised. The role of the waqf as a welfare mechanism declined to the point that in many countries awqaf became a liability and a burden on the public purse.

The third economic sector

Recessions and economic downturns have drawn attention to the Islamic economic system and its faith-based institutions of zakat and waqf. Many Muslim countries embarked on reforming the administration of awqaf by separating the custody (*nazara*) function from awqaf asset management by establishing separate entities to develop and manage awqaf properties. They conceded that the waqf has a separate personality "*thimmah*" and that awqaf funds should not be commingled with public funds. Egypt in 1971 established the "Egyptian Awqaf Authority" to take over the management of awqaf properties from the Ministry of Awqaf. In Sudan, the "Federal Corporation of Awqaf" was established in 1987. Kuwait, in 1993, founded "Awqaf Public Foundation". In Jordan, the Ministry of Awqaf, Islamic Affairs and Holy Places established "Awqaf Properties Investment Corporation". In Malaysia, at the federal level, the Prime Minister's Department in March 2004 established the Department for Awqaf, Zakat and Hajj (JAWHAR) to coordinate the activities of the states' religious councils in matters relating to awqaf development.

The majority of Shariah jurists are of the view that once a property is donated as a waqf, it should remain a waqf forever. The conditions of perpetuity and inalienability of a waqf asset have led over the years to a considerable accumulation of societal wealth that played an important role in improving the lot of Muslim society. As a reflection of its increasing contribution to the economy, awqaf as a non-profit institution is considered to be one of the most important components of the third economic sector.[4] The distinction of this third sector from the other two economic sectors – the government sector also known as the first sector, and the private sector sometimes called the second sector – is characterised by being voluntary, and by its social, cultural and humanitarian mission.

Awqaf organisations are Islamic not-for-profit entities with a wide diversity of structures and purposes. They are not part of government although many perform a public service. They generate economic value that is more impactful than quantifiable. Their operations dovetail into all sectors of the economy and include a wide range of industries including real estate, education, healthcare, social services and recreation. They undertake a broad range of social, cultural and economic activities especially in areas where public services are lacking or insufficient, and where the private sector does not find it profitable to invest.

Custody and management of awqaf

In principle, the *waqif* through a deed determines the objectives of the waqf and its management and succession processes. The waqf manager or trustee (*mutawalli/nazir*) holds the title of the waqf property, exercises legal control and is bound by fiduciary responsibility and moral obligation to protect and administer the waqf for the benefit of the beneficiaries in accordance with the terms of the waqf deed. *Mutawallis* are expected to comply with both the letter and spirit of the waqf condition. The importance of the conditions of the *waqif* is indicated by the often quoted maxim: "The conditions of the *waqif* have the same legal weight as the edicts of the legislator". However, some flexibility is afforded through the differences of the schools of jurisprudence. Abu Hanifah, for example, allows changing the conditions of the *waqif* if there is an overriding public benefit (*maslahaa'ama*), or when the beneficiaries or the purpose of the waqf come to an end.[5]

The authority of *mutawallis* to act and make decisions on behalf of the waqf carries an immense responsibility and their duties are wider and more onerous than they were assumed to be. As trustees, *mutawallis* have the primary responsibility for prudent management of assets in their custody. As such, *mutawallis* are expected to have a certain level of business skills and investment knowledge to support their role in monitoring the safety and performance of assets under their control. However, because of the nature of awqaf, its religious message and social application, it seems logical that those who are entrusted with the custody and management of awqaf properties are more religiously conscious and tend to employ their faith when managing. But the operating environment is rapidly changing and as a consequence the role of the *mutawalli* is also changing. *Mutawallis* are required not only to act in good faith for the best outcomes for the waqf, but also to be seen acting diligently and ethically, and build trust among those they deal with. However, due to the unscrupulous behaviour of some *mutawallis* awqaf had lost some of the respect and trust of the community. *Mutawallis* have to overcome image problems. They need to develop behavioural characteristics to uphold awqaf ethos and change the branded image as persons who are insular, sceptical and a business risk. *Mutawallis* have the responsibility to safeguard and grow assets in their custody and produce returns, hence rendering it harder to act solely on their beliefs.

Creating an enabling legal environment

Without a good sustainable environment, it is difficult to develop an economic sector. The major challenge faced by awqaf is ensuring that the huge treasure of waqf assets is preserved, developed, continues to grow and serve humanitarian and social needs. This can be met only by creating an enabling legal environment – one that creates a level playing field that enables awqaf to fulfil their obligations to donors, beneficiaries and all other stakeholders.

Awqaf is a global sector and many awqaf organisations have international presence acting as trustees and custodians of many assets and cross-border investments, operating across multiple jurisdictions with different legal systems, regulatory requirements and cultural norms. It is not unusual to find the waqf property in one country and the beneficiaries in another while the waqf organisation is based in a third country. In a globalised environment, a waqf has a much broader exposure than it does domestically. Therefore, the regulatory environment should foster public confidence in the waqf, encourage donors and promote ethical and proactive behaviour of employees, volunteers and *mutawallis*. Donors usually are more generous and financiers more willing to provide capital for projects of organisations that adopt the best practices of corporate governance.[6]

Unlike commercial corporations, the services delivered by awqaf may often be intangible and difficult to measure. Companies have clear delineations about shareholders, with all operations and reporting geared towards profits. The position is not so simple for awqaf organisations. Regulated mainly by Shariah and restricted by *waqif* conditions, many awqaf foundations consider regulatory and compliance issues of corporate governance as costly and unnecessary administrative burdens. Unlike commercial corporations, staff in an awqaf foundation comprises low-paid professionals or volunteers who have chosen to work in awqaf for less tangible rewards. They are mainly concerned with social aspects and pay little attention to financial efficiency or accountability. They claim that by legislating what is effectively an issue of faith, the very fabric of awqaf will be undermined.

Strategy formulation in an awqaf foundation can be subject to a unique and complex set of influences. What is deemed to be appropriate strategy will be conditioned by concern not to violate the conditions of the *waqif*, the wishes of the donors and the legal environment. The concerns of non-beneficiary stakeholders should also form part of awqaf foundations' responsibilities and as such *mutawallis* should have the duty to act in the interest of the entire community. These days no organisation is immune from public scrutiny, not even a shelter nor an orphanage that does not have a blemish to its name. Therefore, the impact of awqaf's performance on the community must be positive and the organisation must be seen to be operating in conformity with community standards and expectations.

The business face of awqaf

Awqaf is rapidly developing as a vital economic sector accounting for a substantial share of the Islamic financial system. Contrary to popular belief, awqaf organisations have many similarities to private sector corporations. In some ways, it seems there is very little difference from the corporate world – assets need to be managed, bills to be paid, revenues to be earned and reports to be made. Awqaf also undertake a wide range of activities such as investment, project management, fund raising and maintenance of key banking relationships. Other than the lack of shareholders, it could be difficult to tell a waqf foundation from a for-profit corporation.

There are however differences between awaqf organisation and a commercial enterprise. Where companies have shareholders and boards, awqaf organisations have waqifs, donors and trustees. The most fundamental characteristic of awaqf organisation, compared to a commercial enterprise, is that its primary mission is to provide some form of social service which primarily impacts on the quality of life. The members of awqaf organisations are trustees and custodians, but not owners. Awqaf beneficiaries are entitled to the usufruct of the asset but have no claim on the asset itself. The waqf system separates beneficial ownership from legal ownership, and beneficiaries remain entitled as long as they remain qualified as beneficiaries. In addition to the poor and needy, awqaf purposes include non-humans and public utilities such as mosques, schools, cemeteries, roads, bridges and water wells.

Awqaf organisations need a steady stream of revenue in order to fund their operations. They cannot achieve financial sustainability by relying entirely on donations. Many waqfs are finding it necessary to expand their revenue base to include steadier forms of income from investments and commercial activities to ensure their financial independence and long-term sustainability. This spills over into the overly competitive environment of the marketplace where awqaf have to compete with the private sector and this means selling goods and services and be profitable. Thus, awqaf's social work is getting more closely entwined with business endeavours.

While most of the corporate governance and management practices of commercial companies can be applied, a thorough understanding and application of awqaf principles will yield better results. Shariah provides the basis for awqaf regulations and the sector shows great concern for ethics based on fundamental values such as honesty, integrity, fairness, trust and commitment. These principles are especially important as it is through these values where awqaf social impacts are more visible. Awqaf has also to deal with the vagaries of the market and the demands for more transparency and accountability. Over the decade, there has been a growing realisation that although the Shariah serves to provide a general framework for regulating the awqaf sector, it is becoming increasingly important to put forward a comprehensive regulatory framework that is more attuned to current market requirements.

Sustainability and profitability of awqaf

The dichotomy between sustainability and profitability is false. There is a misconception among some that making a profit and doing good are contradictory objectives. Just because an organisation is a waqf does not mean that it should not seek profits. The main difference between awqaf and the private sector is that in the corporate world, profit is used to create individual wealth. In awqaf, profits are used to deliver social benefits, accomplish a mission and support future activities. Some stakeholders see the waqf as a conduit of income to beneficiaries and not a receptacle to hold it. They believe that awqaf foundations should not retain any earnings.[7]

There is also a fundamental difference between awqaf and the commercial world in rationalising business decisions. In companies, decisions are justified in terms of their short-term effect on profitability and shareholder value. Awqaf organisations, as trans-generational carriers, have different purposes for generating revenues. The system of waqf converts money to spend into money to invest. Responsible awqaf organisations take a long-term view when investing. Their business decisions are commonly considered good if they achieve long-term benefits for their beneficiaries.

Awqaf stakeholders include donors, *waqifs*, *mutawallis*, beneficiaries, clients, employees, volunteers, the local community and government. Each of these groups consists of individuals of diverse nationalities, culture, age, education, social and economic status. Each group has its own values, interests, goals and perceptions of acceptable performance. Awqaf is capable of responding to the needs of all these groups. But in order to do so, awqaf organisations will have to maintain a balance between their mission objectives and their financial pursuits; in other words, they have to seek a balance between being financially efficient and socially effective. There is little use in being a highly cost-efficient operation if the foundation is proving to be ineffective in delivering successful outcomes in operational terms. Likewise, an awqaf foundation that is highly effective in meeting its operational objectives, but is inefficient financially, may soon find itself unable to continue delivering services as its resources are drained.

Achieving financial sustainability is a goal that all awqaf organisations should strive for. Imagine, for example, an orphanage operated by a waqf foundation. If it does not have any surplus funds to meet ongoing operating and capital costs, the orphanage may be forced to close down. The inability to access any surplus funds from its own reserves may result in the withdrawal of a much needed community service.

Awqaf public and private sector partnerships

Lately, awqaf is getting more attention from both the public and the private sectors. Governments across the Muslim world are becoming more aware of awqaf's potential as an economic driver. The sector is regarded as relatively resilient and recession proof. Awqaf organisations are resistant to market downturns because their assets are unencumbered freehold. They have access to free funds and *pro bono* services. Awqaf's social mandate is to serve the poor, redistribute wealth and correct the imbalance between social strata. Awqaf projects create jobs, produce economic output, stabilise prices and stimulate the economy.

Lately, there has been a growing level of interest and interaction between awqaf and the private sector. Awqaf is rich with one of the important factors of production – land, but is short on other factors such as capital and labour. Funding for development is a constant quest for awqaf. To date large parcels of awqaf land are undeveloped due to lack of funding. This calls for a strategic cooperation between awqaf and the private sector which can bring in capital and entrepreneurship. However, companies are attracted to awqaf projects because of the business opportunities they represent.

Awqaf represent a market niche with good returns. The awqaf sector, albeit not-for-profit, and despite its role as a welfare mechanism, or perhaps because of it, appears to have an edge over other sectors because of the many concessions and privileges granted to awqaf projects. At the same time, commercial companies may see their involvement with awqaf as a way of discharging their corporate social responsibility. Doing social good is good for business and a socially connected project generating a cash flow has a special appeal to the private sector. Partnerships between awqaf and the private sector are more than "marriages of convenience" where under such wedlocks, it is usually one party that stands to benefit more than the other. Awqaf/private sector partnerships are win-win arrangements that bridge the worlds of private finance and awqaf social responsibility with benefit to both.

From an awqaf perspective, a BOT agreement is a means of developing awqaf properties through self-financing of projects. The private sector can assist awqaf to deal with the complexities of project development. The private developer finances the project, carries the risks and operates the project for an agreed period during which the project's cash flow is the only source for repayment of the investment and profit. At the end of the concession period, the facilities are returned to the waqf trustees to become a permanent source of revenue to the organisation. Through these arrangements, awqaf organisations are able to pare away non-core functions so they can focus more keenly on their core mission of social work.

Awqaf support of SMEs

The SME sector provides many opportunities for awqaf to fulfil their objectives of community development. The objectives to be served are a blend of social and profit goals that serve multiple stakeholders. Awqaf can help establish and nurture small- and medium-scale revenue-producing projects that aim at creating jobs and improving the lives of the poor.

Awqaf's support is not a matter of just providing finance or lending money to existing or start-up small businesses. Awqaf organisations can be the "business angels" entering into partnerships with start-ups and early-stage enterprises. Such partnerships can be of enormous benefit to the project, and to the waqf organisation. Awqaf's aim is to build new capabilities and sustainable ventures.

Awqaf's financial support

Awqaf can raise capital and channel funds into the hands of competent management who have business propositions with good prospects of success. Rather than compete with banks, awqaf can fill a gap in small business financing. Awqaf's financial support can be in any one of the three main Shariah compliant modes: participatory, concessionary and project financing. Within these modes are various contractual forms that comply with the principle of risk and profit sharing.

Participatory financing is the most flexible and most common as it adheres to the Islamic principles of sharing of risks and profits. Instead of lending money to an enterprise, awqaf actually gets involved as a partner or shareholder in the business. The more commonly used participatory modes are *musharaka* (equity participation) and *mudaraba* (trust financing). From an SME stance, participatory funding is a good alternative to higher cost borrowing. *Musharaka* participation by awqaf facilitates the transfer of a pre-determined share of the risk in return for a share in the profit. In *Mudarabah*, awqaf as the finance provider (*rabul mal*) promotes business development by extending financing to capable but cash-strapped entrepreneurs, based on awqaf carrying the financial risk and sharing the profit at a pre-agreed percentage.

Concessionary financing is money advanced mainly in the form of *qard-hasan* (benevolent loan) where only the principal is to be repaid, or loans at below-market rates – usually at a small service fee to cover administrative cost. The *cash waqf* is the main source for concessionary SME financing. Concessionary lending can only be considered in very low risk operations and with adequate safeguards to ensure repayment.

Project financing modes are usually non-profit sharing as they are based on cost plus a pre-determined mark-up. The financing contracts used include *baimuajjal* (instalment sales), *baisalam* (forward sale contracts), *ijara* (lease financing), *ijarawaiqtina* (hire purchase), *istisna'a* (construction/manufacturing finance) and *murabaha* (procurement financing). The choice of the mode of financing and the type of contract depends on the nature and needs of the project, on the risk profile and expected returns, and on the waqf organisation's own investment policy and guidelines.

Awqaf's non-financial support

Awqaf can also provide a whole gamut of non-financial support for the smaller enterprise. The most common in-kind contribution is land. The provision of land for a project serves awqaf developmental objectives of waqf properties and ensures permanent connection of the project to the waqf. In such arrangements, the appraised current market value of the land is used to determine awqaf's share in the project. Other in-kind support includes services such as consultancy, training, monitoring and insurance.

Awqaf organisations can also serve as business incubators for new ventures, nurturing and helping them to survive and prosper. Awqaf can provide advice and guidance and help in areas of strategic planning which can be particularly helpful during the early stages of a business development.

Microfinance by awqaf

Awqaf organisations need not spend inordinate amounts of money in order to assist small projects. Awqaf can offer small incentives to drive simple outcomes. Microfinance is the making of small loans, usually less than $500 to individuals to establish or expand a small, self-sustaining family business. Funds for microenterprises can be collected through crowdfunding contributions and allocated as loans for microenterprises. There are many examples of loans ranging from $100 to $500 for micro-projects such as a broom factory, a laundry, cake shop, and supporting artisans, costermongers and other self-employed persons with tools and training.

Policy implication

With the rise of popular movements like "human rights" and "economic equality", governments in the Muslim world assumed direct responsibility for the welfare of their citizens and the role of awqaf was effectively marginalised. However, in spite of government's domination, awqaf remained more firmly tied to society than to the state. Government's welfare programmes have been unable to serve efficiently all of the social needs, especially the delivery of speedy aid and humanitarian support to vulnerable groups who perceived government's actions with a lot of dissatisfaction and suspicion. However, faith-based charity institutions such as waqf and zakat enjoy a higher degree of popular trust, having grass-roots knowledge and much better access to people in need of support than any government agency. Being an act of worship, the practice of waqf as an instrument of benevolence gave the awqaf sector public support that contributed to a large degree in shaping its independence.[8]

Given the apparent support for awqaf at the local and national levels, the sector needs not operate at the periphery of socio-economic activity, but should rather be mainstreamed within the state's legal, social and economic systems. The waqf has relations with all areas of social and economic development such as housing, employment, social amenities, investment and commercial activity at zero cost to the state. Therefore, a great deal of thought should go into government policies which impact on the awqaf as it intersects with other sectors of the economy. It is imperative that the impact of any policy of government on awqaf should be positive and not a hindrance to the sector's capacity to grow. Policies which restrict free cash flow could affect awqaf's ability to be of service to its beneficiaries and ultimately to the state.

Since awqaf's charitable and social programmes ease the pressure on government's budget, it is fair to assume that the government is in fact an indirect and undeclared beneficiary of awqaf. If the awqaf sector is doing well, the overall economy will benefit. It is therefore in government's interest to create the supporting environment that promotes public awareness and facilitates the establishment of more waqfs. Both the public and awqaf institutions should be incentivised and encouraged through mechanisms such as subsidies and tax relief programmes.

Awqaf projects exhibit the combined characteristics of being socially responsible, value adding and market oriented. Islamic banks and financing institutions should be encouraged to finance awqaf projects. Both the government and awqaf institutions should work together to dispel the myth that bankers cannot do awqaf projects and be profitable, and that financing awqaf projects is not just a good idea; it is part of a good business policy.

Conclusion

Awqaf institutions are effective organisations for the socio-economic, cultural and religious development of a country. They have no direct or indirect political involvement although they have considerable influence on the country's political and social life. The development of the awqaf sector is on the national agenda of many Muslim countries as a strategy to boost the economy and complement government's social programmes.

One of the most critical problems facing the efforts to develop the awqaf sector is the widespread lack of awareness of awqaf as a viable and effective economic sector. Despite the sector's awesome size and significant contribution to the economy, there is hardly a mention of it in the financial pages of newspapers. Awqaf remains one of the most misunderstood sectors of the Islamic financial system. Awqaf institutions are perceived to lack the organisational discipline and the entrepreneurial acumen of for-profit corporations. This has resulted in a very slow pace of developing awqaf properties. Hence, it is the reason we see many awqaf properties often in prime locations remaining idle or underdeveloped.

On many fronts, the awqaf sector in many countries has taken steps towards reinventing itself. In doing so, it has been able to reverse the tendency to write off awqaf as being inherently inefficient and shows no entrepreneurial behaviour. Today, most awqaf foundations have a broad business focus. They are taking responsibility for a wider range of activities in the commercial, industrial, agricultural and services sectors. Areas where guidance is required include institutional, legal and corporate governance frameworks. This entails the skilling and empowerment of *mutawallis* and managers to be effective gate keepers and responsible stewards of the assets under their control, and to enable them to charter the continued growth of their organisations.

The renewed interest in awqaf offers an opportunity to learn from the mistakes of the past and to construct a modern regulatory and corporate governance framework. Recognising that awqaf foundations are non-profit entities holding valuable assets and providing essential social services, government as a beneficiary should create the enabling and supporting environment for the awqaf sector to grow and be more effective. Awqaf's real reform agenda should have succinct, relevant, understandable and implementable standards that optimise efficiency and effectiveness of the sector, and the knowledge, expertise and leadership of awqaf professionals.

With the right transparency, stability, long-term planning and guidance, the prospects for awqaf are great and the more the government assists awqaf, the better the awqaf sector is placed to alleviate the pressure on the public purse and contribute to the country's economic development.

Notes

1 Sheikh Mohammad Abu Zahra Awqaf Lectures "*Muhadarat Fi L-Waqf*" P5, 2nd Edition, Dar-Ulfikr Al-Arabi.
2 Zarqa, Sheikh Mustafa "Ahkam Al Waqf" University of Damascus Press, 1947, P10–15.
3 Cizakca, Murat "Awqaf in History and Its Implication for Modern Islamic Economies" *Islamic Studies*, Vol. 6, No. 1, Nov. 1998, P2.
4 Ahmad, Habib, "Legal Environment and Nonprofit Sector: Implications for Growth of Awqaf Institutions" IRTI/IDB P.3.
5 Zaki, Eissa "A Summary of Waqf Regulations" Kuwait Awqaf Public Foundation, Department of Studies & External Relations, 2006AD-1427AH, P7–9.
6 O'Halloran, Kerry "Creating an Enabling Environment for Private Philanthropy: The Role of Charity Law in Northern Ireland" *The International Journal of Not-For-Profit Law*, Vol. 1, No. 3, March 1999.
7 Flow-through entities, also known as pass-through entities or "Fiscally Transparent Entities", are legal entities where income "Flows Through" to beneficiaries.
8 Bello, Dogarawa Ahmad "Poverty Alleviation through Zakah and Waqf Institutions, a Case Study for the Muslim Umma in Ghana". MPRA Paper No. 23191, Posted 10. June 2010 13:38 UTC.

References

Ahmed, Habib (2004), *Role of Zakah and Awqaf in Poverty Alleviation*, Islamic Research and Training Institute, Islamic Development Bank, Jeddah.

Ahmed, Habib (2007), *Legal Environment and Nonprofit Sector: Implications for Growth of Awqaf Institutions*, Islamic Research and Training Institute, Islamic Development Bank, Jeddah.

Ahmed, Hasanudddin (1998), *Strategies to Develop Waqf Administration in India*, Research paper No. 50, Islamic Research and Training Institute, Islamic Development Bank, Jeddah.

Bello, Dogarawa Ahmad (2009), *Poverty Alleviation through Zakah and Waqf Institutions: A Case for the Muslim Ummah in Ghana*, MPRA Paper No. 23191, posted 10. June 2010 13:38 UTC, Ahmadu Bello University, Zaria-Nigeria. http://mpra.ub.uni-muenchen.de/23191/

Brody, Evelyn (2005), Charity Governance: What's Trust Law Got to Do with It?, *Chicago-Kent Law Review*, 80, 641–687.

Chapra, M. Umer (1985), *Towards a Just Monetary System*, The Islamic Foundation, Leicester.

Cizakca, Murat (2000), *A History of Philanthropic Foundations:/The Islamic World from the Seventh Century to the Present* (Istanbul: Bogazici Univ).

DallahAlbaraka (1994), *Fatawa: Shari'ah Rulings on Economics*, DallahAlbaraka Group, Research and Development Dept., Jeddah.

Edelman, Lauren B. and Mark C. Suchman (1997), The Legal Environments of Organisations, *Annual Review of Sociology*, 23, 479–515.

Gerber, Haim (1983), The Waqf Institution in Early Ottoman Edirne, *Asian and African Studies*, 17, 29–45. http:/www.oecd.org/dataoecd/56/36/1922428.pdf.

International Fellows in Philanthropy Program (IFPP) (2000), *Toward an Enabling Legal Environment for Civil Society*, Institute for Policy Studies, Center for Civil Society Studies, Johns Hopkins University, Baltimore.

Kahf, Monzer (1999), Towards the Revival of *Awqaf*: A Few *Fiqhi*, Issues to Reconsider, Presented at the Harvard Forum on Islamic Finance and Economics, October 1, 1999.

Kahf, Monzer (2004), *Shari'ah* and Historical Aspects of *Zakah* and *Awqaf*, Background paper prepared for Islamic Research and Training Institute, Islamic Development Bank.

La Zakat et le Waqf: Aspects historiques, juridiques et economiques. Actes de seminairetenu au Benin du 25 au 31 Mai 1997, edite par Dr.BoualemBendjilali, BanqueIslamique de Developpement, et IstitutIslamique de Recherches et de formation.

Makdisi, John A. (1999), The Islamic Origins of the Common Law, *North Carolina Law Review*, 77, 1635–1739.

Management and Development of Awqaf Properties – Islamic Development Bank/Islamic Research and Training Institute (IRTI) Seminar No. 16 held in Jeddah from 24/12/1983 to 5/1/10984 edited by Dr. Hassam Abdullah Alamin.

Mohammed, Sadig Hammd (2006), Types of Alarsad and Trusts: A Comparative Study from Islamic Sharia Perspective, paper presented at Seminar on Endowments (Awqaf) in Europe, Birmingham, U.K., March 20–22, 2006.

Paul Cook and Fred Nixon, Finance and Small and Medium-Sized Enterprise Development. http://www.galrc.com/icm/micro/fin-sme.html

Poire, M. and Sabel, C. (1984), *The Second Divide: Possibilities for Prosperity*, New York: Basic Books.

Salamon, Lester M. and Stefan Toepler (2000), Influence of the Legal Environment on the Development of the Nonprofit Sector, *Working Papers Series No. 17*, The Johns Hopkins Center for Civil Societies Studies, Baltimore.

Schwarcz, Steven L. (2003), Commercial Trusts as Business Organisations, *The Business Lawyer*, 58, 1–27.

Thomas, Ann Van Wynen (1949), Note on the Origin and Uses of Trust—Waqfs, *Southwestern Law Journal*, 3, 162–66.

UN-HABITAT (2005), *Waqf (Endowment) and Islamic Philanthropy*, Paper 7 –Islam, Land & Property Research Series, Nairobi, Kenya.

Usmani, M Taqi (1999), *An Introduction to Islamic Finance*, Idaratul Maarif, Karachi.

Zarqa, Shaikh Mustafa (1947), *Ahkam al Waqf*, University of Damascus Press, Damascus (in Arabic).

5 The perception of waqf as a financial institution – a lesson from the French literature on Ottoman Empire

Abderrazak Belabes

Introduction

For more than five years, free and chosen consultation of old journals dedicated to the Muslim world, far from the bubble of big data and artificial intelligence, has allowed me to discover information, unimaginable until then, which mentions that the Muslims of Bosnia-Herzegovina were planning to establish an *awqāf* bank to collect the income necessary for the operation of the pious foundations inherent to places of worship and schools. Does this mean that not everything has yet been discovered and that this somewhat neglected region of Europe has not yet revealed all its secrets?

To gather the substance necessary for the exploration of the subject, I had to contextualize the information collected in all possible aspects by cross-checking the data from different sources and similar facts – first of all, the establishment of a *waqf* bank (*Evkafbankasi*), in Istanbul in 1914, during the reign of Sultan Mehmed V Reşâd. The contact with a region that until then had remained almost unknown to me, apart from reading a few books by Alija Izetbegović (1994, 2002), seemed to me a very motivating challenge that offers the opportunity to renew with research in the noblest sense of the term and to go off the beaten track, knowing that the rarer the documentation, the more the opportunities to deepen knowledge, to sharpen the analytical tools.

After reviewing the literature to clarify my epistemological posture, I will describe the data collection protocol between 1900 and 1910, for then identify the main ideas which serve as a starting point, put them in their context, before cross-checking them with those contained in the statute relating to the autonomous administration of affairs concerning Muslim worship, the *awqāf* and education, published on April 15, 1909, by the Austro-Hungarian colonial administration, to finally address the effect of the project to establish an *awqāf* bank in Bosnia-Herzegovina on that of the *Evkafbankasi* launched in Turkey in 1914. The conclusion briefly summarizes the main ideas of the study and proposes a line of thought on the use of the Islamic referent in the world of finance, as well as a new field of exploration to the Umberto Eco's open work theory, to finally invite the Bosnian historians to study the project of *awqāf* bank further by consulting the archives and newspapers dating back to the early 20th century.

Literature revue and epistemological posture

The *waqf* has played an important role in the religious, educational, cultural, social and humanitarian life of Muslims in Bosnia-Herzegovina. Its role is particularly significant in the founding and development of cities (Zajimović, 2010: 9–10; Alarnaut, 2019: 15–22; Smolo, 2019: 94–95). Despite this importance, the literature on the waqf as an institution and its importance in the history of the country remains relatively few (Traljić, 1983: 178; Kolaj-Ristanović, 2019: 220). In this regard, it should be noted that the *waqf* is a universal human phenomenon that is found, in all cultures, under different names.

According to the literature consulted to this day, no study has been dedicated to the emergence of the idea of establishing an *awqāf* bank in Bosnia-Herzegovina in 1900. A few short indications mention an attempt to create such a bank in 1906 (Omerčić, 2018, 84, 345–346), without reference to any ancient source that has been consulted and can be consulted. However, in 1906, local newspapers, founded by Muslims, refer to the establishment of a credit society dedicated to the Muslim community (prva muslimanska kreditna zadruga) in Tešanj (Rešidbegović, 1997: 62). This prompts a distinction between the existence of the object, its conscious or unconscious representation and the way of knowing it (Belabes, 2016: 13), as illustrated in Table 5.1.

Hence, the importance of this study is in shedding light on the crucial importance of how ideas, as social constructions, emerge beyond the conventional conceptual frameworks assimilating the idea of *awqāf* bank – sometimes to purely technical considerations in the extension of the cash *waqf*, sometimes to philanthropic considerations in the context of non-profit or social financial institutions.

However, many studies refer to the project concerning the establishment of an *awqāf* bank – in this case *Evkafbankasi*, in Turkey in 1914, during the reign

Table 5.1 Methodology of the historical approach to the project of a bank of awqāf which appeared in Bosnia–Herzegovina in 1900

Aspects of the methodology	*Definitions*	*Applications*
Ontological existence	Existence of the object	Bank of *awqāf*
Existence of an imago	Conscious or unconscious representation	Islamic bank, Muslim bank, bank dedicated to Muslims
Epistemological existence	How to reach knowledge of the object	Through an ancient source or a contemporary source

Source: Elaborated by the author.

of Sultan's Mehmed V Reşâd (Bayram, 1987: 215; Şeyhun,[1] 1992: 25–46; Toprak, 1995: 60–61; Dawletschin-Linder, 2003: 50; Özcan, 2003: 87–88, 2008: 128; Özdemir and Özdemir, 2017: 83; Karagedikli and Tunçer, 2018: 247; Ortabağ, 2018: 94), without highlighting the role of the external factor, if only as a hypothesis, apart from the classical conceptual framework of the cash *waqf* as a major reference.

The theme of *awqāf* bank is often associated with the theme of cash *waqf* (Arda, 1994: 71; Bilici, 1994: 51, 1996: 86; Çizakça, 1995: 346; Özcan, 2008: 128; Özdemir, 2017: 83; Karagedikli and Tunçer, 2018: 247) to support the idea of putting an end to a revolutionary system of financing in favour of a system based on commercial banking, or, on the contrary, the idea of moving from solidarity funds to a modern banking system based on the market economy and ensuring an optimal allocation of resources. This amounts to considering the form of self-regulated markets as the pinnacle of evolution (Polanyi, [1977]2011: 38), ignoring the fact that in human history the *waqf* appeared before the birth of markets (Belabes, 2019: 8), in their original form: real places locally integrated where goods are exchanged to benefit the community (al-Kanānī, 1975: 31). In other words, there was not a market system but markets, geographically localized and socially embedded.

If everything has been discovered, or if everything can be traced back to a founding fact such as the cash *waqf*, what is the point of studying facts from different and varied temporal and spatial contexts? After having raised the cash *waqf* to the rank of unparalleled legal revolution in the history of the Muslim world (Mandaville, 1979: 289; Alarnaut, 2018: 43), progress in research on associated subjects, under the effect of reasoning by analogy, which consists in relying on an analogy, a resemblance or an association of ideas between two situations, seems minimal, if not negligible.

The main purpose of the study is not to show that this or that country initiated the idea under the effect of the '*virus of precursor*' (Clark, 1959: 103), but to grasp all the subtleties of the financial language relating to the Islamic referent in an explicit or implicit way, within the framework of a research programme initiated a few years ago (Belabes, 2013, 2016, 2018), around the following question: does the word '*Islamic bank*' (or in this case '*bank of awqāf*') mean a financing institution dedicated to a particular community? Does the word refer to financial products that are not specifically identifiable to the notion of *ribā*, whose real meanings need to be clarified in relation to the perceptions of the stakeholders? Or does it refer to a '*home-made*' that expresses a desire to stand out from the colonizer or the majority population?

It is obvious that this questioning also applies to other expressions such as that of 'Islamic finance', 'Islamic social finance', 'Islamic financial market', 'Islamic *sukūk*' and 'Islamic insurance', to name just a few of the most famous. It is a question of distinguishing the use of the Islamic referent, explicit or implicit, as a lexicon – or a way of speaking used by a social group – from its use as a grammar that describes facts and behaviours in a faithful and well-considered manner, which must be distinguished from rhetoric or the art of good communication. The ultimate aim is to develop a typology of the use of the Islamic referent, formal or tacit, to be refined through case studies resulting from a careful examination of historical facts that are often forgotten or overlooked. If it turns out that the use of such a referent emits more smoke than it sheds light, it should be used with great care in order to understand the real dynamics of financial practices associated with the Islamic referent.

Data collection protocol

The study is based on two ancient documents dating back to the beginning of the 20th century, which are as follows:

> In a very brief note on Bosnia-Herzegovina published in the French journal *Revue de l'Islam* as part of a general review of major events relating to the Muslim world, André Ricaud (1900: 188) wrote: "*The Muslims of Bosnia have decided to found a bank to improve the conditions of Muslims from the point of view of religion and education*".
>
> In a note on the Ottoman press, published in the French journal *Revue du monde musulman*, Lucien Bouvat (1910: 692) wrote: "*The Mashaykha*[2] *has just taken an important decision, which could considerably influence the future of the economic policy of Islam. The Bosnian Muslims had planned to found a bank to defend their interests. But was such a foundation permitted by religious law? They asked Mechyakha about this issue. The latter, by a fetwa dated 8 Shawal 1328*[13 October 1910], *declared the establishment of the bank lawful, and authorized it to make all the financial operations, on the condition of conforming to the prescriptions of the Shari'ah. It will therefore come as no surprise to learn that a bill will soon be tabled for the establishment of a waqf bank, responsible for collecting the income of the pious foundations of the Empire. This income is estimated at five million pounds, about 115 million francs. The bank, which would have its headquarters in Constantinople, with branches outside, would be constituted with a capital of 900,000 pounds, about 20 million francs*".

The cross-checking of this information indicates, at first glance, that the Bosnian Muslims had asked the *fatwa* authority of the *Sublime Porte* their opinion on the creation of an *awqāf* bank that seemed to be in danger or to be offered an opportunity for progress. The question then arises: what is the source of this danger or opportunity for progress?

Contextualization and analysis of fundamental ideas

The Congress of Berlin from 13 June to 13 July 1878, which began the process of reducing or even eliminating the European possessions of the Ottoman Empire, proclaimed the occupation of Bosnia-Herzegovina by Austria-Hungary. On 5 October 1908, the emperor Franz Joseph decided to annex Bosnia-Herzegovina. As shown in Table 5.2, the Muslim population of Bosnia-Herzegovina fluctuated between 1879 and 1910 from 448,613 to 612,137 inhabitants. In percentage terms, the Muslim population fell from 38.72 to 32.25, mainly due to emigration to Turkey (Gravier, 1911).

In order to separate the Bosnian Muslims from the Ottoman Empire with the aim of Europeanizing them, in 1882, the Governor of Bosnia-Herzegovina, Benjamin Kállay, appointed Mustafa Hilmi Hadžiomerović as the first Bosnian *Reis ul-'ulema* (head of the *'ulema*), assisted by an *'ulemamedzhlis* (Council of the *'ulema*) and later by the Assembly of the *vakuf-mearif*. The establishment of such bodies led to the bureaucratization of the religious and educational foundations. At the beginning of the 20th century, representatives of traditional elites demanded the right to elect the *Reis ul-'ulema*, *'ulemamedzhlis* and the *vakuf-mearif* council. This was the first political mobilization of the Bosnian Muslim community which resulted in the establishment of the Muslim's People Organization (*Muslimanska Narodna Organizacija*) in 1906, and the promotion by the Austro-Hungarian authorities of a Statute for Autonomous Administration of Islamic Religious Waqf and Educational Affairs (*Štatutzaautonom nuupravuislamskihvjerskihivakufsko-mearifskihposlova*) in 15 April 1909. Faced with the interference of the occupying forces, the Muslim community is mobilizing more around its land and religious elites around the demand for religious and cultural autonomy (Bougarel, 1996: 28). In 1910, 91.1% of landowners in Bosnia-Herzegovina were Muslim (Popovic, 1997: 97), and 80% of the Muslim population was composed of peasants (Pavloviç, 2009: 170).

With regard to financial activity, in past centuries, the *waqf* was the major source of financing for urbanization and the building of basic infrastructure and services. It financed the construction of religious buildings, schools, hospitals, bridges, waterways, cobbled streets, public squares, water fountains, shops, warehouses and hotels (Zajimović, 2010: 12–13). The cash *waqf*, which dates back to 1534 in Bosnia-Herzegovina, was used to finance the activities of merchants, craftsmen and peasants with an interest rate of around 15% (Kreševljaković, [1940]2018: 63). With the drying up of the cash *waqf*, for reasons that are still poorly understood and little known, the financing of activities was carried

Table 5.2 Number of Muslims in Bosnia-Herzegovina in the years 1878–1918 (census of 1879, 1885 and 1910)

	1879		*1885*		*1895*		*1910*	
Orthodox	496	781	571	250	673	246	865	918
	42.86%		42.76%		42.94%		43.49%	
Muslims	448	613	492	710	548	632	612	137
	38.72%		36.88%		34.99%		32.25%	
Catholics	209	391	265	788	334	142	434	061
	18.07%		19.88%		21.31%		22.87%	

Source: Popovic, Alexandre (1997). Les musulmans de Bosnie-Herzégovine, mise en place d'une guerre civile, *Actes de la recherche en sciences sociales*, Vol. 116–117, mars, p. 97.

out through the informal loan of money granted by merchants, moneylenders and money changers, Jewish, Christian and Muslim, whose interest rate varied between 50% and 100% (Kreševljaković, [1940]2018: 65). Hence the creation, from 1866, of municipal foundations for the financing of agricultural activities, called *Menafi-sanduci*, to counter the exploitation of the peasant by the moneylender (Kreševljaković, [1940]2018: 66–67). These foundations have spread to 38 cities in Bosnia–Herzegovina (Kreševljaković, [1940]2018: 78). Before the idea of the *awqāf* bank emerged, there were a variety of financing methods. They were not limited to cash *waqf*, as shown in Figure 5.1.

During the Austro-Hungarian occupation, dating from the beginning of the 20th century, capital is scarce and the loan granted by the banks is quite expensive with an average interest rate of around 6.5%. The banks are numerous, but of little importance with the exception of the *PrivilegierteLandesbankfürBosnien und Hercegovina* (privileged bank of the country in Bosnia-Herzegovina) in Sarajevo. For their part, the *Unionbank* of Viennaand the *Ungarische Bank und Handels-Aktiengesellschaft* (Hungarian Banking and Trade Company) of Budapest have each opened a branch in Sarajevo. In addition, there are 15 local commercial banks or savings banks organized as joint-stock companies, the largest of which are *Centralbank und Sparkassa* (central and savings bank) in Sarajevo (for Catholics), and *Srpskabanka* in Mostar (for Orthodox). There are also 21 savings and agricultural banks incorporated as limited liability companies, including the first Muslim credit company (*prva muslimanska kreditna zadruga*) founded in 1906 in Tešanj (Archives Diplomatiques, 1909: 321–322), to which some writings on the origin of Islamic banks in Bosnia-Herzegovina (Bukvić, 2013: 22) and others on the origin of banks dedicated to the Muslim community (Höpken, 1994: 217; Marko, 2000: 98) visibly refer. This gives an idea of the plurality of interpretations of the Islamic adjective even when it is associated with the same object. Before the First World War, the Muslim community had six banks, including three large banks in Tešanj, Brčko and Banja Luka and two provincial banks in Foča and Bijeljina (Jelić, 2007: 233; Vujović, 2015: 53).

Starting from the idea that as long as the *awqāf* remain out of market circulation, and therefore out of the optimal allocation of resources, and out of participation in public charges,[3] there will be neither an efficient reorganization

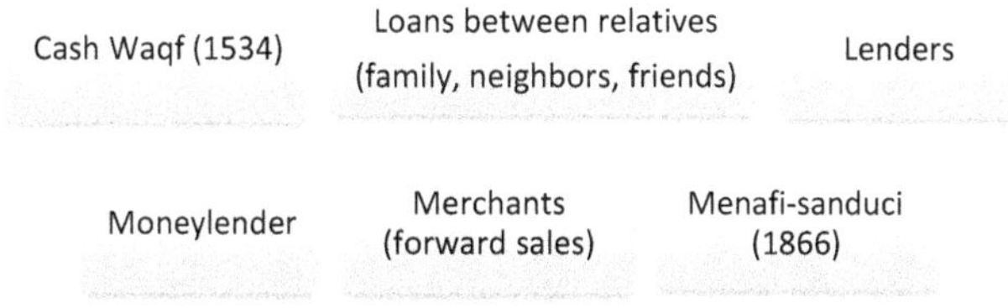

Figure 5.1 Variety of financing methods in Bosnia-Herzegovina before the idea of the awqāf bank emerged.

Source: Elaborated by the author.

of public finances, nor wealth creation based on the use of existing resources that breaks with the feudal organization of production (Blondel, 1911: 82–85); the *awqāf* were placed under the supervision of the colonial administration. However, as Emile de Laveley (1885: 538), professor of political economy at the University of Liège, points out in an article on the agrarian regime and the rural economy of Bosnia-Herzegovina:

> The awqāf are an essential element of civilization; all that is of general utility is due to them. The confiscation of the vakufs would be an economic fault and a crime against humanity. Is it not better to satisfy the needs of charity, education and material improvement by means of the income from an estate than by means of taxation?

The negative perception of the role of *awqāf*, which resulted in the confiscation of some of the most vital assets (Zajimović, 2010: 13–16), had disastrous consequences on the life of the Bosnian populations. As a Muslim from Mostar aptly pointed out in June 1900:

> And as part of the income of the awqāf are used to support the Muslim children who attend government secondary schools, large sums are thus diverted, each year, from the pious and charitable goals for which the awqāf were instituted by their founders.
>
> (UnMusulman, 1900: 163)

According to the latter, the claims of the Muslim population of Bosnia-Herzegovina addressed to the Austro-Hungarian colonial administration can be summed up in two major points: '*Autonomy both with regard to our religious affairs and public education*' (UnMusulman, 1900: 164).

In the face of criticism that lasted for three decades, the colonial administration drew up a statute on the autonomous administration of matters concerning the Muslim faith, *awqāf* and instruction, published on 15 April 1909. According to the preamble,

> this Statute was drawn up with the collaboration of the 'Ulema and representatives of the Muslim people, examined from the point of view of the Shari'ah and approved by the supreme religious leaders of the Muslims of Bosnia -Herzegovina, the 'Ulema-Medjliss.
>
> (Administration austro-hongroise de la Bosnie-Herzégovine, 1909: 9)

This demand for religious autonomy illustrates the specific characteristics of the identity of the Muslims of Bosnia-Herzegovina, which is essentially based on confessional identity, a complex and multidimensional phenomenon that cannot be reduced to a question of strict observance of the rules of *Shari'ah* in all aspects of daily life, particularly in the economic sphere. The Muslim community, like the rest of communities, is vastly varied. In this regard, some modernists emphasize the need to reform the main religious institutions, the administration of *awqāf* and educational programmes, and to lift the ban on interest in banking activities (Bougarel, 2008: 5). To ensure their survival in the post-Ottoman context resulting from the Treaty of Berlin, Muslims must take up the challenges and seize the opportunities offered by European modernity without denying their faith (Bougarel, 2017: 15). The analysis of the Statute is instructive in a number of ways.

Statute for self-governing administration of Islamic religious and *Vakuf-mearif* activities in Bosnia-Herzegovina

The preamble of the statute states the following:

> In our concern to strengthen and ensure the uninterrupted development of Islam in Bosnia-Herzegovina and the well-being of the Muslim people in these countries, we have decided to confer on the Muslims living in these countries the right to regulate themselves, within the framework of the laws of the country, and subject to the exercise of the right, by our Government, of our supreme right of supervision over their affairs relating to worship, vakuf and mearif, to administer vakuf-mearif property in accordance with the provisions of the Shari'ah and to use the income from such property exclusively for religious and educational purposes.
>
> (Administration austro-hongroise de la Bosnie-Herzégovine, 1909: 9)

This confirms that the main demands of the Muslims in Bosnia-Herzegovina concern the administration of places of worship and education.

In the general provisions, the statute indicates that 'all the movable and immovable property vakouf-mearif of the Muslim people in Bosnia-Herzegovina are property of the interested awqāf, they are exclusively affected with the needs for the religion and the education of the Moslim of this country' (Administration austro-hongroise de la Bosnie-Herzégovine, 1909: 9).

The *vakuf-mearif* property consists of the following:

- The independent *awqāf*;
- The central fund *vakuf-mearif* – to which must be added the revenue from the cult tax, the State subsidy, voluntary contributions and legacies (Administration austro-hongroise de la Bosnie-Herzégovine, 1909: 10).

The purpose of the central *vakuf-mearif* fund is:

- To provide for all the needs of the administration of the organs of *vakuf-mearif.*
- To provide for the payment of maintenance costs and public taxes levied on the invested capital.

- To fulfil the mission for which the vacant *awqāf* had been constituted, to the extent that the resulting expenses are covered by that vakouf's share of the income of the *vakouf-mearif* fund.
- To grant subsidies for the repair and construction of mosques for which there are no or insufficient *awqāf* and which are in localities where the Muslim population does not have sufficient resources.
- To assist the staff of mosques, houses of worship and schools, for which there are no or insufficient *awqāf*, to the extent that such staff are unable to obtain relief from the local Muslim population.
- To maintain interest-bearing *waqf* lands, including repairing or, as the case may be, constructing houses.
- To grant subsidies for any other object of general or particular interest – the worship, the education or the Islamic benevolence.
- To meet the extraordinary needs of the central fund *vakuf-mearif*.

In the case of family *waqf* whose surpluses are allocated to the descendants of the founder or to the employees of such *awqāf*, subsidies from the central *vakuf-mearif* fund will be granted only as loans (Administration austro-hongroise de la Bosnie-Herzégovine, 1909: 26).

The central *vakuf-mearif* fund consists of the movable and immovable property accumulated in the *waqf* funds. These include, in particular, sums not used by the central administration itself, all the property of the *awqāf* that is vacant as a result of the disappearance of the object of their foundation, or, for other reasons, donations and legacies. The income of this fund consists of income from deposited and interest-bearing funds, *waqf* taxes, religious taxes, voluntary contributions and other income (Administration austro-hongroise de la Bosnie-Herzégovine, 1909: 25–26).

The terminology '*vakuf-mearif*' used in the Statute is instructive in more ways. It reflects a desire both to secularize and commodify *awqāf* in order to gradually transfer certain *waqf* property into the public and private domain, and to remove certain areas, such as education, from religious influence and place them in the hands of public and private powers. In this respect, *waqf* becomes a power issue between various forces as illustrated in Figure 6.2. It would be useful to study the flows relating to *waqf* and the interactions of their players in relation to the notion of power, i.e. their capacity to influence and/or constrain. Such a new field of study could be described as *geowaqf*.

If the income of the fund is not reduced to the cash *waqf*, the unspoken goal of the project to create the *waqf* bank is the commercialization of *awqāf*, so that in the long term they will be dominated by market forces where financial logic takes precedence over everything else (Trakic, 2012: 342). If such a project materializes, sooner or later the market logic will take precedence over the utopia that animated the pioneers of the *awqāf*. In this respect, secularization is only an intermediate stage, in a process which must ultimately lead to the commodification of *awqāf*, in the name of the sacralization of private property as the basis of social order.

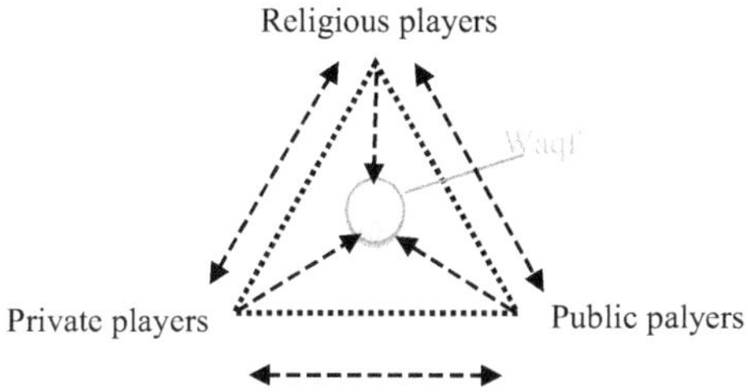

Figure 5.2 Waqf as a power issue between diverse forces.
Source: Elaborated by the author.

But what is the effect of the project to create the bank of *awqāf* in Bosnia-Herzegovina on the one launched in Turkey in 1914; starting from the following question about the contagion of ideas (Sperber, 1997): where do our ideas come from? Some, of ourselves, at least we generally believe, but most are transmitted to us by others, which sometimes seem insignificant, and we in turn pass them on, in one way or another, as well on our friends than those who perceive us as rivals, even enemies, under the effect of mimetic desire.

Effect of the project for the establishment of an *awqāf* bank in Bosnia-Herzegovina in 1900 on the launched in Turkey in 1914

Two events may occur in succession or may be related without having a causal relationship. Most of the writings that mention the project to establish an *awqaf* bank in Turkey, in this case the *Evkafbankasi*, failed to avoid such a trap. Not only do they associate this bank with the cash *waqf* (Çizakça, 1995: 346; Çiftçi, 2004: 97; Özcan, 2004: 63; Toraman et al., 2007: 14; Özdemir, 2017: 83; Gürer and Coşkun 2018: 247; Ortabağ, 2018: 94), but they support the idea that the *awqāf* bank replaced the cash *waqf*, that the purpose of the establishment of the *awqāf* bank was to end the cash *waqf* or the depreciation of the global value of their respective assets. This assertion may apply in some cases and not in others. It cannot be supported absolutely. A distinction must be made between causality and correlation to avoid abusive generalizations. The project must be approached as a social construction that is not reduced to a purely technical question relating to the processes used for the realization of a particular activity.

The note on the Ottoman press, published in the *revue du monde musulman*, sheds new light on this question by showing that the idea of establishing the *Evkafbankasi* in 1914 has its origin in the request of the Bosnian Muslims, to the *Mashyakha* of the *Sublime porte* in Istanbul, on the lawfulness – or conformity to the *Shari'ah*– to establish a bank for financing the activities of the *awqāf* related to worship and education. The fatwa, dated 13 October 1910, issued in this regard declared the establishment of such a bank lawful on condition that it did not violate *Shari'ah* injunctions (Bouvat, 1910: 692). Based on the minority status of Bosnian Muslims and the colonization of the Austro-Hungarian empire, the *Mashyakha* authorized the use of interest rates in bank operations (Omerčić, 2018: 345–346).

The fact of using the *Mashyakha* of *Sublime Porte* to benefit from a status derogating from the *Shar'iah* rules suggests that the initiators of the project to establish a bank of *awqāf* in Bosnia-Herzegovina were in favour of the interest and that they found resistance within the population: the *ribā* seems to take on the meaning of excessive interest to which the initiators of the project to establish a bank for Muslims in Saint Petersburg in 1908 (Belabes, 2016) and in Egypt in 1908 (Belabes, 2018) adhered. This interpretation is in line with Article 1907 of the French Civil Code, initiated by Napoléon after the revolution of 1789, according to which the law does not prohibit the interest loan, whether of money, foodstuffs or other movable things, but only prohibits excessive interest exceeding 5%, as evidenced by the discussions at the Council of State (Jouanneau, 1805: 614–619). This means that in Bosnia-Herzegovina, as elsewhere in the various regions of the world, the conception of finance by Muslims is a changing and plural reality, elusive outside the actors who animate it and the cleavages that structure it. We should therefore be wary of hasty generalizations and conclusions that are not supported by substantial evidence.

As illustrated in Figure 5.3, the existence of the idea of *awqāf* bank in Bosnia-Herzegovina since at least 1900 undermines the assumption that the idea originated with Hayri Efendi (Bayram, 1987: 162; Ortabağ, 2018: 94), Minister of *awqāf* (December 1910–July 2012), and then *Sheikh ul-Islām* or Grand *muftī* (1914–1916), who raised it in 1914. New ideas are created where they are least expected, even if it is always difficult to identify their authors categorically. As such, the idea of the *awqāf* bank may have emerged outside Bosnia-Herzegovina and before the beginning of the 20th century. This prompts further exploration of the subject by examining old writings relating to different regions of the world, especially those that have been neglected until now.

However, if in Turkey the establishment of *VakifBank* in 1954 has its origin in the project of the *Evkafbankasi* of 1914, for the establishment of *Vakufsa Banka* in Bosnia-Herzegovina in 1992 two hypotheses are possible: it is either from an internal source, i.e. from the *awqāf* bank project of 1900, or from an external source, i.e. from the establishment of *VakifBank*. This epidemiology of representations undermines the classic conceptual model of '*centre and periphery*' which shows a relationship of inequality and domination between the Ottoman State and its provinces – in this case Bosnia-Herzegovina. The dynamics of the spread of the idea of a bank of *awqāf* is a counter-example that merits reflection.

For further clarity, Figure 5.4 models the spread of the idea of *awqāf* bank between Bosnia-Herzegovina and Turkey without going into detail on the objects. This modelling relating to the contagion of ideas could be expanded to other regions for a better understanding of the epistemological

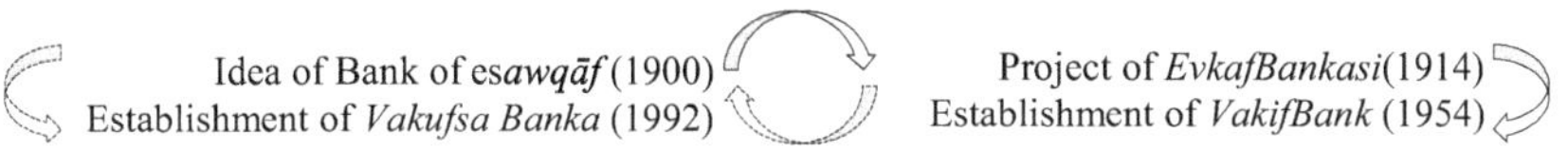

Figure 5.3 Spread dynamics of the idea of bank of awqāf between Bosnia-Herzegovina and Turkey (1900–1992).

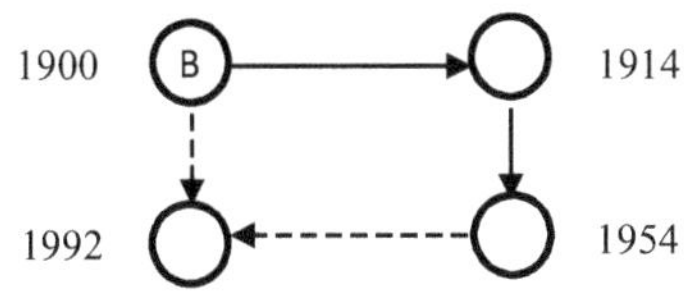

Figure 5.4 Modelization of the spread of the idea of awqāf bank between Bosnia-Herzegovina and Turkey.

presuppositions and give credit to whom it is due, starting with the following questioning: where did the idea come from? How did it get to us? Why does it spread easily today unlike past decades beyond the rapid spread of new communication technologies? Where is it going to lead us with regard to potential opportunities and risks?

After approval of the *Evkafbankasi* project by the Turkish government, a bill was prepared and passed by the Senate and the Assembly. Following the agreement of Sultan Mehmet V Reşad, on 19 July 1914, the authorization to establish the bank, with a nominal capital of 500,000 pounds, was given as a joint stock company that could handle all kinds of banking transactions (Akgunduz, 2015). The law was finalized on 2 August 1914 with some modifications.[4] However, its implementation was severely criticized by some sections of the population, since its mode of operation was essentially based on the interest rate. The project finally failed due to the Ottoman's involvement in the First World War by joining Germany on 31 October 1914 (Ortabağ, 2018: 94). In wartime, innovative projects, regardless of their real effect on the quality of life of the people, were stifled by the noise of the cannons.

Conclusion

With regard to the documents consulted and the data drawn, their cross-checking, their analysis and exploitation, beyond the representations deeply anchored in minds, the major results that emerge from this study are as follows:

- The idea of the *awqāf* bank was born in Bosnia-Herzegovina and dates back at least to 1900, during the Austro-Hungarian occupation, with the idea of increasing the income of the *awqāf* with modern banking techniques, without specifying a particular institutional form between retail bank and investment bank, knowing that banks in their modern configuration are companies offering financing, savings and cash flow management services.

- The idea of such a bank is not the result of a dynamic innovation from an internal process of constant research to improve the quality of *awqāf* products and services, but of a desire to imitate the banking model introduced into the country by the Austro-Hungarian colonizer. The mimetic desire is first carried out in the field of ideas before being reflected in the behaviour.
- The logic of the market takes precedence over social cohesion, which is based on the social relationships between the inhabitants of the city and the capacity of society to integrate its members without exclusion or discrimination of any kind. In this respect, the maximization of return on assets is gradually tending to become an end in itself and not a means to an end initiated by the founding fathers, as evidenced by the first *waqf* document, dating from 1462, attributed to Isa beg Ishaković, founder of the city of Sarajevo, dating from 1462 (Alarnaut, 2019: 27).
- Although the confrontation of ideas is just as important as the struggle for anti-colonial emancipation, this project has not attracted the interest of research on the history of banks in Bosnia-Herzegovina, which is generally limited to listing the banks created for the Muslim community. As such, it is necessary to go beyond the traditional method which presents this history as a linear series of creation of banks in favour of a perspective in which aborted attempts, errors and failures must be studied with as much care as achievements, successes and exploits. Knowing that ideas are more important than institutions that eventually disappear sooner or later. As Alexandre Dumas (1997: 584) pointed out in the *Count of Monte Cristo*: 'Ideas do not become extinct, sire; they slumber sometimes, but only revive the stronger before they sleep entirely'.
- The doctrinal consensus of Muslim legal schools on the prohibition of any fixed return on capital is tempered by a concern to take advantage of the profit opportunities offered by the modern banking credit system. The concept of *ribā* takes an acceptation of excessive interest, and income from bank interest is tolerated, to a certain extent, as long as it is devoted to the realization of common goods or services of general interest. In this regard, in social sciences, the definition of concepts must be based on the vocabulary used in real-life situations.
- Following criticism from a section of the population, the initiators of the project urged, in 1910, the *Mashyakha* – or High Authority in charge of the fatwā according to the rules of the Hanafite rite – of the *Sublime Porte* to issue a legal opinion in line with their interpretation.
- The Turkish Minister of *awqāf* Hayri Efendi took up the idea to launch a similar project in Turkey in 1914 under the name of *Evkafbankasi*. Despite its adoption by both chambers and the promulgation by Sultan Mehmed V Reşâd, the project was in turn criticized because of the suspicion of *ribā*

which weighs on its mode of operation. It is finally put in a drawer, following Turkey's engagement in the First World War alongside Germany.

- Following this epidemiology of representations, it appears that the idea of an *awqāf* bank does not come from Hayri Efendi as generally suggested in the specialized literature. Nor is it '*a newly born idea*' as said in the introduction of the first session on '*waqf bank*' of the workshop '*International Innovative Platform for Islamic Economy Products*', organized by the International Center of Islamic Economy in cooperation with the Dubai Airport Freezone Authority, on 22 November 2015. Those who take credit for the idea, in one way or another, are encouraged to more modesty. History is not erased so easily. Furthermore, innovation is a daily social process – it was not initiated by academic elites, whether they are financial engineers, economists or new financial jurisconsults, most of which given the current trend, bring nothing new and are not specialists in the noble sense of the term.
- Moreover, this epidemiology of representations undermines the classic conceptual model of '*centre and periphery*' which shows a relationship of inequality and domination between the Ottoman State and its provinces – in this case Bosnia-Herzegovina. The dynamics of propagation of the idea of *awqāf* banks is a counter-example worthy of interest.

In view of these unprecedented results, two levels of analysis should be distinguished: on the one hand, the reasons for which the Islamic referent is mobilized in finance in a formal or tacit manner; on the other hand, the diversified uses made of this Islamic referent. In this case, the mobilization of the Islamic referent seems to be linked to a willingness to take advantage of the profit opportunities offered by the banking credit system for the benefit of the Muslim community in the wake of the Austro-Hungarian colonial expansion and the banking credit system introduced in the country. In other words, it would be more appropriate for the profits from loans to Muslims to go into the hands of community banks instead of benefiting others. In this sense, the use of the Islamic referent allows a variety of interpretations that are not limited to a question of strict compliance with normative rules or ethical standards. Time, space and local culture are primordial factors that cannot be underestimated in deepening the understanding of phenomena. This avoids two extreme epistemological postures: on the one hand, systematically consider as futile and derisory '*what is not associated with Islam*' (Al Yahya, 2016: 209); on the other, consider '*what is associated with Islam*' as primitive and backwards (Blondel, 1911: 83; Vujović, 2015: 39).

The message of Kheireddine Pasha, also known as Kheireddine Ettounsi, stated in his book '*Aqwam al-MasālikfīMa'rifatAḥwāl al-Mamālik*' (The Best Ways of Knowing States) – if we do not work to adapt to the dominant system, adaptation will be imposed on us, sooner or later, from the outside (Ettounsi, [1867]2012: 74) – seems to overlap here unexpectedly, with a specific meaning that the author himself probably did not foresee: if we do not take advantage of the opportunities offered by the dominant system by imitating the practices used, it will develop in our countries to our disadvantage. New interpretations of a work do not necessarily result from reading it. This opens up a new field of exploration for the theory of the open work (Eco, 1965: 11).

Bosnian historians are invited to further explore the awqāf bank project by consulting the archives and newspapers of the time, or at least what remains of them, especially after the atrocious civil war that ravaged the country from spring 1992 to autumn 1995. It is of course the ideal situation to rely on documents in local languages, knowing that '*what cannot be completely surrounded must not be abandoned completely*', to quote a famous Arab proverb. The progress of knowledge takes place in stages in a gradual and regular manner, far from any dogmatism which refrains from confronting the theoretical knowledge acquired with new facts discovered through serious research.

Notes

1 I would like to thank Ahmet Şeyhun for giving me the page numbers of his MA Dissertation in History Untitled '*Centralization Process of Cash Waqfs in the Ottoman Empire and Their Legal Framework*', Boğaziçi University, Istanbul, 1992, where he explained the establishment and the functioning of the Evkafbankası and administration of the endowed cash (Nukudparalarmüdürlüğü), by email on 27 December 2019. All authors who referred to this unpublished dissertation do not mention page numbers.

2 *Machyakha:* Assembly of Sheikhs (scholars) responsible for issuing fatwas (legal opinions).

3 Article 3 of the law on the administration of Bosnia–Herzegovina of 22 February 1880 stipulates: '*The Administration of Bosnia and Herzegovina Shall Be Organized in Such a Way That Its Expenses Shall Be Covered by Its Own Revenues*'.

4 Evkafbankasıhakkındakanûn-Imuvakkat, Düstûr, T. 2, C. 6, Ss. 330-331, 3 Cumâdelûlâ1332, 30 Mart [March] 1914 (Akman, 2007: 144); Evkafbankasihakkindakanun, Düstûr, T. 2, C. 6, Ss. 1046–1048, 9 Ramazan 1332, 2 Ağustos [August] 1914 (Akman, 2007: 164).

References

Administration austro-hongroise de la Bosnie-Herzégovine (1909). Statut austro-hongrois relative à l'administration autonome des affaires concernant le culte musulman, les *vakouf* et les *mearif* en Bosnie-Herzégovine [Austro-Hungarian Statute on the Autonomous Administration Concerning Muslim Worship, *vakouf* and *mearif* in Bosnia-Herzegovina], 15 avril 1909, *Bulletin analytiques des principaux documents parlementaires étrangerstransmis à la Présidence de la Chambre des Députes*, No. 23, 20 décembre, pp. 9–36.

Akgunduz, Ahmed (2015). Vakfedenlerinbedduasındankurtuluyoruz [We Get Rid of the Curse of the *Awqāf*], *SonDevir*, 16 January.

Alarnaut, Muhamed M. (2018). *NaḥwaDawrFā'il li-al-Awqāf fi Ḥayāt al-Mujtma'āt al-Muslimah al-Mu'āṣirah* [Toward an Active Role of *Awqāf* in the Life of Contemporary Muslim Societies], *Journal of King Abdulaziz University: Islamic Economics*, Vol. 31, No 3, pp. 33–58.

Alarnaut, Muhamed M. (2019). *Al-Busnawa al-HarsakKhilāl al-Ḥukm al-Uthmānī* [Bosnia and Herzegovina under Ottoman Rule], Amman: Alaan Publishing.

Al-Kanānī, Yaḥya (1975). *Aḥkam al-Sūk* [The Rules of Market], Tunis: al-Charika al-Tunisiya li-al-Tawzi'.

Al-Yahya, Fahad (2016). *Al-Bank al-Waqfī* [The Waqfbank], al-Qasim: Markaz al-Khayr al-Baqī li-al-Awqāfwa al-Wassāyah.

Arda, S. A. (1994). The Establishment, Development and Features of the Turkish Banking Sector)Vakifbank), in BiliciFaruk. Le Waqf dans le monde Musulman contemporain (XIXe-XXe siècles), fonctions sociales, économiques et politiques, Institut français d'études anatoliennes d'Istanbul, IFEA, Istanbul, pp. 71–84.

Bayram, Sadi (1987). Sultan ReşadDevrindeEvkafBankasıKurulmaÇalışmaları [Establishment of Evkaf Bank in Sultan Mehmed V Period], *VakıfHaftasıDergisi*, Vol. 5, pp. 215–222.

Belabes, Abderrazak (2013). Ṣafaḥāt min Tārīkh al-Maṣrafiyah al-Islāmiyah: MubādarahMubakirah li-Inshā' MaṣrafIslāmīfī al-JazāirfīAwākhir 'Ishriniyāt al-Qarn al-Mādhī [A Few Pages from the History of Islamic Banking: An Early Initiative to Establish an Islamic Bank in Algeria in the Late 1920s], *DirāsātIqtiṣādi-yahIslāmīyah* [Islamic Economic Studies], Vol. 19, No. 2, pp. 1–44.

Belabes, Abderrazak (2016). Enquête sur une initiative de création d'une banque pour les musulmans de Saint-Petersbourg au début du XXe siècle [An Inquiry on an Initiative to Create a Bank by Muslim Entrepreneurs in St. Petersburg in the Early Twentieth Century], Paper presented to the Chair '*Ethics and Financial Norms*', University Paris 1 Panthéon-Sorbonne, 20 January.

Belabes, Abderrazak (2018). Istiqṣā' FikratInshā' Bank Islāmī bi-Miṣrfī 'Ām 1908 [An Investigation into the Idea of Establishment of an Islamic Bank in Egypt in 1908], paper presented to the Wednesday Seminar, Islamic Economics Institute, King Abdulaziz University, 17 October.

Belabes, Abderrazak (2019). Ma'ālimManhajiyah li-DhabtIstikhdāmMafhūm al-Waqffī al-Tamwīlwa al-Istithmār [Methodological Guidelines for the Use of the Concept of Waqf in Financing and Investment], in the Book '*Al-Tamwīlwa al-Istithmār fi al-Awqāf*' [Financing and Investment in Awqaf], Jeddah: The Scientific Publishing Center, King Abdulaziz University, pp. 1–44.

Bilici, Faruk (1994). Les Waqfsmonéraires à la fin de l'Empire ottoman et au début de l'époquerépublicaineenTurquie: des caisses de solidaritévers un systèmebancaire-moderne [The Cash *Waqf* at the End of the Ottoman Empire and the Beginning of the Republican Era in Turkey: From Solidarity Funds to a Modern Banking System], in F. Bilici (dir.). *Le Waqf dans le monde Musulman contemporain (XIXe-XXe siècles), fonctions sociales, économiques et politiques*, Institut français d'études anatoliennes d'Istanbul, IFEA, Istanbul, pp. 51–60.

Bilici, Faruk (1996). Les waqf-s monétaires à l'époque ottomane: droit hanéfite et pratique [The Cash Waqfs in the Ottoman Era: Hanafite Law and Practice], *Revue du monde musulman et de la Méditerranée*, No. 79–80, pp. 73–88.

Blondel, Georges (1911). La question agraire de la Bosnie-Herzégovine [The Agrarian Question of Bosnia and Herzegovina], *Séances et travaux de l'Académie des sciences morales et politiques*, tome soixante-seizième, deuxième semestre, juillet, pp. 76–87.

Bougarel, Xavier (1996). *Bosnie, anatomie d'un conflit* [Bosnia, Anatomy of a Conflict], Paris: La Découverte.

Bougarel, Xavier (2008).Farewell to the Ottoman Legacy? Islamic Reformism and Revivalism in Inter-War Bosnia-Herzegovina, in Nathalie Clayer and Eric

Germain (eds.), *Islam in Inter-War Europe*, London: Hurst, pp. 313–343. *Hal Sciences de l'Homme et de la Société*, pp. 1–23.

Bougarel, Xavier (2017). *Islam and Nationhood in Bosnia-Herzegovina: Surviving Empires*, London: Bloomsbury Publishing.

Bouvat, Lucien (1910). Presses ottomanes [Ottoman Presses], *Revue du monde musulman*, Vol. XII, No. IX, septembre, pp. 689–697.

Bukvić, Amer (2013). Evolution of Islamic banking in southeast Europe: A spark from Bosnia & Herzegovina, *Islamic Finance News*, Vol. 10, No. 43, 30 October, pp. 22–23.

Çiftçi, Cafer (2004). YüzyıldaBursa'da Para YaklflariveKrediIşlemleri [Money Approaches and Credit Transactions in Bursa in the 16th Century], *TarihAraştırmalarıDergisi*, Vol. 23, pp. 79–102.

Clark, Joseph T. (1959). The Philosophy of Science and the History of Science, in Marshall Clagett (ed.), *Critical Problems in the History of Science*, Madison: University of Wisconsin Press, pp. 103–140.

Dawletschin-Linder, Camilla (2003). *Diener seines Staates: Celal Bayar (1883–1986) und die Entwicklung der modernenTürkei* [Servant of His State: Celal Bayar (1883–1986) and the Development of Modern Turkey], Otto HarrassowitzVerlag.

Dumas, Alexandre (1997). *The Count of Monte Cristo*, Volume 2, Hertfordshire: Wordsworth Editions.

Eco, Umberto (1965). L'œuvreouverte [The Open Work], Paris: Seuil.

Ettounsi, Kheireddine ([1867]2012). *Aqwam al-MasālikfīMa'rifatAḥwāl al-Mamālik'* [The Surest Path to Knowledge Regarding the Condition of Countries], Cairo - Beirut: Dar al-Kitab al-Masri – Dar al-Kitab al-Lubnani.

Gravier, G. (1911). L'émigration des musulmans de de Bosnie-Herzégovine [Emigration of Muslims from Bosnia and Herzegovina], *Revue de Paris*, tome premier, janvier-février, pp. 212–224.

Höpken, Wolfgang (1994).Yugoslavia's Communists and the Bosnian Muslims, in Andreas Kappeler, Gerhard Simon, Georg Brunner (eds.), *Muslim Communities Reemerge: Historical Perspectives on Nationality, Politics, and Opposition in the Former Soviet Union and Yugoslavia*, Durham, NC: Duke University Press, pp. 214–247.

Izetbegović, Alija (1994). *Al-Islāmbayna al-Sharqwa al-Gharb* [Islam between the East and the West], Kuwait & Munich: Majallat al-Nūr & Bavaria Verlag & Handel GmbH.

Izetbegović, Alija (2002). *Hurūbīilā al-Huriyyah* [Notes from Prison, 1883–1988], Damascus: Dar al-Fikr.

Jelić, Damir (2007). *Provincial Banking in the Austro-Hungarian Monarchy and Successor States 1913–1925*, PhD Thesis, University of Leceister, School of Historical Studies, May.

Jouanneau, L. (1805). *Discussions du Code Civil dans le Conseild'Etat* [Discussions of the Civil Code in the Council of State], tome second, Paris: Demonville.

Karagedikli, Gürer and Tunçer, Ali Coşkun (2018). Microcredit in the Ottoman Empire: A Review of Cash Waqfs, in Marcella Lorenzini, CinziaLorandini, D'Maris Coffman (eds.), *Transition to Modern Banking, in Financing in Europe: Evolution, Coexistence and Complementarity of Lending Practices from the Middle Ages to Modern Times*, London: Macmillan Palgrave, pp. 239–268.

Kolaj-Ristanović, Irena D. (2019). O ustanovivakufaivakufskimdobrima u KneževiniSrbiji 1830–1878: pravno-istorijskiokvir [On Waqf Institution and Waqfs Property in the Principality of Serbia 1830–1878: Legal and Historical Frame], *PravniZapisi*, Year X, No. 1, pp. 201–220.

Kreševljaković, Hamdija ([1941]2018). Menafi - sanduci (Poljodjelskepripomoćnezaklade) u BosniiHercegovini (1866–1878) [Menafi – Sanduc (Fondationsagricolesauxiliaires) enBosnie-Herzégovine (1866–1878)], *Znakovivremena - Časopiszafilozofiju, religiju, znanostidruštvenupraksu*, Vol. XXI, No. 82, pp. 61–78.

Laveleye, Emile de (1885). La Bosnie régime agraire et économie rurale [Bosniaagrarian System and Rural Economy], *Revue des deux mondes*, tome LXX, juillet, pp. 516–552.

Mandaville, Jon E. (1979). Usurious Piety: The Cash Waqf Controversy in the Ottoman Empire, *InternationalJournal of Middle East Studies*, Vol. 10, No. 3, pp. 289–308.

Marko, Joseph (2000). Bosnia and Herzegovina: Multi-Ethnic or Multinational, in European Commission for Democracy through Law, in Council of Europe (ed.). *Societies in Conflict: The Contribution of Law and Democracy to Conflict Resolution*, Strasbourg: Council of Europe Publishing, pp. 92–118.

Omerčić, Jasmin (2017). Waqf in Bosnia and Herzegovina in the 20th and 21st Century, *Islam and Civilisational Renewal*, Vol. 8, No. 3, July, pp. 342–367.

Omerčić, Jasmin (2018). *Socio-Economic Potential of Waqfin Bosnia and Herzegovina*, Sarajevo: Center for Advanced Studies.

Ortabağ, Erol (2018). *Osmanlıİmparatorluğu'ndaBankacılığınGelişimiveRegülasyon* [Development and Regulation of Banking in the Ottoman Empire], TürkiyeBankalarBirliği, Yayin No: 326, Istanbul.

Özcan, Tahsin (2003). Osmanlı para vakıfları: Kanûnî dönemiÜsküdarörneği [The Ottoman Waqfs of Üsküdar during the Kanûniû Period], Ankara: TürkTarihKurumuYayınları.

Özcan, Tahsin (2004). KanûnîDönemiÜsküdar Para Vakiflari [Uskudarcash*awqāf*], in ZekeriyaKurşun, Ahmet EmreBilgili, Kemal Kahraman, CelilGüngör (eds.), *ÜsküdarSempozyumu I*, 23–25 May, ÜsküdarBelediyeBaşkanlığı, ÜsküdarAraştırmalarıMerkezi, Publication No. 10, pp. 57–67.

Özcan, Tahsin (2008). OsmanlıToplumunaÖzgüBirFinansmanModeli: Para Vakıfları [A Specific Financing Model to Ottoman Society: Cash Waqf], *Çerçeve*, Yıl: 16, Sayı: 48, Ekim, pp. 124–128.

Özdemir, Mücahit and Özdemir, Öznur (2017). Bridging the Gap: The Restitution of Historical Cash Waqf through Vakıf Participation Bank, *International Journal of Islamic Economics and Finance Studies*, Vol. 3, No. 2, pp. 74–99.

Pavloviç, Vojislav (2009). La crise de Bosnie 1908, cent ans aprèsCompte rendu du colloque, 26–27 septembre 2008, Paris, *Bulletin de l'Institut Pierre Renouvin*, 2009/2 (N° 30), pp. 165–173.

Polanyi, Karl ([1977]2011). *La Subsistance de l'Homme. La place de l'économie dans l'histoire et la société* [The Livelihood of Man], traduit de l'anglais et présenté par Bernard Chavance, Paris: Flammarion.

Popovic, Alexandre (1997). Les musulmans de Bosnie-Herzégovine, mise en place d'une guerre civile [Muslims in Bosnia and Herzegovina, Setting Up a Civil War], *Actes de la recherche en sciences sociales*, Vol. 116–117, mars, pp. 91–104.

Rešidbegović, Amra (1997). Osnivanjei rad Islamskedioničkeštamparije II Sarajevu do 1918-te godine [Establishment and Operation of the Muslim Press in Sarajevo until 1918], *Bosniaca*, II, pp. 56–67.

Şeyhun, Ahmet (1992).Centralization Process of Cash Waqfs in the Ottoman Empire and their Legal Framework, Master thesis in History, Boğaziçi University, Istanbul.

Smolo, Edib (2019). The Role of Waqf (Endowment) in Economic Development of Bosnia and Herwegovina: A Historical Overview and Future Prospects, in Khalifa

Mohamed Ali, M. Kabir Hassan, AbdelrahmanElzahiSaaid Ali (eds.), *Revitalization of Waqf for Socio-Economic Development*, Cham: Palgrave MacMillan, Volume 1, pp. 85–106.

Sperber, Dan (1996). *La Contagion des idées* [The Contagion of Ideas], Paris: Odile Jacob.

Toprak, Zafer (1995). *İttihat-TerakkiveDevletçilik* [Union-Progrès et Etatisme], Istanbul: TarihVakfıYurtYayınları.

Toraman, Cengiz, Tuncsiper, Bedriye and Yilmaz, Sinan (2007).Cash Awqaf in the Ottomans as Philanthropic Foundations and Their Accounting Practices, paper presented the Fifth Accounting History International Conference, Banff, Alberta.

Trakic, Adnan (2012). A Legal and Administrative Analysis of Inalienable Muslim Endowments (Awqaf) in Bosnia and Herzegovina, *Islam and Civilisational Renewal*, Vol. 2, No. 3, pp. 337–354.

Traljić, Mahmud (1983). Osvrtnadosadašnjuliteraturu o vakufima [A Review to the Literature of Vakufs], *AnaliGaziHusrev-begovebiblioteke*, Vol. IX–X, pp. 171–178.

Unmusulman (1900). Les Musulmans de Bosnie-Herzégovine: leursdoléances – leursvœux [The Muslims of Bosnia and Herzegovina: Their Grievances - Their Wishes], *Revue du monde musulman*, Vol. XII, No. IX, novembre, pp. 161–165.

Vujović, Milan (2015). RazvojBankarstva u HercegovinizavremeAustrougarskeokupacije [Development of Banking in Herzegovina during the Austr-Hungarian Occupation], *Bankarstvo*, Vol. 3, pp. 36–57.

Zajimović, Senaid (2010). *Vakufi u BosniiHercegovini: historijat, trenutnostanjeiperspektive*, [*Awqāf* in Bosnia and Herzegovina: History, Current Situation and Perspectives], Sarajevo: Islamskazajednica u BosniiHercegovini, Vakufskadirekcija.

Lois, Proclamation, Rescrit, Congrès, Statut

Akman, Mehmet (2007). Tanzimat'tanCumhuriyet'e Osmanlı HukukMevzuatı. TertipDüstur'unTarihiFihristveDizini [Ottoman Legal Legislation from Tanzimat to Republic. Directory and Index], *TürkHukukTarihiAraştırmaları*, Sayı 4, 2007 (Güz), pp. 41–368.

Annexion par l'Empire austro-hongrois: Proclamation aux habitants de la Bosnie et de l'Herzégovine [Annexation by the Austro-Hungarian Empire: Proclamation to the Inhabitants of Bosnia and Herzegovina], https://mjp.univ-perp.fr/constit/ba1908.htm

Annexion par l'Empire austro-hongrois: Rescrit adressé le 5 octobre 1908 au président du Conseil des ministres d'Autriche [Annexation by the Austro-Hungarian Empire: Rescript Sent on 5 October 1908 to the President of the Austrian Council of Ministers], https://mjp.univ-perp.fr/constit/ba1908.htm

Congrès de Berlin de 1878 [Berlin Congress of 1878], https://mjp.univ-perp.fr/traites/1878berlin.htm

Loi concernant l'administration de la Bosnie et de l'Herzégovine [Law on the Administration of Bosnia and Herzegovin], 1880, https://mjp.univ-perp.fr/constit/ba1880.htm

Statut relative à l'administration autonome des affaires concernant le culte musulman, les *vakouf* et les *mearif* [Austro-Hungarian Statute on the Autonomous Administration Concerning Muslim Worship, *vakouf* and *mearif* in Bosnia and Herzegovina], *Bulletin Analytique des principaux documents parlementaires étrangers transmis à la Présidence de la Chambre des Députés*, No. 23, 20 December 1909, pp. 9–36.

6 Contemporary approach in productive awqaf development

Hendri Tanjung, Imam Teguh Saptono and Imam Nur Aziz

Analysis

The renowned economist, Milton Friedman, published "The Social Responsibility of Business Is to Increase Its Profits" in *The New York Times Magazine* (September 13, 1970). On a macro-scale, the above symptoms are also increasingly felt, at least the occupied wall street movement, even to the Arab Spring phenomenon. According to some economic and political experts, it is essentially caused by the unity of the interests of the capital owners represented by a handful of the majority group which generally has a level of welfare far below. Therefore, in the CSV concept there are a number of major paradigm shifts, including integrating the interests of companies with the benefits of beneficiaries, so that each company's activities are not oriented toward profit maximization, but are embedded in social and economic benefits (see Figure 6.1).

But in reality, creating an organization that has the spirit of "truly CSV" is not easy because there will always be a tradeoff between profit and social benefits if the business paradigm is not changed. As long as the Key Performance Indicator (KPI) used by the capitalist is still the same, don't expect his or her behavior to be different. Indeed, Islam has known the concept of truly CSV since 1.5 centuries ago, which has been implemented by all Waqf corporations. What was the Waqf corporation 1.5 centuries ago? The main features are told in the stories of Umar Dates Plantation Co., Ustman bin Affan Water Co., Abdur Rahman bin Auf Trading Enterprise, etc. This means the garden of Waqf, Umar, Ustman Well, Abdur Rahman bin Auf's trading business and many more, while the affix behind was solely born from a contextual approach, because at the time of the Prophet and his companions there was no known modern business institutional model as illustrated earlier. Furthermore, referring to Quran, Surat Ali Imran verse 92, the verse which most commentators agree that it is about Waqf, mentioned, "You have never come to the (perfect) virtue, before you spend some of the best treasure that you love. And whatever you spend, surely Allah knows it". Based on this verse, ask the company capitalists, which one do they really love: giving up part of the profits (bottom line) or the engine or the corporation? Of course, all of them mention the corporation. This is actually the form of Waqf itself, namely giving up the engine (productive assets) that is capable of producing or precisely making the company owned as a Waqf corporation by giving up ownership to Allah. Then the riddle is answered about the institutional form that is able to run the spirit of CSV in sincere. It is Waqf corporation.

Furthermore, the turmoil of the world community on the business behavior of the capitalists is increasingly mounting. This is shown by the economic inequality between the rich and the poor; the prosperity of developed countries and poverty in a number of countries, especially in Asia and Africa; education disparity; health services; more.

World economic experts at the United Nations General Assembly on September 25, 2015 in New York have formulated an agreement signed by 193 heads of state including Indonesia. With the theme "Changing Our World: 'Agenda 2030 for Sustainable Development'", the SDGs containing 17 goals and 169 targets are global action plans for the next 15 years (effective from 2016 to 2030) to end poverty, reduce inequality and protect the environment. SDGs apply to all countries (universal), so that all countries, including developed countries, have a moral obligation to achieve the goals and targets of the SDGs.

Sometimes we are too pragmatic and naïve. Have we ever thought why we are busy struggling to eradicate poverty, but do not try to kill the causes of poverty itself? Have we ever thought to retire the interest system, stop the traditional practices of conventional banking which have in fact proven to cause the gaps asset ownership between capital owners and marginal groups is getting bigger? The underdeveloped sectors (such as community fishing, agriculture, MSME) are not touched by formal financial sources, especially banks. Learning from the story of the caliph Umar Abdul Azis (in the book *Musykilah al-FaqrwaKaifa 'Alajaha al-Islam* by Yusuf Qhardawi) mentioned that the state made financing to the people through the funds of Baitul Mal (ZISWAF, kharaj, jizyah), with a pattern adapted to the needs and abilities of the target recipient (not with the interest mechanism). This means that the money is allocated not by the risk and return mechanism alone, but rather because of the objectives of the sharia maqosid, which is very much in line with the concept of cash Waqf. Some libraries even mentioned that money endowments are dwarfed along with the development of modern banking institutions. It is the endowment fund source that has the characteristics and ability to answer its "maqasid" goals because it has practically a very long period of time and without any cost of funds.

Two examples above, namely the need for the presence of Waqf corporation and cash Waqf, are a contemporary approach that needs to be revived amidst a very dichotomous mindset of a business practice. The dichotomy is nothing but the separation between commercial and social activities. This condition has been going on for hundreds of years until now. We are busy having to revive a new quadrant, namely high-impact investment.

As a matter of fact, Islam can distinguish between social and commercial activities, but it never separates between the two because they are all within the framework of worship to Allah. So, it is impossible for religious activities to produce pious people personally without socially pious people, so it is when they do business.

For a devout Muslim, doing business is part of worship, which is based on three main principles, namely Lillah, Fillah, Billah. Lillah is a belief that what we have (resources, capital, technology, networks, customers, etc.) comes from God and is only for God. Fillah is a principle that holds, because everything comes from God and for God, the way to use and treat it (treated by) only in the way of God. The Billah principle is a view that the Lillah and Fillah principles should have been worked out, whatever the results are. If the result is not in accordance with the wishes and expectations, it is solely due to Allah's permission. If it matches or even exceeds that expectation, it is solely because of God's help and at all not because of our greatness. Therefore, the bottom line (profit) is not the ultimate goal (ultimate decision), but only a result and risk arising from the religious struggle. Profit is the result, while endeavor is a form of gratitude. It will never be comparable between what we try and what we get (whatever the result). This concept is certainly far more powerful than John Elkington's triple bottom line approach in 1994 which contained profit, people and planetary parameters and was made an approach to the preparation of Sustainability Report by Shell in 1997.

It is a necessity that if the objectives and Sharia rules of a business entity are fulfilled, then the transactions carried out by the business must be transactions that have a high impact on the social aspect. It is impossible to escape from the sharia maqoshid, namely safeguarding faith, safeguarding souls, protecting offspring, protecting intellect (intelligence) and safeguarding property. In conclusion, in the concept of sharia there will only be high-impact transactions, i.e. transactions that have adequate financial returns on the one hand and have high social impacts on the other hand. So does the investments—it must be impacting investment activities.

Therefore, in conducting business, a Waqf corporation only has a C quadrant. While in the minds of traditional-conventional entrepreneurs they are busy discussing "financial, policy or business instruments" which would be able to meet the quadrant C rules. This is because they are always in the quadrant other than C because of the trap of believing in the paradigm of "trade-off". Indeed, in Sharia Transactions, there is no known "trade-off" between financial and social return. Overall performance parameters are measured by the benefit index, with the sole purpose of being good to Allah.

However, the concept of Waqf corporation is also not entirely the same as Social Preneur in the sense that get as much business as possible (regardless of how to meet the rules of shariah or not) and give a lot to the social field. This is what we call the "Robin Hood Complex". This can explain why CSR is carried out by many large companies, and even multinational companies in all sectors cannot improve the economic condition of the people, poverty and inequality. On the contrary, poverty and inequality continue to grow in a structured, systematic and massive way.

So, how can we revitalize endowments? There is no other event but to ground them into daily economic activity in today's modern context. It must be acknowledged that the legal system of companies, banks, capital markets, taxation and many more cannot accommodate Waqf mechanism into its mainstream activities. However, from the understanding of Waqf fiqh, there is still a narrow and rigid understanding. Some issues such as the process of replacing Waqf assets, nadzir transfers and the definition of lost and losses cause slow growth of Waqf assets and also their utilization. Many uses of Waqf assets become very limited and only dwell on social assets (non-commercial) such as tombs, mosques and madrasas so that the trickle-down effect of the resulting economic activity is limited.

The limitations of the propositions related to Waqf both in the Quran and the hadiths cause the practice of Waqf to become an area of ijtihadi and vary in each school of thought. This limitation should be seen as a mercy and a force for the implementation of Waqf in the field. This means that Waqf should be able to easily accommodate and adjust to the condition of the economic development of the people—ranging from issues of technology, disruptive economy, internet of things, to VUCA. It should be a means of proving that Waqf can be present to answer these challenges, rather than making them marginalized. Waqf stakeholders should prioritize the purpose of prosperity and put aside differences between schools. In order to create a healthy Waqf eco-system, policy makers must adopt two approaches, namely push strategy and pull strategy. Push strategy as much as possible encourages all stakeholders of Waqf (nadzir, Islamic financial institutions, government, ulama). It is concerned about the innovation of Waqf products in accordance with the development of the Islamic financial industry such as the launch of sukuk cash linked Waqf, Waqf sukuk, insurance premium Waqf, Waqf shares, Waqf banks, etc. Pull strategy attracts Islamic financial institutions to care for Waqf.

It must be recognized that in the history of Islamic civilization, one of the economic signs of progress of the people is built through the practice of Waqf as one of the economic pillars. This is marked by the development of Waqf assets, especially productive Waqf in a significant amount. Drivers of Waqf development at that time were generally productive assets such as gardens and business ventures. People need new thoughts and concepts of Waqf in order to be able to give birth to product innovations that are in accordance with the times, while still maintaining the spirit of the sharia maqosid. The belief in the greatness of Waqf as a great and extraordinary celestial instrument in responding to economic problems, if it has not had a significant impact, rest assured that the error lies with those of us who have not been able to apply it appropriately.

Cash Waqf linked sukuk (CWLS)

Indonesia made an innovation by launching a product called cash Waqf linked sukuk (CWLS). In brief, CWLS can be described as follows:

> Waqf linked sukuk (WLS) is a safe and reliable endowment money solution, as well as developing the country. Indonesian waqf Board invests waqf funds in state sharia securities. Sukuk yields paid by the government will be given to maukuf alaih (beneficiaries) to build madrasas, build

health centers or hospitals, economic empowerment programs for the ummah, recovery of disaster areas, and other activities according to the Shari'a. The funds will return 100% to the time when they are due.

Put simply, CWLS is a transaction for a Waqf project. The hope, blessing flows all the time. CWLS tells us that Islamic financial products in Indonesia, even in the world, are increasing again. One of the goals of the launch of this CWLS product is to increase the market share of Islamic finance in Indonesia. Because, according to Perry Warjiyo, the governor of Bank Indonesia, one of the three things that can increase the Islamic financial market share is the launch of a new product. A large and varied product mix will make people have many choices to invest their money. Meanwhile, two other things that can increase the market share of Islamic finance are moving the halal economy and sharia financial economic campaigns to the public.

CWLS products

This CWLS product is actually a temporary Waqf, where people who are waqif only donate their money for several periods of time (minimum five years according to regulations), and after maturity, the money (principal amount guaranteed) will be returned. For example, Person A has one billion rupiah, then Person A is temporarily represented for ten years; after ten years, Person A will get his money back as much as one billion. Profit-sharing results obtained annually from sukuk will be given to Nazirs to be used to build projects (madrasa, hospitals, disaster area recovery, scholarships and others) according to the Shari'a. What's in it for A? A will get the reward for ten years from the temporary Waqf he does. More importantly, the one billion is not lost. The CWLS scheme can be seen in Figure 6.1.

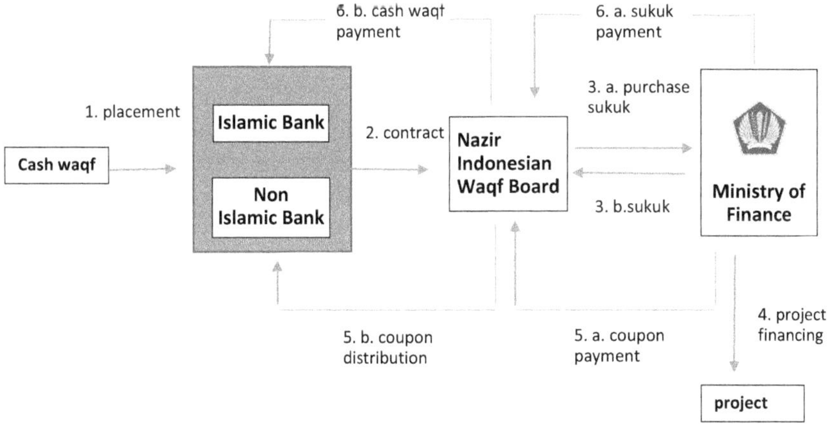

Figure 6.1 Cash Waqf -linked Sukuk (CWLS) scheme.

Risk management of CWLS

In terms of risk management, CWLS is safe, because the form of SBSN investment is guaranteed by the state. Arguably there is zero risk. Waqf core principles (WCP) article 22, concerning market risk, WCP22, states as follows: The waqf supervisor ascertains that waqf institutions (Nazirs) have an adequate market risk management process that takes into account their risk appetite, risk profile, market and macroeconomic conditions, and the risk of a significant deterioration in market liquidity. Nazirs must have a standard valuation mechanism for assets under management that is based on regular changes in their market value. This includes prudent policies and processes to identify, measure, evaluate, monitor, report and control or mitigate market risks on a timely basis. In fact, the vice chairman of BWI said: "given the Nazarite capacity in Indonesia is still limited in managing productive assets, then investment in the form of SBSN, can mitigate it".

Waqf risk management standards outline that voters must be able to calculate risk appetite, risk profile, and market and macroeconomic conditions. Risk appetite is a situation in which an organization chooses to accept, monitor, defend or maximize itself through opportunities. That is, Nazir must be able to see opportunities and use those opportunities to develop Waqf property. One way is to invest in this WLS. With this WLS, Waqf is directly used to develop the country. In terms of risk profile, WLS is considered beneficial, where the ability of Nazir to bear an investment risk is very good. This is because the risk of investment is very small, or it might be said to be non-existent. Risk profile is an assessment or conclusion of the ability and willingness of investors to bear an investment risk (in this case fluctuations or losses). In terms of market and macroeconomic conditions, this WLS is arguably more resilient to macroeconomic shocks. During the recession, for example, where the real sector has underperformed, this WLS can actually help move the real sector economy. Profit sharing obtained from WLS is used for economic empowerment programs, especially for micro-businesses.

Target market of CWLS

This WLS is very suitable for people who have idle money for a certain period of time. During that period, the idle money could be temporarily represented, thus resulting in a reward for him or her. By the same analogy, this will also inspire the land endowment to temporarily endow the land. Instead of the land not being tilled and left stranded, it is better to be presented to Nazarite for a while. After the time is over, the Wakif regains his land. Of course, the Wakif has already printed the reward from the results of his land management which is presented to Nazir. In the area of West Sumatra, the land that is not cultivated is quite extensive. With temporary Waqf, these lands can be managed by Nazir, where the results of their management are used for beneficiaries of Waqf (maukuf alaih).

Beneficiaries of CWLS

The earthquake and tsunami in Palu and around it made us think and try to help our brothers by rebuilding damaged infrastructure. This rebuilding effort is the responsibility not only of the government but of all the people. Indeed, Islam emphasizes the responsibilities of others. Even in the Quran surat Al Maun verse 7, it is explained, including people who reject religion and do not want to provide assistance to others. That is, helping our fellow nation children is our responsibility. Let us help others on the basis of mutual cooperation. Isn't mutual cooperation the essence of Pancasila? Of course everyone wishes this WLS success. Everything depends on us. Let us continue to socialize this WLS with the spirit of mutual cooperation, the spirit of building the country and the spirit of seeking blessing. Surely blessing that flows all the time.

Innovation in Waqf blockchain

Historically, Waqf had significantly contributed to the well-being and educational development of the Muslim societies. It was a successful and exemplary model for funding and sustaining Islamic educational institutions such as universities, schools, madrasahs and other public services in the past that some of these institutions are still in existence. Nowadays, however, the Muslim societies expect that many awqaf institutions should take over more responsibilities to meet the current social and educational problems. There are challenges to be faced by significant numbers of awqaf institutions today. These challenges revolve on how to mobilize and manage their resources to improve Islamic educational institutions and societal economic development, and help preserve the vast liquid assets.

Waqf blockchain as new innovation

According to www.islamichain.com (2019) annually Islamic philanthropy generates up to $1 trillion in charitable funds. However, its beneficial impact is often absent of transparent and accountable delivery mechanisms. With the introduction of new technologies such as blockchain, it brings renewed hope to the revival and management of Waqf properties and assets, especially for the future generation. Now most of you are probably wondering, what does charitable Islamic endowment have to do with a digital ledger of records (or blocks)? A startup company Finterra explains how the two actually live in a symbiotic relationship that has the potential of benefitting one another.

It is noted that in the era of Islamic golden years, specifically the Ottoman era, the establishment of Waqf derived outstanding results and benefits in terms of enriching the welfare of an individual throughout his or her lifetime. Through the Waqf foundation system, buildings and lands were used to provide education, medical services, water and other essential services to those in need and develop the capital, and as a result the Ottoman Empire succeeded in eliminating poverty for centuries. Waqf used to play this significant role in improving the lives of individuals, societies and economies, but it is no longer the case today. The Waqf landscape in the contemporary world is plagued with issues of liquidity, transparency and mismanagement, all of which constrain the full utilization of the potential of Waqf and impede the complete development of the projects. For years, experts have tried to solve these issues but to no avail. This is of course until February 2019, when a technology-based organization, called Finterra, launched its flagship product, the "WAQF Chain". It had managed to develop a blockchain with Waqf as its use case.

Liquidity

Finterra formulated a platform designed to tackle all of the issues mentioned earlier, by harnessing the blockchain technology to raise capital for the development of Waqf projects. The arrival of technological advancements such as blockchain has given people hope for the revival of the glory days of Waqf in the modern world. Enabling the donation of cash Waqf solved the problem of unproductive and immobilized Waqf properties, because the money donated is used for Projects or Causes which provides never-ending benefits to the *ummah*.

Transparency

One of the main advantages of blockchain technology is the total transparency offered in the distributed ledger, where every transaction is recorded publicly and individuals who are provided authority can view the transactions. Users who donate on the WAQF Chain platform can track their contributions from the moment it is gifted until the beneficiaries have reaped the rewards. Moreover, using the "smart contract"—a computer program or algorithm that automatically executes itself when the predefined conditions are met—could further enhance the performance and efficacy of the Waqf institution, while also increasing the security, providing transparency and adherence to the Waqf stipulations.

Awareness

This relationship between blockchain and Waqf is a two-way street and therefore both reap benefits from one another. One of the key challenges facing blockchain is the lack of knowledge of the technology and how it works, which is why the adoption and applications of blockchain technology garners interest and raises awareness in each sector. As a result, the concept of Waqf can go a long way in enhancing the legitimacy and image of the blockchain technology; therefore, more banks, investors and potential clients would be willing to work with blockchain-based companies.

The key issues are lack of availability of data and historical records, weak transparency and public disclosure, improper audit and compliance practices. The advent of the blockchain has offered a ray of hope for the revival of the Waqf institution. The blockchain has already proved itself as a game-changing breakthrough. Similarly, the Waqf institution could be invigorated with the innovative and efficient use of the blockchain. Moreover, the use of smart contracts on blockchain could further enhance the performance and efficacy of the Waqf institution. It is strongly believed that with the firm Islamic jurisprudential foundations of the Waqf, blockchain and smart contracts will ensure that the Waqf institution could partake in the economic development of the whole Muslim world.

There is no doubt that the blockchain is the building block of the future knowledge economy. Whether it is building blockchain airports or even solving environmental issues, the potential of the blockchain is full of promise. To begin to understand just how blockchain could transform our world, it's helpful to identify its defining characteristics. Most notably, these include its distributed and immutable ledger and advanced cryptography, which bring a powerful new property to large-scale computer networks: *Trust*. This ranges from trust in owning a digital cryptocurrency or good, to trust in its origin, or in the veracity of a transaction. Similar, perhaps, to that false trust the Sassanid soldiers put in those rusty battle chains.

Perhaps more important is our trust in blockchain's decentralized business model, which according to Dr. Mussaad M. Al-Razouki (2018) is similar to the trust exhibited by Ibn Waleed's army in Allah and their general's blitzkrieg strategy which essentially decentralized his army. The blockchain's **decentralized autonomous organization** (DAO) nature is neutral by definition and highlighted by the fact that all data and code that underpins the blockchain technology is open for all to see.

Bringing the blockchain into Islamic fintech

A **Waqf**, also known as *habous* or *mortmain* property, is an inalienable charitable endowment under Islamic law, which typically involves donating a building, plot of land or other assets for charitable purposes with no intention of reclaiming the assets. These donated assets may be held by a charitable trust. The person making such dedication is known as *waqif*, or donor, and the Waqf is usually considered his or her (family) legacy and as a perpetual source of *hasanat* (good deeds) until the end of days.

The term "Waqf" literally means "confinement and prohibition" or causing a thing to stop or stand still. The legal meaning of Waqf, according to Imam Abu Hanifa, is the detention of a specific thing in the ownership of Waqf and the devoting of its profit or products "in charity of the poor or other good deeds".

Another notable scholar, Bahaeddin Yediyıldız, defines the Waqf as a system which comprises three elements: *khayrat*, *a'akarat* and *Waqf*. Khayrat

(خيرات), the plural form of *khayr*, means "goodnesses" and refers to the motivational factor behind a Waqf organization; *a'akarat* (عقارات) refers to corpus and literally means "real estate" implying revenue-generating sources, such as capital markets, land and water wells; and finally *Waqf*, in its narrow sense, is the institution(s) providing services as committed in the endowment deed such as hospitals, schools, mosques, libraries, etc. The beauty of combining the technological concept of the blockchain with the historical and traditional concept of the Waqf is that at their very core, both of these innovations deal in maintaining a sense of public trust for the benefit of society as a whole both presently and toward perpetuity. More on the principle of fidelity to come later.

Islamic finance and its digital economy offer opportunities for Muslims and non-Muslims as both populations now seek a convergent solution to their pressing issues—rebuilding trust and confidence in a financial system that had lost them. Some technologists imagine this world without intermediaries, while others just want a faster and more efficient way of transacting. Either way, the challenge comes from accountability, and embedding that sense of accountability within the new systems that are being built, based on the sharing of risks and profits that anchor the nature of our economies, including the sharing economy of underutilized assets. The blockchain technology is rapidly gaining the attention of Organizations of Islamic Cooperation and Islamic Development Bank. There are various Islamic financial institutes which are planning to use the blockchain system to bring the benefits that come with it.

The authorities in Dubai have revealed their plan that in 2020 they will be using blockchain in public and private sectors. It is no surprise that even government is showing interest in the digital currency. Here we have the information related to the relationship of blockchain in the Islamic finance and banking system.

What is the state of blockchain today?

In PwC's 2018 survey of 600 executives from 15 territories, 84% say their organizations have at least some involvement with blockchain technology. Companies have dabbled in the lab; perhaps, they've built proofs of concept. Everyone is talking about blockchain, and no one wants to be left behind. It's easy to see why. As a distributed, tamperproof ledger, a well-designed blockchain doesn't just cut out intermediaries, reduce costs, and increase speed and reach. It also offers greater transparency and traceability for many business processes. Gartner forecasts that blockchain will generate an annual business value of more than US$3 trillion by 2030. It's possible to imagine that 10%–20% of global economic infrastructure will be running on blockchain-based systems by that same year.

For the Islamic economy, blockchain technology has the potential to make a significant impact. The blockchain in Islamic finance and banking will surely help the Islamic banks and financial institutes to succeed. Without worrying about the interest and other such issues, the Islamic banking system will be able to work more productively. Islamic financial institutions are increasingly using blockchain technology for complex financing terms, Shariah-compliant transactions and Islamic and sharia-compliant alternatives to conventional insurance.

Blockchain's core attributes mean that it has significant potential for use in Islamic finance due to its:

- Transparency: blockchain provides provenance, traceability and transparency of transactions.
- Control: access to permissioned networks is restricted to identified users.
- Security: the digital ledger cannot be altered or tampered with once the data are entered. Fraud is less likely and easier to spot.
- Real-time information: when information is updated, it's updated for everyone in the network at the same time.

The blockchain in Islamic finance and banking will surely help the Islamic banks and financial institutes to succeed. Without worrying about the interest and other such issues, the Islamic banking system will be able to work more productively. Management of loans and other relatable services will become easy. In addition to reducing fraud and risk, it can bring down the high costs associated with Islamic finance. The cost of processing Islamic financial products is higher than regular financial services products, so blockchain is a very effective tool to bring down the cost in the back-end processing systems of Islamic finance companies. To sum up the real challenge in Waqf blockchain, going forward, will be the legality of smart contracts, and the global regulatory framework needed to establish true peer-to-peer lending across borders. This will be a great challenge to the blockchain CWLS case in Indonesia too.

Telkom as GLC (Government-Linked Corporation) of Indonesia will initiate to provide the technology or engine to blockchain the CWLS. However, this project shall attempt to set up all eco-system in Indonesia Waqf Board to install the blockchain technology.

References

Core Principles for Effective Waqf Operation and Supervision. A Joint Initiative of Central Bank of Indonesia, Indonesian Waqf Board and Islamic Development Bank. October 2018.

Dalby, Simon, Susan Horton, Rianne Mahon, and Diana Thomaz (Editor). *Achieving the Sustainable Development Goals: Global Governance Challenges* (Routledge Studies in Sustainable Development) 1st Edition. Routledge, 2019.

Elkington, John. *Cannibals with Forks: The Triple Bottom Line of 21st Century Business.* Oxford: Capstone, 1999. ISBN 9780865713925.
Freireich, Jessica and Katherine Fulton. "Investing for Social and Environmental Impact." *Monitor Institute*, January 2009.
Friedman, Milton. "The Social Responsibility of Business is to Increase its Profits." *The New York Times Magazine*, September 13, 1970.
Porter, Michael and Mark Kramer. "Creating Shared Value (CSV)." *Harvard Business Review Magazine.* January-February 2011 edition.

7 Utilizing awqaf in modern Muslim minority societies

Sheikh Haitham al-Haddad and Umer Suleman

An overview

The term "waqf" or "awqafis" is not specifically mentioned in the *Holy* Quran or in many of the statements and traditions of the Prophet (pbuh). However, the concept was well established in the practice of the Prophet (pbuh) and his companions. In later years, it was widely used by almost all key members of the Muslim community. The key prophetic statement that is quoted in this context is the hadith of Abu Huraira that the Prophet (peace and blessings of Allah be upon him (pbuh)) said: "When the son of Adam dies, all his good deeds come to an end except three: ongoing charity, knowledge from which others may benefit after he is gone, and a righteous son who will pray for him." It was recorded by Imam Muslim in his Sahih collection (Al-Nawawi, 1277).

Several studies consider the Qubamosque in Madina, which was established by the Prophet Muhammad (pbuh) upon his immigration to Madina, as the first waqf in Islam (Kahf, 2015). Following on from these studies, the Prophet's mosque should be considered the second waqf, and possibly the most important waqf in Islam. The researchers could not confirm this through the primary sources that spoke about waqf in Islam (Al-Tarabulsi, 1902). This is because many primary sources, including books of hadith and *sirah*, reported the first waqf in Islam as the waqf of the Prophet (pbuh) from the assets left by a Jewish man who converted to Islam called Mukhairiq. In his will, Mukhairiq had indicated that after his death, his seven orchards in Madina should be given to the Prophet Muhammad (pbuh). According to these sources, Mukhairiq was killed in the Battle of Uhud in the third year of hijra and hence the Prophet (pbuh) took ownership of the orchards, converting them into a charitable waqf.[2] However, this difference is not fundamental and has no real practical consequence.

A well-known *hadith* recounts the donation of an orchard and its fruits to charity by one of the Prophet's (pbuh) close and great companions, upon the direction of the Prophet (pbuh). It was reported that, following the acquisition of land in Khaibar (north of Madina) by Umar ibn Al-Khattab, he asked the Prophet for advice on what he should do with it. The Prophet replied: "If you wish, you can give its benefits to charity whilst preserving it – so that it can no longer be sold, nor bought, nor may it be possible to give it away or bequeath it." Umar went on to dedicate the land to the benefit of the poor and needy relatives, to "set free slaves" in the way of God, and to provide for guests and travellers (Ibn Al-Hajjaj, 2000a).

The proceeds from the sale of fruits, thus, became the revenue-generating waqf for social development. This spurred the creation of awqaf by other companions of the Prophet (pbuh). It also gave birth to the creation of the family waqf, whereby one of the conditions stipulated that the children and relatives of the *waqif* have priority over the revenues generated.

Referring to the Islamic literature and historical resources, we find many quotations from various scholars. These quotations describe the extensive practice of waqf throughout history among the companions of the Prophet (pbuh) and other Muslims. For example, Imam al-Shafei stated, "I came to know that 80 from the Ansar of the companions of the Prophet (pbuh) establish awqaf" (Al-Sherbini, ???).[3] Al-Qurtubi, a prominent Maliki scholar, described the issue of the waqf, i.e. its virtues in Islam, as a matter of consensus between the companions of the Prophet (pbuh). The awqaf of Abi Bakr, Umar, Uthman, Ali, Aysha, Fatimah, Amr ibn al-Aas, Abdullah ibn al-Zubair and Jabir are known in Makkah and Madina (Ibn Al-Hajjaj, 2000b). It is beyond the remit of this chapter to present this historical development in Islamic history. It is enough to confirm that waqf is of one of the key characteristics of Islamic social, political, spiritual and economical life. It is also a characteristic that exists at various points of Islamic history in different geographic regions of the Islamic land. It is worth (although not vital) to mention that waqf can either take the form of *waqfkhairi* – which are awqaf established for the benefit of public charity, or *waqfahli* – wherein specific familial members are stipulated by the *waqif* as primary beneficiaries. There is an ongoing debate among Muslim scholars concerning the latter, i.e. *waqfahli*, and whether it should be accepted and encouraged. This is due to the possibility of circumventing Islamic inheritance laws. However, *waqfkhairi* is a widely accepted form of waqf, and it is the primary focal point of this chapter.

Muslim historians described many examples of waqf. Ibn Battoutah, the famous historian, geographer and traveller, also mentioned both the significance and prevalence of waqf – describing the wonders that he saw when visiting Damascus, stating "Endowments (awqaf) in Damascus were plentiful, uncounted, and unlimited." He added,

> There were endowments (awqaf) for helping those who cannot go for Hajj, there were also endowments (awqaf) for paving and improvement of the streets. There were endowments also for supplying wedding outfits

> to girls of poor families unable to provide them and others for the freeing of prisoners. There were endowments for giving food, clothing, and the expenses of conveyance for travellers as well

and among the most amazing things that he witnessed were the awqaf for utensils for those who were in need of them (Ibn Battutah, 2003, p. 99). In conclusion, the institution and its practice throughout history have demonstrated immense potential for positively transforming society and the economy, and thus represent an underappreciated contribution of Islamic civilisation to our understanding of political economy.

The economic role of waqf

In economics, public goods are defined as goods and services which are non-excludable and non-rivalrous. A public good (or service) may be consumed without reducing its amount that is available for others, and it cannot be withheld from those who do not pay for it (BusinessDictionary, 2019). This means that the consumption of such goods by one person does not diminish the potential for their consumption by others. Moreover, the benefits of such a good cannot be excluded, and thus cannot be restricted to a specific group. The quintessential public good often cited in elementary economics textbooks is that of the lighthouse: once built, its value is not diminished no matter how many ships use it for navigation. Nor can its benefits be restricted to naval vessels which pay for the service. It was not a coincidence that "a lighthouse on the Romanian coast was built and operated by a waqf institution in the 18th century" according to the Turkish historian, *Bahaeddin Yediyildiz*. This is a prime example of how the awqaf system defies the predictions of mainstream economic theory. The provision of a myriad of public goods through the awqaf system throughout Islamic history demonstrates the potential of having a decentralised, private provision of public goods and services independent of state intervention and at no cost to the state. The harnessing of private sector charitable endowments into institutions of perpetuity has resulted in an *oversupply* of public goods and services in many historical instances, rather than the undersupply of such goods and services as predicted by the economic theory (Budiman and Kusuma, 2011).

A profound description of the social-economical contribution gained from the waqf system states:

> …a person would have been born into a waqf house, slept in a waqf cradle, eaten and drunk from waqf property, read waqf books, been taught in a waqf school, received his salary from a waqf administration, and when he died, placed in a waqf coffin and buried in a waqf cemetery.
>
> (Nor, 2019; YediYildiz, 1996)

Hundreds of examples can be found in Islamic history on the contributions of the waqf system to all sectors of people's lives including religious, social, educational, health, financial and political life. According to Marshall Hodgson, a world-renowned historian, Zakah, collected by enforcement of public law, was the original vehicle for financing Islam as a society. However, Hodgson then went on to add that "private waqf foundations largely took its place in this role" (Hodgson, 1977, p. 124). In other words, both Zakat and waqf are the main foundations of the Islamic financial system and are, therefore, the backbone of any society. Many academics and research works in Islamic finance share Marshall Hodgson's conclusion (Al-Martan, 2011).

Waqf may eventually transcend intra-civilisation impacts and may act as an inter- or cross-civilisation tool of cooperation and development. According to Professor Kuran, "not only did the waqf turn into a defining feature of Islamic civilization; it went on to become a source of cross-civilization emulation" (Kuran, 2001, p. 848). Professor Kuran's conclusions is supported by the fact that many classical Muslim scholars described that in establishing waqf, the main beneficiaries were *thimmies*, i.e. Jews or Christians, who resided in the Muslim nation in its early form. It was reported that Safiyyah, the Jewish wife of the Prophet (pbuh), donated a waqf to her brother who was not a Muslim (Ibn Qudamah, 2013, v.5 p. 377).

In his forward for the World Bank Group, INCEIF and ISRA report on maximising social impact through waqf, Dr Mohd Azmi Omar, President and Chief Executive Officer of the International Centre of Education in Islamic Finance (INCEIF), stated:

> The latest statistics in the United Nation's Global Issues report show that almost half the world's population or over 3 billion people live on less than US$2.50 a day; 640 million live without adequate shelter; 925 million people suffer from hunger; 400 million have no access to safe water; 270 million have no access to health services; 10.6 million die before reaching the age of 5, and 1 billion are illiterate. Therefore, the urgency in implementing funding instruments such as waqf that are aligned with the belief system of contributors and needy communities alike, has not been more pronounced than now.
>
> (The World Bank Group & INCEIF & ISRA, 2019)

The economic repercussions of the success of the awqaf system are significant. The private provision of public goods and services, which, in modern societies, constitutes an increasingly larger proportion of public expenditure, has the potential to significantly reduce the fiscal burden on governments.

Since 2009, public social spending had constituted approximately 21% of GDP on average across the countries of the "Organization for Economic Cooperation and Development" (OECD, 2016). Moreover, developments in healthcare technology, ageing populations and demographic changes are placing an ever-increasing burden on state-sponsored welfare systems across the globe. In contrast, the awqaf system provided and maintained almost the entire welfare system of the Islamic empires, stretching from the early Umayyad era until the collapse of the Ottoman Empire in the late 20th century, and this was at no cost to the state (Çizakça, 1998). The potential for reducing public expenditure and the size of bureaucracies and central governments makes the awqaf system an indispensable tool for achieving economic efficiency and reducing state intervention in the free market economy. Such a goal has been pursued by governments and international bodies since the emergence of the neoliberal economic consensus in the 1970s.

Another potentially transformative role for the awqaf system is highlighted by Çizakça (1998). The reduction in fiscal expenditure opens up the potential for drastically lower levels of public borrowing. In 2015, OECD countries' average level of gross public debt reached 112% of GDP (OECD, 2017). In effect, governments are borrowing on average more than the whole of the annual output of their economies, thereby placing an upward pressure on interest rates and dampening investment and economic growth. The potential for lower public borrowing and subsequent lowering of interest rates provides an opportunity to move towards an interest-free economy. An economy sanctioned by *shariah*. Furthermore, awqaf institutions were historically significant sources of employment and wealth redistribution – two factors that are crucial for robust and sustainable economic growth (Çizakça, 1998).

Waqf and social-political development

The efficient functioning of political institutions is not independent of the social fabric of the societies which they govern. The emergence of an institutional political economy in the 20th century, with seminal works such as Robert Putnam's *Making Democracy Work* (1993), emphasised the role of social capital in society as a prerequisite for effective governance. In essence, the presence of networks of mutual cooperation between private citizens allows for effective private sector organisation and cooperation. Consequently, a robust civil society is created. One that can ensure that the rule of law is upheld in society and can also effectively monitor and restrict state action to ensure governments rule in the interest of citizens.

Awqaf are distinct from regular charitable donations. A waqf involves the creation of a corporate body whose activities benefit charitable causes. Moreover, any waqf is financed from the revenues it generates. The extensive array of awqaf which were established by private citizens acting entirely of their own accord, organising themselves in a corporate manner to set up long-lasting institutions for the pursuance of specific objectives, was an important source for the creation of social capital. This social capital forms the backbone of civic participation and facilitates the creation of a strong civil society which can participate in political life. Through this system, checks on executive power can be established, thereby ensuring the formation of inclusive and equal political and economic institutions. The persistence of authoritarianism, corruption and economic underperformance in the Middle East and North Africa (MENA) region has repeatedly been attributed to the active destruction of civil society by colonialism and authoritarianism in the region since the late 19th century (International Islamic University of Malaysia, 2009). Unsurprisingly, this was also the period when awqaf, which represented the ownership of close to a third of all land in parts of the Ottoman Empire, came under extensive attacks by the Colonial powers and the Ottoman central governments. Large swathes of awqaf properties were confiscated and nationalised as a result of this action. It can, thus, be argued that a revitalisation of awqaf presents an opportunity to positively transform societies by promoting civic cooperation, equitable wealth distribution and sustainable economic development.[4]

Waqf in non-Islamic societies and systems

Waqf is an instrument that can function and benefit any society – whether Muslim or non-Muslim. The presence of institutions such as trusts, irrespective of their origins, is sufficient evidence indicating how the concept of waqf can function and flourish even under non-faith–based legislations and systems. The similarities between awqaf and trusts led researchers to conclude that trusts originated from awqaf. This opinion, however, is not shared by all (Gaudiosi, 1988). The key issue here concerns how the efficient establishment and operation of the theory behind awqaf systems is manifested in non-Muslim societies in the form of the trust system, and how this has the potential to extend the aforementioned economic and societal benefits of awqaf to non-Islamic societies. This unique model of the welfare state is not only independent of state expenditure but also independent of the profit-making mindset that is a key motivation for many social-financial activities.

Waqf is an instrument that can function and benefit any society – whether Muslims or non-Muslims. The presence of some institutions such as trusts, irrespective of their origin, is evidence that waqf, as a concept, can function and flourish even under non-faith–based legislations and systems. The similarities between waqf and trust led to researchers believing that waqfs were the roots of trusts and from where they originated. However, others disagree with this opinion. The key issue here is the fact that efficient establishment and operation of the theory behind awqaf systems which is manifested in non-Muslim societies in the trust system has the potential to extend the aforementioned economic and societal benefits to non-Islamic societies. This unique model of the welfare state is not only independent of state expenditure but also independent of the profit-making mindset that is a key motivation for many social-financial activities.

Contemporary awqaf in key non-Muslim countries

Today, awqaf institutions operate across the globe under a variety of legal systems and in numerous forms. Many of the rigidities of awqaf have been amended to allow greater power for *mutawallis* (trustees of the waqf). This is to allow them to adapt the functions of awqaf to ensure their efficient functioning. Furthermore, the prevalence of the English legal system in post-colonial states across the Islamic world has led to the corporatisation of awqaf. This has allowed for their incorporation in legal terms as a corporate entity with juristic personality. The role of *mutawallis* is often analogous to that of a board of trustees, allowing for a much greater degree of operational flexibility which was lacking in the rigidity of the static perpetuity of *traditional* awqaf.

A brief review of the practice and performance of awqaf in a number of selected non-Muslim countries that have specific legislations to recognise and organise awqaf is undertaken. Through this undertaking, we can derive lessons and recommendations that can be applied in other non-Muslim countries with Muslim minorities that have no specific legislation for awqaf such as the UK. Whilst awqaf institutions operate across many non-Muslim countries, the following cases have been studied due to the size and significance of the *waqf* sectors and/or the innovativeness of their operation.

India, a non-Muslim country with one of the largest awqaf in the world

The Indian experience of waqf is unique. Although many parts of India were ruled by Muslims, India is currently a secular country, consisting of a multi-cultural and multi-religious population. Furthermore, it is classified as a non-Muslim country and, thus, it is interesting to study how the awqaf system is functioning there. The Islamic culture has a strong presence and visibility in India, due to the percentage of the population who are Muslim and their role in shaping the Indian history. Several researchers believe that awqaf in India go back to the 12th century CE and they flourished under the Delhi Sultanate (Mahru, 1965). Others, however, believe that the history of the awqaf system in India goes back to the early days of the Islamic presence in the subcontinent when Muslims took over al-Sind (Pakistan now) in the 8th century. One fact that stands out is their justification for this belief. They argue that it is impossible that Islam flourished in India between the 8th and 12th centuries without awqaf which was well established and commonly used to finance many social and educational activities within Muslim lands from the early days of Islam (Al-Nadawi, 2017). Hence, indicating that the awqaf in India went through different stages between flourishment and decline.

According to the Sachar Committee's influential 2006 report, which was commissioned by the Indian government to report the status of Muslims in India, there are approximately 500,000 registered awqaf with 600,000 acres of land in India, with a book value of ₹60 billion (roughly $1 billion). However, the market value of these properties is likely to be much higher. Current estimates suggest that the market value of awqaf lands in Delhi alone reached values in excess of $1 billion. However, the return on such properties is often very low estimated at around 2.7% (Government of India, 2006, p. 219).

S. Khalid Rashid, one of the key and early authors on waqf in India, believes that

> India can boast to be the country with the largest number of awqaf. The total has been estimated as exceeding 250,000. Indian Muslim Awqaf or Trusts are running 2,500 secular and technical schools, colleges, and orphanages and at least 60,000 madrasahs and 200,000mosques.
>
> (Rashid, 1978)

The Sachar report suggests that at current market valuations, waqf properties in India should be able to secure at least a minimum 10% return, yielding more than ₹1,200 billion ($18 billion) annually. The report highlights the immense potential for social development in the country which can be achieved through the revitalisation and efficient management and regulation of awqaf. A key point for Muslims in the West to be aware of is the fact that a major hindrance to the development and effective management of awqaf is the weakness of legal protections and the heavy reliance on federal governmental bodies for the management and regulation of awqaf. Such weakness and reliance have led to institutional neglect and incompetence. Various amendments to the 1965 Waqf Act have taken place over time. Finally, following consideration of the amendments proposed by the Muslim personal law committee, the 2013 Act was approved by the government (Islamic Fiqh Academy, 2014). One report that was presented as a conclusion of one of the large conferences about waqf in India and which was organised by the Islamic fiqh academy of India in 2014, along with many other reports and studies, confirmed that the misuse of awqaf in India was not limited to individuals. Rather, the misuse of awqaf went beyond that. It was found to be carried out by the government itself (Islamic Fiqh Academy, 2014). Numerous other reports, including Sachar, confirmed that there is an urgent need for improvement in the management standards for awqaf to ensure that the potential of such institutions is fully leveraged, stating "to put in place world class facilities such as universities and colleges, hospitals and health centres" (Government of India, 2006). It should be noted that the Indian government established the "Central Waqf Council" as a statutory body under the administrative control of the Ministry of Minority Affairs. The council was set up in 1964 as per the provision given in the Waqf Act, 1954. It acted as an advisory body to the Central Government on matters concerning the working of the Waqf Boards and the due administration of Awqaf (Government of India, 2019).

Singapore, a model for functioning awqaf in a non-Muslim country

It is noteworthy that increasingly in the last few years, Singapore has been mentioned at various international Islamic finance forums as a model for the development of waqf. However, again Singapore is a non-Muslim country with Muslims only accounting for 15% of its population (Department of Statistics Singapore, 2009). Despite their minority, Singapore still recognises Islam as an official component of the society. Majlis Ugama Islam Singapura (Muis), also known as the Islamic Religious Council of Singapore, was established as a statutory body in 1968 when the Administration of Muslim Law Act (AMLA) came into effect. Under AMLA, Muis is required to advise the President of Singapore on all matters relating to Islam in Singapore (Islamic Religious Council of Singapore, 2019).

Singapore's experience with the issuance of Sukuk, and more recently the *waqfIlmu* as a cash waqf, has been cited favourably by several nations (K & L Gates, 2019). The following information has been retrieved and summarised from the *Contemporary Waqf Administration and Development in Singapore: Challenges and Prospects*.

The Administration of Muslim Law Act (AMLA) in Singapore defines a waqf as "a permanent dedication by a Muslim of any movable or immovable property for any purpose recognised by the Muslim Law as pious, religious and charitable." With the creation of the Administration of Muslim Law Act (AMLA) in 1968, and in accordance with Section 58 of AMLA, all awqaf created are vested in Majlis Ugama Islam Singapura (MUIS). In 1968, only six awqaf were registered in MUIS. By 2000, all 100 awqaf in Singapore were registered under MUIS. This allowed for their possessing of a complete database of all awqaf properties, revenues, expenses and disbursement information. The effective and efficient management of waqf assets and properties by MUIS has enabled waqf revenue to increase significantly. The first commercial development of waqf started in 1990, wherein vacant land was transformed into four units of terrace residential housing. This led to the increasing of the revenue from rental income of $681 to almost $36,000 per annum.

The MUIS property department recruited professionals such as civil engineers, architects and quantity surveyor as part of their team, leading to the management of the portfolio professionally and a shortening of the turnaround time and quality of developments. The initial financing for the first project came from the General Endowment Fund managed by MUIS. Developed properties were sold on a leasehold basis for 99 years, and the proceeds from these sales were used for the building of mosques and further waqf commercial properties. The presence of underdeveloped awqaf, which had high asset values, but with limited cash reserves and liquidity led MUIS to issue *Musharakah* bonds to raise $60 million. Details of this arrangement are provided below:

> The project increased the revenue of the particular properties from an annual rental of $19,000 per annum in 1995 to an escalated gross income of $5.3 M in 2006. This equated to an 11.3% annual return on investment. For this innovation, MUIS was awarded the Sheikh Mohammad Bin Rashid Al Maktoum Islamic Finance Awards, 2006.MUIS has further

> created an "internal REITs" (Real Estate Investment Trust) instrument for its *Waqf* properties. The instrument allows individual waqf to own property through shareholding- "A pool of waqf properties now owned a piece of the property at 11 Beach Road in terms of shareholding. The net return from the yield of the particular building was then distributed to the various waqf in terms of the shareholding or investments contributed to the whole assets. There are 24 awqaf which have participated in this structure." The adoption of such a structure increased flexibility in disposing, exiting and liquidating the assets of the shareholders depending on the needs of the particular waqf.

Singapore also has a cash waqf system in the form of the Mosque Building Fund. One lac seventy-five thousand Muslim employees had contributed towards this fund through monthly deductions from their salaries. The deductions are then transferred by the employer to the CPF (Central Provident Fund) that acts as the collecting agent for the contributions. An estimated $6 million is collected annually from this collection. This fund has also enabled MUIS to build 22 mosques with an accumulated worth of $130 million. In conclusion, the Singapore experience of waqf is a rich experience for Muslims in non-Muslim countries to benefit from. However, the key distinguishing factor for this experience and also for the Indian experience is the government's recognition of this Islamic system – waqf. This recognition has allowed the provision of a legal framework through which it can operate safely.

Lessons for Muslim minorities

Having explored the historical and contemporary operation of awqaf, a number of key lessons can be drawn from the experiences. In particular, experiences relating to the development of waqf and its flourishment in non-Muslim countries. First, it should be noted that there is an ongoing debate between different researchers, thinkers, Muslim scholars and even non-Muslims concerning the reason behind the decline of waqf in the last two centuries. The researchers believe that such socio-political-economic and spiritual phenomena are far too complex to be analysed from one perspective alone. There is, undoubtedly, an array of factors behind the decline of waqf in Muslim and non-Muslim countries. Some of those factors are internal and some of them are external. However, Haitam Suleiman concluded that the decline of waqf "cannot be attributable to its foundational basis, nor to the legal doctrine but rather to factors unrelated to its legal theory" (Suleiman, 2016). Prof. Zaleha Kamarudin and Assoc. Prof. Sharifah Zubaidah Syed Abdul Kader summarised the key issues surrounding the application of waqf in India. These issues are also key problems facing other awqaf in other non-Muslim countries. These include:

1 Lack of serious effort to develop waqf properties.
2 Encroachment of waqf properties.

3 Waqf al-awlad being inadequately managed.
4 Absence of democratisation and decentralisation of waqf administration.
5 The problems that come with a redundant Central Waqf Council.
6 Issues arising from excessive government control.

(Kamarudin and Syed Abdul Kader, 2016)

They also highlighted several challenges that face the establishing and the development of waqf in non-Muslim countries.

First, socio-political constraints were indicated. Regarding these, key sub-challenges include islamophobia and associated stigmas, labelling the channelling of external funds as supporting terrorism, lack of diplomacy and political will to engage with Muslim countries. Second, legal constraints were recognised. These include constraints against the donations either coming to the waqf or coming out of the waqf. These constraints can either impact the country of the waqf or the other country, and they function as key legal challenges. Moreover, restrictions on the global nature of Islamic law and the absence of an international model waqf law with clarity on foreign or international waqf are also among the key challenges. Third, the requirements dictating the regulation of the waqf by Islamic law and the lack of recognition of Islamic law in the state laws of the non-Muslim countries is another key legal challenge. Finally, they also noted the existence of certain economic constraints, as waqf is likely to be treated as non-governmental organisations (NGOs) that are restricted in making profits (Kamarudin and Syed Abdul Kader, 2016).

Having mentioned these challenges, whilst also acknowledging that the waqf acts as a fundamental transformation tool for the socio-economic development of communities, it appears that despite such challenges, the Muslim minorities residing in non-Muslim nations have no choice but to revive the sunnah of waqf. Such a revival would secure this socio-economic transformation. To achieve this, their strategy must be multi-faceted. It must function at various levels, including the political, legal, social, educational and economical level. Most non-Muslim countries are secular democratic countries that have adequate levels of legislations to regulate charitable activities. This should provide Muslim minorities with enough legal ground to explore new creative and innovative ideas to establish awqaf within different legal frameworks.

Muslim minorities must also be active. It is only through such political involvement that they can influence decision makers, thereby ensuring they establish sufficient laws that either make way for the establishment of awqaf, or lead to the provision of alternative arrangements such as trusts. The use of private sector firms to provide professional management and investment solutions for awqaf can be beneficial in two ways. First, it can provide a transparent accounting system that alleviates the possible accusations of fraudulent activity and the financing of terrorism. Second, it further maximises the potential returns for awqaf assets, which can then increase the amount of charitable work undertaken. Constructing international organisations that cater for awqaf and campaign for it on different levels is a must in this hostile environment. Muslim leaders in the West or in non-Muslim countries should explore the idea of developing an international organisation that is only active in non-Muslim countries.

Furthermore, it might be wise to limit fund transfer between countries where waqf is practised and other countries. This also necessities the need for each country to have its own awqaf. Raising awareness of the philanthropic function of waqf among Muslims and non-Muslims plays a major role in providing a societal framework that will foster a positive atmosphere for the protection of waqf and its growth. Moreover, it is highly imperative that a solid understanding of waqf and the need for it are developed in the community. This would also include reference to the best means of governance and administration of waqf. Moreover, understanding should extend to sharia rulings concerning many of its details. The simultaneous development of standardised sharia guidelines on awqaf, the effective governance and administration, and an effective legal incorporation of a structure can, therefore, facilitate the growth of awqaf, allowing for better management of their assets. The Accounting and Auditing Organization for Islamic Financial Institutions (AAOIFI) is currently in the process of consultation on a draft standard for awqaf which hopes to clarify a consensus among scholars on technical issues regarding their operation. However, more work must be undertaken concerning the management and governance of awqaf in secular setups. Imams, preachers and scholars play a major role in raising the required awareness

Waqf and UK regulation

As Zaleha Kamarudin and Sharifah Zubaidah Syed Abdul Kader concluded, Muslims in non-Muslim countries have three options to establish awqaf.

1. By the formation of community-based waqf projects that operate within the existing conventional legal framework in such countries – be it in the form of a trust, a foundation, a limited company by guarantee of a NGO.
2. Through the semi-regulation of waqf by means of special laws that relate to regulating the personal law of Muslims in the country.
3. By the regulation of waqf by employing a national legislation on waqf, establishing a central waqf body and then forming state waqf boards at the state level.[5]

As is the case in a few non-Muslim countries, waqf in the UK is similar to an English trust (Marwah and Bolz, 2009) and some awqaf run as normal charities.

> From the socio-economic perspectives of these two institutions, waqf and trusts played similar, if not identical roles. They provided the means and the mechanism for permanent charities. The institutions of waqf

and trusts served a plethora of social and charitable objectives including funding infrastructure.[6]

Under both systems, property is held, and the usufruct is derived for the benefits of specific individuals (English trusts) or for a general charitable purpose (both). The charity commission in the UK is the body that regulates the work of such trusts, hence providing it with a certain degree of legal protection (Islamic Relief Academy, 2015).

Major differences between the two systems do exist. One such example regarding English trusts concerns the position of the trustee who is considered to be the owner of the trust. Under an Islamic waqf, the trustee (mutawalli) is not considered to be the owner. The trustee is no more the owner of a trust than the mutawalli could be the owner of a waqf. The main function of both is to administer the property for the benefit of another entity, specifically the beneficiaries as stipulated by the trust or waqf, and not for themselves. Another cited difference pertains to perpetuity, which is a mandatory feature of a waqf. A trust, however, cannot be perpetual – with the exception of a charitable trust. Additionally, another difference arises from the superiority of the system being employed over inheritance laws. Under English law, the trust will supersede inheritance obligations, whereas under Islamic law, the rules of inheritance must be honoured first (Cizakca, 2000). However, English trust law does provide a workable basis for operating a waqf in the UK, if the correct legal clauses are incorporated.

Towards reviving the practice of waqf, the model of the National Waqf Fund (NWF) in the UK

Muslims are the most charitable community in the UK, donating over £100 million during Ramadhan alone (2017 est.) (ITV, 2018). Muslims have been known to be more likely to donate to individual projects and international disaster relief campaigns rather than to the specific charities that deliver them. This has been exemplified by the rise of charitable fundraising platforms, which aren't charities themselves, but that connect fundraisers of specific causes with potential donors. An example of such a platform is Muslim Giving, which raised £1.5 million in its first year alone (UK Fundraising, 2019). This may be an alternative form of the Just Giving platform which has raised $2 billion in the last four years. This clearly demonstrates the size of the opportunity. Building on from the altruistic nature of the Muslim community in being charitable, the next step is to develop a strategic outlook. There is no better strategic approach in making sadaqah as a socio-economic transformation tool than through waqf.

The National Waqf Fund (NWF) was born from realising that in the next 30 years the Muslim population will approximately make up 10% of the UK population. Measures need to be put in place today to ensure that the evolving needs of the Muslim community as a whole are met. In the UK, there are a few organisations that aim to revive the Islamic practice of the awqaf. Yet, they vary in terms of aims, size and governance. They are either regionally specific, or for a specific cause. Examples include the following Sunni organisations: the International Waqf Foundation, the Swansea Mosque and Islamic Community Centre, the waqf by Islamic relief, the Europe Trust, Penny Appeal and the Waqf Fund formed by the East London Mosque. NWF aims to be an exemplary model for waqf management and utilisation not only in the UK but also in other European non-Muslim countries that serve as a socio-economic transformation tools for European Muslims. Taking the historic operation of waqf as the model, NWF seeks to create an operational revenue stream for Muslim charitable causes through the establishment and efficient investment of individuals' and institutions' donated asset pool. The key features of NWF are as follows:

- Provisioning of funds – NWF will be established as a charitable trust to act as a source for funds for Muslim charitable organisations.
- Creating an investment fund that will acquire "waqfable" assets (those that fulfil the criteria of waqf). These would be assets which ownership is transferred into the waqf structure so that income that is derived from those assets can be distributed to relevant causes.
- Adopting a flexible, dynamic, modern yet sharia-based approach in terms of the nature of waqf. Thus, it would be accepting new forms of non-classical and physical assets such as cash and e-assists, temporary waqf, the running of the waqf, developing it and distributing its income.
- Raising funds for direct investment and to receive existing assets.
- Providing an effective avenue for all Muslims irrespective of their financial situation to establish a sadaqah jariyahon on behalf of themselves, their parents and other people whom they want to donate on their behalf.
- Leveraging technology in the fintech space that ensures efficiency and regulatory requirements are met.

A prospective analysis was carried out illustrating the situation of NWF had it been set up 20 years ago, and a modest £1 million was fundraised and invested on an annual basis. In such a situation, the UK Muslim Community today would be benefitting from:

Assets value: £32,892,664
Charitable income raised: £12,448,074
Properties in trust: 145

At the time of writing this chapter, NWF is in the process of launching, by taking a hybrid approach to fundraising and the deployment of income. Patient capital, as the name belies, requires a long period for pay off for monies invested, with a waqf. This is not an issue of concern, since the aim is long-term income derivation to support causes. The challenge will be scaling the process upwards to meet operational expenses. Typically, a good real estate investment in the UK nets around 5% return which would mean significant sums invested initially to meet modest operating expenses. NWF will tackle this by keeping a fund for development and resale that nets approximately 20% return, to meet its operating expenses. This fund will recycle the investment until the main fund has grown to a size that its ongoing income can cover the operating expenses of running the waqf and is below 10% of the entire income generated of the fund. More than a fund for strategic charity giving, the creation of NWF allows the Muslim community in the UK to operate as a collective. This will allow the cross-representation of communities, thereby unifying them on a common ground in the absence of an overarching Islamic regulatory framework.

Notes

1 There are many definition of waqf. It takes us beyond the remit of this research to study them analytically. Some of them can be seen in the following primary sources: Fath Al-Qadeer 5/37, Hashiuatnaibnabdeen 2/391, Al-Hattabmawahib Al-Jalil 6/81, Al-Dardir, Al-Sharh Al-Kabir 4/76, Al-Nawawi Al-Majmu 16/225, Al-Sherbinimughni Al-Muhtaj 2/376, Ibn Qudamah Al-Mugni 5/597, Al-Bahuti Al-Rawdh Al-Murbi 5/531.

See also Al-Fiqh Al-Islamiwaadillatuh Dr Wahba A-Zuhaili, Damascus, Dar Al-Fikr 8/155.

2 This story is mainly reported in Ibn Sad Al-Tabaqaa (1/246) Beirut. Hammad Ibn Ishaaqu Al-Bagdadi, Tarikat Al-Nabisallaallahualihiwasallam read by Drakram Al-Umari E-Copy. See also Abu Bakr Al-Khassaf, Ahkam Al-Waqf, Bulag Egypt P 2–3.

3 Al-Sherbini, Mughni Al-Muhtaj Fi Adillat Al-Minhaj 2/485 (Beirut, Lebanon).

4 See Ganim Al-Bayyumi and others.

5 Such as the Waqf by Islamic Relief and Penny Appeal.

6 Mohammad Abdullah.

References

Al-Martan (2011). Zakat and Waqf Are among the Pillar of Islamic Economy and Their Implementation Ends Poverty and Social Injustice. Interviewed 4th April 2011. Available at: http://www.aleqt.com/2011/04/04/article_522909.html (Accessed: 1 September 2019).

Al-Nadawi, SH (2017). *Al-awqaf Al-Madaniyah Fi Wilayat Delhi: Tarikh'ha, Wa-Idaratha, Wa'Wad'aaha Al-hali.* [Online]. Year 2, (1). Available at: https://www.aqlamalhind.com/?p=468 (Accessed: 3 September 2019).

Al-Nawawi, Y (2018). The 40 Hadith of Imam al-Nawawi. Independent Publisher.

Al-Sherbini and Al-Muhtaj, M. *Fi Adilat Al-Minhaj.* 2(485). Beirut.

Al-Tarabulsi (1902). Al-Isaaf Fi ahkamAlawkaf. Egypt.

Budiman, M and Kusuma, D (2011). The Economic Significance of Waqf: A Macro Perspective. [Online] 8th International Conference on Tawhidi Methodology Applied to Microenterprise Development, January 2011. Available at SSRN: https://ssrn.com/abstract=1844606 (Accessed: 6 September 2019).

BusinessDictionary (2019). *Public Good.* Web Finance Inc. [Online]. Available at: http://www.businessdictionary.com/definition/public-good.html (Accessed:????)

Çizakça, M (1998). Awqaf in History and its Implications for Modern Islamic Economies. *Islamic Economic Studies.* [Online]. 6(1).

Cizakca, M (2000). *A History of Philanthropic Foundations: The Islamic World from the Seventh Century to the Present.* Turkey: Bogazici University.

Department of Statistics Singapore (2009). Wayback Machine. Available at: https://web.archive.org/web/20110124160522/http://www.singstat.gov.sg/news/news/press12012011.pdf (Accessed: 20 September 2019).

Gaudiosi, MM (1988). The Influence of the Islamic Law of Waqf on the Development of the Trust in England: The Case of Merton College. *University of Pennsylvania Law Review,* [Online]. 136(4). Available at: https://scholarship.law.upenn.edu/cgi/viewcontent.cgi?article=3909&context=penn_law_review (Accessed:???).

Government of India (2006). *Social, Economic and Educational Status of the Muslim Community of India – A Report, 2006.* Available at: http://www.minorityaffairs.gov.in/sites/default/files/sachar_comm.pdf (Accessed:???).

Government of India (2019).Central Waqf Council. Ministry of Minority Affairs. Available at: http://centralwaqfcouncil.gov.in/content/introduction (Accessed:???).

Hodgson, M (1977). *The Venture of Islam, Volume 2: The Expansion of Islam in the in the Middle Periods.* Vol. 2. Chicago: University of Chicago Press.

Kahf, M (2015). Waqf: A Quick Overview. [Online] Available at: http://monzer.kahf.com/papers/english/WAQF_A_QUICK_OVERVIEW.pdf (Accessed:???).

KURAN, T (2001). The Provision of Public Goods under Islamic Law: Origins, Contributions, and Limitation of the Waqf System, Law and Society Review, Vol. 35. USC CLEO Research Paper No.C01–13. Available at: SSRN: https://ssrn.com/abstract=276378 (Accessed:????).

Ibn Al-Hajjaj, M (2000a). Sahih Muslim-Book of Bequests. 13. London: Darussalam.

Ibn Al-Hajjaj, M (2000b). Sahih Muslim-Book of Prayers. 3. London: Darussalam.

Ibn Battutah (2003). The Travels of Ibn Battutah in Mackintosh-Smith, T. (ed.). UK: Picador Publishing.

Ibn Qudamah (2013). “Al-Mughni”. Dar ‘Alam al Kutub.

International Islamic University of Malaysia (2009). Can the Waqf System Be Considered Equivalent to the Role of Civil Society in the Arab World? Available at: https://drive.uqu.edu.sa/_/cjsr/files/%20مكتبة%20الأوقاف%20يوازي%20نظام %20الوقف%20دور%20المجتمعدور%20المدني%20في%20الوطن%20العربي.pdf (Accessed: 3 September 2019).

Islamic Fiqh Academy (2014). Seminar on “Awqaf in India” Report of India Report. Available at: http://ifa-india.org/arabic.php?do=home&pageid=awqaf_seminar_arabic (Accessed: 5 September 2019).

Islamic Relief Academy (2015). Comparing the Effectiveness of Waqf and the English Charitable Trusts. Available at: http://library.iracademy.org.uk/comparing-the-effectiveness-of-waqf-and-english-charitable-trusts-2/ (Accessed:??).

Islamic Religious Council of Singapore (2019). Majlis Ugama Islam Singapura (Muis). Available at: https://www.muis.gov.sg/About-MUIS/History (Accessed:???).

ITV (2018).Revealing the Generosity of the UK’s Muslim Community during Ramadan. Available at: https://www.itv.com/news/2018-05-16/ramadan-the-holiest-month-of-fasting-that-reveals-the-incredible-generosity-of-the-uks-muslim-community/ (Accessed:???).

K & L Gates (2019). K & L Gates Straits Law. Available at: https://www.klgates.com/singapore-singapore/ (Accessed:???).

Kamarudin, Z and Syed Abdul Kader, SZ (2016). External Constraints for Awqaf in Non-Muslim Countries. *5th Awqaf Magazine Conference*. Sydney: Islamic Markets. Available at: https://islamicmarkets.com/publications/external-constraints-for-awqaf-in-non-muslim-countries (Accessed:???).

Mahru, AD (1965). *Insha-i Mahru, Lahore, 1965*. Lahore: Shaikh Abdur Rashid (ed.). pp. 37–39.

Marwa, H and Bolz, AAK (2009). Waqfs and Trusts: A Comparative Study. *Trusts & Trustees*, [Online] 15(10), pp. 811–816. Available at: https://academic.oup.com/tandt/article-abstract/15/10/811/1659738?redirectedFrom=fulltext (Accessed: 6 September 2019).

Nor, NM (2019).*Critical Evaluation of Waqf Contribution to Socio-Economic Development: A Comparative Work on Waqf and Foundations*. [Online] Available at: https://www.academia.edu/7063294/Review_Article_-_Critical_Evaluation_of_Waqf_Contribution_to_Socio-Economic_Development_A_Comparative_Work_on_Waqf_and_Foundations. (Accessed: 4 October 2019).

Organization for Economic Cooperation and Development (2016). Social Expenditure Update 2016: Social Spending Stays at Historically High Levels in Many Countries. Paris: OECD Publishing.

Organization for Economic Cooperation and Development (2017). Government at a Glance 2017: General Government Gross Debt. Paris: OECD Publishing.

Rashid, K (1978). *Wakf Administration in India: A Socio-legal Study*. India: Vikas Publishing House.

Suleiman, H (2016). The Islamic Trust Waqf: A Stagnant or Reviving Legal Institution? *The Electronic Journal of the Islamic and Middle Eastern Law*, [Online]. 4, pp. 27–43. Available at: https://www.zora.uzh.ch/id/eprint/123754/1/Suleiman_Haitam_Waqf_Published.pdf (Accessed:???).

The World Bank Group & INCEIF & ISRA (2019). The World Bank Group, INCEIF and ISRA Report on: Maximizing Social Impact through Waqf Solutions. Malaysia: The World Bank Group & INCEIF & ISRA Publishers. Available at: http://documents.worldbank.org/curated/en/930461562218730622/pdf/Maximizing-Social-Impact-Through-Waqf-Solutions.pdf (Accessed: 1 September 2019).

UK Fundraising (2019). Muslim Giving Raises £1.5m in Its First Year. Available at: https://fundraising.co.uk/2019/04/03/muslimgiving-raises-1-5m-in-its-first-year/#.XcB4oS2cbEY (Accessed: ???).

YediYildiz, B (1996). Place of the Waqf in Turkish Cultural System [Online]. Available at: http://yunus.hacettepe.edu.tr/~yyildiz/placeofthewaqf.htm (Accessed: 3 October 2019).

Part II

Awqaf

Its law and policies

8 Gender justice in the law of awqaf

Syed Khalid Rashid

Introduction

Those who have close minds and no knowledge are happy in their fallacious assumption that Muslim women have no property rights. They consider them as the most deprived and miserable beings on the face of this earth. This false notion prospered because of the lack of knowledge of Western languages (English, German and French) among Muslim *ulema*, as it was in these languages that the disparaging remarks were made. It is only now that Muslim response is getting audible. But the earliest note of dissent was sounded by Syed Ameer Ali in his book, who explained, among other things, the status of Muslim women. His credential to write on the subject was beyond any doubt. As a judge of the Privy Council and the author of the famous book on Islamic law in two volumes,[3] he was eminently qualified to write on the subject. In an assertive manner he wrote in *Spirit of Islam*:[4]

> The improvement effected in the position of women by the Prophet of Arabia has been acknowledged by all unprejudiced writers, though it is still the fashion with bigoted controversialists to say the Islamic system lowered the status of women. No falser calumny has been levelled at the Prophet.[5]

He went on to say:

> But the Teacher (Prophet), who in an age when no country, no system, no community gave any right to women, maiden or married, mother or wife, who, in a country where the birth of a daughter was considered a calamity, secured to the sex rights which are only un-willingly and under pressure being conceded to them by the civilised nations in the twentieth century, deserves the gratitude of humanity. If Muhammed had done nothing more, his claim to be a benefactor of mankind would have been undisputable.[6]

Ownership and gender

In Islamic law, both male and female owners are governed by the same legal rules. Both are regarded as trustees, as real ownership of everything in this world and universe belongs to Allah. The Quran addresses everyone "to spend of that whereof (Allah) has made you trustees (*mustakhlafin*)" [*Surah Al-Hadid* (57), ayat 7]. A Muslim male and female may deal with his or her property in any manner which is allowed under *Shariah*. She or her may thus sell, lease, mortgage, exchange, gift or bequeath the property, and do whatsoever she or her is permitted to do under Islamic commercial, contractual and inheritance laws. Her vast powers cover matters of *waqf*: from creation to administration and appropriation (as will be seen in detail in coming pages). It is proposed to study the subject "women and *waqf*" under two parts: Part I is to deal with such provisions of the law of *waqf* which establish the status of women as the creator of *waqf*, as beneficiary and as *waqf* administrator. Part II to look into certain actual cases, both historical and contemporary, where women created *awqaf*, had been beneficiaries and administrators.

Rights of Muslim woman in the law of *waqf*

She may create a waqf

Islamic law allows any woman, Muslim, non-Muslim or even an apostate, to create a *waqf*. What is required is that she must be the owner of the property being endowed as *waqf*, and she should be *aqil*, *baligh* and *hurr* (i.e. sane, adult and free). A *waqf* cannot be created by a minor or guardian acting on behalf of a mirror. If created, such a waqf would be void.[7] Similarly, void would be the *waqf* which is made by a woman who is suffering from *mard al maut (*death, illness), unless it is for a religious or charitable object; then it is allowed to a maximum of one-third of the settlor's property.[8] A non-Muslim female (and also *dhimmi*) is allowed to create a *waqf*. Hanafis, however, require such a *waqf* to be lawful according to the religion of dedicator as well as *shariah*.[9] Shafiis and Hanbalis require *shariah* compatibility as sole criterion.[10] Malik is taken into account the religion of the founder, but without allowing creation of a *waqf* in favour of a mosque.[11] Apostasy of male Muslim renders void a validly created *waqf*, but not so in the case of the apostasy of a woman. This is based on the rule which exempts her from being slain on apostasy.[12]

Pardanashin ladies may revoke the waqf they create – a special privilege

In the Indo-Pakistan sub-continent and probably elsewhere also where similar situation may exist, it is possible to apply for judicial annulment of a *waqf* created by a lady (whether Muslim or non-Muslim) who is adult, same and solvent but who is *pardanashin*, that is

> ...unable to read and write and generally ignorant, as most of her class ... (who) swears positively that she did not understand the meaning of the deed which she executed (can revoke the *waqf* she created) ... it is, moreover, hardly likely that she had known what was the real effect of making a *waqf*.[13]

However, this rule was not followed in a case decided by the Bombay High Court which refused to validate the revocation of a waqf created by a lady who claimed to be Pardanashin[14] but failed to convince the court of her naivety. In principle, the court may allow the revocation of a waqf executed by a Pardanashin lady on the ground that the true import of the waqf – deed – was not brought home to the lady's mind.[15] Thus, each case has to be considered on its own merit. This rule, however, does not extend to Muslim males.

She decides the objects of a waqf she creates

A Muslim woman enjoys the discretion to name the object of the *waqf* she creates. She may even omit to specify an object, without compromising the validity of *waqf*, which will be presumed to be for the poor, as they are the ultimate beneficiaries of every *waqf*.[16] The doctrine of *cy pres* is inbuilt in the Islamic law, and unlike Common law, there is no need to establish the "width of charitable intent" in the case of "initial failure". The concept of charity in Islam is so wide and all-embracing that it treats even such objects as charitable which Common law regards as non-charitable (e.g. giving to one's own children). In Islamic law, if the specific object of a *waqf* fails or becomes extinct, the *waqf* is presumed to be for the poor. All Muslim jurists are in agreement on this, except some of the Hanbali jurists who allow the benefit to go to the relatives of the founder (*waqif*). Another group of the Hanbalis say, it shall go to *bait ul mal* (state treasury).[17] A woman dedicator (*waqifa*) may make a dedication in favour of her own family, or for her own benefit during her life (only under Hanafi law), or for some specified individuals, or for any religious or charitable object. Under Shia law also, a dedicator cannot be a beneficiary.[18] If some of the objects named by a woman dedicator are valid and others invalid, then waqf takes effect to the extent of valid object, provided separation of valid and invalid is possible.[19] It is lawful for the *waqifa* (woman dedicator) to authorise the *mutawalli* (supervisor) to name the object.[20] A *waqf* in favour of the tomb of the saint is valid.[21]

She may appoint mutawalli and lay down the administrative structure of the waqf

A woman may be appointed a *mutawalli*, even if she is a non-Muslim. It is because Islamic law does not put any restriction on the basis of sex or religion in appointing a *mutawalli*. A woman founder of a waqf may appoint herself as the *mutawalli* of the *waqf* she creates. However, where the duties attaching with the office are religious in nature, like leading the congregational prayers, a woman cannot act as a *mutawalli*. A minor girl may be appointed as a *mutawalli*, but she would only be allowed to start acting as such after attaining majority. In Islamic law, the power of appointing a *mutawalli* primarily rests with the *waqif* (dedicator), male or female. If he or she dies without appointing anyone, this power is inherited by the executor, on whose failure or absence, the court is empowered to make the appointment.[22] In a Court judgement it was held in 1868 that where a woman is appointed a *mutawalli*, "She will not be required to do more than her sex permits; and she is entitled to discharge the duties to which she cannot personally attend by deputy or proxy".[23] According to Ameer Ali, "Secretariat or religious differences form no disqualification and accordingly the fact that a person (including a woman) is a *Shiah* does not disqualify him (or her) for the superintendence of a *waqf* made by a Sunni. So long as a person can discharge the duties of the trust personally or through ad deputy, he or she is qualified to hold the office of *towliat* (administration).[24] A *waqifa* (lady founder) may reserve the right of governance of the *waqf* she is creating to herself, or appoint someone as *mutawalli*. She may reserve the right to dismiss the *mutawalli*. But in the absence of such a reservation, only court may order removal.[25] However, Abu Yusuf allows such removal irrespective of the fact whether or not such reservation has been made.[26] A *mutawalli* of a public *waqf* is open to public scrutiny. If found guilty of maladministration or malversation, the court may remove her or him. The court requires solid proof, not mere accusation.[27] A mutawalli cannot discharge herself without seeking court's approval. Similarly, in compliance of the rule – delegatus non potest delegare – a *mutawalli* cannot transfer her title to another person.[28]

Powers of a mutawalli woman

Powers of a *mutawalli*, including a woman *mutawalli*, are confined to fulfilling the objects of *waqf* and to keep the *waqf* property in good repair and to manage it prudently as a person of ordinary prudence and not as an investment wizard or management expert. She cannot undertake any grand scheme of improvement, expansion or beautification without court's approval. The maximum period for which a *mutawalli* may grant lease is three years in case of agricultural land and one year in case of non-agricultural land. A lease for a period in excess of this needs court's approval. Contracting debt is another matter where court's prior permission is needed, so also in case of sale, mortgage or exchange of *waqf* property. Any unauthorised action of a *mutawalli* in any of the above cases will make her or him personally liable for any loss.[29] Remuneration of a *mutawalli* is whatever is reasonable or customary in a given situation. It is up to the *waqif* to fix it. However, where is too low or too high, it may be increased or decreased by the court on the application of the *mutawalli* or the beneficiaries, as the case may be.[30] If in order to lessen the burden of her work, a *mutawalli* appoints a helper, his salary cannot be paid out of *waqf* fund unless allowed by the *waqif* or the court.[31] According to some Maliki jurists, in the absence of any indication about *mutawalli's* remuneration, it should be paid out of *bait ul mal* (state treasury) as it is state's responsibility to administer *awqaf.*[32]

A few historical and contemporary evidence of women as dedicators, beneficiaries and administrators of *awqaf*

Woman as founder of waqf

It is a subject which is still to be studied in depth. In historical records, sometimes scanty sketches appear of Muslim women who excelled in their philanthropic pursuits. One of the earliest descriptions of such a woman is that of Siti el-Sham bint Ayub Ibn Shadi (died 614 AH). She created a *waqf* for the benefit of two schools in Damascus: Al-Barraniyya and Al-Juwaniyya.[33] Property rights conferred on women by Shariah consist of right over dower (*mahr*), right to do whatever an owner is entitled to do with the property (sale, mortgage, lease, gift, exchange, will) and right to inherit. Right to endow her property as waqf comes within these rights. Women in Mamluk Egypt had considerable access to property and wealth. As wife, daughter, mother and some close relation of nobles and prominent persons, they possessed enough means to fulfil their philanthropic urges. As historical records show, they indeed fulfilled their urges well,[34] and created hundreds of *awqaf.* Muslim women founders of *awqaf* came from a wide variety of social backgrounds, but mostly they belonged to the upper layer of society. Only about 10% were from the lower class strata. In Ottoman Empire, generally, 20%–50% of the total number of *awqaf* were created by women. For example, in Istanbul of the 16th century, 37% of the *awqaf* were founded by the women.[35] Some of the researchers explain this phenomenon by suggesting that:

> ... women endowed waqfs in order to protect their property and income it produced from encroachment by their own close relatives. The endowed property produced income they could enjoy during their lifetime and dispose of as they preferred. In the sixteenth century some kind of tradition related to women waqfs became widespread in the Ottoman Empire. Namely, women endowed money for salaries of imams, muezzins and other mosque employees... In that way they provided some funding for an already existing mosque... Thus, women seem to have given precedence to religious needs over material things (like building a school, or a house or a shop).[36]

According to Mary Fay, who researched on *awqaf* in Egypt during the 19th-century Ottoman period:

> The Ministry of (of Awqaf) index lists 496 waqfs founded in the 18th century. The number of male donors of waqfs was 393, and the number

> of female donors was 126, which means that women made up to 25 percent of the total number of donors whose waqfiyyat can be found in the ministry's daftarkhana. (out of 126 awqaf), ninety seven were established by women individually, seven by seven women with other women, sixteen by women with husbands or male relatives, and six buy women with unrelated men (e.g. Guardian, freed slave).[37]

A study of Muslim women awqaf in Ayyubid Damascus, Syria shows that 26% of the 160 *awqaf* were created by women.[38] Recently, Kuwait *Awqaf* Public Foundation collected the total number of *awqaf* registered with it in order to ascertain the gender of the dedicators. The total number of *awqaf* dedicators came to 549, which after deducting the number of companies, corporations and anonymous donors in whose cases, naturally, it was not possible to assign any gender, the total dwindled down to 481, out of which 256 were found to be endowed by men and 225, that is 47%, were by women.[39] Looking at the type of *awqaf* created by women, it was found that women predominantly preferred to create charitable *waqf*, followed by *waqfthurri*, *mushtarik* (combined) and mosque, in this order. Table 8.1 provides the percentage of each category.[40]

A closer look at the objects of *awqaf* created by Kuwait Muslim women shows that they placed emphasis on (i) feeding of poor, (ii) *iftar* (food for breaking of fast) during Ramadhan, (iii) manumission of slaves, (iv) care of disabled, (v) student scholarships, (vi) building of mosques, (vii) furnishings of mosques, (viii) salary of imams and other mosque officials, (ix) recitation of the Quran and (x) *sabeel* (free water).[41] The whole of Islamic history is full of instances where *awqaf* were created by women.

> Women were donors of waqfs has already been established by scholars such as Muhammad Amin, who has studied the period 853 AD to the end of the Mamluk Sultanate; by Fanny Davis, Ulka Bates, Gabriel Baer, and others who have studied Turkish women during the Ottoman period; and by Muhammad Afifi, who has studied Egyptian women, also during the Ottoman period. The waqf has also been studied as an institution and as an instrument for social welfare.[42]

Historically, women had more autonomy and power because generally power was created in households rather than in the State. They derived their status

Table 8.1 Women awqaf in Kuwait

Type of waqf	*Female waqf*	*Percentage (%)*
Charitable	180	80
Thurri	20	8.89
Mushtarik (combined)	15	6.22
Mosques	11	4.89
Total	225	100

and wealth from their membership in a Mamluk household and relationship to a Mamluk grandee. This was and still is true even in other Muslim societies as well.[43] Coming to specific cases of individual *awqaf* created by women, it may suffice to give, by way of random sampling, half a dozen or so cases out of hundreds of such *awqaf* scattered throughout the Islamic world and history.

i The *waqf* of Zaynab Khatun – one of the largest dedicated by an elite woman in the 18th-century Egypt, Zaynab, the freed slave of the late Amir Ismail Bey al-Kabir al-Gazdughli – endowed considerable property, including three wakalas, one of them in Khatt Ghuriya; a courtyard (*hawsh*); a *makan* in Khatt al Nasriyya; a workshop for the making and selling of bread; a share (*hissa*) valued at one-quarter in a shop in Khatt al-Ghuriyya; a coffeehouse in Khatt al-Dawdiyya; and three makans and two shops in Khatt Qawsunt. It should be noted that the makans she owned were in two of the most prestigious neighbourhoods in Cairo-Qawsun on the east bank of the Birkat al-Fil, which was inhabited only by beys, and al-Nasriyya, a neighbourhood of Kashifs west of the *Khalij* (canal*) al-misri*.[44]

ii We are told about two women in Cairo: Salha Khatun binti Salim Agha Ikhtiyar Ta'ifat *Jawishan Sabiqan* and al-Sitt 'Aisha Hanim, daughter of the Amir Radwan Agha of the *Ta'ifat Gamaliyyah*. Salha endowed two shops and a storehouse (hasil) in *KhattBayn al-Qasrayn*, a shop in *Khatt al-Shawayyim*, coffeehouse (baytqahwa) and two shops in Bab al-Kharq, another shop in *al-Rab al-Zahari* and another in Bab Zuwayla; while al-Sitt 'Aisha endowed all of a *wakala* in Bulaq, water wheels, a baking oven (furn), a mill (tahun) and unspecified number of *makans*.[45]

iii The *waqf* created by Shawikaz Qadin in Mamluk times was recorded in a 56-page document, each page of which was painted in enamel paint, and the edges of each page were decorated in liquid gold. This *waqf* was huge as it consisted of substantial holdings in urban commercial real estate comprising of two houses, agricultural lands, a number of rental units and shops and shares in *wakala*.[46]

iv One finds numerous accounts of women endowing charitable *awqaf* in Ottoman Damascus. The *waqf* created by Hafiza Khanum al-murahli was for the benefit of five mosques and one religious school in Damascus.[47]

v Women in 16th-century Ottoman Krusevac (Bosnia) owned agricultural lands, which they could sell or endow. The *waqf* of Gale Hatun, wife of HaciHayruddin, consisted of a sum of 2,000 akçes meant for giving loans in *Shariah*-compliant manner and a shop which was to be rented out for 60 akçes for the salary of the *mutawalli*. In addition, she endowed the mosque with arable land and pastures located between the villages of Donje Stopange, Vinarce and Bobiste.[48]

vi Shah Jahan Begum of Bhopal (India) (1868–1901) commissioned the building of a mosque in 1889 in Woking, England and made it a *waqf*. She made sizable donations towards its building and maintenance.

The mosque is located 30 miles southwest of London and was one of the first mosque that was built in Western Europe.

Begum of Bhopal also started building a mosque, known as Tajul Masajid, at Bhopal, the biggest in the Indo-Pakistan sub-continent, but she died before its completion. In the 1970s, it was completed with public donations.[49]

vii In 1420 AH (1999), Haya Abdul Rahman Al-Habib of Kuwait made *waqf* of her building located in Hawalli and dedicated it to provide food to the poor's fasting during the month of Ramadan. The feeding was to be done in the mosque of Haya Abdul Rahman al Habib itself.[50]

viii Princess Fatima binti Ismail of Egypt was foremost among women who spent generously on charitable projects. Major portion of the proceeds of *awqaf* created by her were earmarked to support education in the seat of Ottoman Caliphate. She also helped in establishing the Egyptian University (now the University of Cairo). She made *waqf* of 661 acres of land in Daqahlia governorate for the university. The income from this land forms a big percentage of the income of the university. She offered her own palace to the university.[51]

Women as beneficiaries of awqaf

It is interesting to enquire into the categories of women who benefitted from *awqaf*. These included freed slaves, orphans, children, young unmarried girls, girls who were to be married, widows, women in exile, poor women and women who inherit less or nothing due to some inheritance rules.[52] On the basis of historical records, it is possible to identify the following categories of women beneficiaries:

(i) children, (ii) freed slave women, (iii) wives, (iv) widow, (v) orphans, (vi) women living in exile or refugees, (vii) unmarried young girls, (viii) women or girls married for the bribes and their dowry, (ix) women who inherited less due to inheritance rules, (x) adopted orphans, (xi) orphaned grandchild, (xii) widowed granddaughter, (xiii) *waqifah* herself in Hanafi law, (xiv) dedicator's family and (xv) any other women of dedicator's choice.[53]

Woman as mutawalli

As *nazira* of a *waqf*, either created by herself or someone else, a woman commands considerable power under the law of *waqf*. In this capacity, she has a formal legal relationship with the court and the officials dealing with *waqf* administration grant approval regarding matters concerning *waqf* under her charge, including lease and exchange, repair and upkeep.

Historical records of Mamluk Egypt show the efficacy of women administrators of *awqafwakala* of considerable complexity. Egypt of that time served as an entry point in the international transit trade in which *wakala* served a pivotal role. *Wakala* covered warehouse, retail sales and housing of traders. On the ground floor was the warehouse (*hawasil*), where goods were stored before distribution inside the country and exploitation outside of Egypt, and shops (*hawasil*) for retail sales or even artisanal workshops. On the upper floors were the residential units (*tabaqat or oda*), which were rented to merchants and looked out over the interior courtyard. The value of a *wakala* depended on its size and location. The price of a *wakala* could surpass a million paras, a sum that exceeded by far the value of any other economic investment in Cairo at this time.[54]

> As their waqifiyat demonstrate, elite women not only owned (and endowed) the most lucrative investment property of the period, they also, as owners 9and naziras) had to manage investments of considerable complexity. The various units which made up a wakala were rented out to the merchants, shopkeepers, and various units which made up a wakala were rented out to the merchants, shopkeepers, and artisans who used the various spaces in the building. If the owner of the wakala also owned the rab on top, she had to manage these units, which were usually rented to merchants on a monthly basis. Of the 11 women who invested in wakala, 5 endowed the entire wakala while 6 endowed shares in the wakalas.[55]

An example of a woman *mutawalli* (or *nazira*) administering extensive properties spread over several countries (India, Saudi Arabia, the UK) is that of an Indian lady – Saba, the elder daughter of Mansur Ali Khan Pataudi. In 2011 after the death of her father, she became the first woman *mutawalli* of the waqf properties known as *Awqaf-e-Shahi* (Royal *Awqaf*), created in the past by Sultan Jehan Begum, ruler of Bhopal, a princely state in India. The *waqf* is worth ₹ 300 crores (US$60 million). The waqf consists of numerous properties including the massive mosque – Tajul Masajid – in Bhopal and rubats in Makkah and Medina. Her position has been confirmed by the Madhya Pradesh *Waqf* Board.[56] Sometimes, because of the heavy workload, women *mutawalli* (*nazira*) had male assistants working with them to administer larger *awqaf*. Sometimes, depending on the wishes of the *waqifah*, a freed slave girl was appointed *mutawalli*.[57] Sitti Fayzadah Qadinbinti Abdullah al-Baydah, Aisya Khatunbinti Abdullah al-Baydah and Sitti Zafaran Khatunbinti Abdullah al-Habashiya belonged to this class of fortunate freed slave women.[58]

The normal and routine duty of a Kuwaiti woman *mutawalli* consisted of collection of rent, maintenance of *waqf* property and fulfilling the wishes of the waqif. Such a Kuwaiti woman mutawalli was Fatima binti Ghanim al-Hurais, who endowed her house and earmarked its income for feeding the poor. She remained the *mutawalli* of her *waqf* throughout her life, and after her death, her daughter, Nahyabinti Nasser al-Khurais, became the *mutawalli*.[59] In a description of the working method of the *waqf* administrators of the Imperial soup kitchen in Jerusalem of Ottoman times in the years 1550–1558, it was noticed that payments to the administrators were rarely made out of *waqf* income. Independent sources of income were provided for this purpose. Administrators collected revenues, expanded the sources of income, supervised new constructions and repairs, and allocated resources. Sometimes, they engaged themselves in other economic fields like long-distance trade in grains, soap factories, etc.[60]

Conclusion

It is a matter of great satisfaction that in recent times there has been appearing an increasing resistance to the orientalist's onslaught on the image of Muslim women. The orientalists conveniently assumed that Muslim women passively accept their bleak lives, either because they know of no alternative or because they have no means to fight this faith prescribed by God and administered by their male masters.[61] But in fact

> an increasing number of Muslim women across the globe do not share in resignation regarding their inferior rights in practice of their helplessness with respect to misogynist versions of Islamic rights. They are combating both the traditional restrictive practices as well as challenges to their identity and empowerment through neo-colonialist yardstick.[62]

The Indian Waqf (Amendment) Act 2013 requires that at least two women members be appointed by the Government of India to the 21 member Central *Waqf* Council which is a statutory federal body constituted under the Waqf Act 1995 [Sec, 5.9 (2) Proviso]. In the case of the State Waqf Boards, which supervise *waqf* administration in each state, it is now provided in the amending law that there must be appointed at least two women members in each board [Sec, S.14 (IA) Proviso]. The maximum number of members in a State *Waqf* Board is 11. This development represents an official acknowledgment of the importance of women in *waqf* administration in India. Probably, it may induce other countries to follow suit.

Whatever historical records exist confirm the actual implementation of all such legal provisions of *waqf* which authorised a Muslim woman to act as a *waqifa*, to be a beneficiary and to administrator waqf as a mutawalli. It is noteworthy that nearly all of the historical research works have been conducted by Western scholars, who mainly explored Mamluk and Ottoman history. Now the need is to explore this history in other perspective also – for instance, in the perspective of Indo-Pakistan sub-continent and other geographical contexts, preferably, by Muslim scholars. In India, probably such an enquiry will examine the position of women in the laws of *waqf* during the Sultanate and Mughal periods and later in princely states of Hyderabad, Bhopal and Quadh. Then someone may bring this study to the present status of *awqaf* in the various regions of the world where Muslims reside (e.g. 4SA, Europe and South East Asia) and to examine the involvement of women in *waqf* matters. Producing more literature on the subject may also help in dispelling the myth that surrounds the status of Muslim women generally and in the area of *waqf* particularly.

Before concluding, it seems appropriate to sound a note of caution. Without in anyway belittling the fact that in earlier periods of Islamic history, Muslim women possessed every property right, this should not make us to assume that these are still continuing until today. There is a need of conducting a fresh inquiry into the extent of actual enjoyment of these rights by the Muslim women of today in the fact of contrary customs, practices and legislation; Islamic law tools are still relevant to enhance the status of Muslim women and their access to property. "The strategy of deploying and in some senses reviving these 'authentic' tools is at least potentially legitimate".

Notes

1 Gabriel Baer, "The *Waqf* as a Prop for the Social System (16th–18th Centuries)", *Islamic Law and Society*, Vol. 4 (1997), pp. 265–297.
2 Mary Ann Fay, "Women and *Waqf*: Towards a Reconstruction of Women's Place in the Mamluk Household", *International Journal of Middle East Studies,* Vol. 29 (1977), pp. 33–51.
3 Ameer Ali, *Mohammedan Law*, Vol. 1 (Calcutta, 1892).
4 Syed Ameer Ali, *The Spirit of Islam: A History of the Evolution and Ideals of Islam* (Christopher's, London, 1953 – A Reprint of the Reprinted and Enlarged 1922 Edition).
5 Id. at 255.
6 Id. at 256.
7 Al-Tarabulsi, Burhanuddin Ibrahim, *Kitab Al-Is'af Fi Al Awqaf*, 2nd ed. (Cairo, 1902), p. 10 (hereafter referred to as "Al-Tarabulsi").
8 Ibid.
9 Al-Khassaf, Abu Bakr Ahmad Ibnamr, *Kitabahkam Al-Waqf* (Cairo, 1904), p. 335 Ff.; Al-Tarabulsi, p. 14.
10 Al-Shirwani, Abdul Hamid, *Hawashituhfat Al-Muhtaj Bi Shariah-Al Minhaj* (Cairo, 1938). p. 237.
11 Ameer Ali, *Muhammadan Law* (Bombay, 1885), p. 395.
12 Al-Khassaf, *Loccit Supra* at 351 Ff.
13 *Nawab Asghar Ally V. Delrossbanoo Begun*, [1875] Bengal Law Reporter, 167.
14 *Fatima Bibi V. The Advocate-General* (1886) 6 Bom. 42.
15 See, *Farid- Un- Nisa V. Mukhtar Ahmad* (1952) 52 I.A. 342; See also, *Syed Ahmad Fatima V. Diwan Abdul Halim* (1920) 24 CWN 494 (Privy Council); *Sahuhar Prasad V. Fazal Ahmad* (1933) 60 I.A., 116 at 121; and *Shaikh Muhammad Ibrahim V. Bibi Maryam* (1928) 8 Patna 484 at 488, 489 and 495.
16 Quran: *Surah Al-Baqarah* (2), Ayat 273.
17 Ibnqudamah, Abdullah Ibn Ahmad, *Al-Mughni* (Cairo, 1947).
18 Tyabji, Faiz Badruddin, *Muslim Law: The Personal Law of Muslims in India and Pakistan*, 4th ed. (Bombay, 1968), p. 575.
19 Id. at 550.
20 Id. at 561, citing *Fatawa Al-Hindiyyah.*
21 Id. at 571.
22 *Radd-Ul-Muhtar,* Vol. III, p. 594; *Durrulmukhtar,* p. 241, cited in Syed Ameer Ali, *Mohammedan Law*, 5th ed. By Raja Said Akbar Khan, Vol. 1 (Lahore, 1976), p. 442.
23 *Hussainibibeev. Hussain Sharif,* [1868] 4 Mad, H.C.R. 23.
24 Syed Ameer Ali, *Loccit Supra* at 442–443.
25 Al-Ramli, Muhammad Ibn Ahmad, *Nihayat Al-Muhtaj*, Vol. 5 (Cairo, 1938), p. 396.

26 Al-Tarabulsi, p. 54.
27 *Radd Al-Muhtar*, Vol. III, p. 638, cited in Syed Ameer Ali, Vol. 1, p. 458.
28 Mohd. Zain Bin Haji Othman, *Islamic Law with Special Reference to the Institution of Waqf* (Kuala Lumpur, 1982), pp. 189–192.
29 *Radd, Al-Muhtar*, Vol. III, p. 649,
30 Syed Ameer Ali, *Muhammadan Laws*, Vol. 15th ed. (Lahore, 1976), pp. 468–469.
31 Al-Ramli, *Nihayat Al-Muhtaj*, Vol. 5, p. 387.
32 Abu Zahrah, Muhammad, *Muhadarat Fi-Al-Waqf* (Cairo, 1957), p. 390.
33 Dalal Bint Makhlid Al-Harbi (2001), *Women's Contribution to Book Waqf in Najd, Riyadh*, King Fahad Library, p. 3, cited in Iman Muhammad Al Humaidan, *Women and Waqf* (Kuwait Awqaf Public Foundation, State of Kuwait, 2007), pp. 31–35.
34 Fay, Mary Ann, "Women and Waqf: Towards a Reconsideration of Women's Place in Mamluk Household", *IJMES*, Vol. 29, No. 1 (1997), pp. 33–51.
35 Baer, Gabriel, "Women and Waqf: An Analysis of the Istanbul Tahrir 1546", *Studies in the Social History of the Middle East in Memory of Professor Gabriel Baer*, Asian and African Studies, University of Haifa, 1983, p. 28.
36 Draganaamedoski, "Women Waqf in the Sixteenth Century Sanjak of Krusevac (Alacahisar)", Balcanica (2009), No. 40, pp. 43–55. See also, M.L. Meriwether, "Women and Waqf Revisited: The Case of Aleppo, 1770–1840", In M.C. Zilfi (Ed.), *Women in the Ottoman Empire: Middle Eastern Women in the Early Modern Era* (Leiden, 1997), pp. 128–152; Kerimafilan, "Women Founders of Pious Endowments", In Amilabuturovic and Irvin Cemil Schick (Eds.), *Women in the Ottoman Balkans: Gender, Culture and History* (London, 2007), pp. 99–121.
37 Mary Ann Fay, "Women and Waqf: Towards a Reconsideration of Women's Place in the Mamluk Household", *International Journal of Middle Eastern Studies*, Vol. 29, No. 1 (Feb, 1997), pp. 35–51 at 38, citing Haim Gerber, "The Waqf Institution in Early Ottoman Empire", *Asian and African Studies*, Vol. 17 (1983), pp. 29–45.
38 See, Humphreys, R. Stephen "Women as Patrons of Religious Architecture in Ayyubid Damascus", *Muqarnas*, Vol. 11 (1994), pp. 35–54.
39 *Infra* N. 40 at 55.
40 Iman Mohammed Al-Humaidan, *Woman and Waqf* (Kuwait Awqaf Public Foundation, State Of Kuwait, 2007), pp. 55–56.
41 Id. at 45–58.
42 Mary Ann Fay, Supra N. 37 at 36, where she has cited the following sources: Fanny Davis, *The Ottoman Lady, a Social History from 1718 to 1918* (Westport, CO: Greenwood Press, 1986); Ulku Bates, "Women as Patrons of Architecture in Turkey", In Lois Beek and Nikkiekeddie (Eds.), *Women in Muslim World* (Cambridge: Cambridge University Press, 1978), pp. 245–260; Gabriel Baer, Supra N. 37, Muhammad Muhammad Amin, *Fahrasatwatha'iq Al-Qahira* (Cairo, Institutfrancais D' Archaeologies Du Caire, 1981); and Muhammad Afifi, *Al-Awqafwa Al-Hayat Al-Iqtisadiyya Fi Misr Fi Al 'Asr Al-'Uthmani* (Cairo, General Egyptian Book Organisation, 1991) and Butrusabd Al Malik and Daniel Crecellius, "A Late Eighteenth Century Egyptian Waqf Endowed by a Sister of the Mamlukshaykh Al-Eyey Muhammad Beyabou Al-Dhahah", *Arab Historical Review for Ottoman Studies*, 1–2, (1990), pp. 9–14.
43 Mary Ann Fay, Supra N. 37 at 46.
44 Mary Ann Fay, Supra N. 37 at 39.
45 Id. at 40–41, citing, *Waqf*, No. 2444, Ministry of *Awqaf*, Cairo.
46 Waqf No. 2215, Ministry of Awqaf, Cairo Supra N. 37 at 43.
47 Randi Deguilhem, "Consciousness of Self: The Muslim Women as Creator and Manager of Waqf Foundations in Late Ottoman Damascus", In Amira El-Ezhari

(Ed.), *Beyond the Exotic: Women's Histories in Islamic Societies* (Sonbol, Suracuse NY: Suracuse University Press, 2005), pp. 102–118.

48 *Tahrir Daftar* 567, 428, cited in Draganaamedoski, "Women Waqfs in the Sixteenth Century Sanjak of Krusecae", *Balcanica* (2009), No. 40, pp. 45–55.

49 www.shahjahanmosque.org.uk/ (http://www.shahjahanmosque.org.uk).

50 Iman Mohammad Al-Humaidan, Supra N. 40 at 49.

51 Id. at 33, 34.

52 Muslemapurmul, "Women and Awqaf in Mamluk and Ottoman History" (Unpublished), www.Jamaaldiwan.Com/Blog/Riles/Muslema_Waqf.Pdf. This Section is Mainly Based on this Source.

53 Id. at 4–7, 9.

54 Andre Raymond, *Artisans Etcommercants Au Caire* (Damanscus, Institutfrancais De Damas, 1974), 1: 409, cited in Mary Ann Fay, Supra N. 39 at 40.

55 Id. at 41.

56 http://www.deccanherald.com/content.195347/saba-paraudi-first-woman-patron.html

57 Randi Deguilhem, Supra N. 47 at 106.

58 Shaham, Ron, "Masters, Their Freed Slaves, and the Waqf in Egypt (Eighteenth-Twentieth Centuries)", *Journal of the Economic and Social History of the Orient,* Vol. 43, No. 2 (2000), pp. 162–188. See also, Crecelius, Daniel, "The Organisation of Waqf Documents in Cairo", *International Journal of Middle East Studies*, Vol. 2, No. 3 (1971), pp. 266–277.

59 Iman Mohammad Al-Humaidan, *Supra* N.40 at 54–55.

60 Amy Singer, *Constructing Ottoman Beneficence: An Imperial Kitchen in Jerusalem* (State University Of New York, 2002), p. 123.

61 Hoodfar, H., "Muslim Women on the Threshold of the Twenty-First Century, In *Dossier* 12: *Women Living Under Muslim Law* (London, 1998), p. 112, cited in Sirajsait and Hilary Lim, Land Law and Islamic Property and *Human Rights in the Muslim World* (Zed Books, London, 2006), p. 130.

62 Sirajsait and Hilary Lim, Supra N. 61 at 130, citing Ahmad, L., *Women and Gender in Islam* (Yale University Press, New Heaven, 1992).

References

Crecelius, Daniel, "The *Waqfiyah* of Muhammad Bey Abu Abu Al-Dhahab", *Journal of the American Research Centre in Egypt,* 15 (1978), pp. 83–105.

Crecelius, Danial, "Incidence of Waqf Cases in Three Cairo Courts: 1640–1802", *Journal of the Economic and Social History of the Orient,* 29.2 (1986), pp. 176–189.

Gerber, Haim, "Social and Economic Position of Women in an Ottoman City, Bursa 1600–1700", *International Journal of Middle Eastern Studies,* 12 (1980), pp. 231–244.

Marcus, Abraham, "Men, Women and Property: Dealers in Real Estate in the 18th Century Aleppo", *Journal of the Economic and Social History of the Orient,* 26.2 (1983), pp. 137–63.

Peri, Oded, "Waqf and Ottoman Welfare Policy", *Journal of the Economic and Social History of The Orient"* 35.2 (1992), pp. 167–186.

Shatzmiller, Maya, "Islamic Institutions and Property Rights: The Case of the Public Good Waqf", *Journal of Economic and Social History of the Orient,* 441.1 (2001) pp. 44–74.

9 Developing a waqf market and reconceptualising awqaf governance via regtech

Zakariya Mustapha and Aishath Muneeza

Introduction

The history of modern Islamic finance has been that of success as evidenced by its tremendous growth in assets, developments and diversification in turning out viable alternative financial products and services globally. Islamic finance today, in its journey of more than four decades, is said to have reached a maturity stage where the successes it records in its respective components as a financial system are being consolidated. Regardless of the success story, it is observable that development has not been even across all components of Islamic finance industry. In this regard, the institution of waqf, a social finance component, can be brought within focus particularly in comparison to banking, takaful (insurance) and capital market components.[1] Waqf is an old Shariah-compliant instrument of outstanding track record where people donate assets to create an endowment for religious as well as welfarist purposes such as education, basic healthcare, community development and general financial well-being. Interest of recent renewed on this classical Islamic institution due to its inherent nature and alignment to modern-day development agenda such as the United Nations' sustainable development goals (SDGs) which are aimed at addressing socio-economic challenges.[2] Accordingly, aside being a form of endowment, the potential of waqf instrument has long been recognised as capable of addressing many socio-economic problems in addition to promoting key development factors such as financial exclusion among Islamic nations.[3]

Waqf is an enabler institution that inherently serves as a bridge across the divide between those endowed with wealth in the society and the needy/poor members of the society with view to ensuring wealth redistribution. The institutions of waqf had historically served those ideals in Muslims nations during the golden eras of Islam. The instrument of waqf has been a social finance tool that can be developed to serve and further that goal in Islamic finance. Today, despite recognising the potentials of waqf to address many socio-economic problems that befall developing Muslim nations, the waqf instrument is less researched anymore than its practice promoted in those nations. Moreover, the advent of technological innovations such as blockchain, cloud computing and artificial intelligence for the delivery of financial products and services has presented peculiar challenges to institutions offering Islamic financial services. This means the institutions need to brace themselves for disruption and ways to adapt and outlast the challenges and remain relevant. In the midst of this struggle comes the reawakening for waqf and consequently the need of a market for it. Thus, as long as technology is used to formulate and deliver waqf financial products and services, the regulatory terrain would equally require specially tailored, technology-based regulations and solutions to monitor and supervise a waqf market. Understanding this challenge, the study of waqf and its market in relation to technology-based governance is well timed to ensure purposive deliverability, so that waqf institutions can be revived, sustained and further promoted in the Muslim world. This study is qualitative with exploratory design. Accordingly, relevant social financing and governance principles as well as regulatory technology practices from authoritative data sources including books, journal articles and web resources were examined and analysed. The focus is on regulation and governance in a technology-driven fashion to help renew and reinvigorate waqf assets, formulate and deliver social financing instrument in waqf using emerging innovative technologies.

This chapter examines waqf market as a new component to be developed within Islamic financial ecosystem as facilitated by financial technology, and in relation to its governance through regulatory technology. This is in order to learn how the disruption caused by fintech in traditional finance can be tackled via regtech to reconceptualise the governance of the new waqf market and its instruments. The chapter is divided into five main segments. Following the first segment in the preceding introduction, the second segment provides an overview of the current state of waqf and its potentials in relation to Islamic finance. The third segment highlights the idea of a waqf market and the propriety of the term in alternative to the term Islamic social capital market. In the fourth segment, an explanation is offered on global outlook and impact of regtech, its impact and potential when it comes to waqf governance. The fifth segment touches on waqf market governance and regtech application and solutions therein, while the sixth or last segment of the chapter offers recommendations on the issues addressed and concludes the chapter.

Current state of waqf and its potentials in relation to Islamic finance

Waqf is an Islamic concept of endowment or charity that serves both social and economic purposes. As a form of endowment, waqf is an old Islamic institution that can certainly advance social financing and make a difference in societal welfare and economic development. The concept of social finance comprises approach and practice of managing financial resources and assets which deliver social dividend as economic return. In other word, social finance refers to creation, financing and/or investing in charities, philanthropic ventures, not-for-profit and social enterprises and related channels.[4] Social finance is an area whose importance is emerging and growing as a fundamental of development on a global scale.[5] The institution of waqf is re-emerging in importance consequent to the development of modern Islamic finance in its three main components – Islamic banking, Islamic insurance and Islamic capital market. Waqf is an instrument that would precisely promote socio-economic contexts and objectives of Islamic finance in its own perspective. The institution of waqf, as a social finance mechanism, has accordingly been envisaged to provide a potential fourth component of the Islamic finance ecosystem – hence the idea of a waqf market.[6] In this regard, and when viewed from an economic perspective, waqf holds much potentials as an important component of the Islamic economic system. Nonetheless, waqf assets, save in few jurisdictions, remain globally moribund, due to several governance issues that have constrained their development. These issues range from poor or lack of suitable administrative system coupled with inexpertise, lack of accountability, mismanagement to lack of standard legal and regulatory framework for the administration and management of waqf assets.[7] Therefore, waqf assets worth 100 billion of dollars have been left undeveloped and idle. Given their worth, however, waqf assets are too large to be overlooked. Unfortunately, as it stands, asset managers in real estate investment trusts (REITs) seem to have spared efforts to unlock this sleeping giant. The situation hinders realisation of rewards or gains that waqf assets can generate both for the beneficiaries of the waqf and for their founders or dedicators. It actually threatens workability and sustainability of the institution as a whole. These, among other issues, collectively stand on the way of waqf realising its potentials to contribute in the socio-economic well-being of the people where waqf assets are situated. For these reasons, waqf today has become a stagnant institution of little relevance, where, in spite of its rich history and important roles, much of it is unknown even to many Muslims. Accordingly, waqf no longer performs its intended socio-economic role in Muslim countries. The Global Islamic Finance Report 2015 succinctly describes the situation of the Muslim nation in terms of social challenges amidst the abundance of waqf assets and how development of Islamic banking and finance has left out waqf in these words:

> The current economic situation of almost all Muslim countries in terms of their high illiteracy rate, lack of good healthcare, high unemployment rate, the spread of poverty and low level of food production must encourage one to study the institution of waqf, which has played an instrumental role in addressing a range of socio-economic issues in the Muslim societies of the past. Many contemporary Islamic economists contend that the institution of waqf is still relevant to the socio-economic

> development of the Muslim societies, most of which face a multitude of problems. The relevance of waqf has also been highlighted in the wake of success of IBF... Yet, applications of the principles of waqf in IBF are rather scarce.[8]

Thus, as it is, waqf is seemingly one of the Islamic institutions that has not been opened up in line with developments in the life of Muslims. It is also one area that has been leveraged on modern-day technology to develop and enhance its returns. It is time for this narrative to change as John Sandwick is quoted saying:

> ...people have adopted the most modern technologies in their daily lives, from cell phones to heart surgery to traffic control – yet still Awqaf are managed much like they were 500 years ago. This must change. Awqaf must adapt to modern management and administration.[9]

Therefore, given the state of waqf assets around the world, it is imperative to establish a new system of waqf that focuses on strong governance and professionalism as measures to arrest the decay of this historic Islamic heritage, revive and sustain it. These would promote waqf deliver on its potentials and gain traction as an Islamic finance component with its own niche.

The economic and social challenges in the areas of healthcare, education, unemployment, community development, poverty, food insecurity and hunger can be addressed, to a large extent, through the institution of waqf.[10] With property estimates worth over one trillion US dollars spread across the Muslim world,[11] much of which donated and managed privately, and yet underutilised due to the fact that extant waqf administration is not underpinned by befitting regulatory mechanism that would spell suitable governance system thereto. With that, waqf can potentially address long-term public financing gap among other modern developmental issues and reclaim its role as a tool of social and economic upliftment. As a social financing tool and by virtue of the assets to its credit, the World Bank, INCEIF and ISRA Waqf Report (2019) has affirmed waqf as being poised to effectively contribute in addressing global development agenda as championed by the United Nation's SDGs.

Thus, waqf seeks to advance Islamic redistribution of wealth as a means of ensuring financial equity in societies. In this regard, waqf has been identified as a potential tool to reverse many social menaces in many Muslim countries. For instance, with view to poverty reduction and/or eradication and people economic empowerment, waqf has been appropriately applied in devising suitable instruments in Islamic finance for that purpose. It is along this line that waqf is used to guarantee small and microenterprises as well as establishing micro takaful with social orientation or waqf-based takaful (Islamic insurance). Islamic microfinance institutions have been established based on waqf. Thus, cash realised from a waqf fund for instance is being invested and the profit therefrom is then utilised for microfinance. Alternatively, the cash realised can be used in financing projects and other ventures in the form of interest-free loans. Another way is by utilising waqf funds as capital and setting up microfinance entities in developing the microfinance sector since Islamic banks are not providing microfinancing and tend to be wary generally of lending to small and micro-businesses.[12] For instance, a waqf fund has been utilised in underwriting financing operations of Islamic microfinance bank for micro, small and medium enterprises (MSMEs). This is a demonstration of the hybridisation of waqf and microfinance that offers practicable and innovative ways through which Islamic finance promote access to development finance.[13]

Similarly, waqf-based takaful allows takaful to be spread more widely at microenterprise level by enabling takaful participants to contribute to a waqf fund so that any surplus can be shared between shareholders of the takaful operators and the waqf fund.

Idea of waqf market

The idea of a waqf market centres around waqf being a component of the Islamic financial services ecosystem, precisely the Islamic capital market. The waqf market comprises tangible and non-tangible assets segments respectively. Therefore, in accordance with the market place, tangible assets will come under management and services portfolio, while the non-tangible, mainly cash, will come under financial market portfolio.[14] It is a standardised and fully regulated market for dealing in waqf instruments in all form and manner befitting waqf, within the bound of Shariah and for social financing purpose. By this market, a waqf instrument for products and services can be developed and offered to serve desired socio-economic ends of contributors or dedicators. The waqf market provides an innovative social financing that is positioned to make impact of waqf more beneficial and sustainable in society via an increased access to financial services that were hitherto unavailable or available but affordable only by few people. Thus, waqf market can help waqf beneficiaries, who are often less affluent, turn into savers or investors in more prudent and diversified portfolios such as microfinancing and micro-takaful.

Establishing the waqf market means creation of standardised waqf-based institutions, realising more benefits from waqf assets, increasing access thereto and monitoring the market through regtech. For this reason, powerful regtech needs be deployed to that effect, so that while fintech accelerates fast access, delivery and affordability of waqf products and services, the regtech tackles compliance (with Shariah in particular) and consumer protection among other concerns which regulators need to address in any kind of market, and with corresponding mastery that counters any disruption to financial dealings processes and procedures and bringing same within regulatory bounds.

Moreover, waqf market is a viable solution that addresses liquidity management challenge due to non-availability of practicable investment opportunities in waqf assets. The range of waqf assets spread across Muslim countries today are exceedingly disproportionate in favour of real assets, i.e. land and landed property. Thus, while waqf is highly rich in land or landed assets, one of the key factors of production, it is deficient in other factors including labour, capital and entrepreneurship. It is a fact that almost all waqf lands today are undeveloped as a result of lack of adequate funds and entrepreneurial ingenuity. A waqf market as a component of the Islamic financial services industry would address this challenge and unlock other potential opportunities of waqf.

Waqf market or social capital market?

It should however be noted that, without more, the term 'waqf market', as a subset of the Islamic capital market, may convey a meaning that is not in the true nature of waqf, i.e. that of economic return from an investment. In view of the fact that the true nature of waqf is more of socio-economic and always with charitable underpinning, waqf is a social finance mechanism in Islam. In this regard, instead of 'waqf market' per se, the term 'social capital market' is thus put forward as most suitable for the social finance sector of the Islamic financial services industry. Meanwhile, waqf is the principal and pioneer instrument in the Islamic social capital market. Moreover, unlike the main Islamic capital market where people and other entities participate as investors in instruments such as sukuk, in the social capital market people and entities participate as contributors instead. Consequently, while investors in the Islamic capital market look for economic returns from their investments in form of dividends, waqf contributors in the social capital market would look to social returns of their contributions ensuring some charitable social-economic goals via some not-for-profit organisations.[15] Again, investments in Islamic capital market instruments have maturity date, while waqf social finance contributions are held and go on in perpetuity. It is equally noteworthy that the term 'social capital' needs to be applied contextually and with appropriate caution. This is because, the term has been around for long time and ascribed to other context than finance where it is often associated with productive benefits emanating from social relations or collective social benefits from some investments.[16]

Financial technology (fintech) and waqf delivery: the case of blockchain technology

Financial technology or fintech encompasses all technological innovations applied in the formulation or creation as well as delivery of financial products and services. Fintech involves the use of technology to provide support for and/or enable financial services by financial institutions. Fintech is manifest in the use of mobile wallets, crowdfunding platforms, chatbots, robo-advisors, cloud computing channels and the internet ecosystems among others making wave in the world today in rendering financial services and products accessible, efficient and affordable.[17] Such financial products and services include funding, payment, lending, trading, investing, currencies and/or cryptocurrencies.[18] Fintech presents a wide range of transformation in financial systems and processes so much so that it is becoming the future in financial system operations. Accordingly, fintech is today transforming financial services industries and societies dealing with money, value, financial resources and trust.[19] Among the prominent technologies that underpin and popularise fintech are blockchain, cloud computing and artificial intelligence or machine learning facilitated by big data analytics. Of these, blockchain and the internet ecosystem seem to have so far more practical application in waqf delivery.

Blockchain is commonly described as a decentralised ledger, private or public, that consists of 'blocks' maintained by a distributed computers network that keeps multiple, verified and immutable records of transactions without a third-party or central authority as intermediary.[20] Blockchain fundamentally encompasses a transaction (represented by a block), a transaction record, a system for verification and storage of the transaction. As transactions occur, blocks are generated and information is recorded as to time and the manner the transaction occurs in sequence. Each block comprises a secured hash, generated while taking into consideration the index, timestamp, data inside the block and hash of previous block. After a block has been verified and added to the blockchain, any alteration to that block would produce a new hash which will be inconsistent with the hashes that precede and would therefore be rejected. The blocks sequentially maintain data of all transactions that occur in the chain, hence the name blockchain. The blockchain in essence can be described as a database of trustless, irreversible and immutable time-stamped record of transaction replicated on servers spread across the world.[21] In other word, blockchain establishes an environment where automation of digitalised instructions via smart contracts executes transactions in a transparent yet trustless way with immutable record of same. The blockchain technology could be used in any kind of transaction that involves value.

One significant advantage of the blockchain technology is the 'trust' element of it which dispenses with the need for a central regulator or certifying authority. As the record blockchain generates and keeps cannot be altered, it can confirm ownership, enable transactions with unprecedented transparency and safeguard the sanctity of contracts. These are fundamental requirements in Shariah for contractual dealings. It should be noted, however, that blockchain technology is not yet a matured ecosystem and requires significant application before it can become mainstream for financial services creation and delivery. Thus, for waqf users, specific needs be met in considering the suitable application for regtech solution.[22]

In view of the foregoing, case use of blockchain technology in waqf has already been established by Finterra with its pioneer blockchain waqf. A fintech firm based in Singapore, Finterra has developed a crowdfunding platform that uses blockchain and creates smart contracts linked to specific waqf projects.[23] This blockchain waqf enables participants to create project proposals in order to create, develop and and/or revitalise endowment assets. Other participants can finance the proposed projects by contributing funds thereto. Where the goals of the projects are met, the proposal is then accepted. By accepting a particular project, a certain number of endowment tokens known as Waqf-coin are generated and issued to the funders participating in the project. By having the endowment tokens, participants obtain stakeholder right share in gains from the project. Moreover, the tokens can be exchanged and/or transferred in the expansive Finterra ecosystem and beyond – the Gallactic Smart Chain network.[24] Similar to the Finterra's waqf chain is Ammana's mobile cash-waqf project, a mobile cash waqf developed by PT Ammana Fintek Syariah in 2018, in Indonesia. Ammana provides users, through its mobile application, access to Islamic social financing by crowdfunding services for the production sector using cash-waqf fundraising. The application provides donors or contributors with the option to select a cash-waqf project of their choice. In addition, it offers comprehensive information on trustees and how they use the funds collected.[25] In view of these developments, blockchain technology coupled with the internet ecosystem and mobile computing can be bedrock for unlimited number of innovations that epitomise fintech.

In waqf administration, it is obvious that the most critical challenge of donors is uncertainty in knowing whether the donation is spent on intended purposes. This is due to lack of transparency by trustees managing waqf funds which has created lack of trust among donors in terms of contributing to or donating for charity.[26] This transparency issue is therefore no longer an issue with waqf on blockchain. Already blockchain-based innovation such as the Finterra's Waqfcoin provides a more efficient way to manage, receive and raise funds for donations to different humanity projects. With waqf digitalised, the Waqfcoin provides a fundamental mechanism that enables access and transaction in the Finterra's blockchain ecosystem which facilitates operationalisation and development of the waqf market.

Disruption to existing regulatory regime: regtech to the rescue

The emergence and development of fintech has disrupted existing financial regulatory setups and brought about unprecedented changes in the operations of financial services industry as it is traditional known. By the disruption, it means creation, offering and proliferation of many innovative financial products and services that are unconventional and uncontemplated by the law. Thus, such products and services circumvent the law and same cannot come within existing regulators' confines. The unprecedented changes necessitate rethinking the traditional ways of regulation and governance as well as searching for an alternative in the wake of pervasive yet unavoidable disruption. Such an alternative should be able to provide corresponding system of regulation that would befit the nature and peculiarities of the innovative and technology-based financial products and services. Regtech or regulatory technology evolves in order to address governance and other challenges consequent to the disruptive nature and peculiarities of fintech in the financial services and other sectors as well.[27]

In the case of the waqf market, regtech is required in order to balance up the on-going disruptions resulting from automation in finance generally or capital market in particular to meet up the demand for compliance with Shariah and current regulatory framework. With advent of digital economy and the determination of Muslim countries moving towards its adoption, public authorities need to brace themselves for the deployment of technology in governance circle. In this regard, advanced Islamic finance jurisdictions such as Malaysia, Bahrain and Indonesia among others are reportedly set to move towards digitalisation of waqf administration leveraging on financial technology, particularly using blockchain technology.[28] Simply put, regtech is used to denote the use of technology, specifically information and communication technologies, in regulating a market in the context of compliance, risk management, identity management and control, regulatory reporting and monitoring of transactions. The use of technology to automate regulation became popular in/after the 2008 global financial crisis.

Regtech solutions have been emerging among jurisdictions in an effort to establish an Islamic digital economy which encompasses incorporating Islamic financial services with some versatile technologies including blockchain, cloud computing, big data analytics and artificial intelligence (AI) algorithms among others in response to the myriad of regulatory issues resulting from disruption such as blockchain sukuk (smart sukuk) and blockchain waqf. These defy existing legal regime for the regulation sukuk (Islamic bond) and in the case of waqf, no suitable legal regime exists for its many jurisdictions.

Regtech solution for waqf market governance

As a financial activity, waqf market practice necessarily requires regulations that would establish a standardised waqf assets governance and administration system. It is a fact that traditional governance and administration system of waqf where related assets are left in custody of individual trustees or, in a very few countries, with some government department cannot serve this purpose adequately. Unfortunately, this remains the commonest form of governance of waqf in most Muslim countries today which greatly contributes in leading waqf to its current state of mismanagement, dilapidation and abandonment. In this regard, a market for waqf is envisaged as a concept where waqf institutions, assets and property can be put to commercial use, generate returns and make a positive difference in society. Consequently, in creating a waqf market, a suitably reconceptualised governance system would be needed so that dealing in waqf assets by regulations would be in the fashion of dealing in financial instrument from an economic efficiency standpoint. In essence, the Islamic endowment of waqf, despite being a virtuous act, can be operationalised as an economic activity to contribute in the economic as well as social well-being of Muslim societies.

Against the backdrop of the current status of waqf, such a reconceptualised waqf governance system is also informed by the pervasive and disruptive application of financial technology, otherwise known as fintech, in formulating and delivering financial products and services. This would likewise necessitate providing suitable regulations that also leverages on technology to address issues associated with the governance of these kinds of dealings, products and services. In other words, deploying fintech to facilitate dealings as well as products and services delivery requires a corresponding mechanism of regulation known in this regard as regulatory technology or regtech. It is noteworthy that, for the development and sustainability of waqf market, the use of fintech becomes imperative as it provides unprecedented speed, accuracy and convenience, involving less personnel resources, in handling and delivering more transactions, products and services. Hence, the application of regtech in the governance of the waqf market becomes imperative as well.

It is important to note that design, structures, approaches and procedures of a country's legal and regulatory system always impact on any development that takes place therein. Accordingly, regtech has to take these into cognisance while automating and standardising waqf governance to ensure extant legal regime does not stifle innovation in the name of strict adherence to regulation. This would require that extant legal regime has to be reformed to take considerations of the peculiarities of digitalisation of regulations via regtech. Accordingly, while standardising regulation and governance, key peculiarities of waqf rules and regulations need be encoded into regtech so that issues of authenticity of establishment and/or registration, statutory reporting, dispute settlement and jurisdiction of court among other regulatory matters can be appropriately covered.

Application of regtech in waqf

Respective regulators have various statutory responsibilities in ensuring smooth operations of various markets and industries that constitute a hub around which nations' economies revolve. In this regard, a prime role would always be played by capital market regulator, and any other regulator in that regard, with respect to the establishment, regulation and oversight over waqf market as a subset of the Islamic capital market. Accordingly, regulators all over the world are charged to do all within allowed extent of law to bring aspect of market under their control and within regulatory bound with the primary goal of ensuring stable economy as a baseline for economic growth and development. This facilitates circulation of wealth and promotes welfare of citizens while protecting against market sharp practice.[29] With the fintech revolution, and the emergence of regtech, although the role remains the same, it is enhanced in scope and mode of execution. Therefore, with regtech for regulation purpose, work of regulators would be digitalised as much as the waqf instrument itself being in digitalised asset. Waqf as a financial instrument is designed, structured and offered in a digitalised format. Thus, waqf instruments and participants in waqf market become data-centred and digitalised as well, all information regarding transactions and participants' identity integrated into data-driven avenues and the transactions rendered via fintech avenues including the blockchain among others. This important transformation has its peculiarities that need to be addressed particularly with view to market conditions, monitoring investments therein, consumer and investor identification and protection as well as promoting healthier, stronger and stable economy.

In this regard, the regtech-based solutions can be provided against governance issues in the establishment, operations and supervision of waqf market via designated regulatory function for automated waqf registry, fraud detection, elimination and monitoring, electronic know your customer (KYC) and its data-driven version of know your data (KYD). Moreover, a study by Deloitte analysed 309 RegTech companies and identified five categories of regulatory technology solutions for the governance of financial services and other industries.[30] These are the regulatory compliance, risk management, customer identity management and control (KYC and KYD), regulatory reporting and surveillance and transaction monitoring.

Relevant tools for facilitating regtech in waqf governance regtech

The above regulatory functions, like any other function of regtech, are based on pattern of data in accordance with coded instruction. Thus, to ensure suitable regulation of waqf market, special regtech applications driven by complex and sophisticated artificial intelligence algorithms would be designed to learn and evolve based on encoded data patterns. This may not be understood by compliance and business professionals who mostly do not have the technical skills to understand in detail how the algorithms function. It is also challenging to audit the methodology used by a particular artificial intelligence algorithm in order to generate a specific output or decision. Accordingly, certain potential governance and supervisory areas that relevant waqf market operators may need to be acquainted with while adopting regtech are highlighted below.[31]

- **Cross-functional technology governance structure** – A cross-disciplinary group would be involved in developing, testing and implementing regtech applications. Testing various scenarios and outputs generated by such applications with input from a cross-functional group would help to limit potential issues therein.
- **Simplified summary of regtech tools** – A simplified summary that describes underlying algorithms and related strategies of the regtech application to be adopted should be maintained. This would enable non-technical staff to understand the intended functions of the planned regtech tool and its algorithms so that they are better prepared to detect and assess where outcomes are not aligned with expected results.

- **Programme on data quality risk management –** Integrity and control of data are of paramount importance for many regtech applications, most especially those that employ artificial intelligence to deliver desired results. Developing an appropriate data quality risk-management programme is crucial to help ensure consistency, completeness and accuracy of the data utilised to support the regtech systems.
- **Established process to identify and address errors or malfunctions –** Companies would immensely benefit from having appropriate and established policies and procedures in order to identify, respond to and mitigate material risks that may manifest in the event errors or malfunctions arise associated with the use of a regtech application. This should encompass establishing alternative processes that can be readily employed in the event such a regtech tool fails.
- **Training of personnel –** Training is necessary and of immense benefit for companies to impart and develop appropriate skills in their compliance, supervisory and operational staff on the use of regtech tools they are adopting.
- **Regulatory sandboxes –** Sandboxes are virtual environments used to test and examine the impacts of innovative new processes, products or technologies in less regulated environment or in environment where regulation is lacking. The UK Financial Conduct Authority has made progress in this area with its Project Innovate unit; so also, Malaysia's Central Bank has developed a regulatory sandbox framework; likewise, Australia's Securities and Investments Commission among regulators/administrators in other countries.[32]

Possible concerns and issues in regtech for waqf governance

On regulators' part, it is worthy of note that regtech does not provide solution to all regulatory requirements due to some barriers where its adoption would be difficult. Meanwhile, as technology can be used by businesses to evade regulations and frustrate regulators, regtech alone cannot eliminate all undesired and unethical business practices or resolve ethical issues resulting from corporate culture. Likewise, regtech as a technology operates based on opaque programmed reasoning that is often biased and reflects altered interpretations of the law; it could thus hinder good judgement in governance and risk management decision processes. Waqf institutions on their part need be careful when partnering with third-party firms to include regulators in the conversation before they enter into such partnerships given cyber risks. Financial and technical competence of the regulators is another issue in some national legal and regulatory settings where regulators perform overlapping duties. Ultimately, many of regtech's efficiency and automation gains could not be utilised as a result of expanded regulatory requirements and their costs, such as the increasing number of subsequent information requests from regulators.[33]

Conclusion

Waqf is a social finance tool that contributed immensely in the development of Muslim societies in the past by catering for societal needs in general and the needs of the poor and weaker members of the society in particular. Despite its current situation of dormancy due to neglect, its potential to do the same and even better remains intact. Modern societies, with technologies at their disposal, can equally benefit from waqf as far as those needs are concerned through waqf-based development policies that will ensure revival of the waqf institutions. Importantly, along these lines, technology can be deployed to the waqf governance in its establishment, management and regulation, for modern economies to prioritise their socio-economic goals via waqf. This would enable unlocking the potential of waqf and position it as an instrument for the pursuit of national and global developmental agenda. Already fintech has been transforming the field of finance in a revolutionary fashion. Using mobile and cloud computing technologies, coupled with artificial intelligence algorithm, fintech is poised to make waqf reclaim its role and unlock further socio-economic opportunities therefrom. The leading technologies driving the fintech transformation, including blockchain technology, can at the same time provide solutions to the governance problems, under-utilisation and lack of standard regulations that actually lead waqf to its current status of idleness and dormancy in the world.

Interestingly, the billon dollars' worth tangible waqf assets now lying idle across Muslim countries and even more that can be dedicated to this charitable cause can be reorganised into a market whereby waqf instrument can be created, exchanged and utilised in the fashion of a capital market for promoting socio-economic upliftment of beneficiaries. The waqf market is an additional component of the Islamic financial services industry to comprise of tangible or landed assets and intangible or cash under respective portfolio of the Islamic capital market. In addition to the fintech and regtech required to underpin waqf market, awareness needs to be created towards it via advocacy for the revival and contribution to waqf charities and imparting basic Islamic social finance literacy among Muslim societies as well as acquainting the people with its peculiarities. This is because illiteracy and lack of users' skills and availability of opportunities are at the moment challenges for large-scale adoption of technologies in delivering intended services and/products among the poor who constitute greater number of waqf beneficiaries. Therefore, more user-friendly apps that educate users could create a higher level of understanding of the benefits of fintech, enabling targeted people to potentially benefit in the transformative ways. Peculiarities of waqf with regard to strict Shariah compliance and the need to appropriately regulate the technologies are concerns to be addressed via tailor-made regtech. Fintech and regtech are not just options but imperatives in order to enhance, facilitate and sustain waqf and its market for efficiency in use of resources, accuracy in information/record, speedy transactions, accountability in management, better protection for market participants and enhanced risk mitigation measures. To attain this in the face of the realities of the technologies today, a paradigm shift in waqf regulation and governance is recommended. In this regard, regtech can come to the rescue with solutions directed at eliminating inefficiency and lack of trust, regulatory compliance, risk management, customer identity management and control as well as surveillance and transaction monitoring. On this it is accordingly proposed that fintech and regtech be developed via Shariah-compliant automation protocols specifically for the Islamic financial services and Islamic social finance. With these tailor-made fintech and regtech in place, waqf can resuscitated, its role in Islamic finance continuously promoted and technology-based innovations for an Islamic digital economy can be further supported and facilitated. To this end, purposive synergy and collaborations for further research and knowledge/experience sharing among all stakeholders from Shariah scholars and academia to regulators and industry practitioners are needed and hereby called for by this work.

Notes

1 There is, of recent, a reawakening towards waqf as a social finance mechanism among Islamic financial services experts and scholars with conscientious academic efforts, in developing and advancing its operation in Islamic finance. This has been in response to the seeming neglect of social finance segment in the global wake of Islamic finance industry since the early 1970s and the need to develop avenues that address social and developmental concerns in Islamic economy as advocated accordingly – see for instance Asutay, M. 2012. 'Conceptualising and Locating the Social Failure of Islamic Finance: Aspirations of Islamic Moral Economy vs. The Realities of Islamic Finance.' *Asian and African Area Studies, 11* (2), pp. 93–94; Asutay, M. 2008. 'Islamic Banking and Finance: Social Failure.' *New Horizon, 169*, pp. 1–3, October–December, Institute of Islamic Banking and Insurance (IIBI), London, pp. 1–4; Asutay, M. 2010. 'Islamic Microfinance: Fulfilling Social and Developmental Expectations.' In Qfinance (Ed.), *Islamic Finance: Instruments and Markets*, Bloomsbury, London, pp. 25–29. Asutay, M. and Aksak, E. 2011, December. 'Does Islamic Finance Make the World Economically and Financially Safer.' In *Eighth International Conference on Islamic Economics & Finance: Sustainable Growth and Inclusive Economic Development from an Islamic Perspective,* Doha, Qatar, 19–21 December, pp. 18–20.

2 Abdullah, M. 2018. 'Waqf, Sustainable Development Goals (Sdgs) and Maqasid Al-Shariah.' *International Journal of Social Economics, 45* (1), pp. 158–172.

3 See Ahmed, H. 2014. 'Integrating Waqf for Realising the Social Goals of Islamic Finance.' *Alim - The Shariah Scholars Journal, 4* (7), p. 37; Nadwi, M.A. and Kroessin, M. 2013. *Cash Waqf: Exploring Concepts, Jurisprudential Boundaries and Applicability to Contemporary Islamic Microfinance*, Islamic Relief Worldwide, Working Paper Series No. 2013-0x, Birmingham, UK, pp. 25.

4 Nicholls, A. and Emerson, J. 2015. 'Social Finance: Capitalizing Social Impact.' In Nicholls, A., Paton, R., and Emerson, J. (Eds.), *Social Finance*, Oxford University Press, New York, pp. 4–5. NB: in its broader context, social finance encompasses financing for green ventures and the general notion of the classes of investments termed as socially responsible.

5 Benedikter, R. 2011. *Social Banking and Social Finance: Answers to the Economic Crisis*, [Springer Briefs in Business], Springer, New York, pp. 1–4.
6 Lahsasna, A. 'I Have a Dream: Waqf Market in Addition to Islamic Banking, Takaful and the Islamic Capital Market.' *Journal of Wealth Management & Financial Planning, 5*, June 2018, pp. 47–53.
7 See World Bank Group, INCEIF & ISRA. 2019. *Maximising Social Impact through Waqf Solutions, Waqf Report*. Available at https://www.inceif.org/wp-content/uploads/2019/07/wb-inceif-isra-waqf-report-maximizing-social-impact-through-waqf-solutions.pdf, last accessed October 20, 2019; Shafii, Z., Iqbal, Z. and Tasademir, M. 2015. Governance Regulatory Framework for Waqf in Selected Countries. Available at http://www.tkbb.org.tr/documents/yonetmelikler/governance-regulatory-framework-for-waqf-in-selected-countries-zurina-shafii-zamir-iqbal-mustafa-tasdemir-2015.pdf, last accessed October 27, 2019.
8 GIFR. 2015, 'Waqf and Islamic Banking and Finance: The Missing Link.' *Global Islamic Finance Report 2015*, p. 113.
9 John Sandwick, Text of Interview with Islamic Finance News (IFN). 2012. 'The Waqf Industry: The Sleeping Giant of Islamic Finance.' *Islamic Finance News*, September 26, p. 4. Available at http://islamicfinancenews.com/sites/default/files/newsletters/v9i38.pdf, last accessed October 20, 2019.
10 The World Bank Group, INCEIF & ISRA. 2019. *Maximising Social Impact through Waqf Solutions, Waqf Report*. Available at https://www.inceif.org/wp-content/uploads/2019/07/wb-inceif-isra-waqf-report-maximizing-social-impact-through-waqf-solutions.pdf, last accessed October 20, 2019.
11 Securities Commission Malaysia, 2015; Abdullah, M., *Op Cit.,* N. 2 *Supra*, p. 159.
12 Ahmed, H. 2014. 'Integrating Waqf for Realising the Social Goals of Islamic Finance.' *Alim - the Shariah Scholars Journal, 4* (7), pp. 37–38.
13 This was the practice operationalised by Islamic Relief Worldwide (IRW) Pilot Cash Waqf Programme 2011–2015 in Kenya for the purpose of providing financing to micro, small and medium enterprises and provided livelihood support to the people. IRW set up a fund provided by an institutional donor and treated it in accordance with the rules of cash Waqf. The project addressed high poverty incidence as well as food insecurity in the Kenyan Mandera district. The district was then devastated by internal conflicts and cyclical droughts which disrupted traditional ways of making a living. See Nadwi, M.A. and Kroessin, M. 2013. *Cash Waqf: Exploring Concepts, Jurisprudential Boundaries and Applicability to Contemporary Islamic Microfinance*, Islamic Relief Worldwide, Working Paper Series No. 2013-0x, Birmingham, UK, p. 21.
14 Lahsasna, A., *Op Cit.*, N. 6 *Supra,* p. 47.
15 NB: The concept of social return as used here centres around creation of values not for profit but for some social as well as charitable purposes. See Nicholls, J., Lawlor, E., Neitzert, E. and Goodspeed, T. 2012. *A Guide to Social Return on Investment*, 2nd Edn., Matter and Co., Middlesex, England, p. 8.
16 For ideological and substantive reasons, the term 'social capital' does not have a concise and undisputed connotation – see Dolfsma, W. and Charlie, D. 2003. 'Subjects and Boundaries: Contesting Social Capital-Based Policies.' *Journal of Economic Issues, 37*, pp. 405–413. Accordingly, the meaning associated with the term 'social capital' always depends on the context of usage and discipline. See Robison, L.J., Schmid, A.A. and Siles, M.E. 2002. Is Social Capital Really Capital? *Review of Social Economy, 60* (1), pp. 1–21; Claridge, T. 2004. *Social Capital and Natural Resource Management: An Important Role for Social Capital?* Ph.D. Unpublished Thesis, University of Queensland, Brisbane, Australia; Poder, T.G. 2011. What Is Really Social Capital? A Critical Review. *The American Sociologist, 42* (4), p. 341.

17 Chishti, S. and Barberis, J. 2016. *The Fintech Book: The Financial Technology Handbook for Investors, Entrepreneurs and Visionaries*, John Wiley & Sons Ltd, Chichester, pp. 20 *Et Seq*.
18 Chakraborty, S. 2018. *Fintech: Evolution or Revolution*, 1st edn. Available at https://www.researchgate.net/profile/sumit_chakraborty/publication/328333395_fintech_evolution_or_revolution/links/5bc6c7e0a6fdcc03c78953b4/fintech-evolution-or-revolution.pdf, last accessed October 26, 2019.
19 Freedman, R.S. 2006. *Introduction to Financial Technology*, Academic Press, London, p. 1.
20 Darcy Allen, D. 2017. 'Discovering and Developing the Blockchain Cryptoeconomy.' *SSRN* Augustb18. Available at https://ssrn.com/abstract=2815255, last accessed October 29, 2019.
21 Peters, G. W. and Panayi, E. 2018. 'Understanding Modern Banking Ledgers through Blockchain Technologies: Future of Transaction Processing and Smart Contracts on the Internet of Money.' *SSRN*, Available at https://papers.ssrn.com/sol3/papers.cfm?abstract_id=2692487, last accessed October 30, 2019.
22 Al-Razouki, 2018. 'Crypto-Waqf: Building a Sustainable Islamic Blockchain.' September 27. Available at https://medium.com/@mussaad/crypto-waqfbuilding-a-sustainable-islamicblockchain-6adb2fab9f1f, last accessed October 23, 2019.
23 See Finterra: *Thewhitepaper,* July 7, 2018, Available at https://cdn.finterra.org/finterra_whitepaper.pdf, last accessed October 26, 2019.
24 Ibid.
25 Tanjung, H. and Adhiyansyah, L. February, 2019. 'Waqf and Innovations in Fintech: The Indonesian Experience.' *ISFIRE Review*, pp. 52–54.
26 Albawaba. 2018. 'Waqfcoin: Crowdfunding Platform Uses Blockchain to Serve Humanity.' Albawaba, August 16, Available at https://www.albawaba.com/business/waqfcoin-crowdfunding-platform-uses-blockchain-serve-humanity-1174718, last accessed October 28, 2019.
27 See Ioannis, A. 2018. 'Fintech and Regtech: Impact on Regulators and Banks.' *Journal of Economics and Business, 100*, pp. 8–10.
28 See Adillah, F. 2019. 'Local Waqf Sets to Move into Digitalisation.' *New Strait Times*, July 12. Available at https://www.nst.com.my/business/2019/07/503817/local-waqf-sets-move-digitalisation, last accessed October 22, 2019; Martin, Y. 2018. 'Islamic Endowments to Be Modernized by Blockchain.' *News BTC*, February 12, Available at https://www.newsbtc.com/2018/02/12/islamic-endowments-modernized-blockchain/, last accessed October 29, 2019.
29 See Osborne Clarke. 2018. 'Blockchain in the Financial Services Sector: What's on the Regulator's Agenda?' *Insight*, January 3. Available at https://www.osborneclarke.com/insights/blockchain-in-the-financial-services-sector-whats-on-the-regulators-agenda/, last accessed October 23, 2019.
30 Deloitte. 2019. *Analysis: Regtech Universe – Take a Closer Look at Who Is Orbiting the Regtech Space*. Available at https://www2.deloitte.com/lu/en/pages/technology/articles/regtech-companies-compliance.html, last accessed October 23, 2019.
31 See Financial Industry Regulatory Authority. 2018. '*Report on FINRA Examination Findings*.' December 7, p. 15. Available at https://www.finra.org/rules-guidance/guidance/reports/2018-report-exam-findings, last accessed October 23, 2019.
32 Other countries in this list include Bahrain, Indonesia, Jordan, Kazakhstan, Malaysia, Mauritius, Mozambique, Rwanda, Sierra Leone and Thailand – see the Digital Financial Services Observatory 2018. 'Regulatory Sandboxes.' Available at https://dfsobservatory.com/content/regulatory-sandboxes, last accessed October 23, 2019.
33 Packin, N. G. 2018. 'Regtech, Compliance and Technology Judgement Rule.' *Chicago Kent Law Review, 93* (1), 193–195.

References

Abdullah, M. 2018. 'Waqf, Sustainable Development Goals (SDGs) and Maqasid al-Shariah', *International Journal of Social Economics, 45*(1), pp. 158–172.

Adillah, F. 2019. 'Local Waqf Sets to Move into Digitalisation', *New Strait Times*, 12 July. Available at https://www.nst.com.my/business/2019/07/503817/local-waqf-sets-move-digitalisation, last accessed October 22, 2019.

Ahmed, H. 2014. 'Integrating Waqf for Realising the Social Goals of Islamic Finance', *Alim - The Shariah Scholars Journal, 4*(7), pp. 37–38.

Albawaba. 2018. 'Waqfcoin: Crowd Funding Platform Uses Blockchain to Serve Humanity', Albawaba, 16 August. Available at https://www.albawaba.com/business/waqfcoin-crowdfunding-platform-uses-blockchain-serve-humanity-1174718, last accessed October 28, 2019.

Asutay, M. 2008. 'Islamic Banking and Finance: Social Failure', *New Horizon, 169*, pp. 1–3, October - December, Institute of Islamic Banking and Insurance (IIBI), London, pp. 1–4.

Asutay, M. 2010. 'Islamic Microfinance: Fulfilling Social and Developmental Expectations', in QFinance (ed.), *Islamic Finance: Instruments and Markets*, Bloomsbury, London, pp. 25–29.

Asutay, M. 2012. 'Conceptualising and Locating the Social Failure of Islamic Finance: Aspirations of Islamic Moral Economy vs. the Realities of Islamic Finance', *Asian and African Area Studies, 11*(2), pp. 93–113.

Asutay, M. and Aksak, E. 2011, December. 'Does Islamic Finance Make the World Economically and Financially Safer', in *Eighth International Conference on Islamic Economics & Finance: Sustainable Growth and Inclusive Economic Development from an Islamic Perspective, in Doha, Qatar, on December*, pp. 18–20.

Benedikter, R. 2011. *Social Banking and Social Finance: Answers to the Economic Crisis*, [Springer Briefs in Business], Springer, New York, p. 133.

Cambridge Analytica IF. 2015. 'Waqf and Islamic Banking and Finance: The Missing Link', in *Global Islamic Finance Report*, Edbiz Corporation Ltd., London, p. 280.

Chakraborty, S. 2018. *Fintech: Evolution or Revolution*, 1st Edn. Available at https://www.researchgate.net/profile/Sumit_Chakraborty/publication/328333395_FINTECH_Evolution_or_Revolution/links/5bc6c7e0a6fdcc03c78953b4/FINTECH-Evolution-or-Revolution.pdf, last accessed October 26, 2019.

Chishti, S. and Barberis, J. 2016. *The Fintech Book: The Financial Technology Handbook for Investors, Entrepreneurs and Visionaries*, John Wiley & Sons Ltd, Chichester, p. 20.

Claridge, T. 2004. *Social Capital and Natural Resource Management: An Important Role for Social Capital?* Unpublished Ph.D. thesis, University of Queensland, Brisbane, Australia.

Clarke, Osborne. 'Blockchain in the Financial Services Sector: What's on the Regulator's Agenda?' *Insights*, 3 January. Available at https://www.osborneclarke.com/insights/blockchain-in-the-financial-services-sector-whats-on-the-regulators-agenda/, last accessed October 23, 2019.

Darcy Allen, D. 2017. 'Discovering and Developing the Blockchain Cryptoeconomy', *SSRN* 18 August. Available at https://ssrn.com/abstract=2815255, last accessed October 29, 2019.

Dolfsma, W., & Charlie, D. 2003. 'Subjects and Boundaries: Contesting Social Capital-Based Policies', *Journal of Economic Issues, 37*, pp. 405–413.

Financial Industry Regulatory Authority. 2018. '*Report on FINRA Examination Findings*', 7 December, pp. 15. Available at https://www.finra.org/rules-guidance/guidance/reports/2018-report-exam-findings, last accessed October 23, 2019.

Finterra. 2018. *TheWhitepaper,* 7th July. Available at https://cdn.finterra.org/FINTERRA_WHITEPAPER.pdf, last accessed October 26, 2019.

Freedman, R.S. 2006. *Introduction to Financial Technology*, Academic Press, London, p. 365.

Ioannis, A. 2018. 'Fintech and Regtech: Impact on Regulators and Banks', *Journal of Economics and Business, 100*, pp. 7–25.

Islamic Finance News (IFN). 2012. 'The Waqf Industry: The Sleeping Giant of Islamic Finance', *Islamic Finance News*, 26th September, pp. 1–4. Available at http://islamicfinancenews.com/sites/default/files/newsletters/v9i38.pdf last accessed October 20, 2019.

Lahsasna, A. June, 2018. 'I Have a Dream: Waqf Market in Addition to Islamic Banking, Takaful and the Islamic Capital Market', *Journal of Wealth Management & Financial Planning, 5*, pp. 47–53.

Martin, Y. 2018. 'Islamic Endowments to be Modernized by Blockchain', *News BTC*, 12 February. Available at https://www.newsbtc.com/2018/02/12/islamic-endowments-modernized-blockchain/, last accessed October 29, 2019.

Nadwi, M.A. and Kroessin, M. 2013. *Cash Waqf: Exploring Concepts, Jurisprudential Boundaries and Applicability to Contemporary Islamic Microfinance*, Islamic Relief Worldwide, Working Paper Series No. 2013-0x, Birmingham, UK, p. 25.

Nicholls, A., Paton, R., and Emerson, J. 2015. *Social Finance*, Oxford University Press, New York, p. 675.

Nicholls, J., Lawlor, E., Neitzert, E. and Goodspeed, T. 2012. *A Guide to Social Return on Investment*, 2nd Edn., Matter and Co., Middlesex, England, p. 107.

Packin, N. G. 2018. 'Regtech, Compliance and Technology Judgement Rule', *Chicago Kent Law Review, 93*(1), 193–218.

Peters, G. W. & Panayi, E. 2018. 'Understanding Modern Banking Ledgers through Blockchain Technologies: Future of Transaction Processing and Smart Contracts on the Internet of Money', *SSRN*. Available at https://papers.ssrn.com/sol3/Papers.cfm?abstract_id=2692487, last accessed October 30, 2019.

Poder, T.G. 2011. 'What Is Really Social Capital? A Critical Review', *The American Sociologist, 42*(4), p. 341.

Robison, L.J., Schmid, A.A. and Siles, M.E. 2002. 'Is Social Capital really Capital?' *Review of Social Economy, 60*(1), pp. 1–21.

Sandwick, John. 2012. Text of Interview with Islamic Finance News (IFN). 'The Waqf Industry: The Sleeping Giant of Islamic Finance', *Islamic Finance News*, 26th September 2012, pp. 1–4. Also available at http://islamicfinancenews.com/sites/default/files/newsletters/v9i38.pdf last accessed October 20, 2019.

Shafii, Z., Iqbal, Z. and Tasademir, M. 2015. Governance Regulatory Framework for Waqf in Selected Countries. Available at http://www.tkbb.org.tr/Documents/Yonetmelikler/Governance-Regulatory-Framework-for-Waqf-in-Selected-Countries-Zurina-Shafii-Zamir-Iqbal-Mustafa-Tasdemir-2015.pdf, last accessed October 27, 2019.

Tanjung, H., and Adhiyansyah, L. February, 2019. 'Waqf and Innovations in Fintech: The Indonesian Experience', *ISFIRE Review*, pp. 52–54.

The World Bank Group, INCEIF & ISRA. 2019. *Maximising Social Impact through Waqf Solutions*, Waqf Report. Available at https://www.inceif.org/wp-content/uploads/2019/07/WB-INCEIF-ISRA-WAQF-Report-Maximizing-Social-Impact-Through-Waqf-Solutions.pdf, last accessed October 20, 2019.

Part III

Awqaf

Its applications and experiences

10 Poverty alleviation through Islamic social finance in agro-sectors – an experience of northern Ghana

Abdul-Jalil Ibrahim and Mohd Ma'Sum Billah

Introduction

In Ghana over 60% of the population depends on agriculture for their livelihood and the proportion is even higher in northern Ghana (Al-Hassan and Diao, 2007). In the context of this development, the agricultural sector remains a vital contributor to economic activity, employing more than half of the working population. The agriculture sector's contribution to GDP over the years has shown a steady reduction from 35.4% in 2006 to 34.3% in 2007 and 33.59% in 2008. In 2015, the sector contributed 19%, declining from almost 30% in 2010. Agriculture is predominantly on a smallholder basis in Ghana. About 90% of farm holdings are less than two hectares in size, although there are some large farms and plantations, particularly for rubber, oil palm and coconut, and to a lesser extent for rice, maize and pineapples (MOFA, 2010). The main system of farming is traditional with hoe and cutlass being the main farming tools. There is little mechanized farming, but bullock farming is practised in some places, especially in the north (MOFA, 2010).

The major challenge facing the sector is insufficient access to finance for smallholder farmers and low investment due to perceived and actual risks in lending to agribusinesses which limit the ability of the sector. According to the Bank of Ghana (BOG) report, only 4.7% of total credit to the private sector in 2018 was channelled to agriculture, forest and fishing (BOG, 2019). The financial inclusion landscape in Ghana is uneven with more people of the northern part of Ghana being financially excluded than the southern part. This means that, of the small proportion of the agricultural financing, only a small portion went to the northern part. This contributes to perpetuating poverty as most of the population there are farmers.

Islamic social finance provides the tools that may be used in poverty alleviation of Muslim communities. Zakah, sadaqa, waqf and blended finance provide a source of social institutions that can be used in this regard. Other Islamic finance contracts with embedded compassion such as Qard, Forbearance, Heeba (donation), Kafalah, Wakalah, Dhaman, Takaful, Hawal al dayin and Promise can be used to complement the major institutions for optimal impact. The chapter is aimed at exploring how Islamic social finance can be used to finance agriculture sector in Ghana by providing a catalyst role to attract impact investors into the agriculture sector and more specifically the northern part. The rationale for choosing Islamic social finance is that there is a huge potential in the agriculture sector in northern Ghana but a pure commercial incentive cannot attract the needed finance as it is perceived as a high-risk area. Islamic social finance will potentially unlock the potential by utilizing the funds that will be mobilized to finance the sector and lay the foundation for attracting commercial capital later on to sustain the sector. Islamic social finance intervention will propose a framework for Islamic social finance that will serve as a catalyst to attract impact investors into the agriculture sector in northern Ghana.

It will also enhance financial inclusion by providing an opportunity for farmers to access financing to reduce poverty by providing incentives to impact investors to deploy financing into this area. Findings of this research will provide the needed framework for applying ISF in northern Ghana by discussing how it can be structured and the associated risks and mitigation options. The method of this study is explorative, to understand the social and economic realities and how Islamic social finance can provide an intervention. This study sheds light on its applicability by looking at how practically this can be implemented in northern Ghana. The study will depend largely on secondary data on Islamic social finance, Islamic finance, blended finance and conventional finance. The study will thoroughly review Islamic finance literature, especially the Islamic finance contracts as well as waqf and zakat. The limitation of this study is that the literature may be sparse due to the limited quality research that has been done in this area and more especially in Ghana. The chapter is organized into five sections including introduction in the first section. The second section presents an overview of the Ghanaian economy with a focus on northern Ghana. The third section presents the agriculture sector in Ghana and its role in the economy and challenges. The fourth section discusses how to structure Islamic social finance to support agriculture financing and its impact on poverty alleviation in northern Ghana and the chapter concludes in the fifth section.

Economy of Ghana with focus of northern Ghana

Ghana's GDP stands around US$ 66 billion at the close of 2018 (EIU, 2019). The real GDP growth rate of Ghana reached a record high of 15% in 2011 as oil production started at commercial volumes. Ghana's economic performance has been above the average growth of West Africa and Africa generally (NSEZ, 2016). GDP growth was 3.1% in 2016 and has increased in 2017 and 2018 to 8.1% and 6.3% respectively (Ghana Statistical Service, 2018). The GDP per capita at PPP stood at US$ 4,785 in 2018. Ghana economy is dominated by the service sector, contributing 46.3% to GDP in 2018.

The agriculture sector's contribution to GDP has declined since 2016 to 19.7% in 2018 (see Figure 10.1).

In terms of resources, Ghana is one of the most endowed countries in Africa in terms of natural resources (such as oil, gold, bauxite, manganese, diamonds iron ore, gas, cocoa, fertile land). The untapped and proven mineral resources include about 2.8 billion metric tonnes of iron ore, 960 million metric tonnes of bauxite, 430 million metric tonnes of manganese and 430 million metric tonnes of limestone. Presently, the country produces modest 160,000 barrels of oil and 120 million standard cubic feet of gas per day (World Atlas, 2019).

Northern Ghana

The Northern and Savannah Ecological Zone (NSEZ) covers 54% of the total land area of Ghana and it's a host to a quarter of the Ghanaian population. The area has fertile land for farming various commercial crops and trees including shea trees, and has also iron ore deposits. The HDI for the NSEZ was computed to be 0.116 for 2014 which is far below that for Ghana (0.575). The roots of the relative underdevelopment of the NSEZ broadly lie in its historical legacies, and, to some extent, in geography, the impacts of which have been compounded by economies of spatial agglomeration (UNDP Northern Ghana Human Development Report, 2018). GLSS (2015) report mapping on the incidence of poverty in Ghana shows that there is a high concentration of poverty in northern Ghana where a majority of Muslims reside. With a regional poverty incidence of 55 which is 13 points above the average national poverty incidence of the country of 42, policymakers are concerned. This area is likely to drive the demand for Shariah-compliant AWF as an intervention.

The Muslim population of Ghana is domiciled across the country but it is concentrated in northern Ghana comprising of Northern, Upper East and

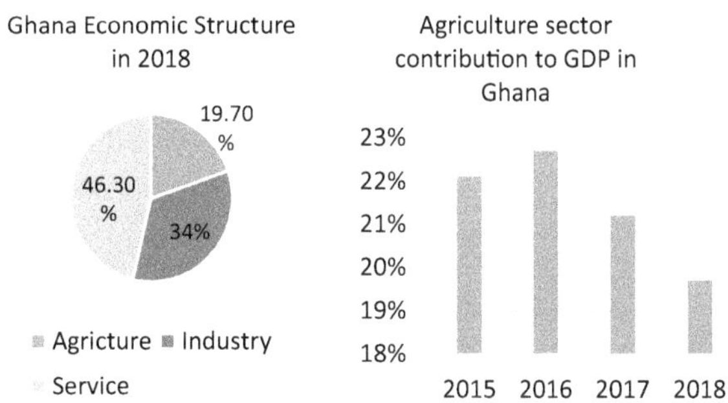

Figure 10.1 Ghana economic structure.

Upper West regions. According to Ghana Statistical Service, Muslims in Ghana constitute 17% of the population with more than 83.6% of household heads in the northern region practising Islam. Islam is also a major religion in Upper East (55.7%) and Upper West (48.0%). Financial institutions are concentrated in the southern part with Accra, the national capital leading with a huge gap. The region with the least access to financial services is the Upper West region located in the northern part. Mobile money provides the highest form of access by most Ghanaians.

According to IBEZ (2015), the most dominant business establishments in northern Ghana is the service sector which is in line with the dominance of the service sector at the national level despite the vast arable and fertile land for agriculture. The northern region has the highest number of business establishments even though it lacks behind the national average. This is partly due to the lack of access to credit for the agriculture sector because of the perceived high risk in the sector which makes it unattractive for banks to finance. The Upper East region has predominantly agricultural-related businesses as service and industrial sector businesses are almost non-existent and these businesses are predominantly in the informal sector. Figure 10.1 shows that the unemployment rate in northern Ghana is higher than the national average as a result of a low number of business establishments and, consequently, a low number of people engaged in employment. In Figure 10.1, whereas Greater Accra has as high as 190,000 establishments with over 1.2 million people engaged in work, the northern region has less than 20,000 and 200,000 establishments and people engaged in work respectively. In a similar analysis, Figure 10.1 shows that even though the three northern regions constitute around 16% of the national population, only 10% of the working population are engaged in work which is lower than the national average of 14%. This shows the enormity of the poverty drivers in the northern regions and the need for a well-thought intervention. Increasing the number of business establishments remains an important approach to countering this and the AWF will help create more businesses and employment.

Overview of the agriculture sector

Ghana cultivates a rich array of staples and cash crops and is the second largest producer of cocoa in the world. The top quantity of the commodity produced in 2012 was cassava and in terms of export value it was cocoa and cashew in the same year (FAO, 2012). The northern savannah zone is a host to the largest agriculture zone. A chunk of the nation's supply of rice, millet, sorghum, yam, tomatoes, cattle, sheep, goat and cotton is grown in the region. In recent times, mango and ostrich commercial farms have also gained popularity in the northern zone (FAO, 2012). The coastal savannah is notable for rice, maize, cassava, vegetables, sugar cane, mangos and coconut, as well as livestock. Sweet potato and soybean crops are viable in this agro-ecological zone, under irrigation. The lower part of this zone is drained by River Volta. Together with other streams and lagoons, these water resources present opportunities for fish farming or aquaculture (FAO, 2012)

Financing modes and challenges

The banking sector consists of 23 banks with 1,225 branches spread across the 16 regions of the country as in June 2019 (BOG, 2019). Over the years formal financial institutions have shown a lack of interest in agriculture finance and several reasons account for this (IFPRI, 2010). One of the reasons is that many agricultural households are located in remote parts of the country and were often widely dispersed which financial institutions find challenging to provide cost-effective and affordable services. Second, a chunk of the agricultural population was subject to adversaries of the weather and climate risks, making it hard for providers of financial services to hedge risks. Third, service providers, mainly urban based, simply did not know enough about the business of agriculture to devise profitable financial products. Fourth, most small agricultural producers in developing countries had little education and little knowledge of how modern banking institutions work. As a result of these difficulties, some innovations have been adopted in recent times – namely, index-based insurance schemes, microfinance, community banking – using modern communication technology to enhance payment system and financial institutions try to bundle financial services with non-financial services as some of the innovations in agricultural financing (IFPRI, 2010).

The reasons mentioned above in part contribute to the perceived high risk of the agriculture sector which constrained the attractiveness of the sector to bankers. Semi-formal and informal sectors are the largest sources of financial access by the rural poor. It is estimated that about 74% of Ghanaians do not own formal bank account and over 60% money supply in Ghana is outside the commercial banking and other regulated financial product system (AfDB, 2013). The role of the semi-formal and informal sector – comprising rural banks, savings and loans companies, and semi-formal and informal financial systems in financing agriculture – becomes even more important in such an environment.

These developments have led the BoG to initiate a national stakeholders' dialogue in 2014 to seek consensus on how to effectively finance agriculture under the topic "Boosting Ghana's Foreign Exchange Resources". The outcome saw the collaboration with the Ministry of Agriculture, with technical support from AGRA to adopt the "Ghana Incentive-based Risk Sharing System for Agricultural Lending" (GIRSAL) as a vehicle for leveraging financial institutions' lending to agriculture in Ghana. GIRSAL aims to minimize lending risks in the full cycle of the agriculture value chain in Ghana and is envisioned to be based on six pillars: (1) risk sharing fund; (2) technical assistance programme, for banks and all involved in the agriculture value chain;

(3) integrated insurance policy, for farmers and agribusiness operators; (4) financial institutions' rating system; (5) bank incentive/reward mechanism; (6) digital financing.

Commodity Exchange (GCE) was designed to address the significant losses in farm produce. This is seen to boost the BOG-initiated GIRSAL in addressing post-harvest losses. This is done by the ready market with professional market institutions that will strengthen the activities of value chain actors. GCE key goal is to link Ghanaian smallholder farmers to agricultural and financial markets in Ghana and across the West Africa region to ensure Ghana farmers secure competitive prices for their commodities, as well as supply good quality commodities which meet the nutritional needs of the Ghanaian people.

Applying Islamic social finance in agricultural financing

The Islamic social funds provide the economic and social tool for inclusive growth and social empowerment of Muslim societies. The Islamic social finance sector broadly comprises the traditional Islamic institutions based on philanthropy, e.g. zakah, sadaqah and awqaf; those based on cooperation, e.g. qard and kafala; and the contemporary Islamic microfinance institutions that aim at making a dent on poverty (Islamic Social Finance Report, 2015).

Islamic social finance

Zakat (alms)

Zakat is the third pillar of Islam which has been made obligatory for to all financially stable Muslims. The compulsory Zakat is divided into two: namely, Zakat al-Fitri, which is paid during the month of Ramadan, and Zakat on wealth. The Asnafaz-Zakat (beneficiaries of zakat) on wealth has been briefly specified in the Quran.[1] According to Maududi (1984), zakat was prescribed to Muslims as other religions before Islam signifying its importance and role in the socio-economic life of Muslims. It helps in redistribution of wealth from the rich to the poor, encourages productivity as idle wealth is zakatable and above all stimulates economic growth through income growth of the poor and the productive use of wealth. Efficient zakat system will ensure that Muslims who are poor are lifted out of the poverty line. The famous hadith where the Prophet encouraged investment by helping a needy person to buy an axe to cut wood instead of just giving a dole to meet the immediate requirements of the needy is worth noting.

Sadaqah (charity)

The Quran affirms: "those who believe, and do deeds of righteousness, and establish regular prayers and regular charity, will have their reward with their

Lord: On them shall be no fear, nor shall they grieve" (2:277). According to the teachings of Islam, the giving of charity and sadaqah helps in many functions. First, the act of sadaqah is an expiation for sins. The believers are asked to give sadaqah immediately following any transgression. Voluntary alms giving can also compensate for any shortcoming in the past payment of zakah. Sadaqah also gives protection against all kinds of evil. It is therefore recommended to give sadaqah by night and by the day, in secret and in public to seek God's pleasure (Quran, 2:274).

Waqf (endowment)

Waqf is an important institution in the Islamic social framework. It can harness the potential of selfless charitable giving in an effective way for better economic impact in the targeted social segments of society. Waqf has played an important role in mobilizing resources for public good in Muslim civilization and has emerged as a credible commitment device that guarantees property owners economic security in return for social services. Throughout the Middle East, it long served as a major instrument for delivering public goods in a decentralized way (Kuran, 2001).[2] According to Kahf (2013), under waqf, an owner donates and dedicates an asset for permanent societal benefit. The beneficiaries enjoy its usufruct and/or income perpetually. In the contemporary application of waqf, it can be established either by dedicated real estate, furniture or fixtures, other movable assets and liquid forms of money and wealth like cash and shares. The cash waqf is usually formed where the pooled donations are used to build institutions, such as schools, hospitals and orphanages (Sadeq, 2002). Aziz et al. (2013) argue that cash waqf can pool more resources and ensure wider participation of individual donors. Besides income support and cash transfers, poor people need training, capacity building and skills improvement to get out of poverty and achieve social mobility. Haneef et al. (2014) argue that the lack of finance and business training requires institutional support to unleash the potentials of micro-entrepreneurs and to establish viable micro-enterprises. Obaidullah (2008) explains that growth-oriented microfinance programmes also need to provide training, insurance and skills enhancement facilities. In this regard, the institution of waqf can improve the chances of socio-economic mobility by providing a rather permanent, effective and efficient funding source for the health and education infrastructure. The increased and improved provision of education and health infrastructure funded through waqf can enhance the income-earning potential of beneficiaries.

Khan (2019) asserts that waqf can be used purposefully for an impactful small and micro business through a Venture Waqf (VW). This is proposed as an institution for the specific purpose of making Shariah-compliant impactful small and micro businesses successful. The chapter argues that the waqf institution established to make impactful businesses successful could blend its resources in a way that can help achieve greater impact. The sources of funds and other resources of the VW could be interest-free loans, charitable grants, waqf contributions, investments, structured and blended financing with philanthropic organizations, voluntary service and advice, compassionate guarantees and any other legitimate contributions.

Leveraging Islamic social finance to attract impact investors into the agriculture sector

Islamic social finance can be leveraged to stimulate investment into the agriculture sector and waqf can be used as a tool in this regard. This will be structured to target investors who are also inclined to impacting their societies and thus do not look for only financial returns but also building social capital. The term "impact investing" was coined in 2007 and is defined by the Global Impact Investing Network (GIIN) as: investments made into companies, organizations, and funds to generate measurable social and environmental impact alongside a financial return. Apart from GIIN, various other global organizations have come out with principles and criteria for measuring the impact of businesses around the world including UN Global Compact, SDGs, ESG, 3Ps and so on. Some scholars proposed Maqasid al-Sharia as a criterion for measuring business impact. In this regard, Islamic value accounting proposed by Obaidullah (2005) is worth mentioning. In more recent research, Obaidullah (2018) asserts that the fact that many Sustainable Development Goals (SDGs) align with Maqāṣid al-Sharī'ah (MaS) means that the MaS-driven Islamic finance would ultimately work towards achieving the SDGs. Hence Islamic finance should naturally be concerned with its impact on society.

Investment is required to build agriculture infrastructures such as irrigation, warehouses and machinery. Also, farmers require inputs to maximize yield but financing is not allocated to the area from investors as the agriculture sector is considered to be of high risk and investors avoid it as noted earlier. This requires intervention and establishing an AWF comes handy.

AWF will be structured to provide a vehicle for incentivizing and serving as a catalyst for attracting private investors into the agriculture sector. With this the waqf fund will be mandated to provide third-party guarantee to investors, carry feasibility studies and arrange for matching of investors with investment opportunities, matching farmers with markets, marketing of farm produce through off-take agreements and providing general advisory services to farmers and businesses in the Agriculture value chain. To sustain its operations, the waqf fund will invest some of its assets through commercial farming and Shariah-compliant funds and assets. When private investors are guaranteed of their investments or provided with income-smoothing vehicles that allow them to make returns subject to future performance adjustments, it will create the requisite environment and assurance for private investors to bring in investments into the sector. With this, the third-party guarantee service of the waqf can provide the needed adjustment to the risk-return profile of the agriculture sector and hence provide a strategic tool of enhancing investment attraction into the area. Waqf fund can also be structured such that blended Murabahah is used to effect the benefiting of non-interest loan to farmers. This will happen by combining compassionate giving and profitability. With this, one party may want to extend a non-interest loan to a farmer when it doesn't make a profit but also interested to share profit with the farmers in case there is profit. This can be an incentivizing instrument that allows the farmer to work hard to earn profit but at the same time it does not put a burden above the principal. Waqf can also bear the cost of funds with regard to Murabahah transactions such that the farmers who are poor only pay back the principal to the Murabahah financier while the waqf bears the markup charge.

The waqf can leverage its mandate to issue a green Sukuk geared towards mobilizing funds for irrigation projects with the government providing some guarantees. Irrigation will be the foundational requirement in maximizing the fullest potential of the productivity in the agriculture sector as it will allow all-year-round farming. It will also see the emergence of commercial farming of cash crops such as mangoes, cashew and cassava within the northern zone. Irrigation projects can be capital intensive and hence investors will want to be assured of recouping their investments as scheduled without any hitches. What it means is that delays or interrupted cash flows will not be welcome. AWF can provide a credit-enhancing role here where they undertake to pay interim returns to investors within the scheme of beneficial ownership. This will be done through an income-smoothing instrument managed by the AWF that will provide the needed adjustment to interim profit and actual profit.

The AWF will also provide agriculture commercial services with a mandate to developing the commercial agriculture ecosystem including developing the market for farmers, commodity traders, buyers and business within the value chain. Farmers can sell their produce to the AWF if they wish to.

The AWF will mobilize funds through multiple ways. The waqf will involve government, traditional authorities, residents of the area, development partners, relevant non-governmental organizations, charities and philanthropists. In Ghana there is no law on waqf, so the waqf will be established as a trust under the company's code. The Northern Development Authority which is mandated by the Government of Ghana to accelerate the development of the North and bridge the development gap between southern and northern Ghana will be an important stakeholder in this. The traditional authorities will donate some strategic lands towards the formation of this waqf. The AWF will issue a regulation that will detail the objectives, vision, mission and programmes. Waqf certificates will be issued matching the projected seed money needed. All parties interested in supporting an impactful business geared towards poverty alleviation will be invited to subscribe to these certificates. Through this, funds can be mobilized for the seed money for the AWF to kick start.

Figure 10.2 presents the structure of the AWF which in summary will make impact investors feel comfortable to invest in various projects in the agriculture sector to alleviate the poverty of poor farmers. Appropriate infrastructure will also be provided and farmers receive financing for inputs to enhance productivity and crop yield (Figure 10.2).

Islamic finance instruments for agriculture financing and risks management

Islamic finance presents quite many instruments that can be used to finance farmers and agriculture businesses in general. Most of the classical sale, lease and sharing contracts, as well as the hybrid contracts can be used to finance businesses by an AWF. It is important to mention that financing agriculture involves, beyond the farms, spanning the entire value chain of the agricultural sector to include production and marketing.

Looking at some of the contracts, it is established that they were inspired by the need for agricultural financing – for instance, Muzara'ah, Musaqat, Mugharasa and Sallam. The other contracts are used to respond to other varied needs of the agriculture sector and some of these contracts include Murabaha, Musawama, Istisna, Ijarah, Musharaka, Mudharabah, Musharakah, Mutanaqisah and the likes. For instance, buying or leasing machines may require Murabahah or Ijarah. Also constructing farm buildings may require Istisna'ah. In AWF investments where equity holding is key, Muharakah may be the ultimate contract that should be used to define the relationship

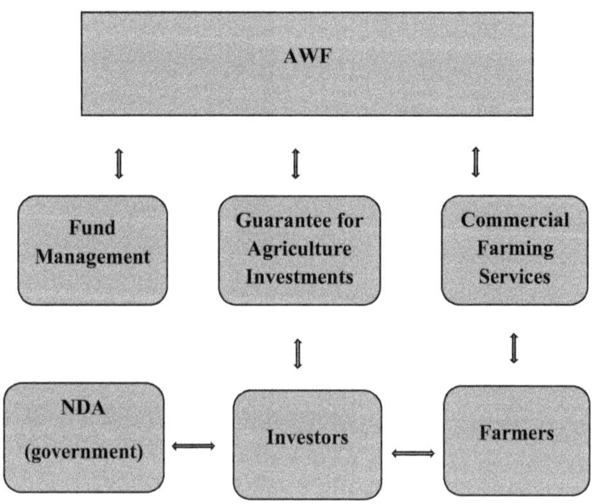

Figure 10.2 Agriculture waqf fund structure and stakeholders.
Source: Author's conceptualization.

between the AWF and the partners. Muzara'ah as a typical agriculture contract can also be used. Other contracts can be used within the operations of the potential investee.

To properly understand how the above contracts can be applied, it is important to dissect the agriculture sector into segments. Also worthy of note is that depending on the crop subsector targeted, different instruments may be used. Usually, commercial trees such as cocoa, cashew, shea nut and the like take more time to mature. Crops usually take three to four months in maturity. The various contracts used are discussed in the next sections. Just like the crops, the various contracts can also be used for livestock and fisheries subsector. For instance, the waqf can provide the needed financing to purchase cattle for rearing by engaging a farmer with expertise in animal rearing for a Musharakah or Mudarabah or Wakalah.

Musharakah (partnership)

Musharakah investors are active, taking part in the management, driving value creation. This trait finds fit with the principles of Musharakah where there is a shared objective of profit-making and shred management. Equity financing structure may be modified so that the investment is not made in full but in tranches. The tranche payments may be benchmarked against the enterprise reaching certain milestones, or just linked to the passage of time. In conventional AWF there is a window for the adjustment of the subscription price if, for example, the milestones are not achieved or forecasts are exceeded (Aggarwal, 2010).

AWF workings will reveal that farmers need more than just finance. It has to be supported especially in the pre seed and seed stage, and that is why the Musharakah contract is key so that the AWF-led investor can provide this added support to the venture to succeed.

A derivative of Musharakah that can be used by AWF in equity financing is a Musharakah line of credit. Musharakah line of credit is a contract of variable capital contribution. With this, an AWF can finance any capital requirement of a prospective business within an accounting year and the business can also pay back funds when they have more than enough cash (Kahf, 2015).

With this, the AWF will be instrumental in putting the necessary measures and strategies to ensure that the venture succeeds. In doing this, the AWF can also leverage existing government institutions. For instance, the Export Development and Agricultural Investment Fund (now Ghana Eximbank) has a facility where businesses in the agriculture sector can acquire machines for production that is geared towards exports. What it means is that the AWF can acquire the needed land and does the feasibility studies of the target plantation which by the way are part of the requirement to qualify for the facility. When this is done they can form a partnership with farmers who may have the expertise in the plant they want to cultivate, for instance, cassava. This will provide an opportunity for the AWF to finance the huge capital requirement that a commercial cassava plantation comes with. In this arrangement, they will be able to pay for the equipment and also share profit from the venture.

Usually, the major problem faced by many farmers in the developing world is post-harvest losses and AWF investing in this area should be aware of this and putting measures to succeed. In Ghana, to make good returns, some businessmen and even companies usually buy farm produce during the bumper season and stock them for some time for the prices to rise so that they can sell. This is impermissible according to Shariah as it amounts to perpetuating riba al-nasi'ah. To ensure that the farm produce is sold profitably, the AWF can source for off-take agreements with local and international buyers of the various commodities that may be produced. This will be easier because the AWF working with many farmers will be able to meet the high volume requirement that is usually required in off-taker agreements. In developed markets, there is a well-functioning commodity market where the prices are not subjected to so much seasonality compared to developing markets. Also, the launch of the Ghana Commodity Exchange (GCE) in the year of 2013 is a positive development towards a more vibrant commodity dealing in the country.

For Musharakah to be effective, some studies call for the standardization of the Musharakah contract. Standardized Musharakah contract will clearly define all the terms as that it is accepted internationally and would ensure that the rights of stakeholders involved in these contracts are well protected (Elsiefy, 2013). Some critiques argue that the Musharakah contract in practice today has many technical and ethical flaws that make it very difficult in using it to raise financing (Choudhury 2001).

Muzar'ah (partnership in crop)

Muzar'ah involves a partnership of crop sharing. In this type of partnership, an AWF can enter into a partnership with a farmer to grow crops where the AWF may provide the land and/or capital and the farmer will provide the labour and/or capital. This contract is typically used for agriculture financing because of its simplicity and the classical roots. The characteristics of this type of partnership include: (a) sharing of gross revenue, (b) investor contribution to capital while farmer contribution to management, (c) different risk scenarios compared with Musharakah, (d) Wakalah-based management, (e) profit/loss sharing linked to gross revenue (Kahf, 2013).

Muzara'ah and its derivatives have an important feature of the distribution of gross revenue. With this, crops, fruits in addition to sharing ownership of trees and land all are expressions of a gross sharing principle. It could also be a tripartite partnership. In this case, one party provides land, the next one provides a combination of required physical inputs and the last of course provides labour. The distribution of gross revenue may not necessarily be in cash as it is allowed to be effected in kind. In Muzara'ah, seeds, fertilizers and pesticides may be contributed by the landowner or the farmer. Also, farm implements may be provided by either of the two partners.

It is noteworthy that in contributing all these additional inputs by either partner, this does not come with payment or compensation to the contributing party out of the gross revenue. This is because the contribution of other inputs is supposed to be incorporated in the ratio of distributing the gross revenue between the two partners. In other words, Muzara'ah does not require, and it does not have, calculation of cost and expenses at the level of the Muzara'ah itself. All cost and expenses are built into the negotiation of the sharing ratio of the partners (Kahf, 2013).Also at the end of Muzara'ah, there is no need for any liquidation of assets as land, as the main fixed asset goes back to its owner and machines also go back to whoever contributes them after the gross products are distributed according to the contractual ratio.

Mugasah and Mugharasah share virtually the same characteristics as Muzar'ah – just that Mugharasah has an added condition of sharing land ownership. Mugharasah is usually applied to plant trees, while Mugasah applies to plants and crops.

Muzara'ah management is based on the principle of wakalah similar to other sharing contracts. The presence of wakalah implies that the manager has an Amanah hand on the property of the other partner. The implication of this is that the farmer is supposed to take appropriate actions to keep the land in most appropriate fertility in the course of the period of the contract and give it back to owner in similar conditions. The expectation is that the Wakil is supposed to take due diligence in protecting the property of the principal. However, the Wakil is not liable for normal wear and tear and any other damage which is not caused by negligence, abuse or contract violation (Kahf, 2013).

In applying Muzra'ah to the agricultural sector in Ghana, the crops sector can be targeted. The AWF can acquire the needed lands from the landowners. In the northern part and many parts of the country, these lands are usually owned by the chiefs whereas in the southern part especially in Accra, lands are owned by families and clans. The AWF can then engage with farmers to provide their labour and expertise to cultivate the land. The AWF can provide the farm inputs and other machinery that may be needed for the farming activity.

Another configuration that may be considered by the AWF is to acquire the machinery needed such as tractors, and combine harvesters, ploughing machines and other assets such as warehousing and buildings. With these assets, the AWF can then reach out to masses of farmers. This will allow optimal use of the investments in these pieces of equipment such that the AWF shares with all the participating farmers of the farm outputs. With this, the AWF can take advantage of the flexibility in Muzara'ah where the partnership doesn't own any of the properties of the venture but rather the ownership is continuously vested in the individual partners.

Wakalah (agency)

Wakalahbil-ujrah takes place in the AWF when other external companies/managers, usual experts in the business area undertaken by the investee, are hired to consult and help the investee company. If the AWF company operates on fee-based contracts, wakalahbil-ujrah will also come into the picture (Al-Rifai and Khan, 2000). Also, Wakalah can be looked at in a situation where the AWF engages directly with other individuals or companies to provide special service for the AWF in its operations. The AWF when investing in cashew farming may contract a cashew research institute or cashew marketing company to carry out the designated task. With this, the wakil is paid its fees when the deliverables are executed.

Salam (sale by differed delivery)

Through Salam form of sale contract the AWF may provide farmers with the necessary financing against their future production. Thus, Salam allows the farmers who produce similar commodities of fixed specifications to enter with the bank into standard Salam contracts under which the bank purchases their products at a price payable in advance. The Salam transactions in Sharia provide that the commodity in question must be in existence at the time of delivery. Certain conditions need to be observed in the Salam contract and the AWF should consider this as it helps in reducing the risk inherent in this contract (see Kahf (2015)). In the case of Ghana, the AWF will sign a contract with farmers by providing the needed cash that is needed to cultivate the land and apply farm inputs. For instance, the AWF can do it with cassava, soybeans, maize, rice, etc. These are short-term yielding crops and there is a well-defined period when crops are harvested. The farmers will then deliver the underlining produce to the AWF on the delivery date. The AWF needs to also sell these commodities when they are received. To have predictable cash flow, the AWF can arrange an undertaking from buyers of these commodities be it local or export market. The AWF can also decide to sell these commodities in the GCE.

Risk management and investment protection in applying Islamic venture capital instruments

AWF investment can be one of the highest risk exposure investments because investment decision is based on potential impact and not on pure commercial motivations. Agriculture investment by its nature is a risky business as there is a high chance of capital loss. Like all real investments in developing countries, Musharakah financing is generally risky given the many adverse effects of changes in the macroeconomic environment and policies, and other factors influencing conditions in the market for the underlining investment. Musharakah is the highest perceived risk-bearing investment among the various Islamic financing modes (Khan and Ahmed, 2001).

The major risk in applying AWF to finance agriculture will be directly related to the contracts used and also the moral hazard of the farmers or businesses in the AWF arrangement. There is an inherent risk in using Musharakah and Muzara'ah and perhaps typical of its nature AWF as risk-bearing entities must be able to deal with these risks. There is also risk associated with a situation where there is a lack of transparency in markets within which the AWF is operating resulting in high monitoring costs. This results in information asymmetry between the AWF and the other partners. These have to be factored into the viability analysis of the AWF investment.

Another important risk that naturally manifests in agricultural activities is the possibility of low yield as a result of bad weather and other uncontrollable events. This is manifested strongly in Salam as the ability to deliver the commodity is directly and indirectly related to the occurrence at production.

There is also a market risk with regard to post-harvest selling of the commodities. As mentioned earlier, there is usually a high supply of commodities during the bumper season thereby driving the prices down and sometimes selling immediately around this time can lead to a loss or lower profit. There has to be a way to minimize the exposure to low prices in bumper seasons by the AWF.

The risk in Muzara'ah is quite different from risks in other types of sharing finance contracts. Here there are several scenarios to be considered depending on the cost of other additional inputs and who provides them (Kahf, 2013). This can be looked at from a scenario when one party provides land and the other farming and the assumption is that all other inputs are zero. In this case, the investor's risk is much less than in Musharakah because gross revenue cannot be negative while net profit may. The same also applies to the farmer under the assumption that the cost of other inputs is zero. In a situation where the arrangement is such that the cost of other inputs is positive and it is divided equally between the two parties, there is a risk of loss to be borne by both parties if the gross revenue turns out to be zero. Lastly, if the cost of additional inputs is positive and it is all contributed by one party there is a risk of loss by one party while the other may make a positive return. This last possible case creates an interesting situation which does not exist in other sharing contracts. That is, one party makes a positive return while the other makes a negative return. This implies that there is a higher risk in Muzara'ah for the party who provides all or most of the additional inputs than in Musharakah.

In providing financing through AWF, to minimize risk relating general non-performance, the AWF may have to segment the farmers by applying different conditions to diversify the risks. This can be done by identifying the various scenarios, in the context of risk assessment and events that may lead to the risks and then appropriately respond to them. The reality is that the AWF may have to bear most of the cost associated with the farm inputs. This can still be contained by segregating the farmers according to income level and appropriately applying a blend of strategies to mitigate the risk. Additionally, to mitigate the risk of non-performance and adverse selection of investees, the AWF can also rely on the guarantees and sureties given by the group members. This approach will work where the AWF encourages the farmers to form groups. These groups are formed such that they share certain characteristics (either age, community ties, family or ethnic or clan). Because these group members know each other, they can vouch for the credibility of one another as well as serve as a subtle guarantee for the AWF to deal with the group members and by far the individual members. This will reduce the risk of adverse selection and also avoidable negative risk evolution of investees.

In partnership, there is an element of wakalah and partners are supposed to act in the best interest of the partnership. The AWF can also put some conditions regarding misconduct by the other partners. Partners are supposed to bear the losses that occur in the course of normal businesses. This loss bearing has the potential of exposing the AWF investment to losses where farmers may act imprudently or negligently. A situation of loss occurrence should be properly spelt out with instances of violation of contract and negligence clearly articulated. This will minimize the risk of moral hazard.

Another important risk that naturally manifests in agricultural activities is the possibility of low yield as a result of bad weather and other uncontrollable events. To tackle this, two tools can be used. The first one is to look at agricultural insurance which is available in Ghana. This is conventional. This may be allowed once the need to insure the farmers becomes necessary and there is no Shariah-compliant alternative. This will give some space for farmers to be able to float above the waters when they are hit by low yields. Another tool that can be used in respect of AWF in dealing with the farmers is to institute a fund or corporative fund where some contributions are made into this fund towards averting any downturn that may affect the yield of any season. The capitalization of this may be an issue for the first years as the farmers may not have the funds to contribute to this. This can still be achievable if it is well planned such that as the years progress, the farmers and the AWF can even set aside part of their shares of the gross output to be invested into this fund such that it can serve as a cushion to non-performing farmers which are linked to the natural occurrences.

The market risk exposed by AWF in terms of the pricing can be mitigated by signing off-taker agreements with buyers in advance. This can be both locally and internationally explored as most of the commodities produced in Ghana are in high demand in the international market. This is especially for commodities which are not regulated. This agreement will define the prices in advance and may not necessarily be exposed to the volatility associated with the seasonality. In well-developed markets, there is a functional commodity market where prices are listed and it is easy to price a commodity and predict the price movements. The launch of the GCE can help in providing the needed pricing signal for investors in the agricultural sector.

Conclusion

The benefit of farming on economic growth is undoubtedly enormous and will particularly be an avenue for poverty alleviation in northern Ghana. There is a need to shift away from reliance on rainfall farming to irrigation to improve productivity. This study explores how ISF can be used as a catalyst to attract agriculture sector investments into northern Ghana. A waqf fund provides an opportunity for income smoothing and guarantee of investments of impact investors. It can then help attract impact investors into the agriculture sector in northern Ghana. This is important because of the reluctant of banks in financing the sector owing to the perceived risks even though it plays a strategic role in responding to the food security needs of the country as well as revenue generation and creation of employment for the people.

Various contracts in Islamic finance can be used to finance the agriculture sector depending on the need. The unique nature of AWF makes Musharakah an ideal contract for AWF. Muzara'ah, Salam and Wakalah are all complementing contracts that can be used depending on the needs of the AWF in the agricultural context. The chapter also discusses the risks associated with the use of these Islamic financing contracts in an Islamic AWF. Diversification, monitoring, farmer's segmentation, insurance (takaful), buyer undertakings and group member guarantees are some of the mitigation measures that can be taken to reduce the risk of capital loss in applying AWF structure in financing the agriculture sector. With this, the farmers will be able to get the needed funding for their farming activities which will lead to enhanced food production and better livelihoods for them and at the same time building an Islamic social finance ecosystem for impact investing.

Notes

1 "Alms are only for the poor and the needy, and the officials (appointed) over them, and those whose hearts are made to incline (to truth) and the (ransoming of) captives and those in debts and in the way of Allah and the wayfarer; an ordinance from Allah; and Allah is knowing, wise" (Quran, 9:60).

2 In 1923, three-quarters of Turkey's arable land be longed to waqfs. Around the same time, one-eighth of all cultivated soil in Egypt and one-seventh of that in Iran stood immobilized as waqf property. In the middle of the 19th century, one-half of the agricultural land in Algeria, and in 1883 one-third of that in Tunisia, was owned by Waqf. See Kuran (2001) for a detailed discussion on the economic significance of Waqf in Muslim societies in the past.

References

African Development Bank. (2013). Financial Inclusion in Africa. http://www.afdb.org/fileadmin/uploads/afdb/Documents/Project-and Operations/Financial_Inclusion_in_Africa.pdf

Aggarwal, V. (2010). A Guide to VC in the Middle East and North Africa INSEAD. www.insead.edu.

Al-Hassan, R. & Diao, X. (2007). Regional Disparities in Ghana: Policy Options and Public Investment Implications. International Food Policy Research Institute, Sustainable Solutions for Ending Hunger and Poverty IFPRI Discussion paper February 2007 Washington D.C, USA.

Al-Rifai, T., & Khan, A. (2000).The Role of Venture Capital in Contemporary Islamic Finance. Proceedings of the Fourth Harvard University Forum on Islamic Finance: Islamic Finance: The Task Ahead Cambridge, Massachusetts. Centre for Middle Eastern Studies, Harvard University, pp. 243–250.

Aziz, M., Johari, F. & Yusof, M.A. (2013). Cash Waqf Models for Financing in Education. Proceedings of the 5th Islamic Economic System Conference (iECONS2013), pp. 835–842. Accessed on 19/10/2019 at www.researchgate.net.

Haneef, M. A., Muhammad, A. D., Pramanik, A. H. & Mohammed, M. O. (2014). Integrated Waqf Based Islamic Microfinance Model (IWIMM) for Poverty Alleviation in OIC Member Countries. *Middle-East Journal of Scientific Research*, Vol. 19, No. 2, pp. 286–298.

Islamic Social Finance Report. (2015). Islamic Research and Training Institute. IDB, Saudi Arabia.

Kahf, M. (2013). Islamic Finance Contract. First edition (February 12, 2013).

Kuran, T. (2001). The Provision of Public Goods under Islamic Law: Origins, Impact, and Limitations of the Waqf System. *Law & Society Review*, Vol. 35, No. 4, pp. 841–898.

Maududi, S. A. A. (1984). The Economic System of Islam. Lahore: Islamic Publications Ltd.

MOFA. (2010). Agriculture in Ghana. http://mofa.gov.gh/site/wp-content/uploads/2011/10/AGRICULTURE-IN-GHANA-FF-2010.pdf

NSEZ. (2016). Northern Ecologival Zone Concept Master Plan.

Obaidullah, M. (2008). Role of Microfinance in Poverty Alleviation: Lessons from Experiences in Selected IDB Member Countries. Islamic Development Bank. Accessed on 19/10/2019 at https://papers.ssrn.com/sol3/papers.cfm?abstract_id=1506077

Obaidullah, M. (2018). Managing Climate Change: Role of Islamic Finance. *Islamic Economic Studies, 26*(1), 31–62.

Sadeq, A. M. (2002). Waqf, Perpetual Charity and Poverty Alleviation. *International Journal of Social Economics*, Vol. 29, No. 1/2, pp. 135–151.

UNDP. (2015). Northern Human Development Indicator. Accessed on 19/10/2019 at https://www.gh.undp.org/content/ghana/en/home/library/human_development/northern-ghana-human-development-report-2018-.html

Worldatalas. (2019). What Are the Major Natural Resources of Ghana. https://www.worldatlas.com/articles/what-are-the-major-natural-resources-of-ghana.htmlBoG, 2019

11 Developing awqaf through cash waqf

Hichem Hamza

Introduction

The concept of waqf reflects multiple dimensions of the solidarity, charity and philanthropy through continuous donations and benefits for the welfare of the society. The waqf, emerged from private property and the free will of individuals to donate their wealth, embodies the spirit of social solidarity (Kahf, 2018, p. 64). The management of orphan wealth is the basis of the management of waqf wealth (Al-Masri, 1999, p. 11), which prevails the social role of waqf institution. Besides, the waqf is driven by the will of charity and the sight of its social impact which requires that the waqf institution realizes this vision with responsibility and transparency.

The waqf institution embodies the pillars of the waqf concept by establishing the relationship between the donor (*waqif*), the waqf assets and the beneficiaries. The waqf institution faces social challenges related to achieving the needs of general public, which requires the development of cash waqf in order to realize the waqf policy goals. Cash waqf appeared in Turkey during the early 15th century has been considered as a revolution in *Fiqh* of awqaf and the contribution of Othman state in the Islamic civilization (Alarnaut, 2018, p. 35). Nowadays, cash waqf is increasing the priority of the waqf institution in terms of financing and investment given its characteristics related to mobilization flexibility, investment choices and liquidity. Cash waqf flexibility could make waqf more attractive for all types of donors enabling the success of waqf to fulfil the social role. The cash waqf development is mainly achieved through the mobilization and allocation of resources which necessitates the involvement of donors and waqf institutions in the realization of waqf objectives.

The mobilization of resources is a recurrent challenge faced by waqf institutions. It ensures the sustainability of waqf and the achievement of the charitable goals. Through the cash waqf, the donors contribute to the redistribution of their wealth derived mainly from the profit sector by channelling a part of it to the non-profit sector (Hamza, 2019, p. 110). The donors are the drivers of waqf resources and the strength of their relationship with waqf institution is determinant for continuous mobilization of resources under the condition of donor and the compliance with sharia objectives. The willingness of the donors increases when they perceive that their funds are being used effectively and with transparency to resolve societal issues. The governance of the relationship between waqf institution and donors based on transparency and social responsibility is most likely among the key factors of cash waqf success. The allocation of financial resources to different investment assets depends on mobilization level and structure of perpetual and temporary cash waqf. In this regard, the waqf institution is intended to realize the balance between charity waqf assets and waqf investment assets to ensure the stability and sustainability of awqaf. A successful waqf is a successful investment of assets (Alarnaut, 2018, p. 46). Besides, the return distribution as a result of waqf investment strategy is another factor that paying attention of the cash waqf donors regarding the social impact of their donations. The rational allocation of waqf return is determinant for the success of cash waqf and the realization of the social vision of awaqf.

The role of awqaf general authority and the degree of its independence with the state are crucial for achieving waqf goals. The case of awqaf central authority in Kuwait is relevant and reveals the effectiveness of the model. Furthermore, the legislative aspects play a great role in attracting people to donate cash waqf. Incentives actions like tax facilities or exemptions encourage donors to donate and to invest in waqf and are important for the continuation of flows of waqf resources and the increase of investment opportunities (Kahf, 2000, p. 133; Al-Douri, 2001, p. 797).The objective of this chapter is to highlight the contribution of the continuous mobilization of resources, the relationship of donors with the waqf institution, the optimal waqf investment and the legislative aspects in developing awaqf through cash waqf. These factors allow us to reach a set of directions on policies and procedures aimed at enhancing the position of the cash waqf as a complement of the property waqf,[1] thus contributing to the efficacity of the waqf policy of waqf institutions. The chapter underlines the commitment and cooperation of waqf institutions, donors and waqf authorities in the revitalization of waqf system.

Growing role of cash waqf

The immovable waqf, especially land and real estate, is the dominant characteristic of waqf assets. However, with the advent of the movable waqf, the waqf has witnessed a change in waqf types, where the most known was the cash waqf,[2] which is no less important than the immovable waqf. The distinction of cash waqf is tied to the flexibility of mobilization and investment of waqf resources, the promotion of the collective donations and the advantages of the liquidity. In view of the importance of cash waqf, several waqf institutions (Kuwait, Saudi Arabia, Bahrain, Turkey, Malaysia) have adopted strategies to attract waqf resources within the framework of perpetual or temporary cash waqf, with the aim of improving the management of financial resources in terms of stability, liquidity, cost and exploitation of investment opportunities (Hamza, 2017, p. 124). The cash waqf is characterized by the flexibility of its mobilization through multiple instruments (waqf funds, waqf shares, corporate waqf, waqfsukuk, waqf deposit, crowdfunding, fintech)[3] used for the investment in projects of economic and social feasibility. Further, the cash waqf is an important tool for financing waqf investment and providing returns that achieve the objectives of all the waqf partners.

Literature regarding awqaf has given more importance to the growing role of cash waqf in terms of mobilization of resources and investment assets. Cash waqf can finance waqf revitalization by attracting funds from all people (Nienhaus, 2018, p. 91). There is evidence that the waqf assets need continuously resources for maintenance in order to remain useful and productive and by consequence to achieve waqf social goals essentially regarding poverty, education and health. These sources flow can be strengthened by the cash waqf given the fact that it allows all public to participate in the donations with whatever amount. In fact, cash waqf allows any person, regardless of his or her financial ability, to participate in the success of the waqf which constitutes a consecration of the concept of collective participation in raising cash funds to contribute to charity by creating and developing awqaf (Hamza, 2017, p. 129). In addition, this culture and awareness of participation promotes the values of cooperation and broadens the solidarity towards waqf beneficiaries. Cash waqf plays a central role in fundraising given the facility of mobilization where not many people can donate a piece of land, but almost anyone can contribute to a cash waqf; in fact, cash waqf gives opportunities for a much wider pool of donors to contribute to social good and reap eternal rewards than waqf restricted to immovable property (WB, INCEIF and ISRA, 2019, p. vi).

Another advantage of cash waqf, with perpetuity and temporary forms, is the liquidity which gives more facilities to optimise the management of resources and assets. The cash waqf contributes to appropriate solutions in the management of immovable and movable assets, thanks to the presence of liquidity. In the current economic situation, liquid funds have an important role in the property waqf (Al-Douri, 2001, p. 783). There is a necessity to give importance to cash waqf given the fact that most of the existing waqf are real estate, while the scope of investment requires liquid funds, labour and raw materials, which necessitates the finding of monetary sources (Al-Douri, 2001, p. 792). The cash waqf can contribute to the financing of the development of a dilapidated waqf and playing the role of a "feeder waqf" for the old waqf (Nienhaus, 2018, p. 95).

The importance of cash waqf is that it complements and supports the property waqf and prevents the use of financial methods that harm the waqf in the long term, as happened in the last two centuries (Al-Omar, 2010, p. 53). The shortage of cash waqf hinders the growth and the sustainability of the waqf assets leading the waqf institution to limit the social role in addition to the research of funds through debt which gives more financial difficulties. Experiences have shown that most of the immovable waqf are difficult to liquidate when the waqf needs to be repaired or restored which sometimes forces the manager (*Nadhir*) to resort to the borrowing. This situation justifies the importance of cash waqf as a complement of property waqf and the choice of Kuwait awqaf authority which has adopted a strategy based on a combination of cash and property awqaf (Al-Omar, 2010, p. 50). The establishment of investment strategy combining cash waqf and property waqf is relevant for the commitment of the waqf institution towards waqf beneficiaries.

Governance of the relationship with donors

The waqf institution seeks to identify donors who share their own values and who have the human and charitable will to contribute to the mobilization of the waqf resources necessary to achieve the noble objectives of waqf. The waqf institution seeks to develop the relationship with the donors in a climate of mutual trust and collective awareness of the challenges of social change, and the need for solidarity among individuals and institutions of the society (Hamza, 2019, p. 112). The establishment and the continuity of the relationship with donors is the essence of the governance objectives given the crucial role of donors in the existence and prosperity of the waqf. In fact, the donors contribute to the redistribution of their wealth derived mainly from the profit sector by directing a part of it to the waqf sector which also indicates the importance of the profit sector in the success of waqf sector (Hamza, 2019, p. 110). In this regard, it is legitimate that the donors through their waqf conditions are involved in the decisions related to the use of funds, investment strategy and return distribution. The law should choose the appropriate balance between the rights and freedom of the donor and the public interest leading to the stability of the waqf; in this context, the donor must be given as much freedom as possible to choose the appropriate conditions of his waqf and achieve all his own purposes in compliance with Sharia (Kahf, 2000, pp. 115–116).

Given the essential role of donors, waqf institution is intended to establish a stable and long relationship with donors and avoid interest conflicts that can occur. Many people are reluctant to donate to waqf institutions because they doubt the honesty of the administrators and do not know how their donations will be used which proves the lack of transparency as a huge problem in waqf administration (WB, INCEIF and ISRA, 2019, p. vi). There is an absence of the principles and rules of good governance in the practices and behaviour of waqf institutions, both in investment and in the return distribution (Al-Omar and Almaoud, 2014, p. 5). Less information about the waqf progress awareness and lack of sharing up-to-date information between waqf organization and the donors could slow down the effort of accumulating the funds and need double effort to appeal the donors (Kasim et al., 2019, p. 1308). Trust and transparency are the pillars of the relationship between the donor and the waqf institution. The manager (agent) is trusted by the donor (principal) to manage donations with accountability, transparency and efficiency. Any misconduct, moral hazard or conflict of interests is harmful for the reputation of the waqf institution and will affect the confidence of the donors towards cash waqf. One of the goals of the waqf administration is to minimize the potential moral hazards such as corruption, embezzlement and trust abuse (Kahf, 2000, p. 306).

The reputation of the waqf institution is based on its reliability and credibility vis-à-vis the society and is an essential factor ensuring donor's confidence. The continuity of cash waqf funds and by consequence the sustainability of the waqf depend on the strength of the relationship with donors. There is a need to improve the fundraising relationship with donors which is "donor-centred" instead of being "organization-centred" (Kasim et al., 2019, p. 1309). The governance mechanisms are intended to resolve any potential conflict of interests in the relationship between waqf institution and donors leading to a critical situation in terms of fund mobilization and waqf investment. Given the importance of wealth donated by donors and managed by the waqf institution, the resolution of potential conflict between the two parties is essential. In this regard, the role of the board of directors (*Majlis al-Nadhara*) and the presence of Sharia board as mechanisms of governance (Al-Omar and Almaoud, 2014, p. 209) can play a crucial role in resolving interest conflict, protecting all parties rights, and ensuring the Sharia compliance of waqf institution.

In the awqaf context, governance effectively ensures that donors' confidence is kept at the highest level in guaranteeing a continuous flow of contributions, thereby ensuring awqaf institution's survival and sustainability (Awaludin et al., 2018, p. 143). Donor's continuous donation is most influenced by donor's trust to the organizations, familiarity with the cause of organization and perceived efficacy of the contribution (Kasim et al., 2019, p. 1305). For charitable institutions like awqaf, the elements of governance, accountability and transparency are equally important as it ensures a continuous flow of resources from donors or contributors (Awaludin et al., 2018, p. 143). It should be ensured that the standards of the governance system are met in the internal environment of the endowments, especially through the main operations, such as polarization, registration, maintenance, disbursement and investment (Salahat, 2018, p. 9). General authority of awqaf should upgrade the governance of the waqf sector and make it more effective, and it should develop channels of financing and investment to support the expansion of awqaf (Asharqia Chamber, 2018, p. 125).

Optimal waqf investment

The flexibility of cash waqf is an interesting advantage for waqf investment choices and opportunities. Cash waqf has opened new horizons for waqf investment which have not been existed with property waqf.[4] Compared to property waqf, cash waqf is characterized by many advantages – the most important is the flexibility in the proper use of waqf assets when there are suitable investment opportunities and high return if funds are invested in certain investment sectors (Al-Omar, 2010, p. 48). Cash waqf is considered as the best means of income generation and capital growth for awqaf (Sabit Haji Mohammad, 2015, p. 43) and has been becoming capital for waqf investment. In fact, the essential role of waqf investment is to serve charitable waqf which needs funds to meet the social functions and to guarantee its sustainability. The philosophy of waqf investment is the support of the charitable awqaf assets and historically, the development of the waqf forced the donor to build income-generating enterprises or waqf investment to ensure the continuation of charitable waqf (Alarnaut, 2018, p. 40). The characteristics of perpetual or temporary cash waqf are important factors in the choice of waqf investment. These two types of cash waqf can be used for real and financial investment and for quardh hassan. In fact, there is a social need for financing microfinance end entrepreneurship through temporary cash waqf which is feasible through quardh hassan.

The prominent indicator of optimal waqf investment is the equilibrium between charitable and investment assets in terms of benefit continuity and financial sustainability. Through equilibrium, there will be an alignment between increasing the size and types of charitable waqf and covering their expenses, thanks to the returns of waqf investment assets. The cash waqf has the capacity to contribute to the equilibrium between charitable and investment assets, on one hand, and perpetuity and temporary waqf, on another hand. The optimal allocation of cash waqf resources is linked to the humanitarian and social objectives of the waqf institution and the lack of equilibrium in this allocation will lead the waqf resources for uses that may not achieve the greatest benefit for the community. The equilibrium between waqf assets is an important factor in achieving the objectives of Sharia and the purpose of sustainable waqf since the donor seeks through their condition to find an equilibrium between charitable waqf and waqf investment to ensure an optimal benefit of waqf assets. Moreover, the equilibrium in waqf assets would stabilize the waqf sector, and any defect in this equilibrium or deficiency in waqf investment leads to a shortage of income, and by consequence, the charitable waqf is regressed, leading the waqf assets to ruin and decay (Alarnaut, 2011, p. 75).

The selection of waqf investment assets is based on the investment strategy and the extent of its compatibility with the conditions of the donor regardless of investment opportunities with high returns. The specificity of waqf and the nature and size of the charitable waqf give an orientation to what should be the investment in terms of strategy to implement and return to realize. In fact, according to Sharia objectives, the waqf resources are affected by investment assets in order to generate a return for waqf beneficiaries. The generation of a reasonable and stable return is a challenge facing waqf institution and is crucial for the future of waqf system given the fact that a successful waqf is a successful investment of assets (Alarnaut, 2018, p. 46). The Western experience in investing waqf assets shows the importance of investing assets through low-risk mechanisms, even though their profits are reduced (Khafagy and Irfan, 2012, p. 14). At the same time, an insufficient return not meeting the minimum need of the waqf compared to the size of the cash waqf allocated poses the efficacity of waqf investment regarding the desired social impact. Such insufficient return may open the door to the indebtedness (*Istidana*) and assets exchange (*Istibdal*) as financial solutions.

The waqf investment required, more precisely the investment project's evaluation, is intended to offer a social return in addition to the economic return. In this regard, the investment climate, available investment opportunities and expected risks should be evaluated (Isbihi, 2015, p. 22). The preference is given to investment projects that fully meet the urgent and permanent needs of the society. The waqf investment could be more useful if funds are channelled to the necessary sectors and small and medium enterprises leading to an economic benefit added to charitable benefits provided that reasonable and stable return is ensured. In fact, there is a possibility to reconsider the management of a part of investment funds so that it can be channelled to entrepreneurship and SMEs rather than to large companies that have more alternatives of financing.

On another side, the waqf return distribution is an important indicator of the waqf investment impact on social need and, by consequence, it is a key motivation for the donors' continuous donations of cash waqf which may reinforce their trust and relationship with waqf institution. Perceived efficacy of the contribution is a crucial internal factor affecting continuous donations among cash waqf donors (Kasim et al., 2019, p. 1308). In fact, donor condition and waqf interest (*Maslaha*) are the two principals' elements guiding waqf return distribution. The logic spending of waqf income with priority to waqf assets maintenance and waqf beneficiaries need is an important factor reinforcing the sustainability and reputation of waqf institution. The increase of waqf resources through investment is necessary and indispensable to ensure the continuity of the waqf in providing its benefits over time, and this is done by allocating a part of waqf return to be reinvested which contributes to the development and sustainability of waqf resources (Asharqia Chamber, 2018, p. 63).[5]

Development of waqf legislation

The development of a legislative environment is one of the priorities of the waqf system that seeks to play a social and humanitarian role efficiently and effectively. Any efforts to revive the waqf necessitate a reformulation of the laws governing the waqf, as well as amending several other laws related to the establishment, management, investment and role of awqaf, such as tax laws, NGO law, and education and health laws (Khafagy and Irfan, 2012, p. 6). The development of legislation and laws is a challenge for the revival of the waqf sector by creating an attractive environment for cash waqf donors and establishing transparency and confidence-building among all the parties of the waqf system. A global legislative approach of cash waqf of the awqaf general authority related to the development of waqf sector is important given the fact that this authority is charged of all legal and regulatory aspects.

The legislative development of cash waqf is fundamentally pertained to the cash waqf products, donor's motivation and tax exemptions. In this regard, it is in the interest of waqf legislation that the state gives more roles and responsibility to the organizations of the civil society to be partners in waqf development planning (Nienhaus, 2018, p. 94). It is recommended that the ministries of awqaf give support and incentive for the development of the waqf, not to be responsible of the management of awqaf (Al-Douri, 2001, p. 793). The Islamic countries need to diversify the waqf legislation and mitigate the authority of the state on the waqf, so that the state becomes a supervisor and trustee regarding waqf role and mission, and achieves the objective of the waqf, and the arrival of benefit to the public (Feddad, 2018, p. 119). In fact, in Kuwait, the awqaf laws are flexible, which makes the awqaf general authority attractive, as an independent government institution, in guiding individuals to a wide range of types of waqf that they wish to participate in managing or following up to ensure that their funds reach their designated destinations (Alarnaut, 2018, p. 48).

In the context of independent awqaf general authority, the cash waqf legislation plays a pivotal role in guiding and facilitating the waqf activity through incentive laws and a roadmap for the most deserving waqf areas regarding development and investment of resources. The legislation related to the creation and development of cash waqf products, as well as incentive measures for donors, will develop waqf activity and encourage turnout on waqf, which contributes to its development and sustainability. Legislative products issued by the awqaf general authorities (Kuwait, Saudi Arabia, Bahrain) provide a package of options for donors to meet their needs and desires away from the state's authority in management and execution (Feddad, 2018, p. 119). The creation and development of the cash waqf products is pertaining to the waqf funds, corporate waqf, sukuk, shares and waqf deposit.[6]

Furthermore, the legislative development can be promoted by the incentive laws regarding cash waqf mobilization and waqf investment. In Morocco, the public awqaf are exempted from taxes where the waqf code in article 151 mentions: "*Public waqf shall be exempted, regarding all their conduct, actions or operations, as well as their related income from all taxes, fee or any other withholding tax of a national or local aspect*" (Al-Zayaani, 2016, p. 294). In the United States, donors receive many tax benefits related to income and capital taxes in order to encourage and motivate them to donate (Kahf, 2000, p. 128). In countries where laws exist with plenty of exemptions, such as the United States, there is an increase of the donations, while we see the opposite in countries where tax exemptions have not been expanded (Kahf, 2000, p. 133). For instance, in Turkey and Malaysia, despite their history and long experience in cash waqf practices, their waqf tax systems remain an issue for the development of the sector (WB, INCEIF and ISRA, 2019, pp. 17, 19). The government should provide financial support to exempt the charitable waqf from taxes in order to have a wide role in serving the society (Al-Douri, 2001, p. 797). A corporate waqf can get advantages, exceptions and tax exemptions more than those granted to profit organizations, which represents a competitive advantage that helps waqf institution and corporate waqf to achieve the target waqf returns and develop their assets (Hamza, 2019, p. 131).

Conclusion

The developing of awqaf through cash waqf is essential for the sustainability of waqf assets and the meeting of the societal need of the public. The social, economic and financial dimensions of cash waqf urge the waqf institution to develop the approach of waqf resources and assets. Historically, immovable waqf and perpetual waqf have prevailed the waqf landscape despite some limits regarding the management of waqf resources and assets. Thanks to movable waqf and precisely cash waqf in perpetual and temporary forms, the property waqf is completed and reinforced by the cash waqf mainly through the flexibility regarding mobilization of resources and waqf investment. The complementarity of cash waqf and property waqf ensures equilibrium in the structure of resources and the optimal allocation of investment assets; besides, it supports the stability of waqf sector through a global risk management approach. The cash waqf is able to promote the waqf investment leading to a stable waqf return which reinforces the social role of waqf institution. The success of cash waqf is highly tied to the trust of donors towards waqf institution and the responsibility of this institution in the donations, investment and return management. The governance of the relationship with donors is the key factor for the continuity of waqf. The legislative development is another factor that can be supported by the waqf authorities for the attractiveness of cash waqf. Finally, the cooperative relationship between awqaf general authority, waqf institutions and donors through their different roles is necessary to reinforce the development of awqaf in Muslim societies.

Notes

1 Property waqf is defined as immovable and movable waqf in tangible form.
2 In 2004, the Islamic Fiqh Academy of the Organization of the Islamic Conference (OIC) authorized the perpetual and temporary cash waqf in the resolution No. 140 (15/6) on investment in waqf and its yields and rents – 15th session of the International Islamic Fiqh Academy, Muscat (Sultanate of Oman) 14–19 Muharram 1425 AH, corresponding to 6–11 March 2004. The Accounting and Auditing Organization for Islamic Financial Institutions (AAOIFI) authorized the cash waqf, stocks, funds and Sukuk Waqf in Sharia standard No. 60 (amended), items No. 2/4/13, 2/4/14 And 2/4/15 (AAIOFI, 2019).
3 These instruments, essentially waqf, funds are increasingly used by waqf institutions and awqaf general authorities (Kuwait, Saudi Arabia, Malaysia, Islamic Development Bank) to mobilize and invest cash waqf.

4 Historically, Ijara with its subsets like *Hikr* and *Ijaratain* were the most known types of assets immovable investment used with restricted conditions and less flexibility.
5 Regarding expenditure from the revenue earned of the awqaf supervised by the Saudi Waqf general authority, it was determined that only 13.1% of it was spent for the beneficiaries designated. The vast majority of revenue (86.9%) was reinvested in order to further develop waqf resources (op. cit., p. 133).
6 Article (7) of the law of the Awqaf General Authority in the kingdom of Saudi Arabia issued by the council of ministers on 09/12/2015 (27/2/1437H) stipulated the approval of the establishment of waqf funds and investment portfolios, the establishment of institutions and corporate waqf, or participating in their establishment, or owning existing shares, in conformity with the regulatory procedures.

References

Accounting and Auditing Organization for Islamic Financial Institutions (2019). Waqf. Shari'a Standard n°60 (amended). Item No. 2/4/13, 2/4/14 and 2/4/15 (AAIOFI, 2019).

Alarnaut, M.M. (2011). Al-waqf fi al-alem al-islamibein al-madhiwa al-hadher (Waqf in the Islamic World between Past and Present). Scales. First edition.

Alarnaut, M.M. (2018). Toward an Active Role of Awqaf in the Life of Contemporary Muslim Societies. *Journal of King Abdulaziz University: Islamic Economics*. Vol. 31, No. 3. pp. 33–58.

Al-Douri, A.T. (2001). Mustaqbel al-waqf fi al-watan al-arabi (The Future of Waqf in the Arab World). Waqf System and Civil Society in the Arab World. Research and Discussions of Intellectual Symposium Organised by Center for Arab Unity Studies. General Authority of Awqaf of Kuwait State. Beirut, Lebanon. pp. 777–799.

Al-Masri, R.Y. (1999). Al-awqaffikhenwaiktisaden (Waqf Jurisprudentially and Economically). Dar Al-Maktabi. Damascus.

Al-Omar, F.A. (2010). Ishem al-waqffil al-amal al-khairiwatanmia al-ijtimaia (Contribution of Waqf in Charity and Social Development). Awqaf General Authority. Kuwait.

Al-Omar, F.A. and Almaoud, B.B.A. (2014). Qawaedhawkamat al-waqf :Nadharatmouassaset al-waqfnamoudhajen (Rules of Waqf Governance: Model of Waqf Institution Management). Chair of Cheikh Rached Ben Dayel for Waqf Studies. IMSIU University.

Al-Zayaani, M. (2016). Moudawanatoal-awqaf al-maghrebia (Code of Moroccian Awqaf). Awqaf General Authority. State of Kuwait.

Asharqia Chamber (2018). Waqf Economics Report. Asharqia Chamber. Riadh. KSA.

Awaludin, N. S., Nahar, H.S., Yaacob, H. and Bakar, N.S. (2018). Exploring Awqāf Governance: Preliminary Evidence of Governance Practices and Disclosure of Two Malaysian Awqaf Institutions. *Journal of King Abdulaziz University: Islamic Economics*, Vol. 31, No. 2, pp. 139–150.

Feddad, L. (2018). Stances with "Toward an Active Role of Awqaf in the Life of Contemporary Muslim Societies" Article by Muhamed Alarnaut. *Journal of King Abdulaziz University: Islamic Economics*. Vol. 31, No. 3, pp. 115–122.

Hamza, H. (2017). Financial Structure of Cash Waqf. *Journal of King Abdulaziz University: Islamic Economics*. Vol. 30, No. 3. pp. 123–141.

Hamza, H. (2019). Al-tamouilwa al-istithmar fi al-awqaf (Financing and Investment in Awqaf). Islamic Economics Institute. King Abdulaziz University. Scientific Publishing Center. July 2019.

Isbihi, A. (2015). Idaretwaistithmarmawared al-awqaf...al-ishkalatwa al-tahadiat (Management and Investment of Waqf Resources...Problems and Challenges). *Awqaf Journal*, Vol. 29. General Authority of Awqaf. Kuwait. pp. 13–35.

Kahf, M. (2000). Al-waqf al-islami: Tatawwuruh, idaratuh, Tanmiyatuh (The Islamic Endowment: Development, Administration and Evolution). Dar al-Fikr Damascus.

Kahf, M. (2018). Islamic Endowments: The Need for a New Charter. *Journal of King Abdulaziz University: Islamic Economics*. Vol. 31, No. 3, pp. 59–66.

Kassim, M., CheEmbi, N.A., Haron, R., and Ibrahim, K. (2019). Internal Factors Affecting Continuous Donations among Cash Waqf Donors. *International Journal of Academic Research in Business and Social Sciences*, Vol. 9, No. 9, pp. 1304–1311.

Khafagy, R. and Irfan, A. (2012). Ihiaanidham al-waqf fi misr ...qiraa fi al-namathej al-alamia (Reviving the Waqf System in Egypt... Reading in International Models). John D. Gerhart Center for Philanthropy and Civic Engagement.

Nienhaus, V. (July, 2018). Awqāf: Social Spending, Development Strategy and Financing. *Journal of King Abdulaziz University: Islamic Economics*. Vol. 31, No. 2, pp. 91–99.

Sabit Haji Mohammad, M.T. (2015). Theoretical and Trustees' Perspectives on the Establishment of an Islamic Social (Waqf) Bank. *Humanomics*, Vol. 31, No. 1, pp. 37–73.

Salahat, S.M. (2018). Hawkamat al-awqafwaidaratamaliatihaaraissia (Governance of Awqaf and Management of Its Main Operations). Saee for Awqaf Development. Riadh. First edition.

World Bank, INCEIF and ISRA. (2019). Maximizing Social Impact through Waqf Solutions. World Bank, INCEIF and ISRA Report.

12 Islamic social finance reform – Hibah a catalyst for Awqaf advancement

Noor Shahalina Binti Jamaludin and Shaikh Hamzah Abdul Razak

Introduction

Islam has a unique dispensation on the concept of wealth, its ownership and distribution. Wealth is regarded as a means to an end and not as an end per se. Essentially material possessions are considered the primary form of wealth. From Islamic perspective, Allah is the true owner of wealth and He (*Allah*) entrusted the wealth to man for beneficial use (Surah *Ta'Ha* (20) verse 6). We are accountable for the manner in which wealth created, amassed, and distributed. The chapter looks at the distribution process of the wealth under the principles of inheritance. Besides the law of inheritance as defined in the Quran in Surah An-Nisa verses 7, 11, 12, 13 and 176, '*Hibah*' instruments could be used in the inheritance distribution process.

This chapter will be discussing the *Hibah* as an important instrument of wealth management for Muslims in Malaysia. The causes of negative perception on doing *Hibah* often have negative impact on public awareness. In this modern day, the greed for wealth is so great that the heirs dispute with each other over the inheritance. Muslims are therefore encouraged to plan and manage their estate while they are still alive to avoid family disputes and unclaimed asset.

Inheritance distribution disputes are increasing in Malaysia. The cases are brought before Syariah Court and are heard under The Administration of Islamic Law (Federal Territories) Act 1993. Syariah High Court's Jurisdiction.[1]

- (Act 505) Part IV Sec. 46: A Syariah High Court shall have jurisdiction throughout the Federal Territories and shall be presided over by a Syariah Judge.
- A Syariah High Court shall:
  - in its civil jurisdiction hear and determine all actions and proceedings in which all the parties are Muslims, and which relate to:
    - gifts intervivos, or settlements made without adequate consideration in money or money's worth, by a Muslim.[2]

It is essential to understand the reasons to this issue: the lack of knowledge and poor awareness on *Hibah* among parties involved. Different forms of *Hibah* are being practiced by different organizations; it must be custom made according to the giver's specification. For that, this research is performed to understand the process of *Hibah* as an important instrument in wealth management. In addition, this study is significant to create awareness of the existence of *Hibah*, and how we could benefit from it. By promoting *Hibah* as an important instrument in the Islamic wealth distribution, we could gain better understanding on the current situation of Malaysian Muslims' best current practice of wealth management throughout the community.

It is very sad to see siblings fighting among themselves for the property left by their parents. Even if the parents left a will, there will be instances when greedy siblings will try to deny other brothers or sisters their fair share. There were cases where one or two siblings would keep the surviving parent in their home and deny other siblings' access. Unless the final distribution is not equitable, implying that the parent had written it under coercion to leave some siblings out, there is no reason to take such cases to court. These parents should state the reasons for doing so in front of a judge before they write their will to ensure that they are not being coerced by another child. Nothing could be fairer than a *Hibah* that names all the children and gives each one of them an equal share of the inheritance, which considered a birth right in many societies and not as payment for looking after one's parents. In fact, children should be happy at being given the opportunity of taking care of their parents and they should do so without expecting a bigger share of the inheritance. Cases where children demanded compensation for looking after their parent should not be entertained by the courts. What if the parent does not have any property or inheritance for distribution? There are also cases of children who force their aged parents to sign over all their property to them and thereafter dump them in old folks' homes. Those who keep their parents in their home for the sole purpose of taking over their finances and controlling their money and getting compensation should be denounced by society.

Estates of the deceased person worth RM60bil have not been claimed by their heirs since independence due to the ignorance and apathy of the heirs. The attitude of not wanting to know the procedures, or which agency should manage the estate distribution, is also a reason for the heirs failing to initiate measures to claim their inheritance. There are also beneficiaries who consider the process of applying for division of property as slow, expensive and inconvenient. Most importantly, this can lead to others claiming the property.[3] Therefore, choosing *Hibah* as a wealth distribution instrument could lead the heirs to enjoy the same quality of life as if the deceased was alive. The reality arises when the heirs are not able to meet with the charges due to financial constraints or disputes among the beneficiaries as to who will be the administrator and who will be making the initial payment.

Hibah as an important instrument in waqf advancement

We can conclude that every alm and gift is *Hibah*, but not all *Hibah* are alms and gifts. *Hibah* on Islamic terms is an agreement that contains the *Hibah* of a property. More specifically, the *Hibah* is a *Hibah* of ain. *Hibah* property from one party to another without repayment (*iwad*) during the life of the person voluntary, not expecting a reward and honoring one, with using the pronouncement of *ijab a*nd *qabul*.

Based on the earlier definition, the characteristics of the *Hibah* are as follows:

i A contract of *Hibah* of property to a party.
ii Assets that can be disbursed are property, not debt or benefits.
iii *Hibah* is made without any repayment (*iwad*).
iv *Hibah* is activated while the giver is alive.
v It is made voluntarily without compulsion.
vi The contract is not meant to reward or glorify certain person.

Hibah provider must have full ownership *(milkutta'am*), full authority over his/her property. Therefore, there is no limitation in the context of rate and *Hibah* can be given to anybody that the donor pleases with one condition that his intention of giving does not violate Islamic law. It is the pronouncement or an act of giving and receiving by *Hibah* provider and *Hibah* recipient (Muda, 2008).

Hibah refers to a transfer of an asset from a donor (*wahib*) to a recipient (*mawhublahu*) without a reward.[4] In terms of law, *Hibah* is a voluntary act of worship and encouraged practice in Islam especially to the immediate family. This practice is based on the Quran, al-Sunnah and *ijmak*. Among the verses of the Qur'an that encourage the practice of *Hibah* is the word of Allah SWT that means:[5]

> Then if they give you part of the dowry happily, eat it (as food) which is good and good.
>
> (Surah *an-Nisa* verse 4)

> … and to give the property he loves to his relatives, orphans, the poor, the traveling people (who need help) the beggar and the (free) slave of the merciful.
>
> (Surah *al-Baqarah* verse 177)

Definition of Hibah

Hibah refers to the gift given to the loved ones while they are alive with no expected rewards for this study research, which leads to a trouble – free claim to inheritance from the loved ones. The result shows that there is room for improvement in marketing *Hibah* product to Malaysian Muslims from the operators to the respondents. Indeed, many Malaysians rely on the distributions by the Shariah court to undertake their inheritance, which may not necessarily be an easy task for the beneficiaries. There have been some inheritance claim disputes made by customers primarily over the distribution portion and the entitlement of the *Fara'id* beneficiaries. But the cases were favorable to the trust company with proper and order documents submitted in court. The companies market their products through certified agents, promotions during Hajj, promotions during 'MingguSaham ASNB' annually and through social media. The *Hibah* trust process is being carried out at both the High Court and Syariah Court. The principle of trust used by the companies is either *Hibah Ruqba* for Wasiyyah Shoppe, Takaful and ASNB or Intervivos (Tabung Haji (TH)). All trust firms use individual power attorneys in their execution of *Hibah* as distribution of wealth is very necessary because the property or asset value appreciates over time. For instance, the current market price of a terraced house in Ara Damansara launched in 2009 at RM380,000 is now valued from RM1.2 mil to RM1.3 mil.[6] As asset prices rise, the question that may arise is whether there is enough money to cover the inheritance claim costs.

Therefore, *Hibah's* awareness as an instrument for the distribution of assets is important to ensure that the beneficiaries will have a comfortable life when the giver is dead. This study benefits society, particularly younger Malaysian Muslims, to realize the importance of the distribution through *Hibah* and the factors that could affect their beneficiaries. Time is an essential part of the *Hibah* distribution, so Malaysian Muslims in this target study group could benefit from this outcome on the suggested appropriate time to start their *Hibah* as an important tool for the distribution of their wealth.

Hibah Al-Ruqba and Al-Umra

Ruqba is derived from the word *ruqub* and *taqarrub*, which means waiting. It is similar to the principle of survivorship clause. *Ruqba* means the condition of gift hinges on death of either party, whereby the survivor shall be the owner of the *Hibah* asset. It can be the settlor or the beneficiary.[7]

An example of *Hibah al-ruqba* pronouncement is when the *Hibah* provider says:

> This land I give to you as ruqba and if you die first then the property will be returned to me and if I die first then the property is for you.

The fuqahas have unanimously agreed that it is not allowed to give *Hibah* ownership for a *Hibah* that will become effective in the future. The majority of Islamic scholars are of the opinion that temporary *Hibah* such as *Hibah* '*umra* and *Hibah ruqba* are considered valid but the conditions are considered void. They debated that if those conditions are applied then they become contradictory to the demand of the solemnization contract of the *Hibah* itself. Prophet Rasulullah (*pbuh*) said:

> Protect your property and do not hibah it away (Hibah) as 'umra for anyone who hibah something away (Hibah) as 'umra, then it becomes the property of the Hibah recipient.

At the meeting of the 56th Federal Committee on Regional Legal Consultation on 5 October 2000 it was decided that the placement of conditions was allowed between the *Hibah*or and the *Hibah*ee after the agreement and *qabul*. Similarly, the Securities Commission's Syariah Advisory Council (SAC) decision at the 44th meeting on 15 January 2003 adopted the *ruqba Hibah* principle as a Syariah basis in the execution of a *Hibah* form for transactions involving joint accounts of unit trust funds, especially accounts held by Muslims.[8] The following are the financial institutions using the *Hibah* principles:

Takaful *Hibah*

Takaful *Hibah* is the compensation money from a Takaful plan which will be given 100% to the heirs according to the wishes of the deceased either through nomination or *Hibah*.

What is the advantage of Takaful using this Hibah distribution?

a The money can be obtained within 21 days (depending on case) without going through the process of obtaining the power of the estate administration, which takes 3 months to 20 years.

b Takaful funds are to be used as a survival money for the heirs to continue living normally when the deceased are no longer around. This is where the importance of Takaful instrument as a source of family income arises.

c Takaful *Hibah* account does not fall under *Fara'id* distribution as the Takaful contract uses the *Ruqba Hibah* for the contract. Once a *Hibah* is done, it is not part of an estate and excluded from *Fara'id*.

In most instances, people leave behind land and home, and it is very difficult to dilute these assets. Yes, the heir has a place to live after they are gone. If there is a Takaful *Hibah*, it would help the heirs to continue living as liquid asset, i.e. cash is there for them as well. Payment of Takaful benefits is done under a family Takaful certificate and a personal accident Takaful certificate. Schedule 10 sets out provisions for the payment of Takaful benefits upon death of a Takaful participant under a family Takaful certificate and a personal accident Takaful certificate, issued in respect of a contract of Takaful entered into by the Takaful participant upon his life.[9]

Hibah Amanah Tabung Haji

In the past, many people save with TH because they wanted to perform Hajj. The price for Hajj pilgrimage costs only RM10,000, but many keep a lot more than that. Deposits at TH look more profitable than savings in regular banks. TH gives you 5%–8% dividend bonus returns every year. With the amount of money deposited, there is a need and concern for estate planning and inheritance subscribing to either *Hibah Amanah* TH or by nomination process.

Unclaimed deposits at TH of approximately 41,000 depositor accounts had reached RM188 million[10] in value; recognizing the problem that involved the Muslims especially, TH recently introduced a new product, namely the *HibahAmanah* ***TH*** as a solution to the depositors to manage their savings while still alive.

HibahAmanah TH

HibahAmanah ***TH*** is a value-added or alternative product for an existing product, Nomination. *HibahAmanah* ***TH*** is a *Hibah Amanah* from TH savings account by Trustee Provider or depositor during his/her life to the *Hibah* Beneficiary on a voluntary basis through *ijab* and *qabul.*

The endowment of *HibahAmanah* property is provided by the depositor out of love during his/her lifetime through *HibahAmanah* ***TH*** Deed of Trust and Power of Attorney (POA). This is a Shariah-compliant service that combines *Hibah* with *Amanah.* The depositor is a Trustee to the recipient of *HibahAmanah* ***TH***. ***TH*** then acts as a Substitute Trustee to administer and manage the property. Following the death of the depositor or recipient, *HibahAmanah* property distribution and payment is carried out (with a fee of 1% based on the current savings balance of the deceased) once a claim is made (Table 12.1).

Wasiyyah Shoppe Berhad

Wasiyyah Shoppe Berhad, the leader in Shariah-based planning and management, became officially a trust company under the Trustee Act 1949 when approved by the Companies Commission of Malaysia on 19 March 2018.[11]

Table 12.1 Total number of depositors of TH[12]

Year	*(Million people)*	*Total deposits (RM million)*
2018	9.3	75,413
2017	9.3	73,522
2016	9.1	67,704
2015	8.8	62,548
2014	8.6	54,358

Source: Tabung Haji.

In December 2015 Wasiyyah Shoppe has provided nearly 25,000 *Hibah* documents to its customers, and it is the largest provider of *Hibah* documents in Malaysia.[13]

As on 31 December 2017, over 50,000[14] Muslims throughout Malaysia subscribed to the estate planning and management services of which 26,400 are *Hibah* documents. Shariah-based products offered in the last 14 years and the effectiveness of documents prepared by Wasiyyah Shoppe were proven in Court when more than 300 *Hibah* judgment orders were obtained from Syariah Courts throughout Malaysia, with 500 cases of inheritance solved within an average of three to eight months. Through Wasiyyah Shoppe nearly all types of assets can be planned for wealth management through strategic cooperation with international trust firms whereby foreign asset customers can also subscribe to this service.

Wasiyyah Shoppe Berhad offers 30 types of Syariah property estate planning and inheritance services that can satisfy almost all the needs of Malaysians. They claimed that they are the only trust company in Malaysia that can provide free services to the beneficiaries after the death of the customer. An heir does not have to pay any fees or inheritance deducted for the purpose of payment of inheritance fees.

Upon being informed by beneficiaries on the death of the customer, Wasiyyah Shoppe Berhad will send representatives from its Legal Department to meet the heirs. They will advise the heirs so that they can clearly understand the legal process they need to go through to claim the estate.

There is no charge for this service to the recipients as it was paid by the giver while alive.[15] All operations and development of Wasiyyah Shoppe Berhad services went through a strict screening process and were introduced to the public only after approval by Wasiyyah Shoppe Berhad's Syariah Panel. With more than 300 *Hibah* clearance orders obtained throughout Malaysia from the Syariah Court and 500 heir cases successfully completed within an average of three to eight months, the service proved its effectiveness.[16]

The concept of cash waqf

Waqf is a significant religious institution. It is a financial charitable institution established by withholding immovable and movable properties to perpetually spend its revenue on fulfilling public or family needs, depending on the conditions set by the founder of the waqf. It is regulated under Shariah for the purpose of Islamic development. The word waqf is derived from the Arabic root verb 'waqafa' means 'causing a thing to stop and standstill'. Once a property is created as a waqf, it can never be given as gift, inherited or sold, since the waqf belongs to Allah (swt), and the waqf property remains intact. Only the generated revenue is channeled to the beneficiaries. The creation of waqf is for the founders to attain righteousness (Surah Al-Imran3:92). In the hadith reported in Sahih Muslim, the creation of waqf is one of the ways to generate continuous rewards for the founder even after his death.

> Abu Huraira (Ra) reported Prophet Muhammad [Peace be upon him (Pbuh)] as saying: when a man dies, all his acts come to an end, except for three things, recurring charity (sadaqahjariyay), or knowledge (by which people are benefited), or a pious offspring, who prays for him.
>
> (Reported by Muslim no.4223)

Waqf assets can be immovable or movable, e.g. cash waqf. In cash waqf, *al-waqif* (donor) endowed cash instead of real estate. Cash waqf began in primeval Mesopotamia, Greece and the Roman Empire. In the 8th century, Imam Zufar had approved cash waqf in the Islamic world for the first time. Cash waqf can be invested through *mudarabah* and profits would be spent for charity. It gained momentum in the 16th century especially among the Ottomans and was supported by the Ottoman Sultans, because funds were financed in the expansion of Islam in Europe (Cizakca, 2010).[17] In advancing the concept of cash waqf, *Hibah* instrument can be utilized for this purpose.

Objectives

Because of the failure to trace legal beneficiaries, in 2011 RM42 billion of assets were frozen and the number then increased to RM60 billion in 2016, and Muslims owned most of the assets (*BH Online*, 2016). *Hibah* is a tool for unlocking this problem, with so many frozen assets in sight and no solutions. A possible reason for this has been that most Muslims in Malaysia do not consider property planning seriously, so previous research has shown that some of them are skeptical about making a Wasiyyah. This is a problem, and ultimately *Hibah* could be the solution.

Hibah is a declaration made by a person during his lifetime concerning his property or its benefit, to be made for the purposes permitted by Islamic law. *Hibah* is very important to the *Hibah* giver; the *Hibah* giver will be able to identify the heirs' problem and solve the problem by distributing *Hibah*. To avoid ignorance of Malaysian legal inheritance procedures and to speed up the distribution process, *Hibah* must be given extensive exposure on a large scale as a solution to Muslims in general.

The objectives of the study are as follows:

i To examine the *Hibah* application by different operators, i.e. Takaful Malaysia, Tabung Haji Malaysia, Wasiyyah Shoppe Berhad, and related issues.

ii To examine the reasons for the Muslim community's low *Hibah* adoption rate.

iii To examine the role of *Hibah* in advancing waqf development.

This *Hibah* study uses a series of questions on awareness about wealth distribution amongst Muslims population. This is to identify and impart the experience on the process of *Hibah* as an instrument for wealth distribution for the group mentioned in order for them to have a better wealth distribution for their beneficiaries when dealing with their inheritance.

Result from this survey would give the society, stakeholder, *Hibah* operators, government and private institutions a better understanding and awareness regarding to the preparedness of *Hibah* as a wealth distribution instrument focusing among Malaysian Muslims.

Literature review

In the context of undistributed inheritance due to failure to obtain the *Fara'id* order for distribution or due to conflict, the amount of undistributed estate comprises of real estate as well as cash. The family of late millionaire businessman Raja Nong Chik Raja Ishak's second wife cannot intervene in the appeal of a civil case relating to his shares and companies, the Federal Court heard. In the suit filed in August 1998, Amanah Raya Berhad (ARB) claimed that the defendants had fraudulently transferred more than two million company shares belonging to Raja Nong Chik after his death. ARB sought the court to declare that the transfer of the shares null and void. Raja Nong Chik, whose properties and assets were estimated to be worth RM16 million, died on 10 February 1994, from the effects of an intracerebral hemorrhage on 27 January, the same year. He died without leaving a will.[18]

The mother of a former minister, the late Tan Sri Jamaluddin Mohd Jarjis, has filed a suit on his estate *Fara'id* distribution against her two grandchildren over their failure to include three company shares worth RM1.3 billion in the list of her son's estate[19] (*The Borneo Post*, 2019).

It was reported by Deputy Finance Minister Datuk Othman Aziz in Parliament that a total of RM5.9 billion has not been claimed by Malaysians as on 31 October 2017. The unclaimed money is mostly made up of inactive bank accounts, unclaimed fixed deposits that have expired, insurance payouts and interests. (NST, 2017)

These include real estate in the name of the deceased, cash and other forms of property. If the cash in the bank is unclaimed, the value may not increase because the savings account and the current account do not normally have any *mudarabah* given to the bank. The property still in the name of the deceased may have multiplied due to the development in the surrounding area.

Kampung Baru housing in Kuala Lumpur, for instance, is a classic case of an estate that has been facing challenges in terms of heritage for so long. Although numerous efforts have been taken by various authorities, including heirs, it is still not easy to manage. The vast number of beneficiaries causes unrestricted access. Indeed, the value of the property is high, but if the inheritance is not managed, the value is not as good as the value of the property around it. If you were to go to the area, you can see the existence of wooden houses surrounded by buildings like KLCC. Although only a few kilometers away, the difference in value is huge. The process of claiming the inheritance is complicated and asset management requires the cooperation of all heirs. If there is only one heir who disagrees with the proposed settlement method, then the deal will be slow, costly and in most cases create the dissatisfaction of the other heirs. It is not an easy task trying to make up to 50 people; it needs lot of patience and great skills. This is because people are not exposed to the process and the importance of property management as opposed to other religious issues such as prayers, ablutions, purges, marriages and crimes. Complicated and difficult procedures are also a factor in which there is reluctance within the Muslims to make property planning. Many are not willing to manage the property because the process involves many agencies such as Syariah courts, civil courts, land and mineral departments, Amanah Rakyat Berhad, Baitulmal and so on. Muslims are encouraged to plan their property intelligently to facilitate the heirs or those who enjoy the property without any hassle. In the meantime, with the development of times saw more and more agencies managing property established in the country.

Ali and Khanom (2014) posited that cash waqf and its investment have the potential to alleviate poverty. An institutionalized waqf charity should be the aim of waqf organization through planning of primary and secondary projects. The primary project can be financed by raising cash waqf with the issuance of waqf certificates of different denominations such as building of schools and clinics. The secondary projects are those that can generate cash flows to finance the regular operational expenses of the targeted projects. The example of developing shopping complex as a secondary project for generating income to finance educational institution for a primary project. An example is the Bencoolen Waqf mosque in Singapore, where the mosque was redeveloped as part of a mixed development comprising commercial block and 12 storey service apartments. The four storey commercial complex provides income for the mosque to maintain and run its operation.[20]

Nurrachmi (2012) proposed the use of cash waqf certificates in various denominations for the participants of waqf projects and the function of waqf institution acting as capital distribution rather than as capital accumulation. Nurrachmi highlighted the issue of unqualified mutawali and proposed for the waqf to have good governance and trust.[21] Mokhtar, Sidin and Razak (2015) identified the collaboration between Bank Muamalat Malaysia Berhad (BBMB) and Selangor Waqf Corporation or Perbadanan Wakaf Selangor (PWS) in implementing the cash waqf scheme known as Wakaf Selangor Muamalat in Malaysia and has become an important tool for Islamic Banking.[22] Under the scheme, the collected cash is channeled for health and education development. They also identified issues such as multi-level decision making process followed by lack of trained personnel as well as the need to comply with the demand of stakeholders followed by underdeveloped secondary projects which led to lack of public trust.

myWakaf is a collective initiative of six (6) Islamic banks to empower the community through cash waqf where the State Islamic Religious Council (SIRC) is able to tap on a larger pool of potential contributors.[23] With this collaboration myWakaf tends to address the issues of efficiency and effectiveness in waqf project management. The Islamic Banks participating in myWakaf are Affin Islamic Bank, Bank Islam, Bank Rakyat, BBMB, Maybank Islamic and RHB Islamic Bank. Their target projects are education, economic empowerment, health and investment. To date they have undertaken six (6) projects with varying success. For example, the Mualaf Centre Renovation in Kelantan was successfully achieved by collecting RM369000. For HTF Hemodialysis Service project under Bank Islam, the target collection is RM6 million; to date collected amount is RM1.458 million, a 24% achievement. myWakaf is addressing good corporate governance, check and balance, transparency as well as ease and convenience. However, marketing and promotion are issues as the general Muslim population have minimal knowledge and there is a need for the Islamic banks and SIRC to be intensive in promoting myWakaf.

Kachkar (2017) proposed cash waqf refugee microfinance (CWRMF) to provide Islamic microfinance and microcredit facilities to refugee entrepreneurs who have potential to manage their own businesses. The model consists of temporary as well as permanent cash waqf for participants or donors to contribute. The collected funds are targeted to be invested in low risk Shariah compliant instruments such as government sukuk or company shares to maintain sustainability, especially for the portion of temporary cash waqf. The donors or participants will receive waqf certificates in the form of sukuk. Sanusi and Shafiai (2015) identified the success of Waqaf An-Nur Corporation and PWS in managing waqf funds to benefit the public such as mosque management and school development as well as public utilities. Waqaf An-Nur Corporation is also embarking on cash waqf concept.

Theory of Planned Behavior

Icek Ajzen (1991) developed the Theory of Planned Behavior (TPB) as an attempt to predict human behavior toward behavioral intention, subjective norm and perceived behavioral control. The theory's first construct is behavioral intention, the motivational factors influencing behavior (Ajzen, 1991). The stronger the intention to engage with a particular behavior, the more likely that behavior is to be performed. The second construct is behavioral attitude, which is the extent to which a person has a favorable or unfavorable assessment of a particular behavior. Attitude consists of convictions of behaviors and evaluations of results. The third construct is the subjective norm that is a social pressure to execute a given behavior or not. Combination of normative beliefs and motivation to comply constitutes subjective norm. Another key role in the TPB refers to people's perception of the ease or difficulty of conducting interest behavior.

These types of survey research highlight several scopes which involve the following.

Demographic profile

From Table 12.2, it can be seen that Bumiputera holds the majority of population with 3,452.9m in Selangor from a total population of 6,472.4m. Therefore, more focus was needed in educating Bumiputera in wealth management, especially in *Hibah* distribution.

Hibah *preparedness confidence*

It was reported that the estates of the deceased worth RM60 billion have not been claimed by their heirs since independence (The Star, 2016). It clearly shows that wealth management is still lacking among Malaysians, which will eventually affect their *Hibah* confidence. This is mainly due to lack of awareness and knowledge on the importance of wealth distribution, fully dependent on the beneficiary to claim the inheritance without realizing the beneficiary's ability in financial status.

Goal clarity

The goal-setting process (Warner, 2012) generally helps you choose where to go. By knowing exactly what we want to accomplish, we know where we need to concentrate our efforts. In order to begin the journey of working toward a goal, we must first ensure complete clarity. Goal clarity can be described simply as one's ability to set a clear and specific goal that all affected parties can understand and work toward it.

Attitude toward Hibah *wealth distribution*

Attitude can be defined as an individual act which is reflected as either positive or negative effect (Chan & Chan, 2010)[25] in evaluating a certain behavior. From the perspective of wealth distribution, attitude is an important

Table 12.2 Population by ethnic group, Selangor (2018)

Population by ethnic group, Selangor (2018)	
Ethnic group	*Million ('000)*
Bumiputera	3,452.9
Chinese	1,563.5
Indians	728.8
Others	49.7
Non-Malaysian citizens	677.5
Total	6,472.4

Source: Department of Statistics, Malaysia.[24] Total added may differ due to rounding estimate.

factor, which influences the behavior of an individual in facing his or her wealth. In the context of Malaysian Muslims, individuals show positive attitude toward wealth distribution with condition of expected family taken care off. Positive attitude of working people toward *Hibah* is also one of the factors that influence them to have a good planning for their wealth distribution.

Hibah *literacy and knowledge*

Kamarudin and Alma'amun (2013)[26] suggested that findings from this study are important to the industry as they can be used to understand the behavior of consumers and to strengthen the Malaysian Islamic estate planning industry.

Boshara, Emmons and Noeth in their Essay No.2: Education and Wealth, May 2015, p. 7[27] concluded that people with more education are more likely to have parents with accumulated wealth and, thus, are more likely to receive an inheritance, thus making a strong relationship between the level of education and wealth management. Moreover, the effective wealth management habits that were inculcated during childhood could help adults make better decisions for their wealth distribution.

Sources of Hibah *as wealth distribution*

In Malaysia, Muslims and non-Muslims are governed by different sets of heritage laws. The estates of deceased Muslims are governed by Syariah laws, while the estates of deceased non-Muslims are governed by acts such as the 1959 Will Act and the 1958 Distribution Act (Amended 2006).[28] Wealth distribution relates to the responsibility of the person to his beneficiaries through different wealth distribution channels, namely *Hibah*, *Fara'id*, Islamic Will and other forms of distribution.

Hibah *as Fara'id denial?*

Fara'id known to be a complicated approach, particularly since the distribution of wealth to legal beneficiaries, must go through several stages involving multiple jurisdictions that the beneficiaries may not fully understand (Abdul Rashid et al., 2013).[29] Under *Fara'id*, the legal recipients have the right to the deceased property and the asset be distributed to the legal recipients in accordance with the Islamic law. In Islam, *Fara'id* is second in settlement of the family inheritance. If the family is unable to reach a settlement itself, *Fara'id* is the law for the distribution of estate upon death. *Fara'id* is a fair solution should the family is unable to reach a settlement. However, if *Hibah* is executed during the lifetime of the giver, disputes over the inheritance will not arise.

Research methodology

The study uses qualitative and quantitative approaches. For qualitative, the information is sourced from related Islamic state authorities, *Hibah* service providers and research previously done. In the quantitative approach data were collected using convenience sampling that involved working adults within Malaysian Muslims. The targeted respondents (among Malaysian Muslims) were selected from a wide spectrum of administrative, management, business, manufacturing and education sectors. Survey questionnaires were distributed through online in the form of Google form within Malaysia. This online survey started on 3 April 2019 and ended on 13 April 2019. The participants were asked to respond to the same set of questions, as it provided an efficient way to collect responses from a large sample of working individuals to perform this quantitative analysis. The study also used data collected from *Hibah* operators such as Takaful Malaysia, Tabung Haji Malaysia and Wasiyyah Shoppe Berhad. Based on the discussion in the literature section, the TPB was proposed as the theory to be used in this research. The data collected will be used to explain the relationship between their preparedness towards *Hibah* and their wealth distribution instrument. Results are derived using IBM SPSS Statistics Data Editor. Most of the questions for each variable were based on the existing literature. However, some items were modified for better understanding.

This study continues in this line of research by evaluating the perspectives of investigating the concept of *Hibah* as an important instrument in cash waqf advancement. The chapter seeks to explain the importance of cash waqf wealth management among Malaysian Muslims based on their inherent (attitude) and marital status to participate in this study on how *Hibah* can be a catalyst in promoting waqf advancement through cash waqf. The study takes the *Hibah* perspective and thus provides an example of the application of this research paradigm in an empirical study. We investigated this phenomenon by providing a theoretical grounded model that explains how *Hibah* adoption can spur cash waqf using data from randomly selected Malaysian Muslims. The results render support for the proposed hypotheses, emphasizing the *Hibah* as an important instrument for waqf advancement.

Research findings

Demographic data analysis[30]

From the data collected through the survey, five categories of variables will be analyzed, namely the demographic backgrounds of the respondents with several significant factors such as the wealth distribution channel, gender, marital status, education background, employment, *Hibah* literacy and knowledge, and whether the respondent agreed that *Hibah* is part of wealth distribution and if they would consider *Hibah* as an important instrument for wealth distribution (Figure 12.1).

The pie chart shows the results of a survey in which Malaysian Muslims were asked about their preferred wealth distribution channel. The question referred to four main distributions: *Hibah, Fara'id*, Islamic Will and others. From the chart most participants preferred to use *Fara'id* and Islamic Will,

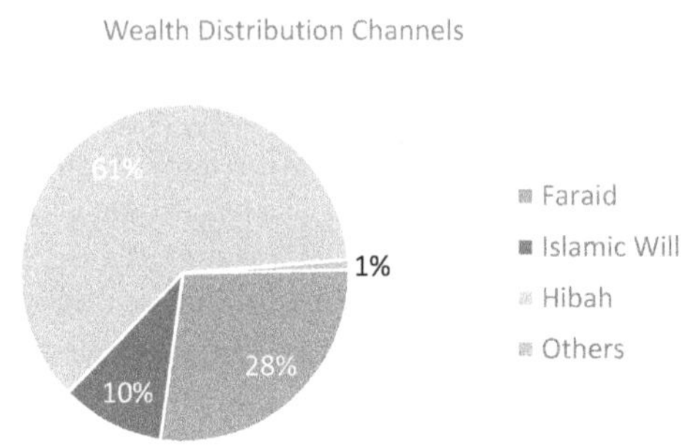

Figure 12.1 Wealth distribution channel.
Source: Authors own.

with 17.4% difference between the two. Nearly two third of participants preferred to use *Hibah*. In conclusion, since *Hibah* was the most popular choice, many participants preferred *Hibah* as an important wealth management. In future, we can probably expect to see more and more people choosing *Hibah* as their preferred choice.

Gender and ethnic

Results showed that most respondents were female (63%) compared to only male (37%) respondents. Ethnic Malay was the highest percentage among Malaysian Muslims with 91%, Chinese (1%), Indians (1%) and 7% among others. *Hibah* is the most popular and preferable method used by the majority of the respondents as compared to other distribution channels. About 60 respondents or 61.2% out of 98% chose *Hibah* as their method of wealth distribution which showed that 19 were males and another 41 were females. From an ethnic and racial perspective, 56 out of 91 Malay respondents preferred the method of *Hibah* as a channel for wealth distribution, followed by one Indian respondent and three for a different race. Meanwhile, 25 out of 27 were Malay and two from other races for *Fara'id's* second highest distribution channel.

Marital status

In terms of marital status, it can be shown that married people had the highest percentage that contributed to the *Hibah* distribution channels which were 70.4% from out of the total respondents where 41 of them chose *Hibah*, followed by 20 people who preferred *Fara'id*, 7 chose Islamic Will, while only 1 respondent opted for other distribution channels.

Ultimately, most of the gathered respondents chose *Hibah*, followed by *Fara'id* and Islamic Will. In this survey, other methods appeared to be the least favored. For cash variables, it showed that the majority of 60 respondents

Table 12.3 Respondents' marital status

Respondents' marital status	
Marital status	*Percentages (%)*
Single	21.4
Married	70.4
Widowed	5.1
Divorced	3.1

Source: Author's own.

chose *Hibah*, 27 chose *Fara'id*, 10 chose Islamic Will and only 1 chose other methods for their cash distribution.

In this survey, Table 12.3 illustrates the marital status of individuals. Majority of the respondents were married, followed by singles and finally followed by widowed and divorced, though it made up only 2% difference.

Education background

The educational background of the respondents involved in this survey shows that 39.8% were bachelors, 31.6% were postgraduates, 22.4% were diploma holders, while the remaining respondents (6.1%) were SPM/Certificate holders.

It shows that for educational background variables, majority of the respondents with degree level education chose *Hibah* as the distribution channel, which were 60 out of 98 of the total respondents. About 27 of them preferred *Fara'id*, 10 preferred Islamic Will and only 1 preferred other distribution methods. Meanwhile, the majority of respondents were those who choose *Hibah* for master's degree graduation, which were 18 out of 31 of the total respondents followed by 13 people who preferred the *Fara'id* method. Eighteen of the respondents chose *Hibah* for diploma level, about three preferred Islamic Will and only one preferred *Fara'id* distribution.

Employment

Most respondents who work in their current position in the organization chose the following channel of distribution of wealth: *Hibah* (27.6%), followed by *Fara'id* (27.6%), Islamic Will (10.2%) and 1% for other methods.

Next, there were about 46 respondents (46.9%) in the private sector. Managing their own business (18.4%) shared the same percentage as other business (18.4%) while the rest were in the government sector (16.3%).

Hibah *literacy and knowledge*

The majority of the respondents responded as neutral as to how to obtain *Hibah* information easily from the wealth distribution channel. 42.9% agreed that they would increase their assets over time. Other distribution alternatives, *Fara'id*, *Islamic Wills*, *Waqf*, and *Sadaqah*, were known to 41.8% of respondents. 43.9% of respondents agreed *Hibah* as a wealth distribution channel to reduce the burden on their beneficiaries. Realizing that the beneficiaries will face various inheritance claim difficulties, 34.7% of respondents agreed that they understood the inheritance claim legal process in Malaysia. Only 4.1% of admitted respondents were unable to manage their assets, while 35.7% were unable to manage their assets. 30.6% were aware of the *Hibah* offered by company/government's distribution benefits.

It can be concluded that respondents are aware of the existence of *Hibah* as a channel for the distribution of wealth management. Comparing married and single respondents as well as widowed and divorced persons indicated that married persons prefer to do *Hibah* for family security when they are dead and to facilitate the process of legal inheritance in Malaysia for beneficiaries. Female for the *Hibah* channel dominates male. Malays are the ethnic people who choose *Hibah* the most. *Hibah* is most likely to be chosen by those working in the private sector. The degree holder prefers *Hibah* as far as education is concerned, and those with cash and assets prefer to use *Hibah* as their channel for wealth distribution. Many of those who are yet to do *Hibah* have some thoughts about doing *Hibah* in the future. In exercising *Hibah*, cost could be an important consideration as some providers are changing upfront fees, whilst others are charging initial fees and for subsequent execution of the *Hibah* document at the courts, the fees could be high.

Hibah *as catalyst for cash waqf*

From the earlier survey, there is great potential for *Hibah* to be a catalyst for cash waqf. We have individuals contributing to mosque funds during Friday prayers. On average collection by most mosques per month is RM20,000. We have a total of 7019 mosques and suraus Friday prayers[31] and we have adjusted the collection in certain areas for low collection periods. The total collection could reach as high as RM140 million per month and RM1.680 billion per year. These are the funds collected by mosques for the activities excluding collection for death benefits. In the same manner we can encourage individuals to contribute funds under *Hibah*. We have a total of 9.43 million of employed Muslims[32] and we can discount 50% for those under B40 leaving us with 4.715 million employed Muslims. If we could derive from them as *Hibah* contribution a minimum of RM50 per year toward creating a permanent cash waqf then that would give us RM235.75 million. We could still get others to create a temporary *Hibah* through investment, where the returns are being channeled to the cash waqf and upon maturity the invested funds would be returned to the waqif or by creating a *mushtarak* waqf for a combination of family as well as public waqf where the funds can be shared 50/50 between the two after deducting investment and administrative expenses.

We can create a Waqf Investment Corporation and it needs to be an independent entity with a *mutawalli* certificate by JAWHAR or any of the SIRC, and all SIRCs can capitalize on the investment expertise of the fund managers and waqf management as well as collaborate with the National Fund Corporation or Perbadanan Nasional Berhad, the investment managers for Amanah Saham Nasional Berhad (ASNB) as advisors or any good investment fund managers (Figure 12.2).

The avenue of possible participants funding is given below (Table 12.4).

The depositors of ASB are as follows.

1 We will be targeting those having units between 50,000 and more than 500,000, which gives a total of 885,674 unit holders with a value of

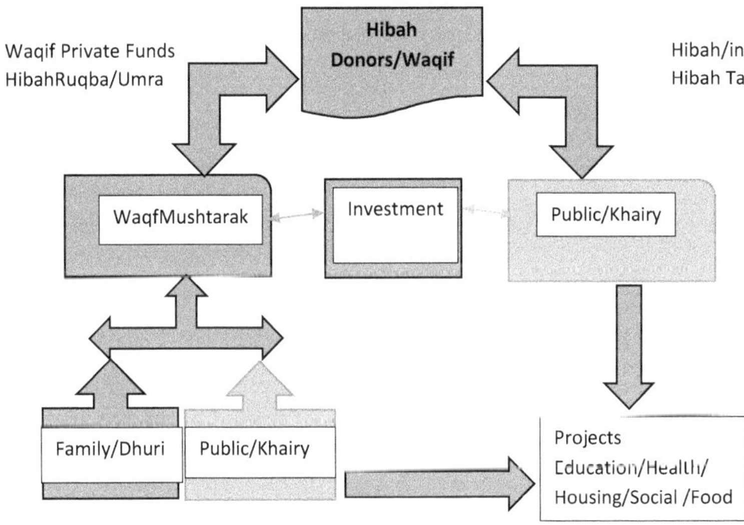

Figure 12.2 Proposed framework: Waqf Investment Corporation.
Source: Authors' own.

Table 12.4 ASNB depositors

Unit size	*Unit holders*		*Unit holding*	
	Nos	*%*	*Units*	*%*
<5000	7.433,271	76.92	4.122.520.378	2.65
5001–10,000	443.439	4.59	2,995,355,075	1.92
10,001–50,000	901,853	9.33	21,184,981,756	13.6
50,001–500,000	862,374	8.92	109,154,775,301	70.06
>500,000	23,304	0.24	18,334,245,603	11.77
Total	**9,664,241**	**100**	**155,791,878,113**	**100**

Source: ASB Financial Report 2018.

127,489,020,904 for a total of RM127,489 million (1 unit = RM1.00). With a dividend distribution of 6.50 sen a unit and a bonus of 0.50 a unit, the total dividend for 2018 was RM9,837.45 million. Based on our target holder dividend received was RM8,924.230 million. If we can get them to contribute 2.5% we will be looking at RM223.11 million for the waqf fund.

2 Voluntary contribution by working Muslims of 4.715 million to contribute RM50.00 a year to the waqf fund; the total amount received would be RM235.750 million.

3 Contributors from *Hibah* Takaful *tabarruq* fund would be another avenue.

4 Individual contributors who wish to investment their funds and *Hibah* the returns for a fixed period under the 'Hibahumra' concept.

All these funds would be channeled to a Waqf Investment Corporation to manage and the proceeds of the investment would be used to finance education, construction or rental of homes for the poor, health and food.

Investment products

The investment products could be Islamic money market, fixed income, Shariah equity and sukuk. The selection criteria would be the fund manager with the best investment performance. Example of fund performance is given below.

Legislation: waqf investment act

The creation of a national waqf investment act is to cater for a universal approach to cash *waqf* administration to minimize the legal issues, especially the *mutawalli* certificate. The intention of creating a Waqf Investment Corporation is to ensure proper management by professionals who are compassionate to the idea. However there are a number of challenges that need to be overcome, given as follows:

a Obtaining the *mutawalli* certificate. This is a major legal consideration; since waqf is a state list category, the *mutawalli* needs to be the SIRC. The need to convince the SRC would be the biggest challenge. So far there are only two *mutawallis* granted the certificate; they are the Johor Corporation where the *mutawalli* was issued by the Johor State Religious Council and Awqaf Corporation Berhad where the *mutawalli was* issued by Negeri Sembilan State Religious Council.

b The corporation will be involved in investment and fund collection; the legislation applicable to it would be the Securities Commission Act, licensed to carry out investment. For taking deposits the license needs to be approved by the Central Bank of Malaysia or Bank Negara Malaysia to overcome the issues of Anti-Money Laundry (AMLA).

c There is need to get public support for such activities and deduct dividend from ASB, *tabarru'* fund under Takaful. The marketing needs to be intensive.

d The setting up of Corporate Social Responsibility (CSR) division within the Waqf Investment Corporation to handle the distribution for education, health, homes and subsistence.
e For the contributors who perform the *Hibah*, a digital waqf certificate or token would be issued for their participation.

Conclusion

The concept and idea of using *Hibah* as a catalyst for waqf investment is feasible with a *mutawalli* certificate. The Muslim community in general is willing to contribute to a good project as can be seen in the collection through the masjid (mosque) and Friday suraus. The selling point for the SIRC is that they did not need to have their waqf cash funds ideal as it can be invested and the proceeds will be given directly to them to carry on with their activities in addition to getting additional funds from the Waqf Investment Corporation. As for the community, there will be available funds to support the education of Muslim children either locally or internationally in the long run and minimize the dependency on the government funding.

Recommendations

Based on the findings, the following are the recommendation:

i Government to provide for a clear common *Hibah Shariah law* in the use of *Hibah Ruqba or Umra*, allowing the giver to make changes during his lifetime as practiced by Takaful, Wasiyyah Shoppe, ASNB when the need arises.
ii Continuous *Hibah* promotion at the mosque, offices and other appropriate events.
iii Need for a fair and transparent *Hibah* fee regulation.
iv The selection of funds and fund managers needs to be transparent and all activities of the Waqf Investment Corporation must be audited and conformed to the mandate of setting up of the Waqf Investment Corporation.

Muslims have the obligation to equip themselves with knowledge of *Hibah* in their wealth distribution for their estate while alive, now for the benefit of their family after their death. From there, the beneficiaries will be able to receive their inheritance within an average of three to eight months; beneficiaries are able to avoid the long and tedious process of claiming the inheritance when it is done through *Hibah* distribution. Just imagine if the RM60 billion in frozen estates could be realized it will benefit the economy, community and our environment.

Research limitation

The statistics from *Hibah* provider are confidential. As the Syariah Court is governed by the State Government and there is no standardized *Hibah*

Act/Enactment in Malaysia, each state has its own way of handling matters with regard to *Hibah*. Therefore, it is highly suggested that future study should focus on standardization of *Hibah* in Malaysia as a law enforcement. We were able to derive information on *Hibah* from operators such as Wasiyyah Shoppe Berhad, Tabung Haji Malaysia and Takaful Malaysia. The process for *mutawalli* is ongoing.

Notes

1 The administration of Islamic law (Federal Territories) Act 1993.
2 Law of Malaysia (Act 505) Part IV Sec. 46 (1) (2) (B) (Vi).
3 https://www.thestar.com.my/metro/community/2016/02/03/estates-worth-rm60bil-left-unclaimed/
4 Part B 8.1 Bank Negara, 2016.
5 http://www.mais.gov.my/perkhidmatan/perkhidmatan-baitulmal/pengurusan-hibah.p1
6 http://www.focusmalaysia.my/property/exclusive-bukit-jelutong-draws-steady-demand
7 Bahari, A. (2014). *Islamic estate, retirement, and Waqf planning.* IBFIM, Kuala Lumpur. ISBN 978-967-0149-43-1 Chapter 6, pp. 172, 173.
8 https://www.mainpp.gov.my/index.php/.../7-hibah?...hibah...
9 http://www.bnm.gov.my/documents/act/en_ifsa.pdf
10 http://www.utusan.com.my/berita/nasional/tabung-haji-lancar-hibah-amanah-th-1.480671
11 https://www.bharian.com.my/bisnes/korporat/2018/04/414573/wasiyyah-shoppe-peroleh-status-syarikat-amanah
12 https://www.tabunghaji.gov.my/en/savings/general-info/data-statistic
13 http://www.utusan.com.my/bisnes/korporat/wasiyyah-shoppe-bantu-urus-harta-pusaka-44-000-orang-1.320070
14 http://wasiyyahshoppe.com.my/
15 Wasiyyah Shoppe Berhad uses front loading method to their clients.
16 http://wasiyyahshoppe.com.my/
17 Cizakca, M. (2010). Incorporated cash Waqf and Mudaraba, Islamic non-bank financial instruments from the past to the future. MPRA Paper. http://mpra.ub.uni-muenchen.de/25336
18 https://www.thestar.com.my/news/nation/2010/05/19/panel-to-decide-on-family-feud/
19 https://www.theborneopost.com/2019/02/13/inheritance-claim-jamaludin-jarjis-mother-sues-two-grandchildren/
20 Mohsin, M.I.A., Dafterdar, H., Cizkaca, M., Alhabshi, S.O., Razak, S.H.A., Sadr, S.K., Anwar, T. And Obaidullah, M. (2016) *Financing the development of old waqf properties: Classical principles and innovative practices around the world.* Palgrave Macmillan, New York, p. 94.
21 Nurrachmi, R. (2012). The implication of cash Waqf in the society. MPRA Paper No.44605. http://mpra.ub.uni-muenchem.de/44605 (accessed on 20/8/2019)
22 Mokhtar, F.M., Sidin, E.M. & Razak, D.A. (2015). Operation of cash Waqf in Malaysia and its limitation. *Journal of Islamic Economics, Banking and Finance*, Vol.11, No.4. https://ibtra.com/pdf/journal/v 11_n_4 Article 8.
23 Mywakaf at https://www.mywakaf.com.my (accessed on 14/8/2019)
24 http://pqi.stats.gov.my/result.php?token=5f957ec0d8e4dfcab2a92eaf94b6a079
25 Chan, C. & Chan, A. (2010). Attitude toward wealth management services: implications for international banks in China. *International Journal of Bank Marketing*, Vol. 209 No. 4, pp. 272–292.
26 http://www.ukm.my/fep/perkem/pdf/perkemviii/pkem2013_5a3.pdf

27 https://www.stlouisfed.org/~/media/files/pdfs/hfs/essays/hfs-essay-2-2015-education-and-wealth.pdf
28 http://extwprlegs1.fao.org/docs/pdf/mal134802.pdf
29 http://gbse.com.my/isijulai16/gbse202(3) 2011-1920(july202016).pdf
30 Refer Appendix 12.1A.
31 http://masjid.islam.gov.my/index.php?data=c3rhdglzdglrlnboca
32 Department of Statistics Malaysia. https://www.dosm.gov.my

References

Ali, M.Y., & Khanom, F. (2014). Understanding cash waqf: Its role towards alleviating poverty in contemporary context. USIM, Seminar Waqf Iqlimi. http://ddms.usim.edu.my/handle/123456789/9911 (accessed on 22/8/2019).

Amanah Saham Bumiputera Financial Report. 2018. http://www.asnb.com.my/pdf/produk/ANNUALREPORT/2019/AR20ASB.pdf (accessed on 1/9/2019)

Bahari, A. (2006). *Panduan Wasiat Islam dan Pentadbiran Harta Pusaka di Malaysia.* Mulia Erat Sdn Bhd. Kuala Lumpur.

Bahari, A. (2014). *Islamic estate, retirement, and Waqf planning.* IBFIM, Kuala Lumpur. ISBN 978-967-0149-43-1

Bank Negara. (2016). *Hibah. Guideline issued as reference on the Syariah rulings applicable to Hibah. Malaysia.*

Buang, S. (1993). *Historic Judgement on article 121 of the federal constitution, Malaysian Law News.*

Chan, C. & Chan.A. (2010). Attitude toward wealth management services: Implications for international banks in China. *International Journal of Bank Marketing.* Vol. 209, no.4, pp. 272–292.

Cizkca, M. (2010). Incorporated cash Waqfs and Mudaraba, Islamic non-bank financial instruments from the past to the future, MPRA Paper. http://mpra.ub.unimuenchen.de/25336

Department of Statistics, Malaysia. https://www.dosm.gov.my (accessed on 23/8/2019)

Hibahdariperspektifundang-undangSyariah di Malaysia.ppt.

Kachkar, O.A. (2017). Towards the establishment of cash waqf microfinance fund for refugees. *ISRA International Journal of Islamic Finance.* Vol. 9, no. 1, pp. 81–86.

Mohsin, M.I.A., Dafterdar, H., Cizkaca, M., Alhabshi, S.O., Razak, S.H.A., Sadr, S.k., Anwar, T. and Obaidullah, M. (2016). *Financing the development of old waqf properties: Classical principles and Innovative practices around the world.* Palgrave Macmillan, New York.

Mokhtar, F.M., Sidin, E.M. & Razak, D.A. (2015). Operation of cash waqf in Malaysia and its limitation. *Journal of Islamic Economics, Banking and Finance*, Vol. 11, no.4. https://ibtra.com/pdf/journal/v 11_n_4 article 8

Muda, M.Z. (2008). Instruments of and Wills: Analysis of the regulations and applications in Malaysia. Paper presented at the Hibah and Faraid National Convention 2008, Kuala Lumpur.

myWakaf. https://www.mywakaf.com.my (accessed on 14/8/2019)

Noor Lizza Mohamed Said & Adnan Mohamed Yusoff. (2017). Wasiat Harta Dalam Islam. UKM Bangi, Selangor.

Nurrachmi, R. (2012). *The implication of cash waqf in the society.* MPRA paper no.44605. http://mpra.ub.uni-muenchem.de/44605 (accessed on 20/8/2019).

Sanusi, S. & Shafiai, M.H.M. (2015). The management of cash waqf toward socio-economic development of Muslims in Malaysia. *Jurnal Pengurusan*, Vol. 43, pp. 3–12.

Warner, J. (2012). Creating goal clarity. http://blog.readytomanage.com/creating-goal-clarity (accessed on 28/2/19).

http://www.bnm.gov.my/documents/SAC/01_*Hibah*.pdf (accessed on 28/2/2019)

https://www.thestar.com.my/metro/community/2016/02/03/estates-worth-rm60bil-left-unclaimed/ (accessed on 5/2/2019)

https://www.nst.com.my/news/nation/2017/11/303548/malaysians-have-rm596-billion-unclaimed-money (accessed on 5/2/2019)

https://www.nst.com.my/news/crime-courts/2018/08/406001/update-jamaluddin-jarjis-mother-seeks-share-sons-rm2-billion-estate (accessed on 5/2/2019)

https://www.thestar.com.my/news/nation/2010/05/19/panel-to-decide-on-family-feud/ (accessed on 3/2/2019)

http://www.utusan.com.my/bisnes/korporat/hubungan-kekeluargaan-putus-kerana-harta-pusaka-(accessed on 3/2/2019)

http://ww1.utusan.com.my/utusan/info.asp?Utusan_Malaysia&sec=Mahkamah (accessed on 3/2/2019)

http://www2.esyariah.gov.my/esyariah/mal/portalv1/enakmen2011/Eng_act_lib.nsf/OpenDocument (accessed on 28/3/19)

http://e-muamalat.islam.gov.my/images/pdf-muamalat/instrumen_*Hibah*_UPDATE.pdf (accessed on 28/3/19)

http://www.mais.gov.my/perkhidmatan/perkhidmatan-baitulmal/pengurusan-*Hibah* (accessed on 28/3/19)

https://www.hmetro.com.my/node/179400 (accessed on 28/3/19)

https://www.hmetro.com.my/mutakhir/2015/01/27353/permudah-urusan-perwarisan (accessed on 28/3/19)

http://www.mpc.gov.my/wp-content/uploads/2017/05/Productivity-Report-2017.pdf (accessed on 1/4/19)

https://www.thestar.com.my/metro/community/2016/02/03/estates-worth-rm60bil-left-unclaimed/ (accessed on 3/4/19)

http://www.focusmalaysia.my/Property/exclusive-bukit-jelutong-draws-steady-demand (accessed on 3/4/19)

https://www.bharian.com.my/bisnes/korporat/2018/04/414573/wasiyyah-shoppe-peroleh-status-syarikat-amanah (accessed on 4/3/19)

http://wasiyyahshoppe.com.my/ (visited 13/4/19)

http://www.utusan.com.my/berita/nasional/tabung-haji-lancar-hibah-amanah-th-1.480671 (accessed on 13/4/19)

https://www.stlouisfed.org/~/media/files/pdfs/hfs/essays/hfs-essay-2-2015-education-and-wealth.pdf (accessed on 14/4/19)

http://www.bnm.gov.my/documents/act/en_ifsa.pdf (accessed on 15/4/19)

https://www.theborneopost.com/2019/02/13/inheritance-claim-jamaludin-jarjis-mother-sues-two-grandchildren/ (accessed on 17/4/19)

https://www.mainpp.gov.my/index.php/../7-hibah?...hibah (accessed on 17/4/19)

http://blog.readytomanage.com/creating-goal-clarity/ (accessed on 24/4/19)

https://www.researchgate.net/publication/235301155_Attitude_toward_wealth_management_services_Implications_for_international_banks_in_China (accessed on 24/4/19)

http://pqi.stats.gov.my/result.php?token (accessed on 27/4/19)

http://www.ukm.my/fep/perkem/pdf/perkemVIII/PKEM2013_5A3.pdf (accessed on 27/4/19)

https://www.bharian.com.my/node/138450 (accessed on 28/4/19)

http://masjid.islam.gov.my/index.php?data=c3RhdGlzdGlrLnBocA (accessed on 25/8/2019)

Appendix 12.1A

Wealth distribution channel findings

		Wealth distribution channel				
		Fara'id	*Islamic Will*	Hibah	*Others*	*Total*
Gender:	Male	11	6	19	1	37
	Female	16	4	41	0	61
Total gender		27	10	60	1	98
Race:	Malay	25	9	56	1	91
	Chinese	0	1	0	0	1
	Indian	0	0	1	0	1
	Others	2	0	3	0	5
Total race		27	10	60	1	98
Employment	Government	7	2	7	0	16
	Private	9	5	32	0	46
	Own Business	5	0	12	1	18
	Others	6	3	9	0	18
Total employment		27	10	60	1	98
Education background:	SPM	2	1	2	1	6
	Diploma	1	3	18	0	22
	Degree	11	6	22	0	39
	Postgraduate	13	0	18	0	31
Total education		27	10	60	1	98
Marital status:	Single	6	2	13	0	21
	Married	20	7	41	1	69
	Widowed	1	1	3	0	5
	Divorced	0	0	3	0	3
Total marital status		27	10	60	1	98
Cash: below RM10,000		3	1	7	0	11
RM10,000–RM50,000		5	4	15	0	24
RM50,001–RM100,000		7	2	11	1	21

(Continued)

	Fara'id	*Islamic Will*	Hibah	*Others*	*Total*
RM100,001–RM300,000	4	1	13	0	18
RM300,001–RM500,000	3	1	6	0	10
Above RM500,000	5	1	7	0	13
Others	0	0	1	0	1
Total cash	27	10	60	1	98

Sources: Result owned by author.

13 Edu-Waqf model – an analysis of selected OIC member countries

Mustafa Omar Mohammed, Mohamed Cherif El Amri and Souhaila Guedira

Introduction

In the early days of Islam, Waqf was used mainly for religious purposes: for building and managing mosques, grave yards, orphanages and hospitals. Subsequently, the role of Waqf was extended to other social and economic areas that included poverty alleviation programs, support for religious education, funding agriculture and water supply services (Mahamood & Ab Rahman, 2015). Waqf was also used to help young men and women get married, help people go for pilgrimage, protect and take care of animals (Kahf, 2011). The role expanded to the provision of essential social services and activities that filled the gap of government budget for education, healthcare, municipality services, housing, construction of public goods and services (Cizakca, 2000). In the areas of economic development, Waqf has been used to finance small community businesses. In these business models, Waqf institutions entered, established by many case studies, into partnership with small businesses that played a vital role in community development (Mohsin et al., 2016). Waqf institutions raise capital and channel it to competent small and medium enterprises (SMEs). The role of Waqf went beyond financing into partnership contracts with start-up entrepreneurs such as "angels".

One of the major sectors where Waqf has played a significant role is education, particularly higher education. History provides evidence of classical Waqf universities such as Ez-Zitouna in Tunisia, Qarawiyyin in Morocco and Al-Azhar in Egypt. These institutions of higher learning were important centers for students and knowledge seekers from all over the world. After the colonization of Muslim countries, this Waqf education system, among others, faced a lot of challenges. Their management malfunctioned, the number of student enrollment drastically declined and the quantity and quality of the educational content provided also suffered. For example, the Qarawiyyin University of Morocco experienced over a decade sharp decrease in the number of courses offered. It used to offer courses that included Arabic literature, sciences, Qur'anic science, Islamic studies, Shari'ah-related courses and history, among others. The university's programs were reduced to Islamic and Shari'ah studies only.

After colonialism hitherto, new models of Waqf-based educational institutions emerged in different parts of the OIC member countries. These models varied from country to country with relative degrees of success and failures. In Turkey, for example, several Waqf-based universities have proven to be resilient while in the case of Malaysia, the Waqf-based AlBukhary International University (AiU) had to close its doors in 2014 due to internal management difficulties and inefficiencies (Bakar et al., 2019).

There are several theoretical studies on developing Waqf-based model and, on the other hand, there are studies that have reviewed extant Waqf-based models of higher education in OIC member countries. Most of the theoretical studies are devoted to developing new models. Meanwhile works on extant Waqf-based models are descriptive and have given little emphasis on the classification and analysis of the various Edu-Waqf models. This chapter has filled these research gaps. It has identified, categorized and analyzed the extant Waqf-based models of higher education in three selected OIC countries, namely Turkey, Malaysia and Indonesia. These three countries represent distinct Edu-Waqf models of higher education. The chapter has also discussed the challenges and prospects of these three Edu-Waqf models.

The chapter is divided into the following six sections including the introduction. The second section provides an overview of the role of Waqf institution in the field of education, highlighting the significance of Edu-Waqf and its roles throughout Islamic history. The third section surveys the literature on theoretical Waqf education models, namely the government allocation-based model, cash Waqf model, Corporate Waqf model and Alumni Endowment model. The fourth section focuses on the experience of Edu-Waqf models of higher education in selected OIC member countries: Turkey, Malaysia and Indonesia. The fifth section discusses the major challenges facing the Edu-Waqf models in these three countries and the prospects of these models. The final section concludes the chapter.

The role of Waqf in education

The role of Waqf in enhancing education has proven successful and effective in Islamic history, across geographical boundaries and Waqf continues to be implemented in different regions from Syria, Egypt, Iraq, North Africa, Turkey, to the West (America, Europe) and the East (Malaysia, Indonesia). Waqf schools and educational institutions since the early days of Islam have been expanding in Palestine, Syria, Iraq, Egypt, reached the regions of Balkan states, Morocco, Andalusian territories, Turkey (since the Ottoman period) and flourished in other parts of the world such as Malaysia and Indonesia (Kahf, 2011; Mahamood & Ab Rahman, 2015). Historical evidence also shows that in Palestine, the city of Jerusalem had 64 schools, out of which 40 were Awqaf. Ibn Hawqal wrote that at Saqalia[1] city alone there were around 300 primary schools, which taught algebra and geometry. As many as 70 libraries were created in Cordoba from Waqf revenues during the 4th-century Hijri (Mohsin et al., 2016). Awqaf provided equal opportunities of free tuition to all classes of the society to receive high quality education. This system of free education is also found in the oldest Waqf University of Zaitouna in Tunis, Tunisia (the first university in the world) established in year 737 AD, followed by Al-Qarawiyyin University in Fez, Morocco (859 AD) and Al-Azhar University in Cairo, Egypt (972 AD). The three universities have existed until today. The significant contribution of Waqf in education continued with Ayubites (1171–1249 AD) and Mamaliks (1249–1517 AD). The primary role of those Waqf-based schools, educational institutions and universities was to support and fund needy students to enable them have access to education at different levels. Moreover, the Awqaf were also responsible for building schools, universities, students' dormitories, libraries and for providing education-related facilities such as furniture.

Waqf in the early days of Islam was instrumental for funding and financing education in general and higher education in particular. This role was a fundamental relief for state budget and household income in meeting the needs of education. In modern societies, the increasing number of students coupled with the high costs of education has led to a decrease in the overall quality of the educational system. The needs of educational institutions are no longer confined to buildings, schools, administrative furniture, tuition fees and scholarships for students, but include facilities such as books, libraries, laboratories and databases. Yet in the majority of societies in the Muslim world (if not all), the responsibility of financing education relies largely on the state (government), which normally has limited resources that are insufficient to cover the needs of education. Hence, Awqaf are now being revitalized in these Muslim countries as alternative funding sources to support education. Modern Muslim states particularly in OIC member countries are motivated by the success of Waqf institutions and the significant role they played throughout Islamic history. The success of Waqf also inspired the West and many universities in America, Europe and other regions of the world to implement the principle of Waqf in the form of endowments, trusts or foundations. Prominent universities that have benefited from the Waqf like experiences are Harvard, Yale and Stanford Universities in the United States, Cambridge and Oxford in the United Kingdom, Melbourne University in Australia and Kyoto University in Japan.

Edu-Waqf models

The diversity of Waqf experiences and its applications in education in different regions of the world underlines the existence of different theoretical models of funding, managing and expanding Waqf-based educational institutions. In the literature, four theoretical Edu-Waqf models are distinguishable: state Waqf-funded model, cash Waqf-funded model, business or Corporate Waqf-funded model and Alumni Waqf-funded model. In practice, some institutions of learning adopt one of these four theoretical models while some may adopt a combination of two or more of these models. In other cases, institutions of learning may switch from one model to the other depending on the needs of the society, changes in the education eco-system and the opportunities and support readily available.

State Waqf-funded model

In this Edu-Waqf model, the main donor and sponsor of Waqf to educational institutions and universities is the state or government. This model was adopted by the classical Waqf-based institutions such as Zaitouna University in Tunisia, Qarawiyyin University in Morocco and Al-Azhar University in Egypt. The Waqf was mainly supported and funded by the government (state) of the respective countries and regions, in addition to some minor contributions from notable individuals in the society, businessmen and businesswomen. In modern states, the Malaysian government for instance provides Waqf funds collected through its designated bodies such as State Islamic Religious Councils (MAIN) and the Department of Waqf, Zakah and Hajj (JAWHAR). The Malaysian government contributed RM 3.5 million (around USD 836,176) toward the establishment of the International Islamic University of Malaysia Waqf fund (IIUMWF) that is used to help needy students (Sulaiman et al., 2009). Another example of state Waqf model is the funding of Al-Abrar USIM Waqf Funds in Islamic Sciences University of Malaysia (USIM). Al-Abrar USIM Waqf Funds is funded by the State Islamic Religious Council of Negeri Sembilan (MAINS) that provided financing facilities in the form of donation of RM 1 million (around USD 238,888) and another RM 1 million as *qard hasan* (interest-free loan) to be returned later (Hussin et al., 2016). The Waqf fund to the University was for the purpose of establishing medical clinics to offer healthcare services for the needy public.

Cash Waqf-funded model

Cash Waqf is defined as "the confinement of an amount of money/cash from the founder and the dedication of its usufruct, according to founder's condition(s), in perpetuity to the welfare of the society". Cash Waqf was largely practiced during the Ottoman Empire and it is still being practiced in Turkey (Cizakca, 1998, 2000; Mohsin, 2009). The income from cash Waqf was used to finance public health, free education, public services and to alleviate poverty, where the beneficiaries were both Muslims and non-Muslims. In Malaysia, cash Waqf was introduced since 1957 and it is now an important model for Waqf projects in different fields, including education. The source of funds for cash Waqf-based institutions for education could be multiple such as donations and endowment from individuals as well as contributions from corporate sponsors (companies, holdings, families, organizations, group of people, institutions, foundations) (Asuhaimi et al., 2013). Cash Waqf funds are used to provide scholarships, finance maintenance and expansion of the educational institutions and universities, to finance establishment of laboratories and libraries and support other education and teaching-related matters. In the case of Turkey, most of cash Waqf universities and educational institutions are sponsored and backed financially by corporations and foundations (companies, holdings, family business holdings). In Malaysia the large contributions of cash Waqf for educational institutions come from individuals as well as from donors in foreign countries. Funds from cash Waqf funds are normally invested in the form of placements on mudharabah investments account in Islamic banks, or some other forms of beneficial income generating projects and investments (Razak et al., 2016; Negasi, 2017). Figure 13.1 illustrates the cash Waqf-based model for funding educational institutions.

Corporate Waqf-funded model

In the Corporate Waqf-funded model for education, private and public business entities sponsor educational institutions in the form of cash or/and physical properties or/and part of the company shares as Waqf. The Corporate Waqf-funded educational institutions are considered and managed as business entities (Hashim, 2009). This model is adopted in many Waqf-based universities in Turkey where the institutions are sponsored by foundations formed by corporate parties like in the case of Sabanci University (sponsored by Sabanci Holding and family), Koç University (Koc Holding and family), Bilkent University (Bilkent Foundation and its companies, Dogramaci family),

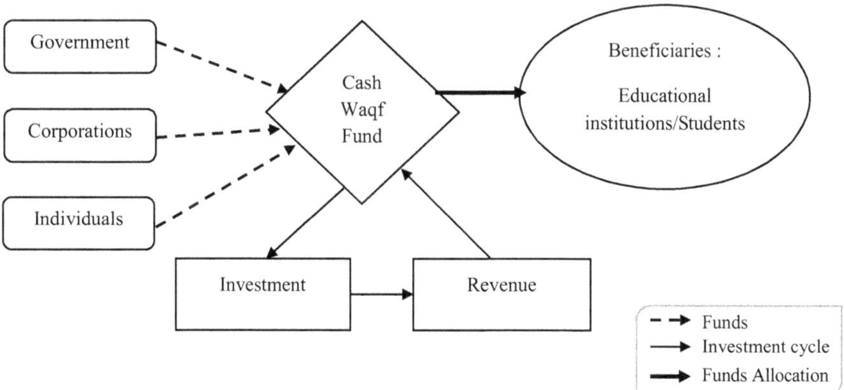

Figure 13.1 Cash Waqf model for educational institutions.

Fatih University (Gulen group), Istanbul Şehir University (BSV – Sciences and Arts Foundation, Ulker Family) (Koç, 2012; Mahamood & Ab Rahman, 2015). In Malaysia, the Corporate Waqf-funded model for education is still at the infant stage and is being tested and implemented in some universities such as the International Islamic University of Malaysia (IIUM) which generate RM 500,000 per year (average USD 119,446) from the rent of Waqf assets inside the university used for commercial purposes (Ali & Wahid, 2014). In contrast, the Corporate Waqf-funded model is mainly and largely being implemented in Indonesia. For instance, Pondok Modern Gontor Darussalam (PMGD) in Indonesian Gontor has several business and SMEs running under its management as many as 31 units in 2012 (shops, restaurants, pharmacies, hospitals, small factories). The business activities are mainly managed and operated by teachers, alumni, staff and employees of the Gontor/Waqf institution or university (Bahroni, 2012). Hilmiyah et al. (2013) confirmed that PMGD rents Waqf land to farmers using ijarah and musharakah contracts.

Alumni Waqf-funded model

In this model, financial support for Waqf (endowment) to fund educational institutions and universities is secured mainly from alumni. This model is not common in many OIC member countries and there is hardly any study that has examined the lack of significant contributions from alumni. Instead, the model in the form of endowment has flourished in Western universities. Prestigious universities in the United States and United Kingdom are best examples. Harvard University for instance is financed by endowment funds reaching more than USD 30 billion in asset (Hussin et al., 2016). In the United Kingdom, Oxford and Cambridge Universities are also partly funded by endowments. Alumni contribute on a monthly basis or on the spot in lump sum one time per year. Oxford University ensures the management of the endowment funds is sustainable through OU Endowment Management (OUEM). The income from the fund is used to provide scholarships, academic award, research and education-related activities (Mahamood & Rahman, 2014).

Edu-Waqf models in selected OIC member countries

This section examines the variations and practices of Edu-Waqf models in the experience of three selected OIC member countries: Turkey, Malaysia and Indonesia. The section will share the modus operandi of these models as practiced in the various Waqf-based educational institutions, schools and universities in these three countries.

Edu-Waqf model in Turkey

The significance and practice of Waqf-based education system in Turkey originate from the era of the Ottoman Empire. In 2016, there were 195 universities in Turkey out of which 68 of them were Waqf based with 38 of these Waqf-based universities located in Istanbul (Mahamood & Ab Rahman, 2015). Waqf-based universities are considered as private non-profit educational institutions, although in Turkey Awqaf funds are also used in financing public universities. The dominant Edu-Waqf model in Turkey is the Corporate Waqf-funded model. In the Turkish Corporate Waqf-funded model the private and public business entities inject assets in the forms of cash and/or properties/or part of shares as Waqf to fund educational institutions. In this model, Waqf-based institutions are managed as business entities (Hashim, 2015). Many foundation-based or Waqf-based universities in Turkey are sponsored by business groups, holdings and family business holdings, individuals, private companies. This Waqf for education in Turkey is regulated by the law, and the government has several requirements for establishing Waqf-based universities. One of the requirements is that educational institutions remain non-profit organizations. The regulation makes sure that the sources of funds for establishing and managing a Waqf-based university are sufficient, and it is a necessity that an agreement be made with state university to back up and assist Waqf-based university in case of crisis. Prominent and high ranking Waqf-based universities include Bilkent University, Koç Univerity, Sabancı University, Istanbul Şehir University, Fatih University, Istanbul Sabahattin Zaim University and Yeditepe University (Mahamood & Rahman, 2013).

Edu-Waqf model in Malaysia

In Malaysia, the largest percentage of Awqaf is used for religious purposes where more than 80% of Waqf related assets are used for building mosques. Contrary to Turkey, the Malaysian Waqf sector is not properly regulated where the majority of Waqf properties and lands as of 2016 were still not registered (Harun et al., 2016). Waqf in every state in Malaysia is managed by religious council. For instance, in Selangor, Awqaf are managed by State Islamic Religious Council of Selangor (MAIS), while in Kedah Waqf is managed by State Islamic Religious Council of Kedah (MAIK). In order to coordinate, empower and ensure the good management of Waqf properties in Malaysia, the JAWHAR has been entrusted to supervise Awqaf in the archipelago, with strong cooperation with the respective State Islamic Religious authorities (MAIN) and other related bodies (Mujani, 2011). Historically, Waqf for education in Malaysia started with traditional religious educational institutions like People's Religious School ("Sekolah Agama Rakyat" SAR), State Religious School ("Sekolah Agama Negeri" SAN), *madrasah* (religious school) and *pondok* (cottage used as religious school and dormitory). Traditionally, the Malaysian individual Muslims would donate and endow their land to religious schools for educational purposes (Mujani et al., 2016). Nowadays, Awqaf funds dedicated for education in Malaysia include also higher educational institutions such as universities. This is an upgrade from the traditional ways of managing Awqaf to a more developed and advanced process. Waqf-based institutions aim to help students in need to finance their studies, provide scholarships and books, finance research activities, and expand educational buildings. There are some Malaysian universities that have implemented and adopted Waqf system in their institutions. Universities create Waqf units or departments. Prominent among the public universities with Waqf departments are the National University of Malaysia (UKM), USIM and Putra University of Malaysia (UPM). As for private universities, there are the examples of IIUM, Islamic University of Malaysia (IUM) and AiU.

Edu-Waqf model in Indonesia

In Indonesia, the Waqf system is widely used in the service of education. The Indonesian Waqf funds are largely and most of the times used to fully support and finance educational institutions at all levels (primary education, middle and high schools, universities). Indonesia adopts a mixture of the four theoretical Edu-Waqf models discussed in section "Edu-Waqf models", although the Corporate Waqf-funded model is largely used, but with a different orientation from the Turkish model. Waqf is used to fund Gontor or Pesantren, an educational institution with indigenous and religious character. After Islam came to the Indonesian archipelago, Pesantren was mainly introduced to the society for teaching religion. Pesantren is considered as a traditional religious school system that was replaced later in many regions by Gontor as a modern version, ensuring quantity and quality of education provided at the same time. Gontor (or Pondok Modern) goes beyond the traditional religious teaching and offers other educational subjects such as sciences, literature, information technology, medicine and agriculture. Gontors in Indonesia are more than the classical educational institution: it is a modern Islamic boarding school, where students and teachers interact together in educational and social activities as subjects and objects of the education at the same time. It is a self-reliance-based system that ensures a smooth and confident integration of the graduates in the real life to undertake their respective roles in the society (Bahroni, 2012). Another interesting aspect of the educational Waqf system in Indonesia is its organization and reliance on SMEs and small business activities developed by the Waqf itself or related departments in order to secure self-financing. Based largely on mudharabah contracts, the SMEs created by the Gontors and Waqf universities are in the forms of restaurants, pharmacy shops, material shops for construction, health centers and hospitals, stationary shops, mineral factories and hotels. The income received from the business activity is used to provide educational facilities, scholarships, building dormitories, financing research, in addition to developing the business activity itself (Hilmiyah et al., 2013). Prominent examples of this Waqf-based model are PMGD and other Gontor-based institutions, Islamic University of Indonesia (UII) and Group of Muhammadiyah Universities (UM) spread across different regions of Indonesia.

Challenges and prospects of Edu-Waqf models

This section discusses pertinent challenges facing the Edu-Waqf models. It also highlights the prospects of Edu-Waqf models.

Challenges of Edu-Waqf models

The salient challenges of the Edu-Waqf models include lack of awareness, trust deficit, financial and administrative autonomy, lack of regulatory framework, management issues, quality of human resource, accounting and reporting, and lack of innovation.

Lack of awareness

The level of awareness about Waqf, its modalities, roles and implications is still very low and sometimes misunderstood in Muslim societies. Waqf in general and Edu-Waqf model in particular is often considered as a "free and unconditional" service. This implies consequently that Waqf does not belong to an organized system and process where there should be rules, regulations, financial and managerial aspects for its development and sustainability. This lack of awareness of the true nature and mechanisms of Waqf, in turn, creates lack of responsibility and leadership among responsible individuals in the society. In Malaysia, for example, a study conducted to test the level of Waqf awareness shows that only 39% out of 350 respondent understood Waqf, while the remaining respondents were not clear or uncertain about Waqf (Wael, 2017).

Trust deficit

This issue is acute in many state or government Waqf-funded institutions in general, and education sector in particular. Individuals and groups no more trust their governments in many countries, especially where a democratic leadership is missing. Individuals are not willing to participate and donate from their wealth to support the existing and new Waqf structures. Individuals and other related parties become doubtful whether their donations are really channeled to Waqf funds and reach the intended beneficiaries. Besides the destination of the funds, there is a serious trust issue about the management and effectiveness of Waqf funds' administration, in the absence of transparence, disclosure and reporting of Waqf schemes and activities.

Financial and administrative autonomy

Lack of financial and administrative autonomy is considered as the most important and critical issue affecting the Waqf-based model educational institutions and universities. Initially, the Waqf educational institution, its vision, mission and management are strongly linked to the interest of the sponsors.

This means that the management board, administration, faculties and other contributors of the Waqf University or institutions are somehow obliged to align and stick to the guidelines and instructions of the donor. Therefore, the financial dependence of the Edu-Waqf University on the donors (the government, corporate entity, individuals or Alumni) leads to lack of financial autonomy as the funding could be reduced or cut off any time if such a university tries to assert its independence. Hence the long-term autonomy of Awqaf and endowment funds for education is not secured. Furthermore, the fact that corporate-based Waqf educational institutions and Waqf universities are supported by sponsors and corporate parties is driving the institutions to be managed as if it were a "company" or "a business unit" of the main sponsor, which is not compatible with the spirit of "foundation (awqaf)" initially (Koç, 2012). In Malaysia, for example, Waqf cannot be managed independent of the religious councils of the different states in the country.

Lack of regulatory framework

Although the Waqf for education in Turkey is regulated by the law, the majority of Waqf-based universities and institutions in many parts of the OIC member countries are not. In the case of Malaysia for instance, the respective authorities of MAIN, JAWHAR, along with Waqf experts and professionals in Waqf for education, cannot ensure good development, management and empowerment of educational institutions and universities' Waqf funds without a sound regulatory framework. Some universities in Malaysia proceed with the appointment of a Waqf management board in order to secure good governance, transparency and effective management in fund raising, but it is still insufficient in the absence of supporting, harmonizing and regulating laws (Bakar, 2018).

Management issues

The management of Waqf in general is entrusted to Mutawallis or Waqf managers. According to Kahf (2011), the Mutawalli has an important role and responsibility in the Waqf management. He is expected to manage the Waqf property in the interest of the beneficiaries and with the aim of maximizing the revenue generated from the assets. The education Waqf managers must ensure value creation for the Waqf, increase free cash flows and returns from the assets and play leading role in managing and reporting to the sponsors and board of Waqf (trustees). This management leadership role is unfortunately missing in the majority of Waqf-based universities and educational institutions. In the study conducted by Kamil and Haneef (2016), the authors found that the majority of Waqf-based universities in Malaysia (according to the sample used) face passive management in regard to their portfolios and lack of risk management practices. In addition, large portion of educational Waqf universities avoid funding departments demanding high investment resources such as civil engineering and mechanical sciences. There is also a lack of necessary space (land) to grow and expand Waqf universities and related educational infrastructures and the fact that Waqf universities and institutions are mainly based in capital cities and large cities in respective countries (Koç, 2012).

Quality of human capital

Pursuant to the previous issue related to the lack of management skills, the problem of human capital expertise in Waqf-based educational institutions and universities is visible in Malaysia and Indonesia where the majority of Awqaf managers and administrators are graduates of Islamic law (Shari'ah) and Islamic studies. This issue is less visible in Waqf and endowment-based universities and institutions in the West and in Turkey, as the managers are from different backgrounds: engineering, law, business administration, finance, accounting. Lack of quality human capital expertise creates the need for strategic planning, administrative management skills, leadership, financial and business skills (Bakar et al., 2019).

Accounting and reporting

Another critical issue with Waqf universities and educational institutions (and Awqaf in general) is the lack for appropriate and specific accounting regulations and standards that are specially developed for Awqaf. There are some "shy" initiatives to come up with accounting and reporting standards suitable for Awqaf; however the related accounting practices are still not fully developed (Ihsan & Hameed, 2007; Masruki & Shafii, 2013; Bakar, 2018; Bakar et al., 2015).The AAOIFI standards for Waqf (Shari'ah standard no.33) highlight some general rules and Shari'ah standards for Awqaf establishment, management and reporting, but the standards are not applied and respected in all "Islamic" institutions and countries. The issue here is the absence of accounting standards applicable for Awqaf in general, and for Edu-Waqf institutions specifically in a way that could be adopted and implemented in Awqaf institutions regardless of the country, the model or the system. In Yayasan Universiti Multimedia (YUM) in Malaysia for instance, the applied financial statements and accounting principles are those of Malaysian Private Entity Financial Reporting Standards (MPERS/MFRS). The administrative and financial reporting are prepared and presented to the Board of Trustee of the Waqf as well as to external auditor. Therefore, there is no doubt that Waqf educational institutions need specific and more compatible accounting standards that are in concordance with its specificities, philanthropic fundamentals and special needs, which are different from any corporate business activity (Bakar et al., 2019).

Lack of innovation

Waqf systems and models adopted for educational institutions and universities in many regions are still based on the traditional and classical approaches of

Waqf management, which is inadequate in the modern era of financial, technological and social development. Innovations like digital payment, fintech and others should be considered in the current education Waqf schemes. This would reduce and minimize the lack of transparency, frauds and misuse of cash Waqf funds in Waqf educational institutions. In addition, the implementation of fintech and digital payment would make payment and flow of cash traceable, management and reporting much faster, easier and efficient (Bakar et al., 2019).

Prospects of the Edu-Waqf models

By now it is clear that Waqf for education sector needs several and serious changes in its different levels and aspects in order to serve its initial objectives and aspirations. The following are some suggestions and prospects for a better development, management and outputs of Edu-Waqf institutions and related parties.

Standardized regulatory framework

There is a primordial need to define the working framework under which the Waqf-based educational institutions could operate and be assessed. Regulatory bodies such as AAOIFI, OIC and Waqf councils in respective countries are highly encouraged to jointly develop standards and regulations for Awqaf, especially the ones that are for educational purposes. The standards should be clear, formulated in a way that suit any Edu-Waqf institution regardless of the country, region, form of Waqf or its sources of funds. This regulatory framework would be then easily adopted by local authorities and included in their local laws and regulations to be applied by Edu-Waqf institutions. The role of the standardized regulatory framework is to organize the Edu-Waqf sector, ensure transparency in terms of the management and use of Waqf funds. Consequently, the release and adoption of such regulatory framework would also solve the issue of trust expressed by sponsors, individuals and funding parties regarding the management and distribution of their donations by the government or the fund managing authorities. Moreover, the regulatory framework would include also accounting and reporting standards for Awqaf and Edu-Waqf institutions.

Sustainability of Waqf funds

Financial source is an important pillar in any Waqf scheme, including in educational field. As discussed previously, Edu-Waqf funds are mainly secured by government, corporations or individuals. These sources are limited most of the times, thus creating dependence on potential sponsors as well as strong exposure to funding cut off. It is clear that Waqf universities and institutions need to diversify their sources of funds, in addition to adopting sustainable financing modes in the long run. Meanwhile financing expensive assets for Edu-Waqf such as laboratories, research centers, high investment needs of departments and purposes could prove challenging as corporate and business sector cannot be involved and engaged in financing and sponsoring such assets (Bakar, 2017). Another important aspect is the normalization and simplification of financing channels, which will enhance and increase the participation of individuals and institution in financially supporting Waqf funds. This is concretized via providing different technological contribution facilities such as online banking in the official website of the Waqf university and direct debit donation. In addition, fundraising programs and activities could be initiated and promoted through marketing and communication unit within the Waqf university. Another interesting element to mention here is the incorporation of Islamic commercial contracts and transactions like "waqf-REITs" (Real Estate Investment Trusts) and "waqf-Sukuk" (Islamic bonds) (Mahamood & Ab Rahman, 2015). According to Musari (2016), a potential Edu-Waqf sukuk could be materialized through different financing schemes such as mudharabah-based Waqf-sukuk, musharakah Waqf-sukuk and/or cash waqf-sukuk. This would support and boost development and expenditure of Edu-Waqf institutions, especially in terms of infrastructure, research, financial sustainability and independence.

Innovation

Innovation requires the initiative of exposing the Edu-Waqf sector to the latest technological tools and channels for a more efficient fund collection and distribution. The future demands the use of fintech technology such as Blockchain, Cryptocurrency and "digital coins", Waqf applications and online crowd funding. Moreover, Edu-Waqf institutions based on cash Waqf model are currently operating using physical Waqf certificates and titles, which can be transformed into a digital form (Bakar, 2017).

Collaboration and specialization

With the growing importance of Waqf in educational field and the increasing need of such a supporting mechanism in educational institution, joint efforts and collaborations become highly imperative. In fact, collaborations between different Waqf educational institutions and sponsors would not only support and strengthen the financial flows for Edu-Waqf institution and "eco-system" but also improve organizational and administrative processes (Suhaili, 2016). This collaboration process relies on the principle of "unity is strength", suggesting that small Edu-Waqf institutions and initiatives could be expanded and developed in a more efficient way through mutual collaboration and mergers. In addition, in order to secure the quality and efficiency of higher education Waqf-based institutions, it is recommended to adopt specialization (Koç, 2012). This suggests that some Waqf universities for instance will focus on undergraduate education, some will tackle postgraduate education levels, while others will specialize in research and development. Such specialization could also be considered based on sectors and subjects of studies (sciences, social sciences, economics and management, medicine, architecture, computer sciences and technologies).

Management

Managing Waqf funds is crucial in Waqf models, especially in educational field. The management board or parties have the responsibility to manage the Waqf funds in a way that ensures the initial and core objectives of the Waqf and the empowerment of educational institutions. Consequently, the choice of managers should be carefully executed. Personal leadership skills and traits should be in line with the Shari'ah, and in conformity with organizational needs of such managerial responsibility that involves charity funds, sponsors' wishes, beneficiaries' rights, moral, social and religious responsibility. Moreover, the "modern" Edu-Waqf institutions are demanding in terms of human capital expertise for a better and efficient management. The administrative parties and individuals are expected to be highly qualified in different managing skills such as financial expertise, legal knowledge, communication and marketing skills and so on, in addition to interpersonal traits (responsibility, honesty, integrity).

Conclusion

It is clearly highlighted that Waqf plays an important role in the field of education and helps in financing scholarships for students, building schools, universities, libraries and funding other education-related activities. In fact, several educational institutions in different regions and countries implemented the Waqf concept in their systems and developed interesting Edu-Waqf models. However, many issues and challenges are observed, affecting the funding, operation and funds' channeling mechanisms of Edu-Waqf schools and universities. The chapter has suggested some reforms and changes in order to solve the issues. These suggestions include regulatory framework, sustainability of funding, management, innovation and collaboration. This would boost the Edu-Waqf sector and ensure its development, efficiency and sustainability.

Note

1 Or *Siqilia* in Arabic, as known today as Sicily in Italy.

References

Ali, S.Z.B., & Wahid, H. (2014). "Peranandan Kepentingan Dana WakafInstitusiPendidikanTinggi di Malaysia". *Persidangan Kebangsaan Ekonomi Malaysia Ke-9*, 9, 216–225.

Asuhaimi, F. A., Shafii, Z., & Alias, M. H. (2013). "The Effort of Selected Public Universities in Developing Awqaf Properties Using Cash Waqf Instrument". *Journal of Chemical Information and Modeling*, 53(9), 1689–1699.

Bahroni, I. (2012). "Streamlining Education Institution through Waqf Enlargement: An Experience of Gontor System". *Jurnal At-Ta'dib*, 7(2), 339–361.

Bakar, R. (2018). "Cash Waqf for Education : Prospects and Challenges". *Journal of Emerging Economies and Islamic Research*, 6(2), 1–4.

Bakar, R. A., Rahman, Z., & Sakinah, W. (2015). "Corporate Waqf University: Practical Model and Challenges Experienced by Yayasan University Multimedia". Paper presented at the International Conference on Waqaf, Trust and Endowment, Malaysia, 2015.

Bakar, R., Sakinah, W., Zaini, R. M., & Sarmin, F. (2019). "Corporate Waqf University: A Sustainability Model". *Journal of Emerging Economies and Islamic Research*, 7(1), 24–36. Retrieved from www.jeeir.comwww.jeeir.com

Çizakça, M. (1998). "Awqaf in History and Its Implications for Modern Islamic Economies". *Islamic Economic Studies*, 6(1), November.

Çizakça, M. (2000). *A History of Philanthropic Foundations: The Islamic World from the Seventh Century to the Present*. Istanbul: Boğaziçi University Press.

Hashim, M.A. (2015). Strategi Jihad Bisnes. Telaga Biru, Kuala Lumpur.

Harun, F. M., Possumah, B. T., Mohd Shafiai, M. H. Bin, & Nor, A. H. M. (2016). "Issues and Economic Role of Waqf in Higher Education Institution: Malaysian Experience". *Al-Iqtishad: Journal of Islamic Economics*, 8(1), 149–168. doi:10.15408/aiq.v8i1.2514

Hilmiyah, N., Mohd Shafiai, M. H., Ahmad, S., Ramzi, M., & Che Hariff, M. R. (2013). "Wakaf Produktif dalam Pembangunan Pendidikan: Kajian di Pondok Moden Darussalam Gontor, Indonesia". *Persidangan Kebangsaan Ekonomi Malaysia Ke VIII (PERKEM VIII)*, 3, 1302–1314.

Hussin, R., Rashid, R. A., & Yaakub, N. I. (2016). "Exploratory Study on Waqf Implementation in Malaysian Public and Private Universities: With Special Reference to Turkish Universities". Paper presented at the Kuala Lumpur International Business, Economics and Law Conference 9, 399–409.

Ihsan, H., & Hameed, S., (2011). "Waqf Accounting and Management in Indonesian Waqf Institutions: The Cases of Two Waqf Foundations". *Humanomics*, 27 (4).

Kahf, M. (2011). "Waqf and Its Sociopolitical Aspects". *Essential Readings in Contemporary Waqf Issue*, 45–55.

Kamil, N.K.M., & Haneef, M.A. (2016). "Investment Practices of Endowment Funds in Higher Education: Lessons for the Developing World". Paper presented at the International Symposium on Waqf and Higher Education (ISWHE 2016), Istanbul, Turkey 28–30 May 2016.

Koç, M. (2012). "Foundation (Awqaf) Universities in Turkey- Past, Present and Future". Paper presented at the 3rd International Conference on Islam and Higher Education (ICIHE 2012) Kuantan, Malaysia; October 1-2, 2012, (October 2012). doi:10.13140/2.1.1010.5280

Laum, B. (1914). "Die stiftungen in der griechischen und ramischen Antika", quoted in Cizakca (1998).

Mahamood, S. M., & Ab Rahman, A. (2015). "Financing Universities through Waqf, Pious Endowment: Is It Possible?", *Humanomics*, 31(4), 430–453.

Masruki, R., & Shafii, Z. (2013). "The Development of Waqf Accounting in Enhancing Accountability". *Middle-East Journal of Scientific Research 13 (Research in Contemporary Islamic Finance and Wealth Management)*, 13, 1–6.

Mohsin, M.I.A., Dafterdar, H., Cizakca, M., Syed Othman, A., Shaikh Hamzah, A. R., Seyed Kazem, S., & Obaidullah, M. (2016). *Financing the Development of Old Waqf Properties: Classical Principles and Innovative Practices around the World.* Kuala Lumpur: Palgrave Macmillan US.

Mujani, W. K. (2011). "The Concept of Law of Gift Inter Vivos under Islamic law and the Contracts Act, 1950". *International Business Management*, 5(6A), 319–325.

Mujani, W. K., Mohd Taib, M. S., & Rifin, M. K. I. (2016). "Waqf Higher Education in Malaysia". Paper presented at the International Conference on Education, E-Learning and Management Technology (EEMT 2016). doi:10.1057/978-1-137-48739-1_31

Musari, K. (2016). "Waqf -Sukuk, Enhancing the Islamic Finance for Economic Sustainability". Paper presented at the World Islamic Countries University Leaders Summit 2016 (November 2016), 1–16.

Negasi, M. I. (2017). "Financing Higher Education in the Islamic World through Waqf (Endowment)". *European Journal of Multidisciplinary Studies*, 5(1), 136. doi:10.26417/ejms.v5i1.p136-142

Razak, D. A., Embi, N. A. C., Salleh, M. C. M., & Fakhrunnas, F. (2016). "A Study on Sources of Waqf Funds for Higher Education in Selected Countries". Paper presented at the International Joint Conference on Islamic Economics and Finance (IJCIEF), 113–128. Retrieved from http://irep.iium.edu.my/52520/

Suhaili, N. A. (2016). "A Way Forward for Reviving Waqf in High Education through Collaboration". Paper presented at the International Symposium on Waqf and Higher Education (ISWHE 2016), Istanbul, Turkey 28–30 May 2016.

Sulaiman, M., Adnan, M. A., & Nor, P. N. S. M. (2009). "Trust Me! A Case Study of the International Islamic University Malaysia's Waqf Fund". *Review of Islamic Economics*, 13(1), 69–88.

Wael, M. (2017). "Waqf Awareness in Malaysia". Unpublished Master Thesis. Multimedia Universiti Malaysia.

Zubaidi, M. (1999). Taj al-'Arus min-Jawahir al-Qamus. Beirut: Dar Sadr, 125.

14 Smart *Waqf* City for Education – an experience in Darussalam Gontor, Indonesia

Magda Ismail Abdel Mohsin and Aminuddin Maruf

Introduction

Reviewing the historical role of *waqf*, it has been realized that it has played a remarkable role in developing Muslim societies. The call for the revival of idle *waqf* properties and the creation of cash *waqf*, at the end of the 20th century and the beginning of the 21st century, witness the emergence of its role in some Muslim societies as it become their economic drivers that improve the welfare of their societies. Examples of such revival, for example, through the revival of idle *waqf* properties, new *waqf* buildings replacing the old properties, have been realized in terms of modern schools and universities, specialized hospitals, commercial areas, residential areas, residential towers, stocks and cash *waqf*. Moreover, the recent creation of cash *waqf* models provides many services that are needed in different Muslim societies such as education, health care, scholarship, feeding the hunger, digging wells. Not only this but surprisingly different kinds of waqf cities have been established in different forums in the Islamic world such as in the case of Sabanci *Waqf* in Turkey, Hamdard *Waqf* City of Health in India, Pakistan, Bangladesh, *Waqf* City in Somaliland and Darussalam Gontor *Waqf* City in Indonesia. This chapter will focus on *waqf* city for education of Darussalam Gontor which has been founded with a masjid and later developed into boarding schools until recently developed into a *waqf* university with all its business units to ensure its financial sustainability. To achieve this, the chapter is divided into five sections; first it presents an overview of the development of the Darussalam Gontor *waqf* city for education, followed by explaining its educational system and then elaborates on its financial sustainability, besides presenting its current and future expansion, and followed with a conclusion.

Development of the Darussalam Gontor Smart Waqf City for Education

Recently the revival of idle *waqf* properties and the creation of *cash waqf* have been realized through many successful projects in the Islamic world.

Indonesia is among those countries that has successfully developed some of its idle *waqf* properties and introduced cash *waqf*. In addition, Indonesia has also established a *waqf* city for education which started with building a small mosque in one of the villages and followed by setting up of boarding schools and a university with full-fledged facilities.

Atiq Waqf Mosque

The seed for the *waqf* city started in 1750 when Sulaiman Jamal, the son in law of Hasan al Besari, built Atiq *Waqf* Mosque in Pendopo. His son, Arham Anom Besari and grandson Santoso Anom Besari continued to develop the mosque after he passed away. Besides holding the prayers, the mosque provided religious lessons to the Muslim families around the area. In 1926, the number of students increased, and this encouraged the founder's family to build a proper school called *Tarbiyatul Athfal* next to the Atiq Masjid. The school later became an established boarding school with more schools opened to accommodate the increasing number of students.

Gontor Darussalam boarding schools

The establishment of *Tarbiyatul Athfal* school marked the start of the chain of boarding schools. Gontor is a village located approximately 3 km east of Tegalsari and 11 km southeast of Ponorogo, East Java, Indonesia. *Tarbiyatul Athfal* was established with a limited source and few number of students who were trained with strong ethical values such as sincerity, tenacity and patience that strengthen the development of the boarding school. It was Ahmad Sahal, one of the Gontor's founding fathers, who taught the students and gave all what he had to provide for free education. In 1931, the total number of students reached 500. The reputation of *Tarbiyatul Athfal* continues to grow along with the increasing interest of the community to send their children to learn about Islam. Such situation motivated the school administrators to open more branches in the villages around Gontor (Gontor.ac).

Looking at the demand for education at that time, the headmaster of *Tarbiyatul Athfal* decided to introduce a new educational programme called *Sullamul Muta'allimin*. Students who had completed at *Tarbiyatul Athfal* continued their studies at *Sullamul Muta'allimin*. The students at *Sullamul Muta'allimin* study subjects such as *Fiqh, Tafsir* and *Hadith* at an advance level. The curriculum also includes other general skills such as arts, sports, scouts and others. The school system attracted many students to study and in 1932 the school had more than 1,000 students.

In 1936, the school introduced another programme called *Kulliyyatul Mu'allimin al-Islamiyyah* (Islamic Teacher Training College). The college was led by Imam Zarkasyi who returned to Gontor after completing his study in Java and Sumatra. The college's programme integrates modern and traditional Islamic school systems. The Islamic subjects were taught in the classes and the students were required to stay at the hostels that were built in designed in the traditional atmosphere of boarding school. The students were taught to learn modern skills such as vocational education, sports, arts and management. The duration of studies at *Kulliyyatul Mu'allimin al-Islamiyyah* is six years.

The founders of Gontor Islamic boarding school referred and adopted four well-established educational institutions to design a strong and robust educational system. These institutions are Al-Azhar University in Egypt for its immortality, Syanggit University in Mauritania for its generosity and sincerity, India's Aligarh Muslim University for its modern educational system which equips students with both general and religious sciences and finally Shantiniketan Group of Colleges of India which is known for its peaceful environment. Gontor Islamic boarding school embraced five core values of sincerity, simplicity, self-sufficiency, Islamic brotherhood and freedom. The school's motto is noble character, sound body, broad knowledge and independent mind (Zarkasyi, 2005a).

12 October 1958 marked the beginning of *waqf* city for education as the founders of Gontor Islamic boarding school endowed the school to the Muslim Ummah. One of the mandates in the declaration of *waqf* is that the school must be further developed into an Islamic university and to become one of the centres for Islamic studies. For such case the *Waqf* Board became the highest administrative body which consists of 15 people who are responsible for all the implementation and development of the school. The schools were led by the headmaster who was elected by the *Waqf* Board every five years. The headmasters were not only responsible for the schools but also all other institutions under the name of Gontor such as *Kulliyyatul Muallimin Al-Islamiyyah,* Darussalam University, Darussalam Gontor Alumni Association, Community Development and many other institutions (Umam, 2013; Zarkasyi, 2005b).

In 2018, Darussalam Gontor Islamic Boarding School had 20 branches with 13 boarding schools for boys and 7 for girls. The main campus which is located in Ponorogo East Java had 20 student hostels that can accommodate more than 4,000 students. The teachers were given accommodation but separate from the students. Besides teaching, the teachers were also involved in the school's business units.

Gontor Islamic Boarding schools are located in various areas of Indonesia, covering from Java to Sumatra Island. The total number of students reaches more than 20,000 and the total number of teachers is almost 3,000 as seen in Table 14.1 (Gontor, 2018).

Darussalam Gontor University

Darussalam Gontor University was the vision of Gontor's founding fathers, namely Ahmad Sahal, Zainuddin Fannani and Imam Zarkasyi. Starting with

Table 14.1 Boarding schools and the number of students and teachers in 2018

No	*Campus*	*Students*	*Teachers*
1	Boys campus 1 (Gontor)	4065	490
2	Boys campus 2 (Madusari)	1295	176
3	Boys campus 3 (Kediri)	1299	231
4	Boys campus 5 (Banyuwangi)	1199	140
5	Boys campus 6 (Magelang)	1214	140
6	Boys campus 7 (Kendari)	246	77
7	Boys campus 8 (Way Jepara)	82	22
8	Boys campus 9 (Kalianda)	571	76
9	Boys campus 10 (Aceh)	100	16
10	Boys campus 11 (Sulit Air)	47	25
11	Boys campus 12 (Jambi)	276	46
12	Boys campus 13 (Poso)	136	44
13	Boys campus 14 (Siak, Riau)	223	50
14	Girl campus 1 (Ngawi)	3423	438
15	Girl campus 2 (Ngawi)	1268	187
16	Girl campus 3 (Ngawi)	2480	269
17	Girl campus 4 (Kendari)	243	69
18	Girl campus 5 (Kediri)	1201	154
19	Girl campus 6 (Poso)	110	42
20	Girl campus 7 (Riau)	812	119
	Total	20.208	2.811

Source: Wardun (Annual Journal of Darussalam Gontor Islamic Boarding School) 2018.

the establishment of *Tarbiyatul Athfal* in 1926, the university was established after 37 years. The establishment of Darussalam Educational Institute (IPD) on 17 November 1963 was the starting point of Darussalam Gontor University.

Darussalam Gontor University initially started with two faculties, Faculty of *Usuluddin* and Faculty of *Tarbiyah*. In his inaugural speech, Imam Zarkasyi, as the University's Chancellor, hoped that the university would have similar qualities to four institutions – the Al-Azhar University of Egypt which continues to be the centre of Islamic studies in the Islamic world for centuries, the Aligarh Muslim University in terms of academics, sincere teachers as those in Syanggit University, Africa and emulation of peaceful environment present in Shantiniketan Colleges in India (UNIDA, 2015).

In 1994, the Faculty of *Shari'ah* was established and with that the IPD was given a new name, Darussalam Institute of Islamic Studies (ISID). In 2010, ISID successfully introduced its postgraduate programme and continuously improved until it became nationally accredited. In 2013, the *Waqf* Board formed a committee responsible for the establishment of Darussalam Gontor University. On 4 July 2014 Darussalam Gontor University was officially established with the issuance Decree Number 197/E/O/2014 from the Minister of Education and Culture of the Republic of Indonesia which is the permit of establishment of Darussalam University. On Saturday 18 September 2014, the

Darussalam Gontor University Inauguration was held by the Secretary of the World Islamic University League, Prof. Dr. Ja'far Abdussalam, in Gontor's Meeting Hall (Unida.Gontor).

Educational system in Darussalam Gontor Waqf City

The educational system in Darussalam Gontor *Waqf* City was designed in a special type of educational environment where students could interact with teachers to gain knowledge and experience. Since both the students and the academics lived together in the so-called *waqf* city, and all their activities are well designed, holistic assessment of the students can be conducted and the potentiality and achievement of the student in various fields during their studies could be identified and monitored. This is to ensure balanced intellectual, spiritual and physical development of the students. The core values adopted by the schools was successfully realised at the boarding schools and the university.

Educational system in Darussalam Gontor boarding schools

The system of teaching in all these boarding schools is different from other traditional boarding schools. It emphasizes on both Islamic and sciences; hence students are taught in both streams of knowledge. The medium of teaching is English and Arabic and the students are required to speak English and Arabic alternately in every two weeks. Any student caught with speaking Indonesian or local languages will be punished by their supervisors. In addition, the students are also taught time management and punctuality is strictly observed. The school follows the Islamic or *Hijri* calendar and students are allowed to go back to their family only twice a year; hence, most of their times they are at the schools (Syamsuri, 2016).

As part of the practical training of the new graduates they will be assigned to teach for one year at the boarding schools. Besides, they can also further their studies at Darussalam University and participate in the school's business activities. Similarly, the way of recruiting new staff is different from other schools or universities. The teachers are also allowed to run the business units of the boarding schools. Though they do not get paid for their job but they are given with free accommodation and free food. The teachers received small salary to cover their monthly basic necessities. With such practices they are trained to work with sincerity and giving back to society. Another unique concept in Gontor's educational system is self-*waqf*. This concept refers to the practice of a person who decided to dedicate their whole life to teaching or running the business units at the boarding school (Muzarie, 2011).

The boarding schools do not only care about the students but also the alumni. Gontor's alumni association has been established in several countries such as Sudan, Turkey, Egypt, Saudi Arabia, Pakistan and Malaysia.

In Indonesia currently there are more than 200 alumni's boarding schools all over Indonesia. In order to connect and strengthen alumni relationship Gontor introduced *Tamam*, which is a trading platform for the alumni (Tamam.id).

As mentioned earlier the highest authority of Gontor Islamic Boarding Schools is the *Waqf* Board. The board acts as a legislative body which is responsible for the development of the education programmes. The headmaster which is the executive body is responsible to implement the *Waqf* Board's mandate into the institutional programmes and report to the board on an annual basis (Zarkasyi, 2005a). The *Waqf* Board consists of well dedicated alumni with some of them being top members of Indonesian parliament while others have dedicated themselves for the cause of education (Muzarie, 2011). The *Waqf* Board has a strong connection with the government and society.

Educational system in Darussalam University

Currently, the university has seven faculties, three master programmes and one doctoral programme. The faculties are Education, Science and Technology, Economics and Management, *Usuluddin*, Humanities, *Shari'ah* and Health. Under each faculty there are two or three departments. The university also establishes centre of excellence to develop student's skills such as the International Centre for *Awqaf* Studies, Centre for Islamic and Occidental Studies, Centre for *Mawarith* Studies, Training for Young *'Ulama'*, Centre for Islamisation of Sciences and Language Centre (Gontor, 2018). The university plans to open two new faculties, which is faculty of medicine and faculty of engineering by the year 2026. Throughout the years, the university has attracted many numbers of students and currently there are more than 3,000 students as shown in Table 14.2.

The university also has students from countries like Malaysia, Thailand, Singapore and Brunei Darussalam. The total number of foreign students is more than 50 students as shown in Table 14.3.

The university also welcomes student exchange programmes with universities from other countries. For instance, in June 2019 there were 11 students

Table 14.2 Number of students based on the faculties in 2018

Faculty	*Programs*	*No. of students*
Tarbiyah	Islamic education	387
	Arabic language teaching	289
Usuluddin	Tafsir and Science of Qur'an	241
	'Aqidah and Islamic philosophy	180
	Comparative religions	435
Shari'ah	Comparative school of laws	149
	Law of Islamic economics	304
Economics and Management	Islamic economics	324
	Management	204
Humanities	International relation	240
	Communication Science	106

Faculty	*Programs*	*No. of students*
Science and Technology	Agro technology	38
	Informatics engineering	102
	Agro-Industrial technology	47
Health Science	Occupational safety and health	52
	Pharmacy	175
	Nutrition Science	125
Master Degree	'Aqidah and Islamic philosophy	62
	Arabic language teaching	62
	Law of Islamic economics	33
Doctoral Degree	'Aqidah and Islamic philosophy	15
Total		3.570

Source: Wardun (Annual Journal of Darussalam Gontor Islamic Boarding School) 2018.

Table 14.3 Number of foreign students based on their origin countries

No	*Country*	*Amount*
1	Malaysia	49
2	Thailand	3
3	Singapore	1
4	Brunei Darussalam	1
Total		54

Source: Wardun (Annual Journal of Darussalam Gontor Islamic Boarding School) 2018.

from Istanbul Sabahattin Zaim Universitesi (IZU) who came to learn Arabic and English languages for two months. Besides the languages, they also learned Islamic studies and about Indonesian culture (Gontor.ac.id).

Financial sustainability of Darussalam Gontor Waqf City for Education

Since 1926 Darussalam Gontor *Waqf* City has been witnessing steady growth until today. This is distinctly because of the cohesiveness of Gontor's *waqf* family. Once they joined as staff or students, they become part of the family and dedicate their lives to support Gontor's *waqf* city. Even though they are not the offspring of the founders of this *waqf* city, yet they contributed their energies, thoughts and services in an attempt to achieve the *waqf* city development and sustainability.

At the beginning of its establishment, the source of funding was initiated by the founders in the form of rice fields which had been endowed to the institution. Later, two other types of funding were created: tuition fees and revenues from a number of business units under the schools.

Tuition fees from the boarding schools

As mentioned earlier 20 boarding schools were established to cater to the demand for quality and friendly boarding schools. Annually, it has been estimated that the fees from the boarding schools are more than 6 billion Rupiahs (USD426,000). This fund is allocated to facilitate the operation and administration of the educational system, besides fulfilling students' needs, including meals, sport facilities and for other student activities (Wardun, 1440).

Income generated from the business units

To finance the operating cost of Darussalam Gontor *Waqf* City for Education 30 different business units were established such as in trade, agriculture and services as shown in Table 14.4.

Table 14.4 Gontor's business units as per 1970–2007

No	*Business units*	*Year of establishment*	*Location*
1	Rice mill	1970	Gontor
2	Darussalam press	1983	Gontor
3	Warehouse KUK	1985	Bajang
4	Building material shop	1988	Bajang
5	Book store	1989	Ponorogo
6	Bakso shop	1990	Ponorogo
7	KUK photocopy	1990	Bajang
8	UKK Grocery	1990	Gontor
9	La Tansa pharmacy	1991	Ponorogo
10	Gambia telephone centre	1991	Gontor
11	Ice factory	1996	Gontor
12	Greengrocer	1997	Gontor
13	Transportation services	1998	Gontor
14	Sudan telephone centre	1999	Gontor
15	Azhar canteen	1999	Gontor
16	DCC (Darussalam computer centre)	1999	Gontor
17	Darussalam guest house	1995	Gontor
18	Asia photocopy	2000	Gontor
19	DDC (Darussalam distributor centre)	2002	Ponorogo
20	DDC (Darussalam distributor centre)	2002	Mantingan
21	Chicken slaughterhouse	2002	Gontor
22	La Tansa Bakery	2003	Gontor
23	Cattle farm	2003	Gontor
24	Darussalam drinking water	2004	Gontor
25	Sport store	2005	Ponorogo
26	Al-Azhar telephone centre	2004	Gontor
27	Confection	2006	Gontor
28	BMT (BaitulMālwaTamwīl)	2006	Mlarak
29	Noodle factory	2007	Gontor
30	Guest house		Gontor

Source: (Muzarie, 2011).

Moreover, the idea of circular economy has been applied successfully in the *waqf* city among the students, teachers and the business units. The students and the teachers are encouraged to buy their daily necessities from the business units which contribute to the financial sustainability of Darussalam Gontor *Waqf* City for Education (Azizah & Kaffah, 2019).

It has been estimated that the income generated from these business units approximately amount to USD9.5 million of which the expenditure is about USD5.5 million for expansion, maintenance and construction (Wardun, 2015).

Expansion of Darussalam Gontor Waqf City for Education

Gontor bought many lands in the past, while planning to expand its business in the future. Recently, Gontor owned 12,643,712 m^2 of land spread throughout Indonesia. Following the mandate of the *Waqf* Board, all assets acquired by Gontor will be considered as an endowment for the Ummah. Currently the total piece of lands owned by the institution is shown in Table 14.5:

Table 14.5 Land owned by Gontor

No	*Locations*	*Area* m^2
1	Ponorogo	678,953
2	Madiun	7,527
3	Ngawi	2,092,995
4	Nganjuk	104,959
5	Tuban	10,600
6	Kediri	240,007
7	TulungAgung	2,254
8	Trenggalek	20,314
9	Jember	17,280
10	Banyuwangi	68,552
11	Yogyakarta	789
12	Solo	100
13	Wonosobo	2,654
14	Magelang	59,716
15	Jakarta	1,173
16	Southern Lampung	119,018
17	Eastern Lampung	82,500
18	Tanjung Jabung (Jambi)	6,091,071
19	Solok	70,000
20	Banda Aceh	126,306
21	Kampar	93,150
22	Siak	750,000
23	Rokan Hulu	71,900
24	Southeast Konawe	527,045
25	Southern Konawe	1,068,259
26	Poso	336,590
	Total	12,643,712

Source: Wardun (2018; Annual Journal of Darussalam Gontor Islamic Boarding School) 2018.

Table 14.6 Expansion of *Waqf* assets (2017–2018)

No	*Location*	*Form*	*Area* m^2
1	East of old La Tansa	Dry land and rice field	2,460
2	North of BKSM	Dry land	5,304
3	South of bridge, front gate of Kepuhrubuh village	Rice field	7,026
4	Precet, Sambirejo, Ngawi	Rice field	850
5	Gontor campus 6	Dry land	67
6	North of stadium	Rice field	1.162
7	Imogiri, Jogjakarta	Rice field	125
8	South of Ikhtiyar Masjid	Building and land	1.388
9	West of BMT Bajang	Rice field	5.389,84
10	South of Brahu village hall	Rice field	93,978
11	South of entrance road of Unida	Rice field	466
12	West of BMT Siman	Rice field	2.487
13	Behind Brahu village hall	Rice field	1.576
14	South of UnidaHote	Rice field	1.645
15	South of Unida	Rice field	1.750
16	In front of AdiSumarmo airport	Building and land	100
17	North of Kepontren warehouse	Dry land	896

Source: Wardun (2018; Annual Journal of Darussalam Gontor Islamic Boarding School).

Moreover, Gontor is expanding its *waqf* assets through acquiring more lands for future development. Thus, there are four sources supporting the development of *waqf* assets owned by Gontor which includes students' cash *waqf*, final grade students' *waqf*, revenue from the business units and *waqf* from the external parties. For the period 2017–2018 the institutions have purchased additional land for expansion of the *waqf* assets as seen in Table 14.6.

Conclusion

A very significant model or example for smart *waqf* city for education has been developed over the past 93 years since 1926. Starting with the intention to provide an Islamic education for children in a small village, it has developed into a chain of boarding schools for both boys and girls in the different states in Indonesia and led to an establishment of Islamic private university, located in the middle of paddy fields in a village in Ponorogo, East Java, Indonesia. Darussalam Gontor *Waqf* University marks the uniqueness of *waqf* university compared to other universities in the country. A distinct feature of Darussalam Gontor *Waqf* City for Education lies in the ways the lecturers, teachers and students live together in a city, in a residential built for teaching staff and hostels for students. They are also encouraged to run the business unites while supporting the business at the same time. This practice does not only allow the wealth to circulate among students, teachers and the business units but it also creates financial independency in raising the funds needed by the *waqf* city without resorting to any external sources of funding.

References

Muzarie, M. (2011). Sukses Memberdayakan Wakaf di Pesantren Modern Gontor (First Edition). Cirebon - Indonesia: STAIC Press.

Syamsuri, J. (2016). Eksistensi dan Kontribusi Pondok Modern Darussalam Gontor Dalam Pembangunan Sumber Daya Manusia. *AT TA'DIB*, 11(2). doi:10.21111/at-tadib.v11i2.776

Umam, K. (2013). Developing Management Standards Based on Islamic Values: Case Study of Darussalam Gontor Modern Islamic Boarding School. *Qudus International Journal of Islamic Studies*, 1(2), 18.

UNIDA, U. of D. G. (2015). University of Darussalam Gontor (UNIDA) Profile. University of Darussalam Gontor.

Wardun. (2015). Warta Dunia Pondok Modern Darussalam Gontor, Ponorogo – Indonesia: Darussalam Press.

Wardun. (2018). Warta Dunia Pondok Modern Darussalam Gontor, Ponorogo – Indonesia: Darussalam Press.

Zarkasyi, A. S. (2005a). Gontor & pembaharuan Pendidikan Pesantren (First Edition). Jakarta: PT RajaGrafindo Persada.

Zarkasyi, A. S. (2005b). Manajemen Pesantren Pengalaman Pondok Modern Gontor (Second Edition). Ponorogo: Trimurti Press.

Websites

Azizah, N. & Kaffah, S. (2019). The Development of Interpersonal Intelligence in Islamic Boarding School Darul Huda Ponorog, At-Ta'dib Journal of Pesantren Education, 14(1), at: https://ejournal.unida.gontor.ac.id/public/journals/4/pageHeaderTitleImage_en_US.jpg

Gontor.ac: https://www.gontor.ac.id/pembukaan-tarbiyatul-athfal-1926

Gontor.ac.id: https://www.gontor.ac.id/uncategorized/mahasiswi-izu-turki-adakan silaturrahim-bersama-pimpinan-pmdg

Tamam.id: https://tamam.id/about-us

Top Universities: https://www.topuniversities.com/universities/universitas-darussalam-gontor

Unida. Gontor: http://unida.gontor.ac.id/history/

15 Empirical investigation on *awqaf* and its socio-economic impact in Malaysia

Muhammad Iqmal Hisham Kamaruddin, Mustafa Mohd Hanefah and Rosnia Masruki

Introduction

The development of *waqf* institutions is consistent with the requirements of *maqasid shariah*. *Maqasid shariah* was defined as the meaning and secrets that can be understood from the Islamic *shariah* in the whole or part of the *shariah* process (IbnAshur, 2006). It can be categorised into three, namely (i) necessities (*dharuriyyat*), (ii) convenience (*hajiyyat*) and (iii) refinement (*tahsiniyyat*). There are five elements under necessities (*dharuriyyat*) consisting of religion, life, mind, offspring and wealth. Laldin et al. (2012) had discussed *maqasid shariah* in *waqf* context whereby it is under the protection of wealth (*hifz al-mal*). Muslims need to preserve, maintain and manage the economic and financial development parallel with *shariah* law including *waqf* management. The *hujjah* of *waqf* are to address ignorance, poverty, ill-health and creation of wealth. *Waqf* has demonstrated remarkable records as shown in historical developments in addressing the prevailing problems at that time. *Waqf* institutions had played a major role in providing social goods such as education and health; public goods (roads, bridges and national security); helping the poor, orphans and the needy, built commercial businesses; utilities (water and sanitation); infrastructure for religious services (building and maintenance of mosques and graveyards); creating employment; supporting agricultural and industrial sector without imposing any cost to the government (Mohsin, 2008).

Learning from the successes of the past, it is believed that *waqf* has great potential in solving the problems facing the *ummah* today. *Waqf* has a built-in dynamism to contribute to the socio-economic development of the *ummah*. The dynamism of *waqf* is inherent in its basic characteristics, namely permanence and inalienability. All the schools of *shariah*

> have stressed the importance of the creation of a *waqf* which had played an important role in ameliorating poverty and in furthering learning in the past and it is expected to play its role in the future provided this institution is reactivated and its management is placed on the sound footing.
>
> (Kahf, 2003)

Besides, *waqf* is one of the mechanisms for wealth creation and distribution developed based on Islamic teachings and principles.

In Malaysia context, State Islamic Religious Councils (SIRCs) are becoming sole trustees and responsible for managing the Muslim wealth revenue derived from *zakat* (alms), *waqf* (endowment) and *mal* (treasury). SIRCs are public service entities established within the confines of Islamic law. The political and social factors affecting SIRCs are unique and have inspired the present research focus. The importance of SIRCs is examined from the perspective of administrators of considerable funds and public accountability paradigm. The former refers to SIRCs, which act as *mutawalli* (*waqf* manager), while the latter urges the public right for information with regard to public services. In the interest of accountability of religious organisations within the purview of Islamic thought, and respecting the public right to have access to information about them, this research provides an empirical investigation on *waqf* management process in selected *waqf* institution in Malaysia. This examination is written under case study format by focusing on the process of *waqf* management practiced in selected *waqf* institution in Malaysia including on *waqf* application process, *waqf* governance, *waqf* monitoring (agents and projects), *waqf* reporting and *waqf* socio-economic impact practices.

Literature review

Background of waqf

Waqf or *awqaf* (plural) is derived from the verb '*wa-qa-fa*'. In terms of language, *waqf* means to stop, to prevent and to hold (Wahbah Zuhaili, 1985). In Islamic terms, *waqf* is an endowment of a portion of one's wealth either in kind or as cash that is permanent and irrevocable (the corpus is detained), done either implicitly or explicitly, for the sole purpose to be close to Allah SWT. The endowed capital is withheld and only its use/benefits are used for specific or general charitable purposes (AbRahman, 2009). Once the asset has been given out as a *waqf*, the right of the endower (*waqif*) over the property ceases. The asset can no longer be subjected to sales transaction or bequeathed or given out as *hibah* (gift) or written as a *wassiyyah* (will). This is supported by narrations of Abu Yusuf, Muhammad bin Hassan, Ahmad bin Hanbal and Syafi'i (AbRahman, 2009). The original *waqf* asset (*mauquf*) may be invested and the usufructs or returns will be distributed to the beneficiaries either for general or specific welfare as specified by the *waqif*. An asset that is endowed as *waqf* may be in the form of fixed/immovable assets such as mosque, madrasah and land or movable assets such as cash, shares and means of transportation. The practice of *waqf* is based on four pillars. First, there is a *waqif* (the one who endows). The *waqif* has to satisfy a number of conditions, namely he is a Muslim who has come of age (*baligh*), he owns the asset, he is sane and he makes the endowment on his own free will. Second, there is a *mawquf*, the asset that is endowed as *waqf*. The conditions on the *mawquf* must be permanent in nature and useful. Third, there are the *mauquf'alaih*, which are the beneficiaries of the *waqf* asset. The beneficiaries are those designated by the *waqif* in his *sighah waqf* (transfer of *waqf*). Last but not least, the *sighah waqf* must be present as a formal exchange of the *waqf* ownership from *waqif* to the *mutawalli* (*waqf* manager) or beneficiaries (Alhabshi, 1984; Yaacob, 2006).

Khalid (1988) had stated that *waqf* in general can be identified into three types which are: (i) *waqf al-i'qar* (immovable assets), (ii) *waqf al-manqul* (movable assets) and (iii) *waqf al-irsod*. *Al-i'qar* or immovable assets refer to any assets which cannot be moved, relocated or changed. Examples for this type of asset are lands and buildings. Meanwhile, *al-manqul* or movable assets refer to assets which can be moved such as cash, books, tables, chairs, equipment, vehicles and poultry. Finally, *al-irsod* refers to the type of *waqf* where the government of a country put a piece of property to be used for the benefits of the citizens of the country. These assets must be used in the community's best interest and for the benefits of Islam.

On the other hand, Khaf (1999) categorised *waqf* into three different types which are: (i) *waqf khayri* (public *waqf*), (ii) *waqf zurri* (family *waqf*) and (iii) *waqf mushtarak* (a combination of *waqf khayri* and *waqf zurri*). In this case, *waqf khayri* refer to a *waqf* that serves the interest of the whole of society or the major part of it. This type of *waqf* is dedicated to supporting the general good and welfare of the poor, the needy, public utilities such as schools, colleges for education, scientific research, shelter houses for orphans and wayfarers and hospitals which provide free services for the sick and poor (Yaacob, 2013). Meanwhile, *waqf zurri* refer to a *waqf* which is endowed initially upon oneself, one's children and one's relatives. In other words, the beneficiaries are either a specific person or persons characterised by the founder or any other specific persons (Yaacob, 2013). Finally, *waqf mushtarak* refer to a *waqf* where *waqif* will specify the target beneficiary (usually the descendants) and later assign the benefit for broader welfare purposes. However, only *waqf khayri* is available and practiced in Malaysia. The existence of *waqf zurri* and *waqf mushtarak* is hardly traceable in Malaysia (Abdul Rahman et al., 1999; Yaacob, 2013).

The term *waqf* has not been specifically mentioned in Al-Quran or Hadith, but the interpretations are made by the *fuqaha* on *sadaqa jariya* (Borham, 2011). Al-Quran and Hadith have enjoined/encouraged Muslims to give out their property as charity in general or as *waqf*. The following is the Quranic verse that encourages Muslims to give out some portion of their property in charity:

> Who believe in the unseen, establish prayer, and spend out of what We have provided for them.
>
> (Al-Baqarah 2:2)

Besides, there is also Hadith that is related to *waqf* which are narrated as follows:

> In the lifetime of Allah's Apostle, Umar gave in charity some of his property, a garden of date palms called Thamgh. Umar said, "O Allah's Apostle! I have some property which I prize highly and I want

> to give it in charity." The Prophet; said, "Give it in charity (i.e. as an endowment) with its land and trees on the condition that the land and trees will neither be sold nor given as a present, nor bequeathed, but the fruits are to be spent in charity." So 'Umar gave it in charity, and it was for Allah's Cause, the emancipation of slaves, for the poor, for guests, for travellers, and for kinsmen. The person acting as its administrator could eat from it reasonably and fairly, and could let a friend of his eat from it provided he had no intention of becoming wealthy by its means.
> (Sahih-Bukhari, Vol. 4, Book 51, Hadith No.26)

Based on earlier Quranic verse and Hadith, the rewards for the good actions including *waqf* are continuous even after the person passes away.

Waqf management in Malaysia

The historic establishment of *waqf* institution in Malaysia is believed to have been in existence for more than 800 years (Alhabshi, 1986). It is believed to have started when the Arab Muslim traders brought Islam to the land in the 10th century. Religious education is the main factor of *waqf* being developed in Tanah Melayu, especially in Terengganu. This is evidenced by one of the early 19th century *waqf* deeds by Sultan Umar, the ruler of the state, stating the objective of his *waqf* is to promote education and the dissemination of knowledge to the public (Yaacob, 2013). During the earlier period, Muslims who wished to *waqf* their property would go to see the village head and they would be the trustee of the *waqf*. However, there are no written documents regarding the first establishment of the *waqf* institution in Malaysia before the 19th century as stated earlier, except for the establishment of the *waqf* of the Masjid Capitan Kling in Penang in 1801, followed by the *waqf* by a member of the Aceh royalty, also in Penang (Yaacob, 2013).

From the legal aspect, *waqf* in Malaysia is under Section 25 of the Civil Law Act 1956 which stated that the administration of Muslim's property shall be in accordance with the Islamic law. There are 14 SIRCs, one for each of the 13 states and one for the Federal Territory. The state Islamic department will enforce all the legislation accordingly. Basically, different states will have different sets of legislations (Harun et al., 2012). Besides that, administration of the *Religion of Islam (Federal Territories) Act 1993* and similar Acts apply for individual provinces.

In Malaysia context, *waqf* properties are mostly developed for common purposes for instance mosques, educational development and social welfare. The government has allocated RM 250 million under the Ninth Malaysia Plan (2006–2010) for Department of Waqf, Zakat and Hajj (JAWHAR) and the Yayasan Wakaf Malaysia (YWM) to develop *waqf* land all over Malaysia for the purpose of building mosques and *musolla*, utilising *waqf* land, or land donated for religious or charitable purposes and used for commercial purpose (Harun et al., 2012). At present, a number of projects benefited from this allocation are shown in Table 15.1.

In terms of *waqf* management, *waqf* affairs are delegated under responsibility of SIRCs of each state. The courts recognised *shariah* as the governing

Table 15.1 *Waqf* projects under the Ninth Malaysia Plan (2006–2010)

No	*Project category*	*Project name/location*	*Project value (RM)*
1	Orphanage	Darul Aitam Wal Masakin Sultanah Haminah Binti Hamidun (JAWHAR-MAIK) Hostel, Alor Setar, Kedah	RM 2.08 million
		Bakti (JAWHAR-MAIK) Hostel, Machang Kelantan	RM 1.5 million
2	Commercial	Office-Lot (JAWHAR-MAIPk), Tambun, Perak	RM 1.6 million
		Shop-Lot (JAWHAR-MAIP), Mukim Utan Aji, Perlis	RM 4.24 million
3	Education Complex	Maahad al-Mashoor, Balik Pulau, Pulau Pinang	RM 41 million
		Wan Mahmood Waqf Student Hostel Complex (JAWHAR-MAIDAM), Besut, Terengganu	RM 8.3 million
4	Health	Hemodialysis Centre (JAWHAR-MAIJ), Batu Pahat, Johor	RM 8 million
5	Welfare	Women Protection Centre Taman Perling (JAWHAR-MAIJ), Johor Bahru, Johor	RM 7.33 million
		Muallaf Complex: Complex al-Sa'adah (JAWHAR-MAINS), Seremban, Negeri Sembilan	RM 4.5 million
6	Hotel	Pantai Puteri Hotel (JAWHAR-MAIM), Tanjung Kling, Malacca	RM 25.6 million
		Seri Warisan Hotel (JAWHAR-MAIPk), Taiping, Perak	RM 19 million
		Klana Beach Resort (JAWHAR-MAINS) and Baitul Hilal Complex, Teluk Kemang, Port Dickson, Negeri Sembilan	RM 18 million
		Grand Puteri Hotel (JAWHAR-MAIDAM), Kuala Terengganu	RM 41.68 million
7	Bazaars	4 units of Waqf Bazaar in Terengganu	N/A
		17 units of Waqf Bazaar in Sabah	
		15 units of Waqf Bazaar in Kelantan	
		42 units of Waqf Bazaar in Pahang	
		32 units of Waqf Bazaar in Johor	
		11 units of Waqf Bazaar in Melaka	
		11 units of Waqf Bazaar in Negeri Sembilan	
		20 units of Waqf Bazaar in Federal Territory	
		25 units of Waqf Bazaar in Selangor	
		28 units of Waqf Bazaar in Perak	
		20 units of Waqf Bazaar in Pulau Pinang	
		32 units of Waqf Bazaar in Kedah	
		27 units of Waqf Bazaar in Perlis	
8	Mart	1 unit of Waqf Mart, Masjid Kariah Panchor Jaya, Seremban, Negeri Sembilan	N/A
		1 unit of Waqf Mart, Masjid Jamek Pekan Gemas, Negeri Sembilan	
		1 unit of Waqf Mart, Masjid Jamek Tunku Besar, Tampin.	
9	Gift Kiosk	1 unit of Gift Kiosk, Masjid Negara, Kuala Lumpur.	N/A
		1 unit of Gift Kiosk, Masjid Putra, Putrajaya.	

Source: JAWHAR (2014) and YWM (2017).

law of property for Muslims including *waqf.* The government of Malaysia has formed JAWHAR on 27 March 2004 with the aim of making the administration systematic and effective. This department however does not have an authority to administer and manage *waqf* properties but rather plays a role as a planning coordinator and observes the *waqf* matter. Later, JAWHAR formed YWM for the sole purpose of identifying the underutilised assets of *awqaf* and planning for their development in coordination with SIRC of each state. One of the important characteristics of *waqf* in Malaysia is every *waqf* shall be registered in the name of SIRC as proprietor in accordance with the *National Land Code 1965* (Yaacob, 2013).

Although SIRCs are authorised for *waqf* management in each state in Malaysia, there are also several other institutions who are authorised by these SIRCs to act as *mutawalli* (*waqf* manager) to administer *waqf* on behalf of SIRCs. This includes the establishment of subsidiary institution of SIRCs such as the Perbadanan Wakaf Selangor (PWS) under the State Islamic Religious Council of Selangor (MAIS) and the Pusat Wakaf MAIWP SdnBhd under the State Islamic Religious Council of Federal Territory (MAIWP). Besides, there are also other institutions that are authorised by SIRCs to administer *waqf* although they are not directly controlled by SIRCs. This includes such as the Waqaf An-Nur Corporation Berhad (WANCorp), the Awqaf Holding Berhad (AWQAF), public universities and even selected Islamic non-profit organisations in Malaysia.

Socio-economic impact disclosure for waqf *institution*

Normally, there are five disclosure elements for socio-economic impact for *waqf*, which are: (i) input, (ii) output, (iii) throughput, (iv) outcome and (v) impact (Arshad & Zain, 2017; Kamaruddin, 2018;[1] Nordin et al., 2017; Shafii et al., 2014). Inputs consist of all possible elements needed in order to carry out *waqf* institution's objective through its activities and programs. Evaluation on outputs refers to quantity and quality of products or services delivered. In the throughput stage, the performance evaluation includes both efficiency and effectiveness measures for *waqf* institution. Evaluation on outcomes relates to results of non-profits organisations that are linked to its objectives. Finally, evaluation at impact stage is an evaluation on the consequences of organisation's activities towards community targeted.

In addition, the result of inputs and outputs is referred to as the efficiency of *waqf* institution, while the result in evaluating throughputs, outcomes and impacts is referred as the effectiveness of *waqf* institution (Medina-Borja & Triantis, 2006). Efficiency of *waqf* institution is measured on how economically all resources are utilised in providing social and economic contributions. Meanwhile, effectiveness of *waqf* institution is measured on to what extent each *waqf* institution's objective and goal is achieved (Beamon & Balcik, 2008). Table 15.2 shows proposed socio-economic impact indicators for the best *waqf* reporting practices as suggested by Nordin et al. (2017).

Table 15.2 Socio-economic impact indicators for the best *waqf* reporting practices

Inputs	*Activities*	*Outputs*	*Outcomes*	*Impacts*
What goes in	What happens	What results –immediate	What results – medium and long-term	What results – effects on root causes; sustained significant change
Cash	Delivery of basic needs (e.g. foods, shelter and medical supplies)	People fed, treated and sheltered	Improved living standard, health	Constant declines in poverty
Real Property	Construction of mosque, cemetery, road and hospital	Infrastructure and hospitality built	Increased income	Islam is widespread around the world
Equipment and supplies	Provision of microfinance	People trained and educated	Expansion of Muslim community	Strong Muslim brotherhood
Knowledge (Modern and Islamic)	Sponsoring disabled, orphans and refugees	Microenterprises formed		Fair income distribution (reduced gap between rich and poor)
Technical Expertise	Awarding scholarship and research. Disaster and accident relief. Conducting training and educational programs. Sponsoring religious activities (*da'wah*, Islamic forum)	Religious activities held		Significant changes in social norms and attributes (social justice, freedom, governance, transparency Achieving objectives of Islamic economic system

Source: Nordin et al. (2017).

A case study in selected *waqf* institution

This chapter is a continuous study from Kamaruddin et al. (2018)[2] which previously conducted research in order to understand *waqf* management practices in selected *waqf* institution in Malaysia. The previous study was focused on: (i) *waqf* governance, (ii) *waqf* application, (iii) *waqf* monitoring and (iv) *waqf* reporting. Therefore, this chapter extends the scope by focusing on *waqf* socio-economic impact disclosure by the selected *waqf* institution in Malaysia. For the purpose of this study, one particular *waqf* institution in Malaysia was studied, namely *Waqf* Institution A. Although there are other *waqf* institutions in Malaysia, this study however decided only to examine *waqf* management practices in *Waqf* Institution A due to several reasons. First, *Waqf* Institution A is well established as compared to other *waqf* institutions in Malaysia. Second, *Waqf* Institution A is among few *waqf* institutions in Malaysia that administer more than RM 500 million of *waqf* assets – thus, significant to be investigated. Third, *Waqf* Institution A is offering various *waqf* programs and activities, which give larger impact towards beneficiaries as compared to other *waqf* institutions in Malaysia. The detail of *Waqf* Institution A is as follows.

Background of Waqf Institution A

Waqf Institution A was established with the consent of its state ruler on 11 January 2011 and was gazetted on 3 February 2011. Previously on 30 October 2009, the state ruler ordered the State Islamic Religious Council A (SIRC A) to empower *waqf* administration by establishing a separate *waqf* entity from the SIRC A, similar to separation of *zakat* administration from the SIRC A previously. Thus, a new separate *waqf* entity known as *Waqf* Institution A is established from this order, parallel with the state enactment where the SIRC A is eligible to establish a body that is suitable to administrate and manage activities that serve its *waqf* initiatives. *Waqf* Institution A is one of the bodies established to carry specifically on *waqf* objectives by the SIRC A which is to administrate *waqf* funds including collection, management and distribution processes. Specifically, *Waqf* Institution A's roles and functions are as follows:

- Advise the SIRC A with respect to the policies, methods, measures needed to be implemented and taken to encourage the development of *waqf* property and products;
- Implement and give effect to such policies, instructions or directives of the SIRC A in respect of property development and endowment products;
- Develop, adopt and implement policies, ways and measures on property development and endowment products;
- Coordinate the implementation of the *waqf* property and product development rapidly;

- Plan, develop, implement and promote the development and implementation of *waqf* property and products;
- Manage and run the operation and maintenance of *waqf* facilities, infrastructure and equipment in the *waqf* area; and
- Promote, coordinate and carry out research and development in all aspects of *waqf* property and products.

Normally, waqf can be categorised into two types which are *waqfam* (general *waqf*) and *waqfkhas* (specific *waqf*). *Waqfam* is a *waqf* contributed by *waqif* (*waqf* donors) without any specific purposes or intention. Meanwhile, *waqfkhas* is a *waqf* contributed by *waqif* with specific purposes and intention on the usage of *waqf*. Under these two types of *waqf*, *Waqf* Institution A currently provides five *waqfam* schemes and one *waqfkhas* scheme. These *waqf* schemes are:

1 Cash *waqf* scheme – this *waqf* scheme is a way for *waqif* to perform *waqf* through cash. In this case, *waqif* will buy the *waqf* share units offered by the SIRC A as the sole trustee of *waqf* property in Selangor and impose such units indefinitely for Allah SWT with the purpose and interests of Muslims.
2 Infaq *waqf* scheme – this *waqf* scheme is a way for *waqif* to perform *waqf* through salary deductions. The *infaq* scheme was created in order to facilitate civil and private employees with a monthly salary deduction at a minimum rate of RM 5.00 and no maximum rate was set.
3 Corporate *waqf* scheme – this *waqf* scheme is focused on private, corporate and government-owned subsidiaries (GLCs) to perform *waqf*. These entities are being called to involve and contribute together in the development of *waqf* property through donations given. Besides providing *waqf* instrument as one of the corporate social responsibility (CSR) to Muslims, this corporate *waqf* scheme will make private and corporate groups as the icon of the Muslims to continue to live the practice of *waqf*.
4 Gold *waqf* scheme –this *waqf* scheme is for *waqif* who are interested to perform *waqf* through gold.
5 Art *waqf* scheme – this *waqf* scheme is similar to cash *waqf* scheme, but this scheme is focused more on artists, actors, singers, film/drama directors, composers, painters and others from art industry to perform *waqf*.
6 *Waqfkhas* scheme – this *waqf* scheme is varying based on *waqif* intention. Normally, *waqfkhas* is highly related to assets such as land and building that are contributed by *waqif* with specific intention. At present, there are about 200 *waqfkhas* projects which are currently in progress status under *Waqf* Institution A that cover various activities such as development of *waqf* land into religious school, cemetery or mosques.

Governance practices of Waqf Institution A

Waqf Institution A is led by a chief executive officer (CEO), who is responsible to report to the *Waqf* Institution A's board of directors (BOD). The BOD consists of 11 members from various backgrounds such as accounting, business, religious, legal, architecture and land. The BOD is responsible in governing and implementing all *waqf* projects and activities run by *Waqf* Institution A. The BOD is also responsible to the *waqf* fund collection mainly endowed by public at large. The list of the current BOD members' designation is as follows:

1 *Chairman* (Deputy Chairman of SIRC A).
2 Deputy Chairman (representative from public listed company – real estate developer company)
3 Board Member (representative from private company – real estate developer company).
4 Board Member (former Director of the State Auditor General).
5 Board Member (State Mufti).
6 Board Member (SIRC A Member).
7 Board Member (Secretary of SIRC A).
8 Board Member (State Legal Advisor).
9 Board Member (representative from private architecture firm).
10 Board Member (Director of the State Land Registry Office).
11 Board Member (CEO of *Waqf* Institution A).

Besides BOD, *Waqf* Institution A has four departments consisting of the Finance Department, the Administration Department, the Marketing and Da'wah Department and also the Research and Investment Department. In addition, *Waqf* Institution A also has a separate Internal Audit Unit which is responsible for internal audit processes. Moreover, although its headquarter is located at the state capital, *Waqf* Institution A has also appointed nine *waqf* officers under the Marketing and Da'wah Department; each *waqf* officer is responsible for *waqf* collection in all nine districts in the state.

Waqf socio-economic impact disclosure

The discussions on *waqf* socio-economic impact disclosure are presented according to three common types of *waqf* schemes in *Waqf* Institution A, which are: (i) cash *waqf* scheme, (ii) share *waqf* scheme and (iii) *waqfkhas* project. Under cash *waqf* scheme, Table 15.3 highlights the findings from the current practices from the interviews with regard to the input, output and impact of cash *waqf* scheme.

Based on Table 15.3, several recommendations are made. For input disclosure, it is proposed for *Waqf* Institution A to vary their input method by considering the introduction of e-wallet or other digital platforms by using QR Code for *waqif* to contribute in cash *waqf* scheme. Meanwhile, for outcome

Table 15.3 *Waqf* socio-economic impact disclosure on cash *waqf* scheme

Level of disclosure	*Details*	*Current practices*
Input	Cash	Offline and online (online banking, PFX, salary deduction)
Output	Disclose the channel of distribution Purposive/specified cash *waqf*	There are three main scopes for the cash *waqf* scheme: *Waqf* Education, *Waqf* Health and *Waqf* Investment
Outcome (*impact – activities based*)	No. of activities Amount spent on activities	Information disclosed is limited on impact for each *waqf* activity/ program by using cash *waqf*
Effectiveness (*output to objectives*)	Ratio on the usage of cash *waqf* for each RM collected	N/A
Efficiency (*input to output*)	Amount of cash *waqf* received ÷ Amount of cash *waqf* disbursed / use	Only disclose amount of *waqf* collection and amount of *waqf* distributed for every three months
Productivity (*benefits to ummah*)	Future/long-term *waqf* activities/ programs benefits towards public	N/A

disclosure, *Waqf* Institution A is required to disclose several indicators for each cash *waqf* activity such as follows:

- Education – number of schools, number of classes, number of students and number of programs.
- Health – number of patients, number of medical equipment, number of medicine contributed (based on medicine types), number of hours for medical consultations (including medicine manpower) and number of disease cured (based on disease types).
- Investment – number and amount of investment (based on investment types), investment returns and number of beneficiaries benefited from investment projects).

In addition, for effectiveness disclosure, it can be done by calculating and analysing cash *waqf* activities/programs conducted with cash *waqf* target (KPI), while for efficiency disclosure, *Waqf* Institution A can make an additional disclosure by computing and analysing the ratio of distributed cash *waqf* for each type of *waqf* activity/program/expense. Last but not least, for productivity disclosure, *Waqf* Institution A is suggested to calculate and analyse outcome indicators (contribution towards nation) as follows:

- Education – comparing number of schools, number of classes, number of students and number of programs with the state statistics.

- Health – comparing number of patients, number of medical equipment, number of medicine contributed, number of hours for medical consultations and number of disease cured with the state statistics.
- Investment – comparing number and amount of investment, investment returns and number of beneficiaries benefited with investment projects with the state statistics.

Meanwhile, under share *waqf* scheme, Table 15.3 highlights the findings from the current practices from the interviews with regard to the input, output and impact of share *waqf* scheme.

Based on Table 15.4, it is found that not much disclosure is made regarding *waqf* share scheme by *Waqf* Institution A. Therefore, several recommendations are made. For input disclosure, it is proposed for *Waqf* Institution A to disclose the amount received for share *waqf* and list of *waqf* projects. Meanwhile, for outcome disclosure, *Waqf* Institution A is required to disclose the list of distribution/completed *waqf* projects. Moreover, for outcome disclosure, it is suggested for *Waqf* Institution A to disclose several indicators for each distribution/completed of share *waqf* including:

- Number of *waqf* projects from *waqf* share.
- Percentage of shares/acquisition from total share for each *waqf* project (ownership status).
- Number of beneficiaries benefited from *waqf* projects.

For effectiveness disclosure, it can be done by calculating and analysing *waqf* project distribution/completed with *waqf* share target (KPI), while for efficiency disclosure, *Waqf* Institution A is proposed to compute and analyse the

Table 15.4 *Waqf* socio-economic impact disclosure on share *waqf* scheme

Level of disclosure	*Details*	*Current practices*
Input	Cash	Offline and online (online banking, PFX, salary deduction)
Output	Acquisition of strategic shares	N/A
Outcome (*impact – activities based*)	No. of *waqf* projects Amount spent on share *waqf* schemes	N/A
Effectiveness (*output to objectives*)	% of Muslim equities at national level	N/A
Efficiency (*input to output*)	Amount of share *waqf* received ÷ Amount of *waqf* share distributed/ acquired	N/A
Productivity (*benefits to ummah*)	Future/long-term share *waqf* distributed/acquired benefits towards public	N/A

ratio on the distribution of share *waqf* for each type of use or acquisition. Last but not least, for productivity disclosure, *Waqf* Institution A is suggested to make an analysis of the contribution percentage made by share *waqf* towards national equities or wealth in general. Last but not least, under *waqfkhas* project, Table 15.5 highlights the findings from the current practices from the interviews with regard to the input, output and impact of *waqfkhas* project.

Similar to share *waqf* scheme, current disclosure practices by *Waqf* Institution A on *waqfkhas* project are limited to only number of land (lots and acres) and list of current *waqfkhas* projects. Therefore, several recommendations are proposed. For input disclosure, it is proposed for *Waqf* Institution A to disclose total value of land acquired (historical cost) and also total number and value of building acquired (historical cost). Meanwhile, for outcome disclosure, besides disclosing the list of current *waqfkhas* projects, *Waqf* Institution A is also suggested to disclose the list of completed *waqfkhas* projects (number of mosques, cemeteries, schools). Moreover, for outcome disclosure, it is suggested for *Waqf* Institution A to disclose performance indicators for each *waqf* land and *waqfkhas* project outcome included as follows:

- *Waqfkhas* project (mosques) – number of prayer spaces created (number of *jemaah*), number of *kulliyyah* conducted and number of activities conducted according to age group.
- *Waqfkhas* project (schools) – number of students and teachers, number of classrooms and number of programs (pre-school, primary, secondary, post teenagers, *tahfiz*, training and skill centre).

Table 15.5 *Waqf* socio-economic impact disclosure on *waqfkhas* project

Level of disclosure	*Details*	*Current practice*
Input	Land/building *Waqfkhas* projects	No. of land (lots and acres)
Output	List of land List of current *Waqfkhas* projects List of completed *Waqfkhas* projects	List of current *waqfkhas* projects
Outcome (*impact – activities based*)	*Waqfkhas* project (Mosques) impact *Waqfkhas* project (Schools) impact *Waqfkhas* project (Cemetery) impact *Waqfkhas* project (Orphanages) impact *Waqfkhas* project (old folks homes) impact	N/A
Effectiveness (*output to objectives*)	Percentage of completed *waqfkhas* projects compared to KPI	N/A
Efficiency (*input to output*)	Amount of *waqfkhas* project created: number of *waqfkhas* projects completed	N/A
Productivity (*benefits to ummah*)	Future/long-term share *waqf* usage/acquisition benefits towards public	N/A

- *Waqfkhas* project (cemetery) – Land square feet (sqft) for cemetery, number of graves used and number of graves available.
- *Waqfkhas* project (orphanages and old folks homes) – number of centres and number of orphans or old folks.

Furthermore, for effectiveness disclosure, it can be done by comparing expected (KPI) with actual completed *waqfkhas* projects, while for efficiency disclosure, *Waqf* Institution A is proposed to compute and analyse ratio on the percentage of completion of *waqfkhas* project for each type of *waqfkhas* project. Last but not least, for productivity disclosure, *Waqf* Institution A is suggested to calculate and analyse outcome indicators (contribution towards nation) as follows:

- *Waqfkhas* project (mosques) – number of prayer spaces created (number of *jemaah*), number of kulliyyah conducted and number of activities conducted according to age group vs state statistic.
- *Waqfkhas* project (schools) – number of students and teachers, number of classrooms and number of programs with the state statistic.
- *Waqfkhas* project (cemetery) – Land sqft for cemetery, number of graves used and number of graves available with the state statistic.
- *Waqfkhas* project (orphanages and old folks homes) – number of centres and number of orphans/old folks with the state statistic.

Conclusion

The findings show that there is still room for improvement especially in *waqf* disclosure practices of *waqf* institutions in Malaysia. At present, *waqf* institutions in Malaysia disclose limited information on *waqf* activities, programs and projects by focusing solely on financial disclosure. This information alone is not enough to satisfy public accountability. For *waqf* socio-economic impact disclosure, it is suggested for *waqf* institutions to disclose all *waqf* activities/programs/projects for all five disclosure elements starting from input, output, throughput, outcome and impact as proposed. Besides, a number of recommendations, especially for socio-economic impact disclosure, are also provided based on these five disclosure elements to enhance the level of disclosure for *waqf* socio-economic impact.

By adopting these recommendations on *waqf* socio-economic impact disclosure, it will advance *waqf* disclosure practices towards a comprehensive disclosure for discharging accountability of *waqf* institution as *mutawalli* (*waqf* administrator). It will also ensure stakeholders are informed on how *waqf* funds and assets are utilised by *waqf* institutions. This is to ensure *waqf* institutions in Malaysia are more accountable, transparent and sustainable. This chapter has laid the groundwork for several strands for future research. Since this study is based on only one *waqf* institution in Malaysia, it is unsuitable to give a picture that other *waqf* institutions had the same good practices in their *waqf* socio-economic impact disclosure practices. Moreover, this chapter just focuses on a *waqf* institution under SIRC type. Other *waqf* institution types that are authorised by SIRCs to administer *waqf* although they are not directly controlled by SIRCs are also potentially to be researched in the future.

Notes

1 Kamaruddin, M. I. H. (2018). A Case Study on *Waqf* Reporting Practices for Governance, Performance and Socio-economic Impact in Malaysia. *International Journal of Management, Accounting and Economics, 5* (9), 693–714.
2 Kamaruddin, M. I. H., Masruki, R., & Hanefah, M. M. (2018). Waqf Management Practices: Case Study in a Malaysian Waqf institution. *World Journal of Social Sciences, 8* (3), 1–12.

References

Abdul Rahman, A. R., Bakar, M. D., & Ismail, Y. (1999). Current Practices and Administration of Waqf in Malaysia: A Preliminary Study. *Awqaf Report* (28/7/1999) (Unpublished).

AbRahman, A. (2009). Peranan Wakaf Dalam Pembangunan Ekonomi Umat Islam dan Aplikasinya di Malaysia. *Jurnal Syariah, 17*(1), 113–152.

Alhabshi, S. O. (1986). Konsep Waqafdan Perlaksanaannya di Malaysia. In *Management and Administration of Waqf Property Seminar.* Perak, Malaysia.

Arshad, R., & Zain, N. M. (2017). Performance Measurement and Accountability of Waqf Institutions in Malaysia. In *SHS Web of Conferences, 36*, 1–15.EDP Sciences.

Beamon, B. M., & Balcik, B. (2008).Performance Measurement in Humanitarian Relief Chains. *International Journal of Public Sector Management, 21*(1), 4–25.

Borham, A. S. (2011). Pelaksanaan Pembangunan Wakaf Korporat Johor Corporation Berhad (JCorp): Satu Tinjauan. In *International Conference on Humanities 2011*, 14–16 June, Penang, Malaysia.

Harun, R., Isa, Z. M., & Ali, N. (2012). Preliminary Findings on Waqf Management Practices among Selected Muslim Countries. In *2012 International Conference on Economics Marketing and Management*, 5–7 January, Hong Kong, China.

IbnAshur, M. A. (2006). *Treatise on Maqasid al-Shariah.* London: International Institute of Islamic Thought (IIIT).

JAWHAR. (2014). *Jabatan Wakaf Zakat dan Haji: Sedekad Membina Tamadun Ummah.* Putrajaya: Jabatan Wakaf Zakat dan Haji (JAWHAR). Available [Online] at, http://intranet.jawhar.gov.my/penerbitan/p_admin/file_upload/CTB%20JAWHAR_FINAL_ONLINE.pdf (Accessed on 21 February 2018).

Kahf, M. (1999). Towards the Revival of Awqaf: A Few Fiqhi Issues to Reconsider. In *Harvard Forum on Islamic Finance and Economics*, October 1, Harvard University, USA.

Kahf, M. (2003). The Role of Waqf in Improving the Ummah Welfare. In *International Seminar on Waqf as a Private Legal Body*, 6–7 January, Medan, Indonesia.

Khalid, A. F. (1988). *Islamic Law and Land in the State of Selangor, Malaysia: Problems of Administration and Islamisation* (PhD Thesis, University of Edinburgh, United Kingdom).

Laldin, M. A., Mahmud, M. W., Sawari, M., & Fuad, M. (2012). *Maqasid Al-ShariahdalamPerlaksanaanWaqaf.KertasKerja 1*, 1–16. Gombak: IIUM Press.

Medina-Borja, A., & Triantis, K. (2006). A Conceptual Framework to Evaluate Performance of Non-profit Social Service Organisations. *International Journal of Technology Management, 37*(1–2), 147–161.

Mohsin, M. I. A. (2008). Cash Waqf a New Financial Product Model Aspects of Shariah Principles on Its Commercialization. In *3rd Islamic Banking, Accounting and Finance Conference (iBAF 2008)*, 28–29 July, Kuala Lumpur, Malaysia.

Noordin, N. H., Haron, S. N., & Kassim, S. (2017). Developing a Comprehensive Performance Measurement System for Waqf Institutions. *International Journal of Social Economics, 44*(7), 921–936.

Shafii, Z., Yunanda, R. A., & Rahman, F. K. (2014). Financial and Operational Measures of Waqf Performance: The Case of State Islamic Religion Council of Singapore and Malaysia. In *Seminar WaqfIqlimi 2014*, 345–359, 29 April, Negeri Sembilan, Malaysia.

Wahbah Zuhaili. (1985). *Al-Fiqh al-IslamiyWa 'Adillatuhu*. Mesir: Dar al-Fikr al-Mu'ashir.

Yaacob, H. (2006). *Waqf Accounting in Malaysian State Islamic Religious Institutions: The Case of Federal Territory SIRC* (Masters Dissertation, International Islamic University Malaysia, Malaysia).

Yaacob, H. (2013). Waqf History and Legislation in Malaysia: A Contemporary Perspective. *Journal of Islamic and Human Advanced Research, 3*(6), 387–402.

YWM. (2017). *Dana Pembangunan Kerajaan*. Putrajaya: YayasanWakaf Malaysia (YWM). Available [Online] at, https://www.ywm.gov.my/dana/dana-kerajaan/ (Accessed on 21 February 2018).

16 Awqaf – its ASEAN experiences and a lesson to learn

Lisa Listiana and Dian Masyita

Indonesia

Indonesia, the largest Muslim population country, is acknowledged by IRTI (2015) as a country that "stands far ahead of others in enacting a law" when it comes to waqf as it has a specific act pertaining to waqf. Prior to the establishment of Waqf Act number 41 in 2004, there were already some regulations related to waqf, especially to the administration of waqf lands. The Waqf Act is therefore considered as a game changer since it offered new perspectives and covered new aspects such as the scope of waqf, type of waqf assets, and also waqf management. Following this Waqf Act, the government of Indonesia has issued other waqf regulations, namely regulation number 42 in 2006 and its amendment number 25 in 2018, and other statutory derivatives.

Within these laws, it is mentioned that people can create waqf in the form of both non-movable and movable assets including cash (Masyita, 2007). It is also allowed to create either permanent or temporary waqf. These regulations became the basis of the establishment of the Indonesian Waqf Board-IWB (Badan Wakaf Indonesia (BWI)) to develop the waqf sector in the country. The main functions of this Board are to supervise and replace the *muttawali*[1] to maintain and develop waqf assets, grant licence for any change in the objectives and objects of waqf assets, and provide suggestions and advises to the government in enacting policy related to waqf. Along with IWB, the Ministry of Religious Affairs is the other authority that regulates waqf sector in the country (Bappenas, 2016). Both of these institutions have representatives in every province and regency.

In terms of numbers, there are around 4,100 km^2 of waqf lands in Indonesia[2] (Saptono, 2019). While the majority of the existing lands are reported to be used as mosques, graveyards, and Islamic schools, he believes that the actual number is much bigger. IWB noted that cash waqf has the potential of collecting up to IDR180 trillion (roughly USD13 billion) annually. However, the actual realization is still less than 1% (Listiana, 2018). The efforts to promote waqf are increasing, especially with regard to cash-based waqf.[3] A number of efforts to promote waqf into mainstream economy have already been started by both government-related institutions and the civil society.

For instance, IWB and Bank Indonesia initiated Waqf Core Principles (WCP) and Cash Waqf Linked Sukuk (CWLS). Furthermore, the number of registered *muttawali* keeps increasing. In early 2019, it is reported that around 201 *muttawalis* in the form of legal body or foundation have been registered in the IWB. In addition, around 19 Islamic banks have been involved in waqf activities by becoming cash waqf receivers. Among the registered cash waqf receivers, two Islamic banks in collaboration with registered *muttawalis* offer platforms to campaign and collect cash-based waqf: Wakaf Hasanah (https://wakafhasanah.bnisyariah.co.id/) and Wakaf Prioritas (https://jadiberkah.id/). Moreover, there are emerging private research and think tank institutions that provide training, research, and seminars about waqf in the country, such as the Waqf Center for Indonesian Development and Studies (WaCIDS), International Centre for Awqaf Studies (ICAST), and the Indonesian Waqf Education Foundation (YEWI in Bahasa).

WCP is a document that was developed as a joint initiative between Bank Indonesia, IWB, and IRTI IDB. It was inspired by the Basel Core Principles. It consists of 29 principles that are categorized into five sections: legal foundation, waqf supervision, good waqf governance, risk management, and Shariah governance. Each principle can be evaluated according to essential criteria and optional criteria (International Working Group, 2018). The existence of WCP may encourage good governance of waqf for versatile waqf investment.

Alternatively, the CWLS has been issued by IWB in collaboration with the Ministry of Finance. The main idea of CWLS is to collect cash-based waqf that can be temporarily invested in state sukuk (SBSN in Bahasa) to fund government development projects. The return of the investment will be given to the *mauquf alayh* through the *muttawali*'s partner. Once the state sukuk reaches the maturity date, the initial fund will be returned to the waqif in case of temporary waqf. However, in case of permanent waqf, the main capital will be re-invested. Currently, the project is still on-going and is expected to end in 2023 (BNIS, 2019). On the other hand, IWB and Ministry of Finance are currently working on developing a mechanism for Sukuk Linked Waqf (Figure 16.1).

Even though the practices of waqf management and development are numerous in Indonesia, Nasir (2017) noted that the literature on waqf in Indonesia within the international scope is limited. So far, waqf development projects by Tabung Wakaf Indonesia Dompet Dhuafa (TWI DD) represent one of the rare examples given in the limited literature about waqf activities in Indonesia written in English.[4] In many discussions, waqf development of properties became the mainstream approach although there are many other waqf projects worth to be learned and which are very relevant to real sector activities.

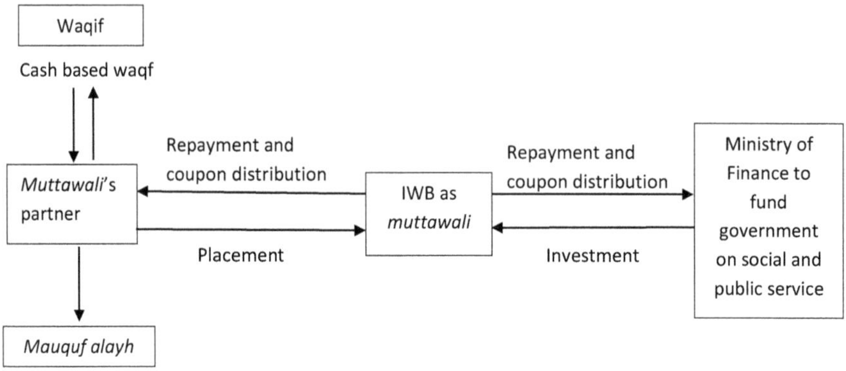

Figure 16.1 Structure of Cash Waqf Linked Sukuk.

For instance, registered waqf institutions invest the collected cash-based waqf to the real sector such as agriculture, animal husbandry, and retail industry. Among the existing *muttawalis*, Global Wakaf is one of the few foundations that invest in those three projects altogether. It has programs on waqf-based food barn, waqf-based livestock barn, and waqf-based retail industry (GlobalWakaf, 2018). Nurrochman (2018) elaborated that when it comes to waqf-based food barn, there are two financing models. The first model consists of giving assistance packages to farmers. The second model is performed through profit sharing by planting either rice or corn, considering the local situation and the main commodity in the surrounding area. In practice, Global Wakaf helps the farmers from the plantation process by buying and standardizing the seed until the harvest process by providing a dryer factory with the capacity of 50,000 tons annually (ACT News, 2019a). While 75% of the produced crop are sold to replace the original investment (to be invested in other areas), to cover operational expenses, and to distribute to the *mauquf alayh*, the remaining 25% of the produced crop is distributed to families living by the project area (Permana, 2019).

One of the six pilot projects is performed in Labangka Sumbawa Indonesia, where there are around 35km^2 lands that are used to plant corn. This project involves 1,200 farmers for the production of 50 tons of corn daily during harvest season (ACT News, 2019a). A similar situation can be observed in the case of Blora project by the same foundation. In this area, tons of rice can be produced during the harvest season in a daily basis and sent to the distributor in weekly basis.

From this project, as of December 2018, 1.742 hectares land were developed, 9.813 tons of rice were produced, 564 farmers were employed, and 16.212 *mauquf alayh* in 49 villages benefited from it (Nurrohman, 2018).

Similar types of waqf projects in agriculture can be found in programs conducted by other registered *muttawalis* such as Sinergi Foundation and Rumah Wakaf Indonesia. While the capital of collected cash-based waqf is invested in agriculture and managed professionally, the profit is generated and distributed for *mauquf alayh* through various social programs (Sinergi Foundation, 2018). In Rumah Wakaf, instead of planting typical one time harvest plant, the cash-based waqf is allocated to buy land and plant long term plantation such as coconut and pepper (RumahWakaf, 2019).

With regard to waqf-based livestock, Global Wakaf run fattening and breeding projects in various locations. Among the existing projects, the one located in Blora is reported to employ 181 people to raise 11,926 sheep. The sheep will later be channelled to supply the annual demand for qurban of Idul Adha. In 2019, 5.104 sheep from this location were used to supply the qurban demand (ACT News, 2019b; Figure 16.2).

Other than investing in the agriculture sector, Global Wakaf also allocates the collected cash-based waqf for investment in retail business projects. The foundation also supplies for micro shops and other shops in the region by being the distribution centre. Their vision is to make of this project a vehicle that distributes their production to end customers. In term of impact/multiplier effect, investing in this type of business may open opportunities for employment and secure the demand side of the produced crops. Up to 70% of the profit ratio, which equals 4.5% of the monthly revenue, will be distributed to the *mauquf alayh*. As of end 2018, there were more than 50 waqf shops and this number is expected to increase gradually (Nurrohman, 2018).

It is worth noting that waqf assets can be significantly developed depending on each country's resources. From Indonesia's experience, it can be learned that cash-based waqf can be channelled for investment in the real sector such as agriculture, animal husbandry, and retail business. Investing in this kind of businesses is promising due to the recurring demand of the production. In addition to that, the nature of these businesses which is labour intensive may make them more impactful for the society.

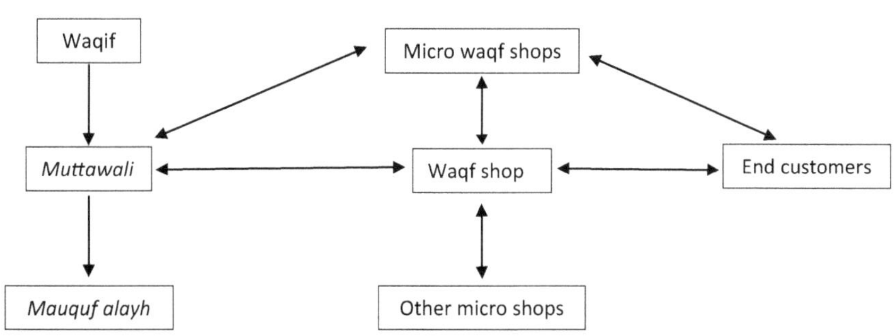

Figure 16.2 Structure of waqf shop.

The existing projects in Indonesia illustrate how waqf empowers people in the waqf project area, generates profit from the investment to be given to the *mauquf alayh*, and in parallel may support the food security program of the country. From the existing cases, channelling cash-based waqf in the real sector represents promising and profitable investments while offering bigger social impact for the community, and thus needs to be promoted. However, considering the risk of investment in these activities, it is important to develop and implement a risk management mechanism to secure the capital of waqf assets and hence benefit the *mauquf alayh*.

Malaysia

In Malaysia, waqf is regulated at the state level where the State Islamic Religious Councils (SIRC) act as the sole trustee of all waqf assets by law (Kadir & Mohamed, 2017). According to Kadir and Mohamed (2017), only five out of thirteen states and three federal territories have specific waqf administration laws, including Johor (1983), Selangor (1999), Negeri Sembilan (2005), Melaka (2005), and Perak (2015). The remaining states and federal territories cover the provisions relevant to waqf in the Administration of Islamic Law Enactments.

In 2004, the federal government of Malaysia established the Department of Waqf, Zakat and Hajj (JAWHAR) with an initial grant of RM256.5 million to undertake 24 waqf projects (Mohsin et al., 2016). This department was established to coordinate the waqf development among Islamic Religious Councils in every state. In addition, the Malaysian Waqf Foundation was established in 2008 by JAWHAR to execute projects related to waqf, including joint waqf projects among stakeholders (YWM, 2019).

In this country, as noted in a published report by the World Bank Group, INCEIF, and ISRA (2019), some waqf assets have been developed either through profit sharing agreement, long lease, Build-Operate-Transfer (BOT) or Rehabilitate-Operate-Transfer (ROT). Cases like Seetee Aisah Waqf and Imarah Waqf (Menara Bank Islam) are examples of waqf development using that kind of contracts. IRTI (2015), in their 2014 Islamic Social Finance Report, has acknowledged the Waqf An-Nur Corporation Berhad (WANCorp) as the innovator of the concept of corporate waqf. Thirteen years after its inception, WANCorp managed waqf assets reaching the value of RM837 million which represents an increase of 494% from the initial capital (WanCorp, 2019).

On 18 June 2017, WANCorp issued a prospectus of waqf shares named Waqaf Saham Larkin Sentral (WSLS) with a total amount of RM85 million. Each share is worth RM0.1 and each person or institution can contribute with a minimum value of RM100 equivalent to1,000 shares. Within this mechanism, WANCorp will then be the trustee of the waqf. The collected amount will be used to upgrade Larkin Sentral transportation terminal and wet market Larkin in Johor Bahru, Malaysia. The dividends and revenue generated from the terminal activities will be distributed to the *mauquf alayh* such as single mothers and the needy (WANCorp, 2017).

While the majority of existing waqf assets in Malaysia are used as mosques, cemeteries, and Islamic education institutions (madrasah), to date, some state waqf authorities have started to collaborate with six participating Islamic banks to collect cash-based waqf under MyWakaf campaign scheme (myWakaf, 2019; World Bank Group, INCEIF, & ISRA, 2019).Using this platform, the collected cash-based waqf can then be managed by the Islamic banks and invested in their financial products or be used to develop the existing waqf assets in education, health, infrastructure, and economy empowerment sectors.

Since the establishment of the scheme, there are six projects that were promoted for raising the funds of RM369,632–RM6,000,000. Among these six campaigns, two have been fully raised and the remaining four are still ongoing. From the two fully funded projects, one has been completed. However, the campaign website only provides pictures of the construction without giving any information about the actual *mauquf alayh* and the sustainability of the project. Other than the MyWakaf campaign scheme, some SIRCs have direct collaboration with specific Islamic banks to collect cash-based waqf.[5]

In addition to the earlier project, Labuan International Waqf Foundation (LIWF) is another case to learn from. LIWF was established in 2015 under the Labuan Islamic Financial Services and Securities Act 2010 to hold and manage waqf properties in accordance with Shariah principles (LIBFC, 2016a; Salmi & Aiman, 2017; World Bank Group, INCEIF, & ISRA, 2019). This foundation enables people from any country to set up waqf and/or benefit from it. LIBFC (2016b) elaborated that the foundation can be a vehicle for Islamic wealth management as it can accommodate cross countries waqf activities in the current era.

Technically, the waqf assets such as real estate (either furnished or unfurnished), movable assets, money or cash, shares and sukuk, rights that can generate income (for example intellectual property rights) or other properties accepted by Shariah will be given to the waqf foundation. LIWF will act as *muttawali* of the respective waqf assets. The income generated from the management or utilization of waqf assets will then be distributed to identify *mauquf alayh*. LIWF can establish different types of waqf, including self-dedicated waqf, joint waqf, charitable waqf, family waqf. Othman (2018) noted that LIWF offers legal certainty and flexibility for the waqif with regard to his/her waqf.

Structure of Labuan International Waqf Foundation

From Malaysia's experience, it is worth noting that the government plays a central role in providing the proper environment for waqf development. The top down support of the government is evident from the establishment of JAWHAR, YWM, WANCorp along with hundred million budgets and capital. The involvement of Bank Negara Malaysia calling for Islamic banks' participation by collecting cash-based waqf and the initiative of LIWF also show the top down support of the respective authorities. The case of Waqf Saham Larkin Sentral illustrates how this support may enhance public involvement in waqf project. It can be a model to adopt or replicate in other countries.

It is important to note that the top down support from the government needs to be complemented with professional management so that the waqf asset along with its benefit can survive. In addition to that, the accountability and transparency of waqf projects need to be enhanced. As in the case of MyWakaf project, pictures of the building itself without information about the actual *mauquf alayh* and sustainability of the project seem to be insufficient to discharge the accountability of the respective *muttawali*. The success indicator of a waqf project is not the completion of building construction. Instead, the sustainability of the assets and on-going benefit for the *mauquf alayh* can be important indicators. Moreover, since cash-based waqf is collected from the public, it is important to ensure that the report is open and accessible to them. Proper accountability and transparency need to be enhanced to encourage people to participate in waqf activities.

Singapore

In Singapore, according to the Administration of the Muslim Law Act (AMLA), all waqf assets are vested under the Islamic Religious Council of Singapore or Majlis Ugama Islam Singapura (MUIS). While MUIS manages most of waqf assets with the assistance of Warees Investments Pte Ltd, it allows some private *muttawalis*/trustees to manage some of them. Most of waqf assets in Singapore are in the form of properties and have been established since 1820 by Arab merchants. In the past, some single waqif created waqf by establishing mosques with specific properties to cover their maintenance costs.

MUIS (2019b) noted that there is no new waqf since 1970. As such, MUIS initiated waqf ilmu with the objective of collecting cash-based waqf from the society. The collected cash-based waqf will then be invested in properties or Shariah compliant funds to generate return that will be distributed to Islamic education institutions (full time and part time madrasahs) as the *mauquf alayh* (MUIS, 2019c). In this mechanism, no minimum contribution is required. People can contribute any amount for the waqf ilmu. To date, MUIS (2019a) reported that SGD14.8 million have been accumulated through the waqf ilmu campaign.

While previous reports and books elaborate only on the development of the Bencoolen complex using sukuk musharakah scheme as a waqf project in Singapore (IRTI, 2015; Mohsin et al., 2016; World Bank Group, INCEIF, & ISRA, 2019), the Red House is another one that is worth to be mentioned. As an effort to enhance the value of old waqf properties, MUIS entered into a joint development agreement with its subsidiary to execute Waqf Revitalization Scheme (WRS) projects (MUIS, 2019d). WRS is a "comprehensive 3-year asset plan by Warees" to revive the waqf assets and enhance their values (Warees, 2014). Institutional Investment Initiative was employed to develop the Red House, the first WRS project in 2012. This project covers the development of 42 residential units, five commercial units, and one iconic bakery shop on the waqf land founded by Sheriffa Zain Alsharoff Binte Syed Mohamed Bin Ahmad Alsagoff.

Technically, with this mechanism, community in the form of mosques and madrasahs can participate in the project and get return (hibah) on the investment. The institutions can either make investments for leasing (retain and use unit) or for building (joint financing for construction). In this project, SGD5 million have been collected from five mosques. Each mosque invested SGD1 million and then got SGD 42,000 hibah which equals 2.1% of the yield that was paid biannually over 24 months. Furthermore, two community institutions invested in a total of SGD 3.75 million and received a similar hibah ratio (Warees, 2014). Among the seven institutions involved in this project, two did not exit the investment after the completion of the construction. Instead, they bought the units to be leased. A similar step to retain and use the units was also taken by two other communities. As such, they are getting rental incomes from the leased units (Warees, 2014).

Other than the aforementioned success stories of waqf development, Finterra Waqf Chain is an initiative worth to be mentioned. With a headquarter in Singapore, Finterra has representative offices in some other countries. In the Internet of Things (IoT) era, waqf needs to catch up with the latest technology so that it stays relevant and is able to meet the expectations of stakeholders. The existence of Finterra Waqf Chain seems to address this requirement.

Basically, the intention of Finterra's initiative is to help addressing the transparency and good governance issues in waqf activities. Finterra will provide a "smart contract multi-chain ecosystem" to enable real time monitoring and tracking of the waqf. In this ecosystem, at least six stakeholders will be involved including a waqf board/*muttawali*, a financial auditor, a takaful/insurance, a fund management, an asset management, and a construction company. The user can be either an individual or a trust/foundation. Rashid (2018) in his work elaborated that the blockchain technology in this ecosystem may help to raise capital for waqf development. It can be a tool to collect more cash-based waqf by offering a transparency mechanism to the public.

From Singapore's experience, it is worth noting that professionals in the field need to be involved in developing and reviving the waqf projects. The involvement of Warees as an agent in managing and developing waqf assets can be a good example for professionals in order to enhance the value of waqf assets. The case of Institutional Investment Initiative which involves mosques and communities in developing the Red House waqf project can be a notable example of collaboration among institutions. Normally, money collected by the well-managed mosques and communities can reach millions of SG dollars. It therefore can be a promising option to use the fund and take a role in the development of waqf assets rather than statically save the money in fixed deposits. In addition, the latest technology such as blockchain and smart contract need to be utilized to enhance transparency and good governance of waqf development.

Conclusion

In many cases, the development of waqf assets is associated with the effort to establish property for leasing. While it may be one solution, there are other alternatives that can be employed. The experiences of the three ASEAN countries illustrate that it is important to consider the local context and resources owned by the respective country so that the waqf can be developed to reach its optimal potential. Waqf can be channelled into the real sector such as agriculture, animal husbandry, real estate and retail business as well as financial sector. In Indonesia for example, as an agrarian country and considering that the waqf lands are not always located in the business district area, the collected waqf assets can be channelled to the agriculture sector. This kind of investment offers a profitable business and may also create a bigger impact on the society and give more benefits to the *mauquf alayh*.

While waqf can be channelled to various sectors, the involvement of professionals is necessary to ensure its sustainability. In addition, this chapter shares lessons on how waqf assets, particularly cash-based waqf, can be collected. For instance, it can be done through the collaboration with other stakeholders such as a government/waqf authority in the case of CWLS and Waqf Saham Larkin Sentral, Islamic banks in the case of MyWakaf and Wakaf Hasanah, crowdfunding and waqf chain platform providers like Finterra, and institutional investors such as mosques and community institutions. While technology needs to be embraced to promote trust and transparency so that people get involved more in waqf activities, the regulatory framework needs to be enacted to facilitate waqf asset mobilization across countries and to promote the involvement of professionals in the waqf sector. Top down support from the government is also necessary.

However, all in all, while the innovation and type of investment and development on waqf may change from time to time involving simple to complex mechanism, it is important to note that the main conditions of waqf need to be maintained. Whichever mechanism is employed to develop the waqf assets, the capital must be protected and the benefit for *mauquf alayh* needs to flow overtime. As such, the impact of the waqf development needs to be measured so that the benefit can be monitored and evaluated. Finally, due to the nature of waqf which should be perpetual, risk management is also among the important areas that need to be addressed in the future.

Notes

1 In Indonesia, *Muttawali* is called as Nazhir. It refers to the persons who manage the Waqf assets.

2 Initially information about Waqf land size is also available in the official website of Mora and IWB. However, it is noted that the information is no longer available in the website during the writing process of this manuscript. As such, this manuscript refers to the available information provided by the IWB's Keyperson in his paper.

3 Ishola and Oseni (2018) in their study emphasise the differences between cash Waqf and Waqf cash (Waqf through cash) due to different legal implications. In this manuscript, both types of Waqf related to cash are mentioned as cash-based Waqf.
4 See for example studies or reports by Ihsan (2014), IRTI (2015), Mohsin et al. (2016), Siswantoro and Dewi (2007), Siswantoro et al. (2018), and World Bank Group, INCEIF and ISRA (2019) which took TWI DD as Example/Topic/ Scope discussed in their studies/reports.
5 Unfortunately, the reports are somehow inaccessible during the writing process of this manuscript.

References

ACT News. (2019a). Kelola Potensi Lokal Labangka dengan Wakaf (Manage Labangka Local Potential with Waqf). Retrieved September 25, 2019, from https://news.act.id/berita/kelola-potensi-lokal-labangka-dengan-wakaf

ACT News. (2019b). Seeing the Preparation of Qurbani Animals from the LTW in Blora. Retrieved October 9, 2019, from https://news.act.id/en/berita/seeing-the-preparation-of-qurbani-animals-from-the-ltw-in-blora

Bappenas. (2016). *Masterplan for Indonesian Islamic Financial Architecture.* Jakarta.

BNIS. (2019). Cash Waqf Linked Sukuk - Wakaf Uang Abadi | BNI Wakaf. Retrieved September 1, 2019, from https://wakafhasanah.bnisyariah.co.id/project/98

GlobalWakaf. (2018). *Waqf Builds Ummah's Welfare.* Jakarta: Global Wakaf.

Ihsan, H. (2014). Accountability Practice in a Waqf Institution in Indonesia: The Case of Dompet Dhuafa. Kulliyyah of Economics and Management Sciences, International Islamic University Malaysia.

IRTI. (2015). *IRTI Islamic Social Finance Report 2014.* Jeddah.

Kadir, S. Z. S. A., & Mohamed, N. A. (2017). The Legal Position of Waqf Lands in Malaysia. In S. K. Rashid (Ed.), *Waqf Laws and Management.* Kuala Lumpur: IIUM Press.

LIBFC. (2016a). *A Guide to International Waqf Foundation.* Labuan: Labuan International Business and Financial Centre.

LIBFC. (2016b). Waqf Foundations – A Unique Shariah-Compliant Wealth Management Solution - Wealth Management - Malaysia. Retrieved August 29, 2019, from http://www.mondaq.com/x/527384/wealth+management/Waqf+Foundations+A+Unique+ShariahCompliant+Wealth+Management+Solution

Listiana, L. (2018). Promoting Role of Islamic Banks for Cash Waqf Collection in Indonesia. In *Shariah Economic and Finance Research Forum (FREKS).* Jakarta.

Masyita, D. (2007). Religious Practices: Waqf: Southeast Asia. Brill Netherlands.

Mohsin, M. I. A., Dafterdar, H., Çizakça, M., Alhabshi, S. O., Razak, S. H. A., Sadr, S. K., … Obaidullah, M. (2016). *Financing the Development of Old Waqf Properties.* Springer.

MUIS. (2019a). *Annual Report 2018.* Singapore.

MUIS. (2019b). History of Wakaf in Singapore. Retrieved September 3, 2019, from https://www.muis.gov.sg/wakaf/About/History-of-Wakaf-in-Singapore

MUIS. (2019c). Wakaf Ilmu for Education. Retrieved September 3, 2019, from https://www.muis.gov.sg/wakaf/Creating-My-Wakaf/Wakaf-Ilmu-for-Education

MUIS. (2019d). Waqf Revitalization Scheme. Retrieved September 3, 2019, from https://www.muis.gov.sg/wakaf/Strengthening-Wakaf/Wakaf-Revitalisation-Scheme

myWakaf. (2019). myWakaf – A Collaboration between the Islamic Banks and Majlis Agama Islam Negeri (MAIN) Mainly Dedicated to the Empowerment of Communities. Retrieved August 29, 2019, from https://www.mywakaf.com.my/

Nasir, F. M. (2017). Bibliography and Review of Selected Waqf Literature in Indonesia: Origins, Past and Current Trends. In *Global Waqf Gateway: Bridging the Waqf Agenda For Nusantara*. Pekanbaru: ICWR.

Nurrohman, M. I. (2018). *Waqf Based Economic Empowerment: Experience and Innovation Global Wakaf.* Jakarta: WaCIDS.

Othman, A. (2018). *Managing the Transition of Wealth Across Generations via Shariah-Compliant Solutions.* Kuala Lumpur: ZICO Shariah.

Pattanaprichawong, A., & Dorloh, S. (2019). Analysis of the Law of Waqf in Thailand. In K. M. Ali & M. K. Hassan (Eds.), *Revitalization of Waqf for Socio-Economic Development* (Volume II). Palgrave Macmillan.

Permana, F. E. (2019). Program Global Wakaf Bebaskan Petani dari Tengkulak (Progam by Global Wakaf Free the Farmers from Brokers. Retrieved August 31, 2019, from https://khazanah.republika.co.id/berita/dunia-islam/wakaf/19/01/14/plbhtn384-program-global-wakaf-bebaskan-petani-dari-tengkulak

Rashid, S. K. (2018). Potential of Waqf in Contemporary World. *Journal of King Abdulaziz University: Islamic Economics*, *31*(2), 53–69.

RumahWakaf. (2019). Wakaf Kebun Produktif (Productive Garden Waqf). Retrieved August 23, 2019, from https://www.rumahwakaf.org/wakaf-kebun-produktif/

Salmi, M., & Aiman, M. (2017). Administration of Labuan International Waqf Foundation (LIWF) in the Labuan IBFC: Legal Issues & Challenges with Reference to Assets Managed in Malaysia.

Saptono, I. T. (2019). *Revitalizing Cash Awqaf as a Core of Impact Investing Instruments.* Jakarta: Indonesian Waqf Board (Badan Wakaf Indonesia).

Sinergi Foundation. (2018). Wakaf Sawah Produktif (Productive Farm Waqf). Retrieved September 2, 2019, from https://www.sinergifoundation.org/campaigns/wakaf-sawah-produktif/#1546855685248-a43a8298-1f2c

Siswantoro, D., & Dewi, M. K. (2007). The Effectiveness of Waqf Fund Raising through Mutual Fund in Indonesia. In *Singapore International Waqf Conference* (Vol. 7).

Siswantoro, D., Rosdiana, H., & Fathurahman, H. (2018). Reconstructing Accountability of the Cash Waqf (Endowment) Institution in Indonesia. *Managerial Finance*, *44*(5), 624–644. doi:10.1108/MF-05-2017-0188

WanCorp. (2019). *Waqaf An-Nur Annual Report 2018.* Johor Baru.

WanCorp. (2017). Waqaf Saham Larkin Sentral. Retrieved August 29, 2019, from https://www.waqafsahamlarkin.com/pages.aspx?Content_Name=Pengenalan&p_Id=2

Warees. (2014). *Institutional Investment Initiative (3I) Hibah Disbursement Ceremony.* Singapore.

World Bank Group, INCEIF, & ISRA. (2019). *Maximizing Social Impact through Waqf Solutions.* Kuala Lumpur.

YWM. (2019). Portal Rasmi Yayasan Waqaf Malaysia - Utama. Retrieved September 6, 2019, from https://www.ywm.gov.my/home

17 Integrated social and productive awqaf in Indonesia

Ascarya, Raditya Sukmana and Muhamad Nadratuzzaman Hosen

Introduction

To the best of author's knowledge, there are few recent previous studies relate to the use of waqf for microfinance. Two papers, Haneef et al. (2014) and Abdullah and Ismail (2017), have adopted a literature study approach and the studies reveal that waqf is possible as an important financing for microfinance. The other two studies, Haneef et al. (2015) and Thaker et al. (2016), conduct empirical research to get the view from financing recipients of the waqf-based financing model which confirms that the model can be applied.

Haneef et al. (2014), after extensively looking at the relevant literature studies pertaining waqf and microfinance as well as conducting the field survey, attempt to propose a model that can integrate the role of waqf and microfinance. The advantage of this model is its use of cash waqf, takaful and assistantship along with the microfinance institution which can be utilized to provide affordable cheap financing to the active poor. However, as the chapter suggests, the model needs to be tested in an empirical way. This model would then be empirically tested by Haneef (2015) in the case of Bangladesh. The result shows that there are significant relationships among the variables taken for the proposed model; hence the model is expected to reduce poverty.

Rose et al. (2015) using content analysis examine the various literatures specifically looking into the possibility of using cash waqf for microfinance. The finding shows that in order for the cash waqf to work properly for microfinance, corporate governance is vital to ensure sustainability.

A field survey study using Theory of Reasoned Action by Thaker et al. (2016) has attempted to obtain the perspective of microenterprise on the model that they proposed, namely Integrated Cash Waqf Micro enterprise Investment (ICWME-I) model. It is basically a model that utilizes cash waqf for microenterprise using the contract of musharakah mutanakisah. The study reveals that attitude and Subjective norms are positively significant to the micro-entrepreneurs' intention of using ICWME-I.

This study attempts to advance the knowledge particularly on the relationship between waqf and microfinance. The previous studies have resulted in a normative way (Haneef, 2014; Rose, 2015) and empirical studies by getting perspective on the integrated model of waqf and microfinance (Haneef 2015; Thaker 2016). The uniqueness of this study is that it attempts to identify the various possible models developed by Islamic microfinance institutions (IMI) applying waqf for financing in Indonesia. This study conducts in depth interviews with the top management.

Model and structure of waqf

Based on the return or profit orientation, waqf could be divided into three models, namely: (1) social waqf, which is socially motivated and not-for-profit oriented; (2) productive waqf, which is commercially motivated and for-profit oriented; and (3) integrated social and productive waqf (ISPW), which is a combination of socially motivated not-for-profit oriented and commercially for-profit oriented, in order to maintain social waqf sustainability. Social waqf, such as mosque, is the most popular among Muslims, since the first waqf by Rasulullah SAW was Quba Mosque and a popular hadith saying "...Anyone who built a mosque because of Allah, then Allah will build for him such as in heaven..." (Narrated by Bukhari, no. 450; Muslim, no. 533). Productive waqf has seen revival in many Muslim-majority countries, since it could be long lasting, as well as could have been continuously expanding, so that the reward for the waqif is also increasing. Meanwhile, ISPW has been growing in importance, since social waqf does not always depend on zakat-infaq-sadaqah to sustain and develop.

Social waqf

Social waqf is intended to establish social waqf facility needed by the ummah, which is not intended to gain economic benefits but to gain social benefits, while maintaining the principal of waqf assets to be able to serve the ummah sustainably, so that social waqf is socially motivated and not-for-profit oriented.

There are several types of social waqf, including: (1) worship facility such as mosque, Islamic center and prayer house (musholla); (2) education facility such as pondok pesantren (traditional Islamic boarding school), madrasah (traditional Islamic school) and integrated Islamic school; (3) healthcare facility such as hospital, healthcare center and clinic; and (4) other public facility, such as cemetery, civic center and public park.

The development of social waqf can be initiated by waqif who endows waqf asset (land, cash) to nazir to be managed for certain social activity, or it can also be initiated by nazir who plans to establish certain social waqf facility by collecting waqf (land, cash) from waqif. Subsequently, nazir would sign a contract with contractor or developer to build such social waqf facility on the waqf land financed through cash waqf generated. Social waqf facility, then, can be run and managed by nazir. Common people can utilize this social waqf facility (mauquf 'alaih) for free. The characteristic of social waqf is cost center, since it does not generate income, so that the operational cost must be covered by other sources of social funds, such as zakat and infaq, collected by licensed zakat institution or amil (see Figure 17.1). Social waqf usually relies entirely on waqf collected by nazir, especially direct cash waqf, and does not depend on commercial external financing.

Almost all mosques (or Islamic center) in Indonesia are considered as social waqf. The operational costs of these mosques are covered by voluntary infaq and obligatory zakat of jamaah who pray in those mosques. The mosque management council or "Dewan Kemakmuran Masjid" (DKM) usually acts as Amil or zakat institution that collects zakat and infaq.

Productive waqf

Productive waqf is waqf used for productive activities in the real sector to generate economic benefits, while still maintaining the principal of waqf assets to be sustainable, so that it is commercially motivated and for-profit oriented within the corridor of Shariah law and guided by maqashid Shariah. The return can be extended to finance social programs needed by general ummah, reinvested to productive waqf and/or distributed for nazir benefit. Productive waqf can enter in any halal real sector business such as construction, property, transportation, agriculture, plantation, farming, processing, manufacturing, trading, hotel and restaurant, education and healthcare. Productive waqf can also enter in any halal financial sector business such as Islamic financial institution, Islamic micro-finance institution and Islamic capital market. Any business developed using productive waqf has the potential to compete with regular business, since the cost of capital of productive waqf is essentially nonexistent (zero), so that the price of goods/services produced by productive waqf is always lower than that of the competitor. Moreover, productive waqf

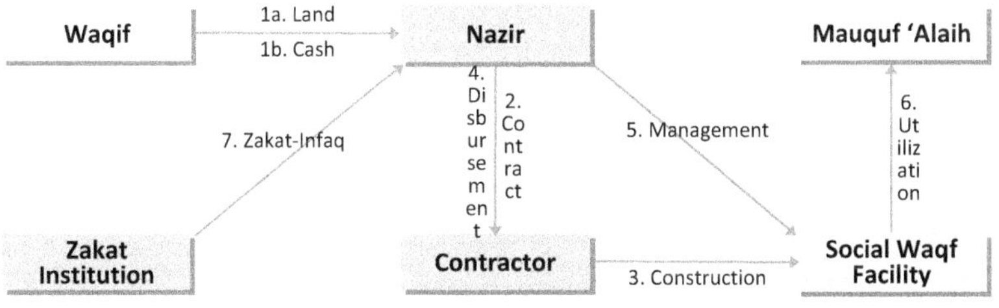

Figure 17.1 General scheme of social waqf.

is very flexible since there are plenty of productive waqf models, which could be adopted in every business sector.

The development of productive waqf is usually initiated by the nazir who has plans to establish certain commercial waqf business by collecting waqf (land, cash) from waqif. Subsequently, nazir will sign a contract with contractor or developer to build such commercial waqf facility on the waqf land financed through cash waqf and/or external financing (such as co-investor, Islamic bank, sukuk and/or international financing). Additional external financing is highly needed to develop medium and large productive waqf. Commercial waqf business, then, could be run and managed by nazir. However, nazir can also hire third party professional/institution to run and manage the business, since nazir generally does not have experience in this particular business. The commercial waqf business should be managed by prioritizing the maintenance of principal waqf assets in balancing risk and return. Net profits received by nazir, after deduction of management fee for third party and profit share for external financing, will be distributed as mentioned before, especially for mauquf 'alaih (see Figure 17.2).

For example, many pondok pesantrens (traditional Islamic boarding school) in Indonesia produce their own bottled mineral water by one of their productive waqf business units, at least to serve their own demand and the surrounding community, with competitive price lower than its competitors, including the market leader.

Integrated social and productive waqf

Another type of waqf is ISPW, which combines social waqf with productive waqf, i.e. combining cost center waqf with matching profit center waqf to ensure the sustainability of social services provided by social waqf needed by the general ummah, especially needy and poor people. Therefore, commercial motivation is blended with social motivation, and for-profit orientation is mixed with not-for-profit orientation.

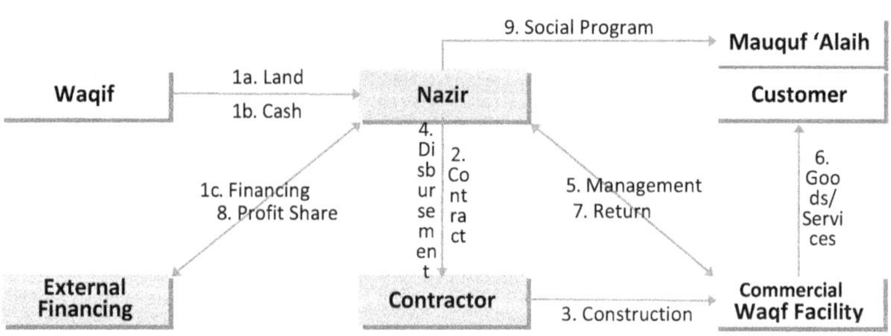

Figure 17.2 General scheme of productive waqf.

The idea of ISPW is initially needed to establish social waqf to provide quality services for the needy and poor people free of charge, such as healthcare and education, which nowadays have become more and more commercially oriented, especially in emerging Muslim majority countries. In order to cover the operational costs of these services, there should be sustainable sources of funds, which could be fulfilled by productive waqf profits. There are, at least, two models of ISPW. First is the social-commercial waqf facility serving social customer (mauquf 'alaih) and commercial customer since the product/service provided is exactly the same such as hospital. The second model consists of two separate social waqf facility serving mauquf 'alaih and a commercial waqf facility serving commercial customers such as Islamic school financed by real estate development.

The development of ISPW model-1 is usually initiated by waqf institution as nazir who develops social project/program financed by waqf, so that nazir starts to announce the project to general public and to collect waqf (especially cash waqf) from waqif. Parallel with waqf collection, nazir will start to build the social-commercial waqf facility, with or without contractor or developer. If urgently needed, nazir will find additional external financing to cover the cost of waqf development. Upon completion, nazir will run and manage the social-commercial waqf facility by himself or by hiring a third party professional/institution. Commercial customer will pay for the goods/services, while social customer or mauquf 'alaih will receive the goods/services free of charge. The income from commercial customer will be used to cover all operational costs (see Figure 17.3).

The difference of developing ISPW model-2 is that social waqf facility and commercial waqf facility are two totally different facilities. Social waqf facility could be hospital, Islamic school, while commercial waqf facility could be any commercial business such as palm oil plantation, hotel and restaurant (see Figure 17.4).

ISPW is usually built/financed by waqf, especially cash waqf. The social waqf facility is always built/financed entirely by waqf (land waqf and cash waqf). The productive waqf facility is also mostly built/financed by waqf. However, it does not rule out the possibility of productive waqf be built/

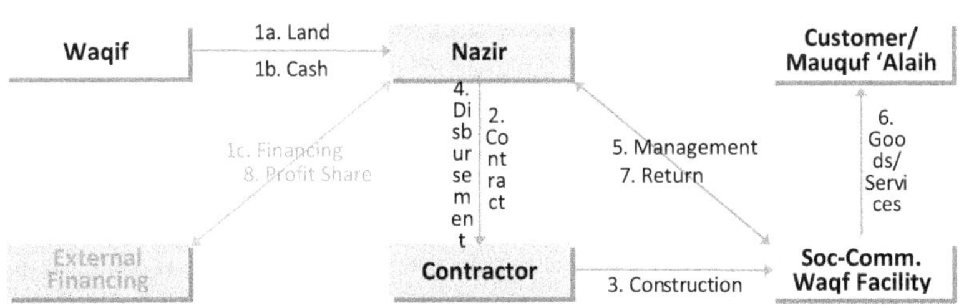

Figure 17.3 General scheme of integrated social and productive waqf model-1.

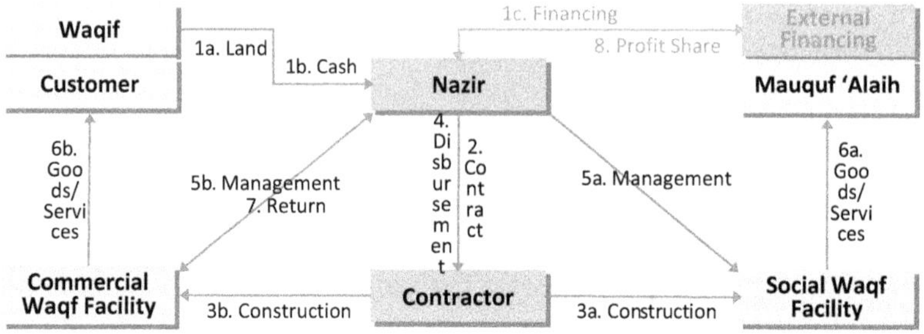

Figure 17.4 General scheme of integrated social and productive waqf model-2.

financed by additional external financing, if urgently required, to speed up the completion of the development.

Integrated social and productive waqf in Indonesia

There are many examples of ISPW in Indonesia providing free education and healthcare services to general ummah, especially the poor and the needy, financed by various productive waqfs. Many charged-free pondok pesantren (traditional Islamic boarding school) have been built based on this model. Many charged-free hospitals, clinics and Islamic medications have also been built using ISPW model. There is also foundation, which is specialized in developing various ISPW models. In this chapter some examples of ISPW models will be discussed, including Firdaus Memorial Park (FMP) (cemetery), Rumah Sehat Terpadu – Dompet Dhuafa (general hospital), Jogokariyan Islamic Center (JIC) and Kuttab Al-Fatih – Sinergi Foundation (SF) (Islamic school). All of these waqf facilities provide charged-free services to the ummah (general public), especially the poor and the needy.

Firdaus Memorial Park

FMP, located in Bandung District, West Java, Indonesia, is an integrated public cemetery built and managed by SF, through its waqf division Wakaf Pro99, based on the ISPW model, which was planned to include cemetery and facilities for visitors, Al-Firdaus mosque and pondok pesantren for tahfidz Al-Qur'an, agriculture and livestock waqf, as well as business units. FMP located in Bandung, West Java covers an area of 21 hectares, where 10 hectares is dedicated for the cemetery (5 hectares for waqif and 5 hectares for the poor and needy), and the rest is dedicated for other facilities. One of the main productive waqf is located outside the FMP complex, namely Ampera Restaurant serving Sundanese cuisine in Bandung city (see Figure 17.5).

Since 2012, SF has collected cash waqf along with 10% infaq from waqif, up to a maximum capacity of 5000 waqif. Each waqif will give IDR15.0 million of waqf plus IDR1.5 million of infaq for operational and promotional costs, which amounts to IDR75.0 billion cash waqf and IDR7.5 operational and promotional infaq fund. Each waqif is entitled to two cemetery plots for waqif and spouse, as well as one plot of cemetery waqf for the poor and needy people. All costs of burial process have been included in this package. The FMP officially was opened in December 2013.

Parallel with the waqf collection, SF started to build the FMP facilities, starting with the cemetery, visitor facilities and rice field, as well as entered into joint investment in the establishment of Ampera Restaurant. Rice field is intended to empower and improve the income and welfare of Islamic community surrounding the FMP and of those who work for FMP by providing support and technical assistance.

With current stage of development, registering 1300 waqif, acquiring 13.0 hectares of land, developing one hectare of cemetery, developing one hectare of visitor's facilities, developing one hectare of rice field, and joint investment in Ampera Restaurant, FMP has been able to operate sustainably (see Figure 17.6).

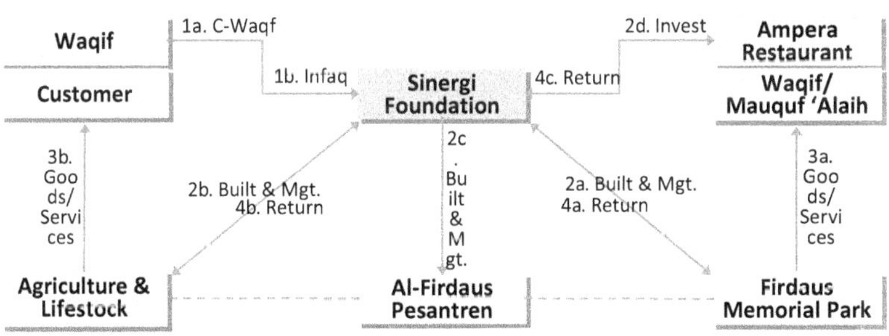

Figure 17.5 The scheme of Firdaus Memorial Park.

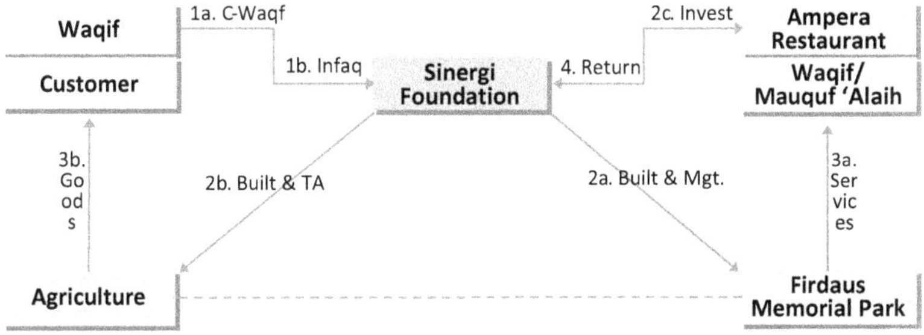

Figure 17.6 Current development of Firdaus Memorial Park.

Integrated healthy house

Rumah Sehat Terpadu (integrated healthy house) – Dompet Dhuafa (RST-DD) Hospital, located in Bogor District, West Java, Indonesia, was established by Dompet Dhuafa (DD) Foundation in July 2012 through its waqf division Tabung Wakaf Indonesia – Dompet Dhuafa (TWI-DD). RST-DD hospital was originally started as Layanan Kesehatan Cuma-Cuma (charged free medical services) – Dompet Dhuafa (LKC-DD) in 2001 to provide free basic healthcare services for the poor and needy people (*dhuafa*). As time passed by, LKC-DD had to deal with *dhuafa* patients needing further specialist treatments, inpatient care, and operative actions, so the existing service facilities were felt to be inadequate and need to be upgraded to hospital level. DD Foundation through TWI-DD collected cash and land waqf from waqif, and subsequently started to build the hospital building on 7803 square meters waqf land through its subsidiary DD Contractor. Simultaneously, DD Foundation established RST-DD Foundation responsible to operate and manage the hospital. RST-DD inaugurated and started its full-fledged medical services in July 2012 free of charge for *dhuafa*, financed by zakat and infaq funds collected by DD Foundation. Every month RST-DD provides healthcare services to 15,000 patients.

Initially, operational costs of the hospital were financed by zakat and infaq funds collected by DD Foundation, since RST-DD strictly served *dhuafa* or mustahik. In later development, the government required hospitals to accept patient holding government health insurance (BPJS), so that RST-DD can also start to accept BPJS patients and generate income from these patients. Dhuafa patients were then registered as BPJS holders paid by DD Foundation/RST-DD Foundation using zakat and infaq funds, and still received free healthcare services from RST-DD hospital. This new scheme made RST-DD transform from social waqf to ISPW generating waqf income for RST-DD Foundation. The illustrated scheme of RST-DD hospital is shown in Figure 17.7. RST-DD hospital has become a reputed hospital providing healthcare services in professional and Islamic way for the community, especially the poor and needy people or *dhuafa*.

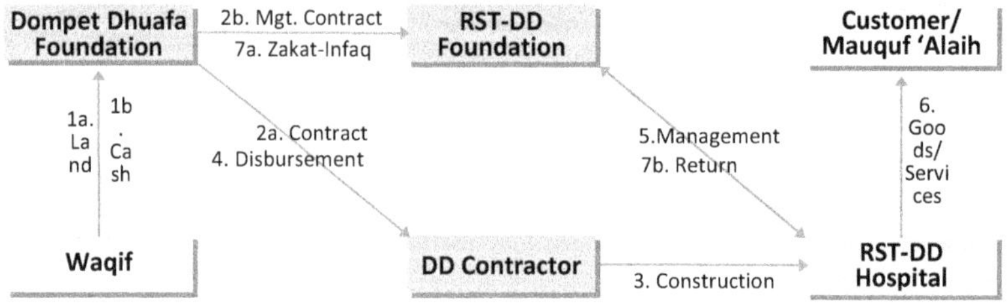

Figure 17.7 The scheme of Rumah Sehat Terpadu – Dompet Dhuafa (RST-DD) Hospital.

RST-DD hospital serves patients with professional, family and heart approaches. In contrast to hospitals in general, RST-DD provides holistic well-being services to the community, which includes physical, economic and spiritual well-being.

DD Foundation has made RST-DD hospital as an ISPW hospital to be replicated in other areas in Indonesia. Currently, DD Foundation has established other ISPW hospitals, such as AKA Medika Sribhawono hospital located in Metro Lampung District, South Sumatera, Indonesia, as well as Ahmad Wardi Eye Hospital located in Serang District, Banten, Indonesia, in collaboration with Badan Wakaf Indonesia (Indonesia Waqf Board). DD Foundation has also been developing Hasyim Asyari Hospital located in Pondok Pesantren Tebuireng, Jombang District, East Java, Indonesia.

Jogokariyan Islamic Center

JIC, located in Yogyakarta, Indonesia, was initially established as small musholla; in 1966, it was upgraded to become a mosque by the Muslim community, by collecting cash waqf to buy 660 m^2, as well as to build 9×9 m^2 mosque and 9×6 m^2 main hall. The waqifs were the local community comprising "batik" entrepreneurs who were members of Batik Cooperative "Karang Tunggal" and "tenun" entrepreneurs who were members of Tenun Cooperative "Tri Jaya".

The mosque became too small, since larger numbers of Jamaah (Muslim who pray in congregation) were coming for prayer in the mosque, so the mosque was enlarged several times in 1999, in 2003, and in 2009, so that it can be transformed into a three-storey Islamic center on 1478 m^2 land and 1118 m^2 building, including Mosque with 1,200 congregation capacity, as well as two meeting rooms in the second floor and 11 lodging rooms in the third floor for rent. The Mosque Management Council (Takmir Masjid) also established several business units such as mini mart, fertilizer production and processed chicken. The business entered by JIC must be different from the business of local residents, so that it will not hurt or compete with local residents' businesses. When JIC needs something, it will try to buy from local resident's first.

The income from these businesses was used to finance operational costs and social programs of the Islamic center, as well as to finance social programs and empowerment programs. Social programs include free basic health services, home improvement, rice ATM and replacement of lost items in the mosque (such as, sandal and motorcycle). JIC completed 18 home improvement in 2017, 22 home improvement in 2018 and 30 home improvement in 2019 for the poor and needy people (*dhuafa*) in the local community. Starting 2019, the home improvement program will build two-storey home for *dhuafa*, where the first floor will be used for business, while the second floor will function as home. Empowerment programs include trainings, Qardh financing and technical assistance. To promote micro/small enterprises (MSE) of the community, JIC conducts Ramadhan Fair every evening in the month of Ramadhan. Hundreds of MSEs participate every year, where 50% of them are owned by local residents (Figure 17.8).

JIC has unique programs, which no mosque has implemented before, namely "Replacement of Lost Item", "Gerakan Jamaah Mandiri" (Independent Jamaah Movement) and "Gerakan Saldo Nol" (Zero Balance Movement). Replacement of Lost Item program was initiated to ensure the Jamaah to be able to pray with peace of mind, without worrying about his/her belongings such as sandals, shoes, and even motor cycle. If one Jamaah loses his/her belonging, JIC will be held responsible and will have to replace the lost item with a new one in exactly the same brand using collected infaq/donation funds.

Independent Jamaah Movement program was launched to support financial independence of JIC operation. First, JIC calculated the monthly cost per capita (CPC) of each Jamaah by dividing its monthly operational cost by 1,200 (congregation capacity). For example, CPC was IDR50,000 (equivalent to USD3.50). Subsequently, JIC will post a message or banner saying that "If you donate less than IDR50,000 you are subsidized by other Jamaah. But if you donate more than IDR50,000 you are subsidizing other Jamaah". This program has successfully increased weekly infaq/donation by 400%. Eventually, every Jamaah can now donate at least IDR50,000 per month to not to be embarrassed. Zero Balance Movement program means that the balance of every month expense and income must be zero, which means that all income received from infaq/donation and businesses must be used to finance operational costs and social programs. With this program, JIC will always stand ready to serve and help the Jamaah and the local community to solve their socio-economic problems.

To be able to serve the needs of local community, JIC regularly conducts census of its community, so that JIC has the database of its community. The census not only record personal data of each member of the community but also record who prayed and who has not prayed, who prayed in the mosque and who has not prayed in the mosque, who has paid zakat and who has not paid zakat, who has given qurban and who has not given qurban, who has

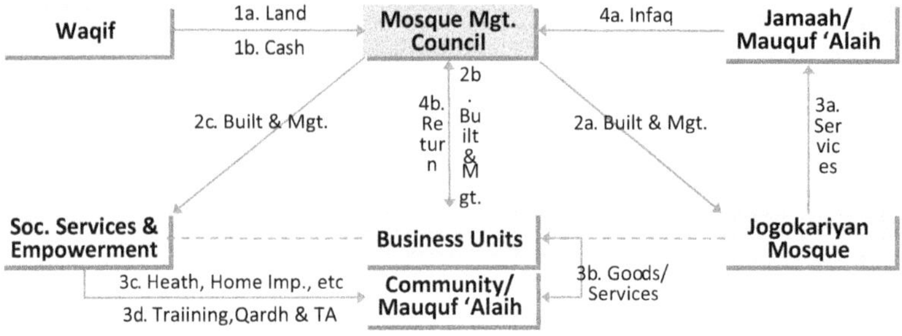

Figure 17.8 The scheme of Jogokariyan Islamic Center.

been involved and who has not been involved in mosque activities, who has offered qurban (*udhiyyah*) and who has not offered qurban. With this database, the JIC recorded, for example, that there were 127 residents who did not pray, while in 2010 there were 17 residents who did not pray. These data showed the development of dakwah in JIC. The database could be used also for Fajr Prayer Movement, by extending formal invitation letter for each resident or Jamaah, similar to invitation for wedding, adding hadith the priority of Fajr prayer. This movement resulted in the number of congregations of Fajr prayer to resemble the number of congregations of Friday prayer. Currently, JIC has also become one of the favorite religious tourism destinations for national and foreign tourists. JIC has also become the role model of mosque management, where Mosque Management Council from other mosques in Indonesia has visited JIC to study how to effectively manage the mosque.

Kuttab Al-Fatih – Sinergi Foundation

Kuttab is a concept of education that has a long history of producing great people. As the Kuttab disappeared from the Islamic world, the earth began to lose light from the scholars and scientists. The Kuttab comes from Arabic word Katatib, which means "Teaching Writing" a type of learning place that was born in the Islamic world. Appearing for the first time at the time of the Prophet, the Kuttab then spread to various countries along with the spread of Islam. The Kuttab was established purely as part of the series of Islamic amal. Kuttab is the main place in the Islamic world to teach children. Its existence is so great in the life of the Islamic community, especially because the Kuttab is a place where children learn the Al-Qur'an and the glorious knowledge in Islamic law.

In the past, the Kuttab gave birth to scholars who became references to Islamic institutions today. Historical records about the Kuttab are still neatly stored; references and field applications are perfectly arranged. The Management and Development Criteria of the institution are well conceptualized. Even the curriculum is mentioned without being covered. The Kuttab has been regenerated by Al Fatih Pilar Peradaban Foundation and has established 28 Kuttab Al Fatih (KAF) spread across 28 different locations in Indonesia. The KAF curriculum refers to the Al-Qur'an and As-Sunnah which are reviewed and translated to be applied in the education of children aged 5–12 years (kindergarten – K6), including Kuttab Awal (Kuttab Awal 1, Kuttab Awal 2 and Kuttab Awal 3), as well as Kuttab Qanuni (Kuttab Qanuni 1, Kuttab Qanuni 2, Kuttab Qanuni 3 and Kuttab Qanuni 4). KAF also reviews the books of the scholars who discussed about the generation of education such as Sirah Nabawiyah, Al-Jami 'Li Syuabil Iman, Ar-Rasul Al-Mu'allim and other books of scholars believed to be good.

SF, in collaboration with Al Fatih Pilar Peradaban Foundation, has established KAF-SF to regenerate this Islamic educational institution, free for everybody, based on ISPW. KAF-SF was launched in March 2018 to provide quality Islamic education free for all people, located in Bandung District, West Java, Indonesia. SF started the development of 1.3 hectares KAF-SF complex by collecting cash waqf combined with 10% infaq needed to finance IDR3.6 billion construction, which was done by SF itself by hiring surrounding qualified people. KAF-SF complex comprises several buildings including Mosque and its tower, school building and yard, teacher's (asatidz/asatidzah) building, management building, teacher's houses, guest houses, as well as field and garden. Simultaneously, SF has also started to invest in real estate development of productive waqf. This free education will be financed by the return of real estate development. Also, affluent parents are suggested to give waqf and infaq (Figure 17.9).

In the current stage of development (second year), SF has built the Mosque; four classrooms in teacher's building; two classrooms, teacher's room and principal room in management building; two teacher's house for Al-Qur'an coordinator (principal) and Iman coordinator; as well as IDR 1.5 billion investment in real estate development. KAF-SF has opened three classes (Kuttab Awal 1, Kuttab Awal 2 and Kuttab Awal 3) with 72 students or santri (24 students for each grade), 12 teachers, one principal and one Shariah Board. Every year, KAF-SF accepts 36 students for three classes. KAF-SF is able to operate sustainably.

Challenges faced by Nazir

Funding

The ISPW models mostly have been financed entirely by waqf, including cash waqf and/or land waqf. The collection of waqf takes time, which could slow down the construction of social waqf facility as well as productive waqf facility. In a worse case, the amount of waqf collected could be smaller than projected, so that the ISPW project must be downsized, or the project has to be extended and delayed. The delayed project would be exposed further to inflation risk which could increase the project costs. Other funding problem

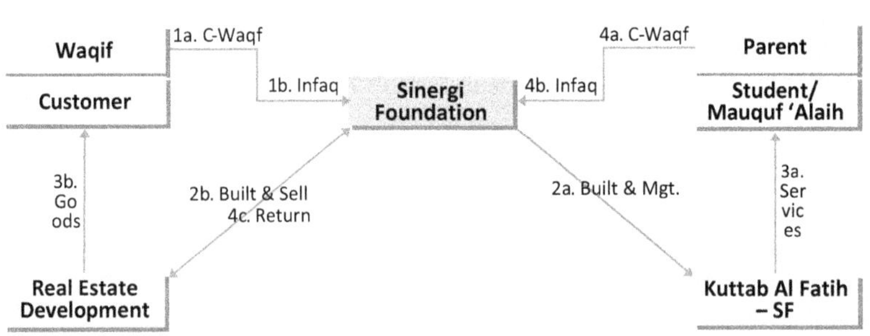

Figure 17.9 The scheme of Kuttab Al-Fatih – Sinergi Foundation.

could also arise when the projected budget to build the ISPW project was too small, while the realized costs were higher than expected. One way to solve this problem is to accelerate the waqf collection using various channels, including personal approach to wealthy Muslims, social media, crowdfunding P2P (peer to peer) social through fintech company and open the booth in e-commerce platform. Another possible way is to raise temporary cash waqf or to borrow Qardh financing from wealthy Muslims for certain period of time, which will be returned at specified agreed time. The least preferred option is to find commercial financing from external parties to accelerate the development of productive waqf, so that the net returns after installment payments could be used to accelerate the development of social waqf facilities.

Sustainability

Businesses in micro level have always noticed frequent ups and downs. Productive waqf, as part of ISPW, can also get exposed to business upturn and downturn, which could affect the sustainability of productive waqf as well as social waqf operation. Meanwhile, in the macro level, businesses will be affected by macroeconomic shocks such as financial crisis, economic crisis and political crisis. Sometimes the changes in central and/or regional government regulations can also affect certain business sectors. For example, the new regulation on health insurance in Indonesia have made the profits of many commercial hospitals to decrease and some of them can even go bankrupt, while this very regulation has made the income of social hospitals to increase. To mitigate these risks, productive waqf should be large enough to be able to stand the ups and downs wave of business cycle. The productive waqf should be diversified in several different sectors to be able to minimize the risks with optimum portfolio. Islamic insurance or takaful could also be used as an option to mitigate the business risks. Moreover, since productive waqf is also a waqf where its assets have to be preserved, the goal of productive waqf should not be to maximize profits, but it should be to minimize risks, so that productive waqf should not enter into high risk businesses.

Human resource

The ISPW, especially on the social waqf side, is operated on tied budget, so that the human resource of ISPW could only be remunerated marginally, which could result in high turnover and/or second-best quality of human resource. The best fresh graduates always choose to work in reputable public or private institutions. They might never think to become ‘amil of zakat institution, nazir of waqf institution or social worker of social institution. The profession as ‘amil, nazir and social worker is still considered as second-class jobs. However, human resources of waqf institution usually are those who have idealism and passion in philanthropy works to help others. Nevertheless, the remuneration of such social workers should be at par with those who work in reputable public or private institutions, since as a full-time job, nazir and worker in contemporary waqf institution have to work professionally in this field to safeguard, maintain and develop the waqf assets entrusted to the nazir/waqf institution.

To attract the best human resources in quality, professionalism and passion, waqf institution has to provide comfortable working environment, career path, as well as attractive fringe and benefits, especially fair and competitive salary. To be able to do that, waqf institution should increase productive waqf assets by increasing productive waqf fundraising, as well as allocating a portion of productive waqf profits to be re-invested or re-waqf to the pool of productive waqf. For example, Waqaf An-Nur Corporation Berhard (WAN-Corp) in Johor Malaysia allocates 70% of its profits to be re-invested or re-waqf to the pool of productive waqf, which has made the productive waqf of WANCorp grew faster.

Technical experiences

Nazir and waqf institution manage productive waqf in various business sectors such as real estate, restaurant, farming, trading, car rental, agriculture, hotel, education, health services and many other sectors. Naturally, nazir has no experience and competence in all of those business sectors entered by the waqf institution. Productive waqf could be managed by the waqf institution itself, while productive waqf could also be managed by professionals hired by the waqf institution. Both options have their own benefits and costs. Nevertheless, business has to be managed by someone who has competence and experience in that particular business sector. One way to solve this problem is that the waqf institution as nazir should start to manage productive waqf in small scale business that naturally has low risk such as real estate. As the nazir is moving forward along the learning curve, the assets managed would be gradually increased by raising more productive waqf funds. For example, many waqf institutions in Indonesia have started raising productive waqf and managing it by themselves, including waqf institutions who manage ISPW. Other option is that the waqf institution would collaborate with professional who would act as *mudarib* (entrepreneur) in managing the business. For example, SF chipped in some portion of capital to establish restaurant managed by professional to open a new Ampera Restaurant branch. Other possible option is that the waqf institution would establish separate institution to manage the productive waqf professionally. Another option is that the waqf institution would hire or collaborate with specialized institution in managing productive waqf business.

References

Abdullah, R. & Ismail, A.G. (2017). "Taking Stock on the Waqf-Based Islamic Microfinance Model." *International Journal of Social Economics*, doi: 10.1108/IJSE-06-2015-0176

Haneef, M.A., Aliyu, D.M., Ataul, H.P. & Mustafa, O.M. (2014). "Integrated Waqf Based Islamic Microfinance Model (IWIMM) for Poverty Alleviation in OIC Member Countries." *Middle-East Journal of Scientific Research*, 19(2): 286–298.

Haneef, M.A., Pramanik, A.H., Mohammed, M.O., Amin, Md. F.B., & Muhammad, A.D. (2015). "Integration of Waqf-Islamic Microfinance Model for Poverty Reduction." *International Journal of Islamic and Middle Eastern Finance and Management*, 8(2): 246–270.

Thaker, M.A.M.T., Mohammaed, M.O., Duasa, J. & Abdullah, M.A. (2016). "The Behavioral Intention of Micro Enterprises to Use the Integrated Cash Waqf Enterprise Investment (ICWME-I) Model as a Source of Financing." *Gadjah Mada International Journal of Business*, 18(2) (May-August, 2016): 111–130.

18 Waqf-led social finance in poverty alleviation – an experience in Khyber Pakhtunkhwa, Pakistan

S. Ghisaul Haq and Suhail Ahmad

Introduction

Waqf-led Islamic social finance has played an important role in poverty eradication. It facilitates improvements and perfection of the well-being on social justice, which has a positive impact on the welfare of the general masses. The financial problems seem to be serious one; therefore, the year of 2010 is renowned as the year of Islamic microfinance, sharing the spirit of helping microenterprises through micro financing (Riwajanti, 2013). It has been observed that microfinance has played a vital role in poverty alleviation over the last few decades. It is a powerful tool of poverty eradication, because of its strategy and income distribution for social as well as for economic development of a nation. Microfinance is not limited to developing countries, but also spread to the developed nations across the world (Mahjabeen, 2008). Interest free micro credit is important for poverty alleviation in the society. Like Qard al Hassan, Bay Salam and micro Takaful to overcome the burden of the poor, resulting from shocks like the death of a family member, illness of some major diseases such as cancer, HIV and the like. Similarly, microfinance plays a key role in overcoming the loss of assets such as housing, livestock and agriculture loss due to unforeseen situation like flood and fire. Instruments of mobilization of funds can be divided into three types. First one is charity, which consists of zakat, sadaqah, awqaf and gifts including Hiba and Tabarru. The next one is deposited in the form of wadiiah, Qard al Hassan and Mudarabah. The last one is equity, which is in the form of Musharakah (Obaidullah & Khan, 2008). Human development is attained through social financial practices of Islamic micro financial institutions of an economy. Human development includes health and educational facilities, foods, security and shelter (Saad, 2010).

Need for Waqf-led social finance

Waqf is playing an important role in poverty eradication. The World Bank has a vision to eradicate poverty by 2030 from the world. Therefore, much attention is required for social finance at the micro level for poverty eradication. It imposes justice and unity irrespective of age, gender, status and race (Chapra,

2007). Islamic finance prohibits transaction based on interest, bribery, gambling, corruption, fraud and similar practices (Odeduntan & Oni, 2016). Waqf-led Islamic social finance is based on the real social justice of a society and which is the main purpose of it. When there is economic social justice in the world, there will be no such gap between the wealthy and the poor in a society. Wealthy people should have the will to help the poor in the form of zakat, sadaqah, Qard al Hassan and similar practices to improve the lifestyle of the poor in the society. Qard al Hassan is a loan without interest and the aim of it is to help the poor and needy person in order to overcome poverty and fulfill their basic needs and other necessities (Khan, Hassan, & Shahid, 2007).

Islam strongly encourages the rich and wealthy community to take active part in poverty alleviation programs such as zakah and awqaf (Ahmed, 2004). Through Zakah the rich community donates some portion of their assets to the poor community. Similarly, the waqf is another form of contribution given to the poor by the rich community. The waqf is a charitable social sector institution which has the main aim to provide welfare services to the poor community of the society. Contribution can be in the form of assets like cash, car, land, building and similar things necessary for poor. It is in the form of cash that poor community can purchase their necessities (Ahmed, 2004). Zakah and awqaf have played an important role in poverty eradication. A model is proposed that combines zakah and awqaf as a tool for poverty eradication in an Islamic micro financial system of an economy (Hassan & Ashraf, 2010).

Islamic microfinance and waqf

The term "Microfinance" literally means small amount of loans. The primary objectives of microfinance are to change and improve the lifestyle of the poor and helping them live a better life, fulfill their basic needs and play a key role in the economic development of a country. Islamic microfinance is the provision of financial and non-financial services based on Islamic values and has the aim to promote justice for all irrespective of their race, gender and economic conditions. Islam commands cooperation and unity as a fundamental rule. In this basis group-based financing and mutual guarantee within the group are accepted and adopted (Obaidullah, 2008). It is suggested that the most suitable method of implementing Islamic moral economy in Islamic business and finance is by conducting social banking and Islamic microfinance. Islamic finance has two moral approaches: one approach is about profit and loss sharing approach, namely Musharakah and the other one is Mudarabah mode of financing (Asutay, 2010).

Waqf-led Islamic microfinance is important for alleviating poverty in a society. The rich pay Zakah to reduce poverty in the country through upliftment of the poor and enabling them to live like how other individuals in the society live (Aslam, 2014). Because every individual has equal right to live in this world, so being Muslims, Almighty Allah obligates each and every Muslim who have the Nisab (a particular amount of wealth/assets) to pay the

Zakah, which will, in turn, help the poor community in a society to fulfill their basic necessities of life.

The Islamic microfinance can be classified into the following categories.

- i **Informal Groups:** Individuals such as friends, neighbors, relatives, money lenders, saving collectors and traders.
- ii **Member-Based Organizations:** Member-Based Organizations (MBOs) include village banks, credit unions, finance cooperatives, and self-help group formed by individuals in a community which help in providing microfinance to the needy person.
- iii **Non-Governmental Organizations:** It includes Islamic non-governmental organizations (NGOs), i.e. charitable organizations, which manage zakah and sadaqah in a society and promote Islamic social finance.
- iv **Formal Groups:** It includes institutions such as Islamic banks and Islamic financial institutions like Takaful and Sukhuk organization, which plays a major role in improving Islamic moral economy in a society.

Impact of Waqf-led Islamic microfinance in poverty alleviation

Poverty is the scarcity of resources to fulfill the basic needs of individual and community. In an individual context, poverty is the lack of resources such as food, money (financial scarcity), shelter, health and nutrition, education facilities and other social aspects of life. On the other hand, in a community context, poverty is the lack of resources at the community and societal level because of poor economy, poor human resources and social activities and policies.[1] The Nobel Prize winner Muhammad Yunus (Yunus, 2007) has worked for micro-credit and microfinance. He said in his speech in 2007 that poverty is not created by the poor people but it is imposed by the system influenced by policies and institutions. In an Islamic perspective, poverty is not only from material aspect but also from moral and spiritual aspects. Therefore, poverty alleviation strategies should study both aspects of a society (Riwajanti, 2013). The spiritual aspect of poverty includes mental peace, happiness and social harmony. Waqf-led microfinance has a positive impact on an individual's life in order to overcome and alleviate poverty in terms of expenditure, food and nutrition, health care, education and empowerment (Bakhtiari, 2006; Brannen, 2010; Hossain, 2012; Mawa, 2008; Mohindra & Haddad, 2005). The impact of Islamic microfinance can be seen in two aspects, i.e. economic and social. It is expected that financial access will help the poor to increase their income level, improve their standard of living, and overcome their difficulties and weaknesses, thereby playing a major role in the development of the nation (Obaidullah, 2008).

As far as the impact of Islamic microfinance is concerned, it is seen by empirical study in (Islamic Bank Bangladesh Limited) impact on rural poverty finds which considerably improves household earnings, output of harvesting and cattle and employment (Ahamad, Bakar, & Lubis, 2016). According to a study by Shirazi (2012) on Islamic microfinance in Pakistan, it was found that, in terms of income growth, poor borrowers of the loan benefited more from Islamic microfinance as compared to non-poor borrowers. Pakistan Poverty Alleviation Fund (PPAF), a not-for-profit company, in 2005 covered 3,000 households to alleviate poverty in the country. There are positive impacts of Islamic microfinance in reducing poverty of a nation. Ahmad et al. argued in their study that social impacts include improvement of Islamic knowledge and relationship with others in terms of enhancing their skills; similarly Islamic microfinance has brought about a positive change in the standard of living of poor people as they have now access to clean drinking water and proper sanitation. Similarly in a study undertaken by Ahmed (2002), it was concluded that Islamic microfinance not only benefited in economic development of the poor but also contributed in their social development such as improvement of Islamic knowledge and their relation with other social groups, family members and especially with their spouses. It is clear from these earlier studies that Islamic microfinance focuses not only on financial aspects, but also on social development of individuals in a society.

As far as the social impact of Islamic microfinance is concerned, it offers market-based services, innovation in products and services, and operational efficiency. It is further stated that Islamic microfinance offers loans not only for productive matters but also for consumption to improve health facilities, education facilities and social responsibility of a society where an individual lives (Wajdi Dusuki, 2008). Islamic microfinance is playing an important role in poverty alleviation in Pakistan. Due to Islamic microfinance practice, standard of living has improved of individuals such as income, consumption, food, health and education. It has also improved ethical norms, values and social development of an individual (Aslam, 2014).

Waqf and its impact on economic and social development: a case of Peshawar, Khyber Pakhtunkhwa, Pakistan

Waqf plays a vital role in the economic and social development of a community. Its role should not be limited to only the economic and financial aspects of life of an individual, but also to the social aspects of an individual's life.[2] The role of waqf cannot be ignored in the economic and social development of a community. Peshawar, the capital of the Khyber Pakhtunkhwa (KP) Province of Pakistan, has a total population of up to 35.53 million, covers 101,741 km^2 area, and consists of 35 districts.[3] Awqaf and zakat are managed by the Provincial Department of Awqaf, Zakat and Minority under the Government of KP. The provincial department manages all types of awqaf and zakat of the province. Awqaf and zakat are managed and distributed in the Province of KP of Pakistan, as shown in Figure 18.1.

The Awqaf and Zakat Department of KP published their five year development plan for 2013–2018 (1,463 million). These figures clearly show progress

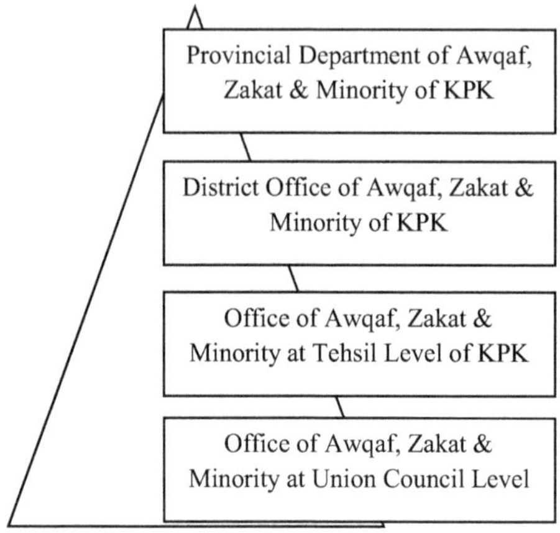

Figure 18.1 Management and distribution of awqaf and zakat in the province of Khyber Pakhtunkhwa (KP) of Pakistan.

and a 100% increase in the annual budget as compared to the previous five year plan 2008–2012, which was 731.331 million.[4] The Provincial Department of Awqaf, Zakat and Minority of KP works in a different manner for the economic development of the community. The following is the detailed sector wise progress and development in different sectors.[5]

S.No.	*Sector/sub sector*		*Sector wise progress and development*
1	Minority (ADP 2013–2014)	i	Enhancement and development of educational institutions for minority in the province
		ii	Financial grants for the minority under the welfare package in the province
		iii	Marriage grants for the minority under the welfare package in the province
		iv	Medical allowances and help for the minority under the welfare package in the province
		v	Scholarships for the children of minority group in the province
		vi	Construction and development of religious places for the minority group in the province
		vii	Special Package for the Kalash Community in Chitral District of KP
		viii	Enhancement and development of Catholic Church in Peshawar
2	Religious (ADP 2013–2014)	i	Enhancement and development of existing darulum in Swabi and Mardan District of KP
		ii	Special arrangements by the awqaf department for the promotion of religious and minority activities in KP
		iii	Enhancement and construction of different religious institutions and mosques in KP

S.No.	*Sector/sub sector*	*Sector wise progress and development*
3	Minority (ADP 2015–2016)	i Special package for the Kalash community in Chitral District of KP ii Financial grants for the minority under the welfare package in the province iii Marriage grants for the minority under the welfare package in the province iv Medical allowances and help for the minority under the welfare package in the province v Construction and maintenance of Mandar (holy place of Hindu community) in Karak District of KP vi Providing textbooks and uniforms for the poor and needy students of minority group in the province vii Trainings in different trade centers for the youth of minority group under the skill training program in the province viii Make arrangement for the security cameras and instruments for the religious places of minority groups in the province
4	Religious (ADP 2015–2016)	i Scholarships for the students in madrassa under the scholarship program in the province ii Construction of mosques and madrassa in KP iii Maintenance of mosques and madrassa in KP iv Land for graveyards for the need of the community in the KP v Construction of graveyards in the KP vi Maintenance and construction of darulum, madrassa and mosques in the KP
5	Establishment of planning cell	The Government of KP established planning cell in 2016–2017. The planning cell is directly linked to the Awqaf Department of the province. And it works and focuses for the betterment and annual development plan for the awqaf and zakat management and efficient allocation of resources. The main responsibilities of the planning cell are to look after the developmental funds for the Awqaf Department, its transparency, and progress and development for the achievement of large scale benefits for the community. It also plays a major role in the target plan achievement by the government towards their target in the province
6	Establishment of model Deeni Madrassa	The Awqaf Department of KP set up a model Deeni Madrassa in 2013–2014 in village Koga of district Buner in KP. The main motto of this model institution is to promote religious as well as Asri education
7	Statistics for Imam of mosques	By the directives of the Chief Minister of KP, the Awqaf Department collects data for the Imam of mosques from different districts of the province. The Awqaf Department collects more than 21,000 statistics of the Imam and leaders of the religious institutions, including mosques and madrassa within four months of short notice

(Continued)

S.No.	Sector/sub sector	Sector wise progress and development
8	Statistics of religious leaders for the minorities groups	By the directives of the Chief Minister of KP, the Awqaf Department collects data of the religious leaders of the minority groups from different districts of the province. The Awqaf Department collects more than 273 statistics of the religious institution leaders of the minority groups within four months of short notice
9	Financial help for the Imam of mosques	The Awqaf Department of KP paying 10,000 as monthly salary to the Imam of mosques
10	Financial help for religious leaders of the minorities groups	The Awqaf Department of KP paying 10,000 as monthly salary to the religious leaders of the minority groups in the province

Conclusion

Islamic finance is a new industry that offers services to a specific market that is not practicing conventional financing and enables Islamic principles in shape of Islamic financing practices. Islamic social finance has contributed in poverty alleviation, financial, and economic and social development. According to the teaching of Islam, every Muslim has the obligatory duty to help others, especially the needy and poor ones. Almighty Allah and His Prophet Muhammad (Peace Be upon Him) is pleased with Muslims who help others; in return Allah will give more and more when they contribute some part of their wealth and asset to the needy in the form of zakah, sadaqah, Qard al Hassan and similar course of actions. There must be social justice for poor in the world because each and every human being has the right to live a better life. Due to this reason the poor and needy individuals have the right to food, health, education, sanitation, security and shelter. In order to improve their standard of living, governments, NGOs, mutual groups, and other institutions need to facilitate the poor and overcome their financial as well as social problems by offering them waqf in different forms like cash, land, building and other assets. The overall performance of waqf-led Islamic microfinance is good when the rich have the will to improve the life of poor and needy. Impact studies show that waqf-led Islamic microfinance plays a vital role not only in improving financial aspects but also in offering social development programs and enhancing the skills of the poor, thus making them become socially responsible individual of the society. Waqf-led Islamic social finance not only improves the living standards of individuals but also strengthens their knowledge of Islamic values and principles. However, an improvement is still needed in waqf-led Islamic microfinance in terms of their regulations and social development.

Recommendation

Besides these practices of Islamic finance, Islamic social finance must contribute more by focusing on economic and social development. It is further suggested that training has to be provided to borrowers and institutional employees who use Waqf-led Islamic micro financial products and services. It is argued that Waqf-led Islamic microfinance requires great attention and needs to be improved to the desired level. Government should take all necessary actions to set up an efficient Waqf-led Islamic microfinance system in the country in order to fully aware the general masses about the benefits of Waqf-led Islamic microfinance. Once the system is fully developed the overall community can get benefit from microfinance.

Similarly State Bank of a country can help and assure that Waqf-led Islamic finance systems can be effectively planned, managed and undertaken according to the rules and regulations laid down by the government. The consensus of State Bank of a country is required to promote and develop a comprehensive setup of the Islamic microfinance system in the country.

Islamic microfinance products and services have the potential to incur losses as compared to conventional microfinance products; to mitigate such risk associated with Islamic microfinance products and services, it is needed to employ committed, experienced and competent staff for efficient operations and management and to formulate strategies and directions for better implementation of Islamic microfinance systems in the country. Similarly, the government can change and innovate their existing Islamic microfinance systems according to the needs and good implementation of the rules and regulations set by the government according to the Shariah principles. More products and services can be introduced and developed for Islamic microfinance systems in the country in order to alleviate poverty and in the best interests of the community.

Notes

1 Savas Alphay and Mohamed Aslam Haneef (2015). Integration of Waqf and Islamic Microfinance for Poverty Reduction: Case Studies of Malaysia, Indonesia and Bangladesh. The Statistical, Economic and Social Research and Training Centre for Islamic Countries (SESRIC) and International Islamic University Malaysia (IIUM), Gombak, Kuala Lumpur.
2 (2019). The World Bank Group, INCEIF and ISRA report on Maximizing Social Impact through Waqf Solutions.
3 Province Wise Provisional Results of Census, 2017.
4 Annual Development Plan of 2013–2014; Department of Awqaf, Hajj, Religious and Minority Affairs.
5 Annual Development Plan of 2013–2018; Department of Awqaf, Hajj, Religious and Minority Affairs.

References

Ahamad, S., Bakar, R., & Lubis, Z. (2016). Islamic microfinance and its impacts on borrowers: A systematic review from 1995–2015. *Mediterranean Journal of Social Sciences, 7*(6), 113–120.

Ahmed, H. (2002). Financing microenterprises: An analytical study of Islamic microfinance institutions. *Islamic Economic Studies, 9*(2), 27–64.

Ahmed, H. (2004). Role of Zakah and Awqaf in poverty alleviation (occasional paper) (pp. 1–150), The Islamic Research and Teaching Institute (IRTI).

Aslam, M. N. (2014). Role of Islamic microfinance in poverty alleviation in Pakistan: An empirical approach. *International Journal of Academic Research in Accounting, Finance and Management Sciences, 4*(4), 143–153.

Asutay, M. (2010). Islamic microfinance: Fulfilling social and developmental expectations. *Islamic Finance Institution and Market*, 25–29. London.

Bakhtiari, S. (2006). Microfinance and poverty reduction: some international evidence. *International Business and Economics Research Journal, 5*(12), 65–71.

Brannen, C. F. (2010). An impact study of the Village Savings and Loan Association (VSLA) program in Zanzibar, Tanzania, Master Thesis. *Wesleyan University, USA.*, 1–175.

Chapra, M. U. (2007). The Islamic vision of development in the light of Maqāsid al-sharī ʻah. *Jeddah: Islamic Research and Training Institute*, 1–52.

Hassan, M. K., & Ashraf, A. (2010). *An integrated poverty alleviation model combining zakat, awqaf and micro-finance.* Paper presented at the Seventh International Conference–The Tawhidic Epistemology: Zakat and Waqf Economy, Bangi, Malaysia.

Hossain, M. K. (2012). Measuring the impact of BRAC microfinance operations: A case study of a village. *International Business Research, 5*(4), 112–123.

Khan, M. S. N., Hassan, M. K., & Shahid, A. I. (2007). Banking behavior of Islamic bank customers in Bangladesh. *Journal of Islamic Economics, Banking and Finance, 3*(2), 159–194.

Mahjabeen, R. (2008). Microfinancing in Bangladesh: Impact on households, consumption and welfare. *Journal of Policy Modeling, 30*(6), 1083–1092.

Mawa, B. (2008). Impact of micro-finance towards achieving poverty alleviation. *Pakistan Journal of Social Sciences, 5*(9), 876–882.

Mohindra, K. S., & Haddad, S. (2005). Women's interlaced freedoms: A framework linking microcredit participation and health. *Journal of Human Development, 6*(3), 353–374.

Obaidullah, M. (2008). *Of the book: Introduction to Islamic microfinance*: The Islamic Business and Finance Network, IBF Net (P) Limited, India.

Obaidullah, M., & Khan, T. (2008). Islamic microfinance development: Challenges and initiatives. *Islamic Research & Training institute Policy Dialogue Paper*(2).

Odeduntan, A. K., & Oni, T. A. (2016). Islamic social finance: A sustainable means of alleviating poverty. *Journal of Islamic Banking and Finance, 33*(3), 96–106.

Riwajanti, N. I. (2013). Islamic microfinance as an alternative for poverty alleviation: A survey. *Afro Eurasian Studies, 2*(1–2), 255–271.

Saad, N. M. (2010). Achieving human development objectives through microfinance institution: The case of Amanah Ikhtiar Malaysia *Journal of Islamic Economics, Banking and Finance, 6*(2), 65–78.

Shirazi, N. S. (2012). Targeting and socio-economic impact of microfinance: a case study of Pakistan. *Islamic Economic Studies, 130*(608), 1–56.
Wajdi Dusuki, A. (2008). Banking for the poor: The role of Islamic banking in microfinance initiatives. *Humanomics, 24*(1), 49–66.
Yunus, M. (2007). The Nobel peace prize 2006-Nobel lecture. *Law and Business Review of the Americans, 13*(2), 267–276.

19 Youth empowerment and the application of cash waqf – an experience in Kano State, Nigeria

Nura Abubakar Gwadabe and Asmak Binti Ab Rahman

Introduction

Nigeria as a nation is facing different kinds of challenges, the most important among the challenges is the one that affects the economy. Consequently, the decline of the per capita in GNP, the widespread of poverty and the prevalence of the phenomenon of unemployment represent a grave danger that is persistent in these nations. The growing rate of unemployment requires necessary and urgent attention, if not it will result in acts of terrorism, corruption and other kinds of social vices. The best method of treating unemployment according to world experience is through the rehabilitation of the unemployed by empowering the youth to enable them to carry out their small projects. But these types of projects require funding which government fails to provide. Islam as a universal religion has covered all human endeavors, Islam has encouraged Muslims in the various verses of the Qur'an and prophetic traditions with regard to distributive justice and societal support from the wealthy individuals to the less privileged ones. Islam has made various provisions for poverty reductions such as zakat, waqf, sadaqa, gift, booty among others, but the main obstacle is the utilization of such.

Marshall Hodgson describes the role of waqf in an Islamic society as "the vehicle for financing Islam as a society".[1] It is mainly done to assist the socio-religious, socio-economic, political and traditional activities of the people. Waqf contributes to human civilizations in a Muslim community, as it is more vital than other forms of charities.[2] The flexibility of waqf makes it beneficial to a wider society unlike zakat that has the specific eight recipients as prescribed by Qur'an.

Empowerment means a multidimensional social procedure and it enables individuals to deal with their very own lives. Further, it tends to be called as a procedure that cultivates powers in individuals for use in their own lives in the public, by following up on issues they think as significant. "Empowerment refers to increasing the spiritual, political, social, or economic strength of individuals and communities"[3] (Keshab, 2013). Youth empowerment has been an issue of concern widely debated and it is a seeming problem in the country. The concern authorities in Nigeria have made different efforts since the country's independence in providing the citizens with employment through various empowerment programs. However, the efforts seem to be fruitless. Sadeq describes the causes of poverty as not only the unemployment and this include education and better health care facilities. Mostly poor people were denied better health care and good education, and this makes them not a good material for employment.[4]

Kano State is the most populous state in all the 36 states of Nigeria, with a total population of about 9.3 million inhabitants, and more than 2,163,225 people are living in the six local government areas of the Municipality.[5] Young people are categorized the most active group; therefore they need much attention and concern to achieve the desired goals of social, political and economic development of the state. The awqaf institutions are purposely established to subsidize their sufferings to cater to the needs of the community religiously, socially and economically.[6] Kahf defines waqf as "holding a Maal (an asset) and preventing its consumption for the purpose of repeatedly extracting its usufruct for the benefit of an objective representing righteousness or philanthropy".[7] The term cash waqf refers to a form of endowment of amount of money for religious dedications. Cash waqf also means an amount of money contributed or gifted as a capital to the needy to start up some business and generate some income.[8] Cash waqf has no limit; any amount of money can be donated as cash waqf. This kind of waqf makes a significant impact in reviving the waqf in present days in some of the Muslim nations such as Malaysia, Singapore, Kuwait and Qatar. It is a better way of gaining the capital and a means of borrowing money; it is also a source of injecting money into the economy.[9] The application of cash waqf can be vital in effective schemes to empower the youth in the state toward achieving the peace and economic progress of the state.

Unemployment rate in Nigeria

Nigeria's unemployment rate data recorded 22.728% in June 2018; the unemployment rate rose to 23.132% in September 2018. The record shows that there has been an increase in the rate of unemployment in the country; the indicators show that youth between the ages of 15 and 34 recorded the highest number of unemployed nationwide.[10]

Impediment to youth empowerment in Kano

Empowerment is regarded as a technique: the instrument by which individuals, associations and community get strength over their lives (Rappaport, 1984).[11] Empowerment refers to developing a sense of confidence in people and society to engage them to address their interests in an able and self-chosen course, following up without anyone else control. It is the route toward getting the opportunity to be more grounded and increasingly certain, especially in controlling one's life and affirming one's rights. Empowerment as action implies both to the technique of self-reinforcing and to the capability to provide assistance to people, which helps them to overcome their sentiment of weakness and absence of effect and to see and use their assets.[12] There are some factors that are responsible for the backwardness in youth empowerment, which are mentioned below.

- Lack of political will: There is no justification for poverty and unemployment among the youth in Kano State, Nigeria; there are available natural resources in the country. Nigeria produces the highest wealth from natural resources such as crude oil and Gold; despite this the youth suffer from unemployment and poverty due to the unwillingness of the political class and those with the authority to provide them with basic amenities such as schools, hospitals, roads and others, but rather engage in different programs that are not significant for youth empowerment or divert the country's wealth into personal property.[13]
- Marginalization due to schisms: One of the banes affecting youth employment is the experiences they encounter in the struggle to change and improve their lives through securing a job. Often because of the quota system which many do not know about they are discriminated in educational placements and getting a job. The idea of merit does not count to place someone but religious background, sectional/ regional place of origin, as well as tribal/ethnic affiliation. These schisms and primordial sentiments block the chances for youth on employment and education. In many host communities "non-indigenes" in cities in Nigeria, complain of lack of access to their children in admission to tertiary institutions, empowerment programs and job opportunities.
- Corruption: It is one of the biggest problems affecting youth's accessibility to employment and empowerment programs. There are allegations of corruption which was why it was not decentralized. Many issues on being employed nowadays come with having the money to pay for an appointment letter. There are several cases in our immediate environment. People are asked to pay before being employed. The basic question is what happens to majority of youth seeking for jobs, as they do not have anything to pay. Impliedly they are denied to the advantage of those that offer to give.
- Sectoral distribution: Nigeria's agricultural sector continues to be the primary sector of employment. Young people in poor rural areas have an option of either working in low-paid work in agriculture or else migrate to the already crowded urban areas, where they can find work in the informal sector, jobs that are not formally paid.[14]
- Indiscipline among the youth: Nigerian youth of today lack moral discipline, fortitude and willingness, which are vital aspects in order to achieve and succeed in their quest to socio-economic development and

sustainable security of the country. Further to this was the unrealistic demand for public sector employment. In Nigeria, many youths still favor public sector employment since they believe it carries higher status and higher wages/salaries, benefits, including that of job security. However, public sector employment is saturated or shrinking and most jobs are being created in the private sector (Osakwe, 2013).[15]

Waqf and good governance

The application of waqf governance in Kano State is timely to ensure accountability so that waqf institutions could be revived and its potential could be further promoted in the state. Good governance serves as a panacea to all administrations. Awqaf are the institutions established for the sake of Allah. Mutawalli must ensure accountability of the endowed assets, cash or property. Islam has advocated the principles of Ikhlas, amanah, adala and shura in which governance could be derived. Allah's consciousness (Ikhlas) makes the waqf administrators to make perfection and manage the endowed resources with sincerity in anticipating the reward from Almighty Allah, and to satisfy the community. Second, Amana which is one of the principles of good governance, impels the awqaf administrators to administer the waqf assets with utmost trust as trustee to Allah and beneficiaries and consider this waqf property as trust. Justice (Adalah) is very vital in the utilization and the distribution of waqf resources to the deserving beneficiaries. The Administrators must perform the act of justice (adala) in determining the waqf resources and to checkmate those that will benefit from the waqf. Shura is the consultation or decision making body which consists of the representatives of various stakeholders of waqf; they are the ones making decision on governing waqf institutions.

Efficacy of cash waqf

Cash waqf is not much familiar with the people of Kano State as much as they know the properties, estate or land awqaf; but presently the attention of people is drawn toward the endowment of cash waqf. The flexibility of cash waqf makes it popular and accepted by the public. The flexibility of cash waqf makes the contributions to be easier and affordable to many people, and it has the potential benefit to the less privileged people where ever they are in the state. Cash waqf has been recognized among the prospective and operative mechanism for youth empowerment and social development. The State Government in Kano cannot afford to employ or empower the teeming youth of the state; therefore, there is a need of financial interventions from wealthy individuals and the philanthropist in the form of waqf to curtail the menace of unemployment in the state. This is where the cash waqf can play its role. Waqf administrators will collect the donation from the donors in cash and invest them in any profitable and shariah-based investment. The profit realized will be used to finance some students to study, establish schools, provide capital to train entrepreneurs and other initiatives that support youth empowerments.

Many people in Kano express their view on the cash waqf and its relevancy in the present-day situations. The features of cash waqf happens to be more "friendly" to the people particularly those who could not afford to endowed big assets or properties as waqf. Benefits to be derived from cash waqf are as follows:

- Cash waqf is affordable and it requires no big land, estate or properties; with little amount of money you can participate and help your community.
- More funds can be generated through cash waqf and can easily be used for youth empowerment and social developments.
- Cash waqf can be utilized to support education and educational institutions such as giving scholarships to the outstanding students and building libraries, classes or schools.
- Cash waqf has the potential of reducing the level of dependency of people in government and can assist in establishing investments that will empower the youth to be self-dependent.

However, to ensure the success and efficiency of the application of cash waqf in Kano State, an organized framework must be setup.

Application of cash waqf in Kano

Cash waqf can be used to overcome the challenges of youth empowerment toward greater security and financial stability.

Four instruments will be used to actualize the role of cash waqf for youth empowerment, as shown in Figure 19.1.

- Access to credit facility: Cash waqf can provide the credits needed to finance Murabaha, even without collateral and high interest rate from banks.
- Provision of capital: Cash waqf can be the source of capital using Musharaka and Mudaraba that can be used to offer micro-finance to start small-scale business and entrepreneurship among youth.
- Source of income generation: Income for the waqf fund will be made by investing some portion of its money in Islamic Equity.[16]
- Societal welfare: Education and health care services will be funded through short term Qard al Hassan.[17]

Through the application and implementation of these proposed methods, youth empowerment in Kano can be achieved and will be successful.

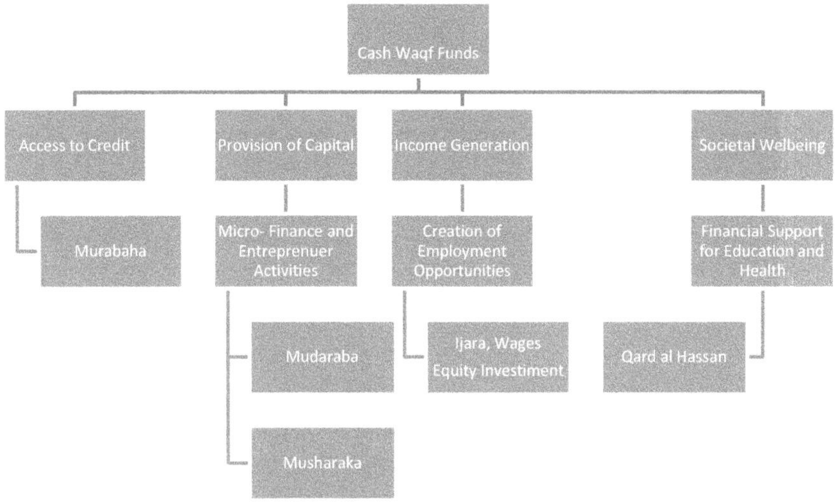

Figure 19.1 Prototypical application of cash waqf for youth empowerment in Kano State.

- Access to credit facilities: It can be provided to the trained youth to finance a desired business through Murabaha Mode of Financing by purchasing the required items which may have been very expensive for the youth to acquire and give it to them in an agreement of paying in a later date or in installment. The profit margin charged will be little because the model is based on charity and to enable the youth to repay without difficulties while helping the business progresses well, not as in the conventional banks where higher interest rates are charged.
- Capital – It can be provided to the youth by the cash waqf to start a business and support themselves, establish peace in the state and attain economic prosperity, with application of Musharakah and Mudarabah Modes.[18] Cash waqf in mudaraba finances can be utilized to support the youth in Kano to start a small-scale business venture, as the institution of waqf would serve as Rabbul-Mal (Capital Providers) to the youth as recipient. The agreement would be made on the ratio of which profit would be shared. And subsequently the waqf institution may sell its shares of partnership to the youth for the progress of his business and become the sole owner of the business.

  Musharakah partnership can be applicable and can provide the business capital to the youth to establish a small-scale business venture. In a situation whereby a youth has little and insufficient amount of money as capital to start a business, cash waqf fund can contribute significantly and support him with some capital to form the partnership. The profit earned in the business would be shared on the agreed ratio based on the capital contribution.

- Equity venture: Investments in equity would make the cash waqf sustainable; reasonable amount of money received as cash waqf donations should be invested in Islamic-Based Equity group. The equity portfolio needs to be diversified into different productive shariah-based investments.[19] This will maximize the profit and minimize the risk that could be detrimental to the value of cash waqf fund. The profit earned from the equity investment can be utilized to finance some business where youth in the state can start their business using the funds provided by waqf fund through micro finance mode. Opportunities for employment can be created by this business by employing youth in the management and administrative positions. The sale of equity shares can be invested into business center and be used to generate employment opportunities for the youth.
- Social welfare: Cash waqf funds can be utilized in the form of Qard al-Hassan to finance some emergency cases that may arise to the youth in the health care or unexpected incidences and due to lack of required funds to tackle the cases. Qard al-Hassan should be repaid with equal principal money. No charges will be incurred to the beneficiary, although the beneficiary may be encouraged to contribute some funds based on his ability to the institution of waqf when he is financially capable to help other beneficiaries. Qard al-Hassan does not have any profit and can only be financed by the activities of other income generations.[20] The generated incomes from the cash waqf investments can be used for scholarship and youth training in various skills, for youth development and nation's progress.

Suggestions and recommendations

In a period where authorities are applying unconventional programs to empower the youth, it has been identified that cash waqf has the potential to solve the menace of youth unemployment in Kano State. The potentialities of cash waqf will be effective in sustaining the programs and strategies of empowering the needy youth in various fields of endeavor.

However, for the better participation of more people, awareness is very vital; stakeholders need to educate the public about the importance and potentials of cash waqf in the provision of social welfare and economic growth. The people's notion of waqf that it can only be used for religious purposes should be changed likewise; not only estates or property can be donated as waqf but also cash can be endowed as waqf. The Kano State peoples understanding of waqf is limited to building of mosques, construction of well, buying cemeteries and others; it is the duty of religious leaders and all the stakeholders to take charge in educating the general public on the role of waqf in providing youth empowerment and social development in the society. With the understanding of cash waqf, numerous recommendations can be given in re-forming the cash waqf and in promoting the living standard of the unemployed youth and the less privileged people in Kano State. Cash waqf could be utilized into investments that would generate employment to the Kano youth, ensure provision of educational institutions and provide the youth with the required capital to start their own business.

Conclusion

Youth in Kano State are facing difficulties in the empowerment process which make the state backward in terms of economic development, peace and human development. Cash waqf funds can be used to transform the lives of many unemployed youth in Kano State, in the educational sector, health care, entrepreneur, and vocational skills. The methods stated earlier can be applied to empower the less privileged youth in the state to cater to the youth's need of empowerment and reduce the destitution and criminal activities among the youth.

Notes

1 Singer, A. (2008) *Charity in Islamic Society*. New York: Cambridge University Press.
2 Hoexter, M. (1998) Endowments, Rulers and Community: Waqf al-Haramayn in Ottoman Algiers. *Studies in Islamic Law and Society* 6.
3
4 Sadeq, A. H. M. (2002) Waqf, Perpetual Charity and Poverty Alleviation. *International Journal of Social Economics* 29(1/2), 135–151.
5 National Population Commission, 2006.
6 Habib, A. (2004) *Role of Zakat and Awqaf in Poverty Alleviation*, Jeddah, Saudi Arabia: IRTI, Occasional Paper No. 8, 19–72. Saudi Arabia
7 Kahf, M. (1998) Waqf of the Muslim Community in the Western Countries: A Preliminary Thought on Reconciling the Shariah Principles with Laws of the Land. Paper Presented at a Seminar on Development of Awqaf. Kuala Lumpur.
8 Khademolhoseini, M. (2008) Cash Waqf a New Financial Instrument for Financing Issues: An Analysis of Structure and Islamic Justification of Its Commercialization. Imam Sadiq University.
9 Ahmed, H. Waqf- Based Micro Finance: Realizing the Social Role of Islamic Finance. In: Integrating Awqaf in the Islamic Finance Sector, Singapore.
10 Quarterly Report (2018) National Bureau of Statistics of the Federal Republic of Nigeria.
11 Rappaport, J. (1984) Studies in Empowerment: Introduction to the Issue. *Prevention in Human Services*, 3, 1–7.
12 Adams, R. (2008) *Empowerment, Participation and Social Work*. New York: Palgrave Macmillan, p. 6.
13 Abdullahi, H., Abdullah, Y.Z. & Mohammed, Y. (2013) Youth Participation, Unemployment and Poverty in Democratic Nigeria: Towards a Policy Response for Sustainable National Security and Economic Development. *Journal of Economics and Sustainable Development*, 4(10), 171–182.
14 NIYEAP, Nigerian Youth Employment Action Plan 2000–2011. Abuja: Federal Ministry of Youth Development (2008).
15 Osakwe, C. (2013) Youth, Unemployment and National Security in Nigeria. *Journal of Humanity and Social Sciences*, 3(13), 259–267.

16 Marzuki, M. U. M. (2012) Tackling Poverty: A Look at Cash Waqf. *Prosidingpersidangankebangsaanekonomi Malaysia*, 2(2), 1611–1623.
17 Amuda, Y. J. (December 2013) Alleviation of Poverty among OIC Countries through Sadaqat, Cash Waqf and Public Funding. *International Journal of Trade, Economics and Finance*, 4(6), 405–407.
18 Kahf, M. (2006) Role of Zakah and Awqaf in Reducing Poverty: A Case for Zakah-Awqaf-Based Institutional Setting of Microfinance. Paper presented at the Conference on Poverty Reduction in the Muslim Countries, Nov.
19 Marzuki, Tackling Poverty: A Look at Cash Waqf.
20 Ahmed, H. (2007) Waqf- Based Micro Finance: Realizing the Social Role of Islamic Finance. In: Integrating Awqaf in the Islamic Finance Sector, Singapore.

References

Abdullahi, H., Abdullah, Y.Z. & Mohammed, Y. (2013). Youth Participation, Unemployment and Poverty in Democratic Nigeria: Towards a Policy Response for Sustainable National Security and Economic Development. *Journal of Economics and Sustainable Development*, 4(10), 171–182.

Adams, R. (2008). *Empowerment, Participation and Social Work*. New York: Palgrave Macmillan, p. 6.

Ahmed, H. (2007). Waqf- Based Micro Finance: Realizing the Social Role of Islamic Finance. In: Integrating Awqaf in the Islamic Finance Sector, Singapore.

Amuda, Y. J. (December 2013). Alleviation of Poverty among OIC Countries through Sadaqat, Cash Waqf and Public Funding. *International Journal of Trade, Economics and Finance*, 4(6), 405–407.

Habib, A. (2004). *Role of Zakat and Awqaf in Poverty Alleviation*, Jeddah, Saudi Arabia: IRTI, Occasional Paper no. 8, 19–72.

Hoexter, M. (1998). Endowments, Rulers and Community: Waqf al-Haramayn in Ottoman Algiers. *Studies in Islamic Law and Society* 6.

Khademolhoseini, M. (2008). Cash Waqf a New Financial Instrument for Financing Issues: An Analysis of Structure and Islamic Justification of Its Commercialization. Imam Sadiq University.

Kahf, M. (1998). Waqf of the Muslim Community in the Western Countries: A Preliminary Thought on Reconciling the Shariah Principles with Laws of the Land. Paper presented at a seminar on Development of Awqaf. Kuala Lumpur.

Kahf, M. (2006). Role of Zakah and Awqaf in Reducing Poverty: A Case for Zakah-Awqaf-Based Institutional Setting of Microfinance. Paper presented at the Conference on Poverty Reduction in the Muslim Countries, Nov.

Mandal, K. C. (2013).Concept and Types of Women Empowerment. Paper presented at the International Forum of Teaching & Studies.

Marzuki, M. U. M. (2012). Tackling Poverty: A Look at Cash Waqf. *Prosiding Persidangan Kebangsaan Ekonomi Malaysia*, 2(2), 1611–1623.

National Population Commission. (2006). The Historic Events of Kano State; Published by National Populations Commission, for the National Population and Housing Census.

NIYEAP, Nigerian Youth Employment Action Plan 2000–2011. (2008). Abuja: Federal Ministry of Youth Development.

Osakwe, C. (2013). Youth, Unemployment and National Security in Nigeria. *Journal of Humanity and Social Sciences*, 3(13), 259–267.

Rappaport, J. (1984). Studies in Empowerment: Introduction to the Issue. *Prevention in Human Services*, 3, 1–7.

Sadeq, A. H. M. (2002). Waqf, Perpetual Charity and Poverty Alleviation. *International Journal of Social Economics*, 29(1/2), 135–151.

Singer, A. (2008). *Charity in Islamic Society*. New York: Cambridge University Press.

Index

Note: Page numbers followed by "n" denote endnotes.

a'akarat 80
AAOIFI *see* Auditing Organisation for Islamic Financial Institutions
Abdur Rahman bin Auf Trading Enterprise 71
Adalah 12
Administration of Islamic Law (Federal Territories) Act 1993 166, 186n1
Administration of Muslim Law Act of 1968 (AMLA) 91; Section 58 91
administrative structure of *waqf* 105–106
agro-sectors, poverty alleviation through Islamic social finance in (northern Ghana) 137–153; economy 138–140; financing modes and challenges 141–142; impact investors, attraction of 144–146; Islamic venture capital instruments, risk management and investment protection in applying 150–152; *Musharakah* (partnership) 147–148; *Muzar'ah* (partnership in crop) 148–149; overview 140–142; risks management 146–147; Sadaqah (charity) 142–143; *Wakalah* (agency) 150; *waqf* 143–144; Zakat (alms) 142
Ahmad Wardi Eye Hospital 253
Ahmed, H. 263
'Aisha Hanim, al-Sitt 109
AiU *see* AlBukhary International University
AKA Medika Sribhawono hospital 253
Al-Abrar USIM Waqf Funds 194
Al-Azhar University 191, 194, 209
Al-Barraniyya 107
AlBukhary International University (AiU) 192, 198
Al Fatih Pilar Peradaban Foundation 255
al-ibahah 28
Aligarh Muslim University 209
Ali, M.Y. 175
Ali Imran 71
Al-Juwaniyya 107
Al Maun 76
Al-Quran 220
Alsagoff, Sheriffa Zain Alsharoff Binte Syed Mohamed Bin Ahmad 241
Alumni Waqf-funded model 196
Amanah Raya Berhad (ARB) 174
Amanah Saham Nasional Berhad (ASNB) 183, 185
Ameer Ali, Syed 103, 106
AMLA *see* Administration of Muslim Law Act of 1968; Anti-Money Laundry
Ammana Fintek Syariah, P.T. 123
Ampera Restaurant 250, 251
Anti-Money Laundry (AMLA) 184
'*Aqwam al-Masālikf īMa'rifatAḥwāl al-Mamālik*' (The Best Ways of Knowing States) (Ettounsi) 65
ARB *see* Amanah Raya Berhad
ASNB *see* Amanah Saham Nasional Berhad
assets exchange (*Istibdal)* 161
Atiq *Waq f* Mosque 208
Auditing Organisation for Islamic Financial Institutions (AAOIFI) 23, 94, 163n2, 201, 202
Awqaf: within classical discourse and their modern implications 23–36; Development Centre (*see* Waqf Development Centre); as economic driver 39–50; emergence of 5–10; flagships 7–8; issues and problems 6–7;

strategic plan 9; *see also waqf; individual entries*
Awqaf Corporation Berhad 184
Awqaf-e-Shahi (Royal *Awqaf*) 111
Awqaf General Authority in the kingdom of Saudi Arabia, Article 7 164n6
Awqaf Holding Berhad (AWQAF) 223
Awqaf-led neo-endowment, in supporting socioeconomic development 11–21; case 17; critical success factors (*see* critical success factors); funds from management of *waqf* 18; important considerations 16–17; literature review 11; recommendation 20; *waqf* project, benefits of 18–20; *waqf* proposal 18
Awqaf Public Foundation (Kuwait) 41, 108
Ayubites 193
Azis, Umar Abdul 72
Aziz, Datuk Othman 174
Aziz, M. 143

Badan Wakaf Indonesia (Indonesia Waqf Board) 253
baimuajjal (instalment sales) 47
baisalam (forward sale contracts) 47
Bait al-Muqaddas 25
Baitul Mal 72
Bank Indonesia 234
Bank Islam 176
Bank Muamalat Malaysia Berhad (BBMB) 175, 176
Bank Negara Malaysia 184, 240
Bank of Ghana (BOG) 137
Bank Rakyat 176
Basel Core Principles 235
al-Baydah, Sitti Fayzadah Qadinbinti Abdullah 111
BBMB *see* Bank Muamalat Malaysia Berhad
Begum, Shah Jahan 109–110
Bilkent University 195, 197
Billah 73
blockchain technology 121–123
Board of Trustee of the Waqf 201
BOG *see* Bank of Ghana
Bosnia-Herzegovina: *awqaf* banking, establishment of 61–63; *awqaf* in 52–66; data collection protocol 55; epistemological posture 53–55; fundamental ideas, contextualization and analysis of 55–59; literature revue 53–55; self-governing administration of Islamic religious and *Vakuf-mearif* activities, statute for 59–61
BOT *see* Build-Operate-Transfer
Bouvat, Lucien 55
BPJS *see* patient holding government health insurance
Build-Operate-Transfer (BOT) 46, 238
business face of *awqaf* 43–44
Byr al-Rumah 24, 28

Cambridge University 193, 196
cash *waqf* 47; application of 274–276; *awqaf* development through 155–164; concept of 172–173; definition of 194; efficacy of 273–274; governance of relationship with donors 158–159; growing role of 156–158; legislation, development of 161–163; optimal *waqf* investment 159–161; socio-economic impact disclosure on 228
Cash Waqf-funded model 194–195
cash Waqf linked sukuk (CWLS) 74–77, 234, 242; beneficiaries of 77; products 75; risk management of 76; structure of 236; target market of 76
cash waqf refugee microfinance (CWRMF) 176
Central Bank of Malaysia 184
Centralbank und Sparkassa (central and savings bank) 57
Central Provident Fund (CPF) 92
Central Waqf Council 90
challenges, Edu-Waqf model: accounting and reporting 201; financial and administrative autonomy 199–200; lack of awareness 199; lack of innovation 201–202; lack of regulatory framework 200; management issues 200–201; quality of human capital 201; trust deficit 199
Civil Law Act 1956, Section 25 221
Çizakça, M. 87
collective participation 157
Commodity Exchange (GCX) 142, 150
concessionary financing 47
Contemporary Waqf Administration and Development in Singapore: Challenges and Prospects 91
corporate social responsibility (CSR) 185, 226
Corporate Waqf-funded model 195–198
CPF *see* Central Provident Fund

creating shared value (CSV) 71, 72
critical success factors: accountability 16; state interference 15–16; transparency 16
CSR *see* corporate social responsibility
CSV *see* creating shared value
custody of *awqaf* 41–42
CWLS *see* cash Waqf linked sukuk
CWRMF *see* cash waqf refugee microfinance

DAO *see* decentralized autonomous organization
Darussalam Educational Institute (IPD) 210
Darussalam Gontor University 209–211
Darussalam Gontor *Waqf* City 207–208; educational system in 211; expansion 215–216; financial sustainability 213–216; income generated from business units 214–215; tuition fees from boarding schools 214
Darussalam Institute of Islamic Studies (ISID) 210
Darussalam University: educational system in 212–213
decentralized autonomous organization (DAO) 79
demographic data analysis 179–180
Dewan Kemakmuran Masjid (DKM) 247
Dewi, M. K. 243n4
dharuriyyat (necessities) 218
DKM *see* Dewan Kemakmuran Masjid
donors, governance of relationship with 158–159
Dumas, Alexandre 64

economic role of *waqf* 85–87
education, role of *waqf* in 192–193
Edu-Waqf model 191–204; challenges of (*see* challenges, Edu-Waqf model); collaboration and specialization 203–204; in Indonesia 198; innovation 203; in Malaysia 197–198; management 204; standardized regulatory framework 202; sustainability of *Waqf* funds 202–203; in Turkey 196–197
Efendi, Hayri 62, 64, 65
Egyptian Awqaf Authority 41
Egyptian University (University of Cairo) 110
Elasrag, H. 15
Elkington, John 73
Ettounsi, Kheireddine 65
Europe Trust 96
Evkafbankasi 52, 61, 63
Ez-Zitouna University 191

Fannani, Zainuddin 209
Fara'id denial, *Hibah* as 178, 179
Fatih University 196, 197
fatwa 55
Federal Corporation of Awqaf (Sudan) 41
Fillah 73
finance: Islamic social finance (*see* Islamic social finance); impact on poverty alleviation 262–263; microfinance 47–48; social 117–118; *waqf* and 261–262; *Waqf*-led social finance (*see* *Waqf*-led social finance)
financial support 46–47
financial technology (fintech) 121–123
Finterra Waqf Chain 241
fiqh 26, 74, 155, 208
Firdaus Memorial Park (FMP) 250–251; current development of 251; scheme of 251
FMP *see* Firdaus Memorial Park
French Civil Code, Article 1907 62
Friedman, Milton 71

al-Gazdughli, Amir Ismail Bey al-Kabir 109
GCX *see* Commodity Exchange
gender: justice 103–115; ownership and 104
General Endowment Fund 91
genesis of *awqaf* 52–66; data collection protocol 55; epistemological posture 53–55; fundamental ideas, contextualization and analysis of 55–59; literature review 53–55; self-governing administration of Islamic religious and *Vakuf-mearif* activities, statute for 59–61
ghallah 28
Ghana: Agricultural Investment Fund (now Ghana Eximbank) 147; Export Development 147; Ghana Commodity Exchange (GCE) 148; Ghana Statistical Service 140; northern (*see* northern Ghana)
Ghana Health Service and Teaching Hospitals Act of 1996, Act 525 of 17
Ghana Incentive-based Risk Sharing System for Agricultural Lending (GIRSAL) 141–142

GIIN *see* Global Impact Investing Network
GIRSAL *see* Ghana Incentive-based Risk Sharing System for Agricultural Lending
Global Impact Investing Network (GIIN) 144
Global Islamic Finance Report 2015 118–119
Global Wakaf 236, 237
goal clarity 177
Gontor Darussalam boarding schools 208–209; educational system in 211–212
Group of Muhammadiyah Universities (UM) 198

al-Habashiya, Sitti Zafaran Khatunbinti Abdullah 111
Al-Habib, Haya Abdul Rahman 110
Hadith 27, 208, 220–221
Hadžiomerović, Mustafa Hilmi 56
hajiyyat (convenience) 218
Hamdard *Waqf* City 207
Hanbal, Ahmad bin 219
Haneef, M.A. 143, 200, 245
Hanifah, Abu 42
Harvard University 193, 196
Hassan, M. K. 219, 260, 261, 266, 274
Hasyim Asyari Hospital 253
Hatun, Gale 109
Hibah (gift) 5, 166–187; cash *waqf* 172–173; as catalyst for cash *waqf* 182–184; characteristics of 168; definition of 168–169; demographic data analysis 179–180; education background 181; employment 181; as *Fara'id* denial 178; gender and ethnic 180; investment products 184; limitations 185–186; literacy and knowledge 178, 181–182; literature review 174–176; marital status 180–181; objectives of 173–174; preparedness confidence 177; recommendations 185; research methodology 178–179; Takaful 170; in *waqf* advancement 168; *waqf* investment act 184–185; Wasiyyah Shoppe Berhad 171–172, 179, 185, 186; wealth distribution, attitude toward 177–178
Hibah al-ruqba 169–170, 185
Hibah Al-Umra 169–170, 185
Hibah Amanah Tabung Haji 171
hifz al-mal (protection of wealth) 218
Hikr 164n4
Hilmiyah, N. 196
Hodgson, M. 270
Hodgson, Marshall 86
historical overview of *waqf* 40–41
hujjah 218
humanitarian 1, 2, 41, 42, 48, 53, 160, 161

IADC *see* International Awqaf Development Center
Ibn Battoutah 84–85
Ibn Shadi, Siti el-Sham bint Ayub 107
ICAST *see* International Centre for Awqaf Studies
ICWME-1 model 245, 249
ICWME-2 model 249
ihsān 12
Ihsan, H. 243n4
IIUM *see* International Islamic University of Malaysia
IIUMWF *see* International Islamic University of Malaysia Waqf fund
ijara (lease financing) 47, 164n4
Ijaratain 164n4
ijarawaiqtina (hire purchase) 47
Imarah Waqf (Menara Bank Islam) 238
impact investing 144
INCEIF *see* International Centre of Education in Islamic Finance
indebtedness (*Istidana)* 161
Indian Waqf (Amendment) Act 2013 112
India, utilizing *awqaf* in 89–90
Indonesia: *awqaf* in 234–238; Independent Jamaah Movement program 254; integrated social and productive *awqaf* in 245–258; Firdaus Memorial Park 250–251; Jogokariyan Islamic Center 253–255; Kuttab Al-Fatih – Sinergi Foundation 255–256; model and structure 246–250; Rumah Sehat Terpadu – Dompet Dhuafa 252–253; Ministry of Finance 235; Mosque Management Council (Takmir Masjid) 253, 255; Nazir, challenges faced by (*see* Nazir, challenges faced by); Zero Balance Movement program 254
Indonesian Waqf Board-IWB (Badan Wakaf Indonesia (BWI)) 234
Indonesian Waqf Education Foundation (YEWI in Bahasa) 235
infaq 26
integrated social and productive waqf (ISPW) 245–258

Internally Generated Fund 18
International Awqaf Development Center (IADC) *see* Waqf Development Centre
International Center of Islamic Economy 65
International Centre for Awqaf Studies (ICAST) 235
International Centre of Education in Islamic Finance (INCEIF) 86, 119, 238
International Innovative Platform for Islamic Economy Products 65
International Islamic University of Malaysia (IIUM) 196, 198
International Islamic University of Malaysia Waqf fund (IIUMWF) 194
International Waqf Foundation 96
Internet of Things (IoT) 241
IRTI 234, 239, 243n4
ISF *see* Islamic social finance
Ishola, A. S. 243n3
ISID *see* Darussalam Institute of Islamic Studies
Islamic Development Bank 80
Islamic Relief Worldwide (IRW) Pilot Cash Waqf Programme 2011–2015 (Kenya) 130n13
Islamic Religious Council of Selangor (MAIS) 197, 240
Islamic Religious Council of Singapore *see* Majlis Ugama Islam Singapura (Muis)
Islamic Religious Waqf and Educational Affairs (*Štatutzaautonom nuupravuislams kihvjerskihivakufsko-mearifskihposlova)* 56
Islamic Sciences University of Malaysia (USIM): Al-Abrar USIM Waqf Funds 194
Islamic social finance (ISF): in northern Ghana agro-sectors, poverty alleviation through 137–153; reform 166–187
Islamic University of Indonesia (UII) 198
Islamic University of Malaysia (IUM) 198
Islamic venture capital instruments, risk management and investment protection in applying 150–152
Ismail, Fatima binti 110
ISPW *see* integrated social and productive waqf
ISRA 86, 238
ISRA Waqf Report 119
Istanbul Sabahattin Zaim University 197
Istanbul Şehir University 196, 197
istisna'a (construction/manufacturing finance) 47
IUM *see* Islamic University of Malaysia
Izetbegović, Alija 52

Jawishan Sabiqan (Ta'ifat) 109
JIC *see* Jogokariyan Islamic Center
Jogokariyan Islamic Center (JIC) 253–255; scheme of 254
Johor State Religious Council 184
Joseph, Franz 55–56

Ka'aba 25
Kachkar, O.A. 176
Kadir, S. Z. S. A. 238
KAF–SF *see* Kuttab Al-Fatih – Sinergi Foundation
Kahf, M. 143, 200, 271
Kállay, Benjamin 56
Kamarudin, Zaleha 92–93, 94
Kamil, N.K.M. 200
Kano State, Nigeria: unemployment rate 271; youth empowerment 270–278
Key Performance Indicator (KPI) 71, 228
Khalid, A. F. 220
Khanom, F. 175
Khan, T. 143
al-Khassaf, A. B. 25
Al-Khattab, Umar ibn 84
khayrat 79–80
al-Khurais, Nahyabinti Nasser 111
Koç University 195, 197
KPI *see* Key Performance Indicator
Kulliyyatul Mu'allimin al Islamiyyah (Islamic Teacher Training College) 208–209
Kuran, T. 153n2
Kuttab Al-Fatih – Sinergi Foundation (KAF–SF) 255–256; scheme of 256
Kyoto University 193

Labuan International Business and Financial Centre (LIBFC) 239
Labuan International Waqf Foundation (LIWF): structure of 239–240
Labuan Islamic Financial Services and Securities Act 2010 239
Laldin, M. A. 218
Laveleye, Emile de 69
Layish, A. 30
legal environment, creation of 42–43
LIBFC *see* Labuan International Business and Financial Centre

Lillah 73
LIWF *see* Labuan International Waqf Foundation

Madhhab, M. 15
madrasah 197
MAIWP *see* State Islamic Religious Council of Federal Territory
Majlis Ugama Islam Singapura (MUIS) 91–92, 240
mal (treasury) 219
Malaysia: *awqaf* in 218–232, 238–239; background 219–221; case study 225–227; management 221–223; National Land Code 1965 223; Ninth Malaysia Plan (2006–2010) 222; socio-economic impact disclosure 223–224, 227–231; Department for Awqaf, Zakat and Hajj (JAWHAR) 41, 182, 194, 197, 221–223, 239
Malaysian Private Entity Financial Reporting Standards (MPERS/MFRS) 201
Malaysian Waqf Foundation 238
Mamaliks 193
management of *awqaf* 41–42
Maqāṣid al-Sharī'ah (MaS) 6, 9, 31, 32, 144, 218
maslahaa'ama 42
Maududi, S. A. A. 142
mauquf (*waqf* asswt) 219–220
mauquf alaih (beneficiaries) 7, 220
mauquf alayh 235–240, 242
Maybank Islamic 176
Melbourne University 193
Menafi-sanduci 57
microfinance 47–48; impact on poverty alleviation 262–263; *waqf* and 261–262
Ministry of Agriculture 12
Ministry of Awqaf, Islamic Affairs and Holy Places (Jordan) 41
modern Muslim minority societies, utilizing *awqaf* in 83–97; contemporary *awqaf* in key non-Muslim countries 88–89; economic role of *waqf* 85–87; India 89–90; lessons for Muslim minorities 92–94; non-Islamic societies and systems 88; Singapore 90–92; social-political development 87–88; UK regulation 94–97
Mohamed, N. A. 238
Mohsin, M. I. A. 243n4
Mokhtar, F.M. 175
Mosque of Quba 25, 28
MPERS/MFRS *see* Malaysian Private Entity Financial Reporting Standards
Mualaf Centre Renovation, Kelantan 176
mudaraba (trust financing) 47
mudarabah 21n10, 174
MUIS *see* Majlis Ugama Islam Singapura
Mukhairiq 83
murabaha (procurement financing) 44
al-murahli, Hafiza Khanum 109
Musari, K. 203
musharaka (equity participation) 47
Musharakah (partnership) 21n11, 91, 147–148
mushtarik 108
Muslim's People Organization (*Muslimanska Narodna Organizacija)* 56
Musykilah al-FaqrwaKaifa 'Alajaha al-Islam (Qhardawi) 72
mutawalli (*waqf* manager) 6, 32, 41–43, 45, 49, 89, 186, 219, 220, 223, 235, 236, 239–241, 242n1; appointment of 105–106; certificate 184, 185; women 110–112; powers of 106–107
Muzar'ah (partnership in crop) 148–149
MyWakaf campaign scheme 239, 242

Nasir, F. M. 235
National Fund Corporation 183
National University of Malaysia (UKM) 198
National Waqf Fund (NWF, UK) 95–97
Nazir, challenges faced by: funding 256–257; human resource 257–258; sustainability 257; technical experiences 258
Negeri Sembilan State Religious Council 184
The New Waqf Law 11
non-financial support 47
non-Islamic societies and systems, *waqf* in 88
Northern and Savannah Ecological Zone (NSEZ) 139
northernGhana: agro-sectors, poverty alleviation through Islamic social finance in 137–153; Northern Development Authority 145
NSEZ *see* Northern and Savannah Ecological Zone
Nurrachmi, R. 175
NWF *see* National Waqf Fund

Obaidullah, M. 143, 144
OECD *see* Organization for Economic Cooperation and Development
Omar, Mohd Azmi 86
optimal *waqf* investment 159–161
Organization for Economic Cooperation and Development (OECD) 86, 87
Organizations of Islamic Cooperation 80
Oseni, U. A. 243n3
Othman, A. 239
Ottoman Empire 40
OUEM *see* OU Endowment Management
OU Endowment Management (OUEM) 196
ownership, and gender 104
Oxford University 193, 196

Pakistan Poverty Alleviation Fund (PPAF) 263
Pardanashin ladies 104–105
participatory financing 47
patient holding government health insurance (BPJS) 252
Penny Appeal and the Waqf Fund 96
People's Religious School ("Sekolah Agama Rakyat," SAR) 197
Perbadanan Nasional Berhad 183
Perbadanan Wakaf Selangor (PWS) 175, 176, 223
PMGD *see* Pondok Modern Gontor Darussalam
policy implication 48–49
policy recommendations 31–35
pondok 197
Pondok Modern Gontor Darussalam (PMGD) 196, 198
poverty alleviation: through Islamic social finance in agro-sectors (northern Ghana) 137–153; *waqf*-led social finance in 260–267
PPAF *see* Pakistan Poverty Alleviation Fund
PrivilegierteLandesbankfürBosnien und Hercegovina (privileged bank of the country in Bosnia-Herzegovina) 57
productive *awqaf* development, contemporary approach in 71–81; analysis 71–74; cash Waqf linked sukuk 74–77; innovation in Waqf blockchain 77–81
productive *waqf* 247–248
profitability 44–45
public and private sector partnerships 45–46
public 20, 28, 29, 35, 43, 48, 49, 57, 58, 60, 65, 122, 124, 155, 157, 158, 166, 172, 175, 176, 191, 195, 197, 198, 240, 241, 246, 250, 257, 258, 270, 273, 276; accountability 219, 231; benefit 42; borrowing 87; charity 84; dent 87; disclosure 79; goods 31, 85, 86, 143, 218; property 38; services 41, 77, 194, 219; utilities 1, 24, 30, 36, 40, 44, 220, 221, 223, 227; *waqf* 106, 162, 182, 220
PwC 80
PWS *see* Perbadanan Wakaf Selangor

Qadin, Shawikaz 109
Qarawiyyin University 191, 194
Qhardawi, Yusuf 72
Qurtubi, A. 84

Rahman bin Auf, Abdur 71
Raja Nong Chik Raja Ishak 174
Rashid, S. K. 90, 241
Razak, D.A. 175
Al-Razouki, Mussaad M. 79
real estate investment trusts (REITs) 92, 118
Red House waqf project 241
refugee crisis management 33
regulatory regime, disruption to 123–124
regulatory technology (regtech): to the rescue 123–124; for *waqf* governance (*see waqf* governance)
Rehabilitate-Operate-Transfer (ROT) 238
Reis ul-'ulema 56
REITs *see* real estate investment trusts
Religion of Islam (Federal Territories) Act 1993 221
RHB Islamic Bank 176
ribā 64
rights of Muslim women 104–107; administrative structure of *waqf* 105–106; *mutawalli*, appointment of 105–106; *mutawalli*, powers of 106–107; objects of a *waqf* 105; Pardanashin ladies 104–105; *waqf*, creation of 104
Robin Hood Complex 73
ROT *see* Rehabilitate-Operate-Transfer
RST–DD *see* Rumah Sehat Terpadu – Dompet Dhuafa
Rumah Sehat Terpadu – Dompet Dhuafa (RST–DD) 252–253; scheme of 252
Rumah Wakaf Indonesia 237

Sabancı University 195, 197
Sabanci *Waqf* 207
SAC *see* Syariah Advisory Council
sadaqah(charity) 25, 26, 28, 142–143
sadaqahjariyah 27
Sadeq, A. H. M. 271
Sahal, Ahmad Sahal 209
Sanusi, S. 176
SDGs *see* Sustainable Development Goals
Securities Commission: Syariah Advisory Council 170
Seetee Aisah Waqf 238
Selangor Waqf Corporation 175
SF *see* Sinergi Foundation
al-Shafei, Imam 84
Shafiai, M.H.M. 176
Shantiniketan Group of Colleges 209
share *waqf* scheme, socio-economic impact disclosure on 229
Shari'ah 7, 20, 23, 24, 33, 58, 61, 62, 87, 104, 129, 218; compliant business model of the Waqf 14; in *waqf*, objectives of 28–31
Shirazi, N. S. 263
Sidin, E.M. 175
sighah waqf (transfer of *waqf*) 220
Sinergi Foundation (SF) 237, 255–256
Singapore: Administration of the Muslim Law Act (AMLA) 240; *awqaf* in 90–92, 240–241; Institutional Investment Initiative 241; Islamic Religious Council of Selangor 197, 240; Majlis Ugama Islam Singapura 91–92, 240–241
SIRC *see* State Islamic Religious Council
Siswantoro, D. 243n4
smart contract multi-chain ecosystem 241
smart *Waqf* City, for education 207–216; Atiq *Waq f* Mosque 208; Darussalam Gontor University 209–211; Darussalam Gontor *Waqf* City 207–211, 213–216; Darussalam University 212–213; Gontor Darussalam boarding schools 208–209, 211–212
SMEs, *Aqwaf* support of 46
social capital 130n16; market 120–121
social finance 117–118; Islamic (*see* Islamic social finance); *Waqf*-led (*see* *Waqf*-led social finance)
social impact 44, 73, 86, 155, 156, 161, 238, 263
social investment 40
social-political development, *waqf* and 87–88
social return 130n15
social *waqf* 246–247
Spirit of Islam (Ali) 103
SRI sukuk 2
Srpskabanka 57
Stanford University 193
State Islamic Religious Council (SIRC) 6, 175, 176, 182–185, 194, 197, 219, 221, 223, 225, 227, 238
State Islamic Religious Council of Federal Territory (MAIWP) 223
State Islamic Religious Council of Kedah (MAIK) 197
State Islamic Religious Council of Negeri Sembilan (MAINS) 194
State Islamic Religious Council of Selangor (MAIS) 223
State Religious School ("Sekolah Agama Negeri," SAN) 197
state Waqf-funded model 194
Sukuk 91
Sukuk Al-Waqf 9
Suleiman, Haitam 92
Sultan Mehmed V Reşâd 52, 63, 64
Sullamul Muta'allimin 208
sunna 39
sustainability 44–45; of *Waqf* funds 202–203
Sustainability Report (Shell) 73
Sustainable Development Goals (SDGs) 31, 36, 72, 119, 144
Swansea Mosque and Islamic Community Centre 96
Syafi'i 219
Syanggit University 209
Syariah Advisory Council (SAC) 170
Syed Abdul Kader, Sharifah Zubaidah 92–93, 94

tabarru' 184, 260
tabarruq 184n3
Tabung Haji Malaysia 179, 186
Tabung Wakaf Indonesia Dompet Dhuafa (TWI DD) 235
Tabung Wakaf Indonesia – Dompet Dhuafa (TWI–DD) 252
Tafsir 208
tahsiniyyat (refinement) 218
Ta'ifat Gamaliyyah (Aisha Hanim) 109
Ta'ifat, Salha Khatun binti Salim Agha Ikhtiyar 109
Takaful *Hibah* 170
Takaful Malaysia 179, 186
The Tamale Teaching Hospital (TTH) 17–19
Tan Sri Jamaluddin Mohd Jarjis 174

Tarbiyatul Athfal 208, 210
Telkom 81
Thaker, M.A.M.T. 245
Theory of Planned Behavior (TPB) 176–178
thimmah 41
third economic sector 41
TPB *see* Theory of Planned Behavior
Treaty of Berlin 59
Trustee Act 1949 171
TTH *see* The Tamale Teaching Hospital
TWI DD *see* Tabung Wakaf Indonesia Dompet Dhuafa

UII *see* Islamic University of Indonesia
UKM *see* National University of Malaysia
UK regulation: National Waqf Fund (NWF) 95–97; *waqf* and 94–97
'*ulemamedzhlis* (Council of the '*ulema*) 56
Umar Dates Plantation Co. 71
ummah 78, 218
UM *see* Group of Muhammadiyah Universities
Ungarische Bank und Handels-Aktiengesellschaft (Hungarian Banking and Trade Company) 57
UN Global Compact 144
UPM *see* USIM and Putra University of Malaysia
USIM and Putra University of Malaysia (UPM) 198
Ustman bin Affan Water Co. 71

VakifBank 62
vakuf-mearif 56; activities, stature for self-governing administration of 59–61
Venture Waqf (VW) 143, 144
VW *see* Venture Waqf

WaCIDS *see* Waqf Center for Indonesian Development and Studies
Wakaf are Affin Islamic Bank 176
Wakaf Hasanah 235, 242
Wakaf Prioritas 235
wakala 110–111
Wakalah (agency) 150
Waqaf An-Nur Corporation Berhad (WANCorp) 176, 223, 239, 258
Waqaf Saham Larkin Sentral (WSLS) 238
waqf 5, 9, 79, 80, 143–144; classifications of 26; conceptual mechanism of 24–28; current state of 117–120; definition of 12, 23, 271; delivery 121–123; funds from management of 18; issues and problems 6–7; market 120–121; model of 13–15; origin of 24–28; potential of 13; productive 247–248; project, benefits of 18–20; proposal 18; public 106, 162, 182, 220; in *shariah*, objectives of 28–31; social 246–247; usage of 12–13; *see also Awqaf; individual entries*
Waqf Act 1995 (India) 112
Waqf Act 2004 (Indonesia) 234
Waqf Act of 1965 90
waqfahli 84
waqf al-i'qar (immovable assets) 220
waqf al-irsod 220
Waqf An-Nur Corporation Berhad (WANCorp) 238–239
waqf blockchain: awareness 78–79; into Islamic fintech, bringing 79–80; liquidity 78; as new innovation 77–79; today, state of 80–81; transparency 78
Waqf Board 212
Waqf Center for Indonesian Development and Studies (WaCIDS) 235
WAQF Chain 78
Waqfcoin 123
Waqf Core Principles (WCP) 235
Waqf Development Centre 5, 10n1
waqf governance: application of 125–126; concerns and issues in 127; solution for 124–125; tools for facilitating 126–127
waqfIlmu 91
Waqf Investment Corporation 184, 185
waqfkhairi 84
waqfkhas scheme, socio-economic impact disclosure on 226, 230–231
waqf khayri (public *waqf*) 106, 162, 182, 220
Waqf-led social finance: economic and social development 263–266; microfinance 261–262; impact of 262–263; need for 260–261; in poverty alleviation 260–267; recommendation 267
waqf mushtarak 220
waqf return distribution 161
Waqf Revitalization Scheme (WRS) 241
Waqf Saham Larkin Sentral 240
waqf shop, structure of 237
waqfthurri 108
waqf zurri (family *waqf*) 220
waqif (donor, endower) 155, 219
waqifs 41–45, 75
Warees Investments Pte Ltd 240, 241
Wasiyyah Shoppe Berhad 171–172, 179, 185, 186

wassiyyah (will) 219
WCP22 (Waqf core principles article 22) 76
WCP *see* Waqf Core Principles
wealth distribution channel 189–190
Well, Ustman 71
woman: as founder of *waqf* 107–110; *mutawalli* 110–111; rights of (*see* rights of Muslim women)
women, as beneficiaries of *awqaf* 110
World Bank Group 86, 119, 238
WRS *see* Waqf Revitalization Scheme
WSLS *see* Waqaf Saham Larkin Sentral

Yale University 193
Yayasan Universiti Multimedia (YUM) 201
Yayasan Wakaf Malaysia (YWM) 221, 223, 239
Yeditepe University 197
Yediyildiz, Bahaeddin 85
youth empowerment (Kano State, Nigeria) 270–278; cash *waqf*, application of 274–276; cash *waqf*, efficacy of 273–274; good governance 273; impediment to 271–273; suggestions and recommendations 276–277
YUM *see* Yayasan Universiti Multimedia
Yunus, M. 262
Yusuf, Abu 219
YWM *see* Yayasan Wakaf Malaysia

Zaitouna University 194
Zakat (alms) 5, 142, 219, 270
Zaman, S. M. 26
Zarkasyi, Imam 209
Zarqa, Sheikh Mustafa 40

www.ingramcontent.com/pod-product-compliance
Ingram Content Group UK Ltd.
Pitfield, Milton Keynes, MK11 3LW, UK
UKHW022217190926
475702UK00003B/403
* 9 7 8 0 3 6 7 4 0 5 3 7 3 *